IDLE HANDS:
THE EXPERIENCE OF
UNEMPLOYMENT, 1790–1990

Idle Hands is the first major social history of unemployment in Britain during the period of its industrialization from the late eighteenth century to the present. Unemployment has been an outstanding problem of modern society and, at times, the overwhelming concern of domestic politics. Although many economists have attempted to analyse its causes, no historian has previously written a history of unemployment which focuses on the experiences of people without work. That is the present aim – not to produce further explanations or remedies, but to recover, from direct evidence, the impact of unemployment on ordinary lives. *Idle Hands* asks how unemployment happened to individuals, how they and their families reacted and coped with it, what steps they took to find work and what remedies were available to them if they failed. And because life is not only about physical survival, how did people feel about their unemployment and what were its psychological effects?

The distinctive feature of this book, and the main source of evidence, is the use of autobiographies and memoirs of working people who experienced and described periods of unemployment as part of their wider life histories. Such writings are a unique historical source, almost unknown until recently. More than 200 autobiographies have been used in the present book, covering a range of occupations from agricultural labourers to skilled workers: they provide moving personal accounts, supplemented by extensive use of other contemporary documents, Parliamentary Papers and secondary sources.

John Burnett is Emeritus Professor of Social History at Brunel University. His publications include *Plenty and Want* ([1966] 1989), *A Social History of Housing, 1815–1970* ([1978] 1986), *Useful Toil* ([1974] 1994) and *Destiny Obscure* ([1982] 1994).

IDLE HANDS

The Experience of
Unemployment, 1790–1990

John Burnett

London and New York

First published 1994
by Routledge
11 New Fetter Lane, London EC4P 4EE

Simultaneously published in the USA and Canada
by Routledge
29 West 35th Street, New York, NY 10001

Phototypeset in Baskerville by Intype, London
Printed and bound in Great Britain by
TJ Press (Padstow) Ltd, Padstow, Cornwall

British Library Cataloguing in Publication Data
A catalogue record for this book is available from the British Library

Library of Congress Cataloging in Publication Data
Burnett, John
Idle hands: the experience of unemployment, 1790–1990 / John Burnett.
p. cm.
Includes bibliographical references and index.
1. Unemployment–Great Britain–History. 2. Labor market–Great
Britain–History. 3. Great Britain–Social conditions–18th
century. 4. Great Britain–Social conditions–19th century. 5.
Great Britain–Social conditions–20th century. I. Title.
HD5765.A6B88 1994
331.13′7941–dc20   93–40069

ISBN 0–415–05500–8 (hbk)
ISBN 0–415–05501–6 (pbk)

CONTENTS

LIST OF TABLES

ACKNOWLEDGEMENTS

The research for this book was made possible by a grant from the Economic and Social Research Council, and its completion and preparation for publication was greatly aided by the award of a Leverhulme Emeritus Fellowship: I am grateful to both institutions for their valuable support. The book draws extensively on previous research into working-class autobiography in which my collaborators, Professor David Vincent and Dr David Mayall, took major parts. In recent years oral history has added importantly to the written record and I acknowledge my debt to those who have worked in this field, especially Dennis Marsden, Jeremy Seabrook and Nigel Gray. I also wish to thank colleagues at Brunel University, particularly Drs Helen Bolderson, Barbara Goodwin and Johnstone Birchall, for many helpful suggestions, and a graduate student, Stanley White, for a preliminary investigation in the university archive of autobiographies. The Inter-Library loan staff were invaluable for their willing perseverance in obtaining obscure publications, while in typing my manuscript Valerie Radford and Annemarie Maggs battled intelligently and uncomplainingly with my illegibility. Last, but foremost, I thank my wife for voluntary research assistance, grammatical corrections and domestic forbearance.

INTRODUCTION

Unemployment has been an outstanding problem of modern Britain, and, at times, the overwhelming concern of domestic policy, overshadowing all other economic and social issues. Not surprisingly, many economists have attempted to analyse and explain its causes, and many politicians, past and present, have offered remedies for one of the most disturbing features of the modern state. No historian, however, has written a history of unemployment which focuses on the experience of people without work. That is the present aim – not to propose further explanations or social policies, but to recover, so far as possible from direct evidence, the impact of unemployment on ordinary lives. Familiarity has led to treating unemployment almost as a 'numbers game'; whether the current rate is two, three or four million becomes a statistical exercise, sanitized and dehumanized, though with powerful political overtones. The concern of this book is the reverse of that – to ask how unemployment happened to individual people, how they and their families reacted to and coped with it, what steps they took to find work and what remedies were available to them if they failed. And, because life is not only about physical survival, what was it like to be without work, and what did one feel about it? 'The real, central theme of History', wrote G. M. Young, 'is not what happened, but what people felt about it when it was happening'. Inner lives, thoughts and emotions may be particularly difficult to recreate, but that, too, is part of the aim of this book.

Three main types of contemporary evidence are used in order to try to answer these questions. The principal source is the autobiographies of working people who experienced and described periods of unemployment as part of their wider life histories. Such writings are a unique historical source, almost ignored until recently, but providing direct, first-hand accounts of ordinary lives, filtered by memory and the passage of time so that they record the most significant events and the sharpest emotions. Recent research has now uncovered more than two thousand such autobiographies, published and unpublished, written by working

1

people whose lives covered the years 1790 to 1945.[1] Though varying in quantity between occupations and regions, and in the quality of detail provided, they cover the whole range of working-class experience. At least 200 autobiographers suffered and described periods of unemployment, and their testimonies constitute the core of primary material in the following chapters. For more recent years the written accounts are supplemented by oral testimonies of witnesses whose experiences were recorded by others, sometimes in response to a set of directed questions. Autobiographical history and oral history are thus different but complementary approaches to reconstructing the past, and both are used here.

A second contemporary source of evidence about unemployment lies buried in Parliamentary Papers – the vast accumulation of 'Blue Books', Reports of Royal Commissions, Parliamentary Committees, government and departmental enquiries in which Britain is especially rich.[2] A thirst for social enquiry became a characteristic of the nineteenth century, and as the problems of an industrializing, urbanizing society increased, almost every aspect of life fell under public scrutiny as experts in administration, law, medicine and other disciplines were called to give evidence on, and propose remedies for, contemporary ills. These enquiries therefore tend to represent the other side of the coin from autobiographies, reflecting 'official' opinion and attitudes and more rarely calling for the views of those directly affected. Although only a few Parliamentary Papers were primarily concerned with unemployment, many dealt with poverty and poor relief, with industries in decline, depressions in trade and labour conditions, and these necessarily included discussion of those without work.

A third major source of contemporary evidence is the social investigations undertaken by concerned individuals, groups and societies. Again, Britain has a long history of such enquiries, ranging from the pioneering studies of David Davies and Sir Frederic Eden in the 1790s to Henry Mayhew's survey of London labour in the 1850s – 'the first attempt to publish the history of a people from the lips of the people themselves' – and the researches into poverty of Charles Booth and Seebohm Rowntree at the end of the century. The onset of unprecedented levels of unemployment in the 1920s and 1930s produced a flood of enquiry, including for the first time studies of its psychological impact, while its return in the 1970s and 1980s has prompted similar investigations, aided now by tape-recording and television as well as the written word.

In total, then, we have a mass of documentary material, some of it central, some more tangential to the social impact of unemployment. To be meaningful as history, the experience of individuals has to be set in the wider context of the social, economic and occupational changes of the period, and this book therefore also draws on the work of other historians, principally specialists in the history of labour, poverty and poor

2

relief. The changing attitudes of the state towards unemployment, and the remedies – or lack of them – which it undertook, form an essential part of the contextual background against which the experiences of individuals are discussed.

A recent author on the economics of unemployment has commented:

> Unemployment is like an elephant: easier to recognize than to define. Definitions abound. Practices differ between countries. They are apt to change within countries, too; politicians beset by a sharp rise in unemployment on a given definition sometimes yield to the temptation to redefine their problem away.[3]

Fortunately, we do not need to penetrate far into this technical jungle, since it is not too difficult to arrive at a commonsense meaning of the term which carries general acceptance.

'Unemployment' was not honoured by inclusion in the Oxford English Dictionary until 1888, significantly during the so-called Great Depression, though both 'unemployment' and 'unemployed' were used occasionally in official reports of the 1830s, if not earlier. In the early nineteenth century more descriptive expressions such as 'want of employment' and 'out of employ' were generally used, as were phrases such as the 'surplus' or 'superfluity of labour'. The meaning, nevertheless, was clear: that there were people who normally worked but who, for various reasons, were unable to find work. Certain categories immediately became excluded from the definition. A slave could not be unemployed as he was bound to work for life: so too was another unfree, dependent worker, the medieval villein or serf. At the other extreme, people of wholly independent means who do not need to work in order to live – members of the 'leisured class' – cannot be said to be unemployed in the ordinary sense, though they may be idle. Independent workers such as writers or artists cannot strictly be unemployed as long as they have the tools of their trades, though they may be poor, and neither can owners of businesses, shopkeepers or farmers unless prevented from working by legal process. 'Unemployment' refers essentially to those who have to sell their labour in return for a wage or salary. They are not technically dependent, because they can withdraw their labour, but neither are they protected, because they can normally be dismissed by their employer. Unemployment is therefore a characteristic of a free labour market which, in turn, is a feature of a capitalist economy.

Within this broad definition there are clearly some groups which have to be excluded. People may be too young or too old to work, though in the two centuries covered by this book there were no generally applicable age requirements for either group. In the early nineteenth century some children from the age of five or six upwards worked in certain occupations until legislation setting minimum ages of eight to ten years was gradually extended to factories, mines, workshops and agriculture between 1833 and 1867: after 1880, when attendance at school to the age of ten became compulsory, this, in theory at least, established a minimum age for full-time employment. At the other end of the scale, there was no general retirement age outside the public services such as the civil service, local government, teachers, police and postmen: in the later nineteenth century larger industrial employers set their own retirement ages, though there was nothing covering agriculture or the host of casual trades. Before the introduction of old age pensions for those over the age of seventy in 1909, most workers worked as long as they were able, sometimes on reduced wages in their declining years. Given the lower expectation of life, retirement was not an option for many people: as late as 1901 less than 8 per cent of the UK population was aged sixty or more, compared with 20 per cent in 1985.[4]

Henry Mayhew subtitled the fourth volume of his study of London labour and the London poor, 'Those That Will Not Work'. There were always some who, though poor, chose not to work, preferring the life of a tramp or beggar, perhaps combined with some occasional work or criminal activity. This was a sizeable group in the nineteenth century, many perhaps unable or unwilling to adapt to the new requirements of town life and factory work, but since they chose, at least in some sense, not to be part of the labour force, they excluded themselves from the possibility of employment. 'Tramping' was not, however, necessarily an indication of unwillingness to work: on the contrary, as subsequent chapters will show, it was often a genuine search for work organized by craft unions for their workless members, and as such occupies an important place in the social history of unemployment. The activities of professional criminals – thieves, burglars, swindlers and the like – can hardly be regarded as 'work' in the normal sense of the word, even if their illegality does not place them outside the definition. Although Mayhew's investigations into the poor were highly innovative, he was sufficiently bound by the morality of his time to include the estimated 80,000 London prostitutes among 'Those Who Will Not Work' (though he devoted over a hundred pages to their various categories and haunts): his view hardly seems justifiable, particularly since prostitution was officially sanctioned and licensed at certain times and places during the Victorian period.

Finally, one must exclude from the unemployed those unable to work through physical or mental disability. Many of the more serious cases could be treated as indigent poor, and maintained in public institutions such as workhouses and lunatic asylums, though the less afflicted would often be supported by their families and might even do occasional, casual work: the borderline of 'unemployability' is a narrow one. But regularly employed workers suffered from periodic illnesses or accidents, many of the latter arising directly out of their work in mines, factories or on the land, and involuntary unemployment of this kind clearly comes within the usual meaning of the term.

Enough has been said to indicate some of the definitional difficulties. The discussion may be summarized by saying that a person is unemployed when he or she is of an age to work, is fit and available for work, needs and wishes to work, is seeking it but is unable to find it. This inelegant definition is the one that will be used.

Unemployment has many causes and takes many forms, and economists have distinguished a number of different types. At the simplest level, people changing jobs, either voluntarily or involuntarily, may be unemployed for a brief period, perhaps only for a few days or a week or two. This is frictional unemployment, an inevitable consequence of mobility of labour and of changes in the demand for it. Indeed, William Beveridge in his classic study, *Unemployment: A Problem of Industry* (1909), believed that an expanding economy required some small degree of unemployment, an 'irreducible minimum' which he put at about 2 per cent for skilled trades and rather more for unskilled. There could never be zero unemployment because demands for labour were always fluctuating, people were always changing jobs, and there always appeared to be 'a general and normal excess of the supply of labour over the demand'.[5]

Beveridge believed that there must also always be some underemployment – that is, people who work fairly regularly throughout the year in the sense of doing some work each week but rarely, if ever, are able to put in a full week. Underemployment applied particularly to the casual trades which required little more than strength – general labouring, portering, navvying, dockwork, carting, roadwork and the like for men; laundrywork, cleaning and sweated domestic trades for women. In Charles Booth's monumental survey of *London Life and Labour* (1889–1902) casual labourers were located in the two lowest classes, A and B. Class A consisted of occasional labourers, loafers, street-sellers and semi-criminals: 'Their life is the life of savages. . . . They degrade whatever they touch. . . . It is now hereditary to a very considerable extent'. Class B were dock-workers and other casual labourers: most worked less than three days a week, and Booth thought it doubtful whether many could work full time. They were 'inevitably poor' from shiftlessness, helplessness, idleness and drink, and could not stand the dullness and regularity of modern industrial life. Booth saw this group as a permanent sub-stratum or 'residuum' of society, the only remedy for which was removal to some form of labour colonies.

Underemployment and frictional employment are distinguishable from a third category, seasonal unemployment, though all share the characteristic of irregularity. Seasonal unemployment takes two main forms – climatic and social. Agriculture, the largest occupation of the British people in the first half of the nineteenth century, was especially subject to variations in demand for labour at different times of the year, heaviest in hay and corn harvest from June to September, least in winter months from December to March. Farmers met this difficulty by keeping small numbers of permanent men for specialist work all the year round, and employing day labourers as needed for the busier seasons. This often meant unemployment or underemployment for labourers during several months in the year. Many other occupations besides farming also had regular alternations of busy and slack seasons, normally showing a trend from slackness in winter to activity in spring and summer: this was especially true of outdoor constructional work, building, bricklaying, painting and trades which depended on building activity such as furnishing. The reverse applied to coal-miners, iron- and steel-workers and gasworkers, who were busiest in winter and slackest in summer, following seasonal demands.[6] Here were cases where unemployment could not be laid at the door of shiftless workers, and for whom the only remedy seemed to lie in a system of insurance against the slack times.

So far, the types of unemployment considered were traditional in the sense that they had existed, though in less acute form, before the vast economic and industrial changes which gathered speed from the late eighteenth century onwards. Other, more 'modern' types of unemployment – technological, cyclical and structural – were principally associated with the new forces of production, the mechanization of industry and the expansion of world markets as a result of the Industrial Revolution. Rapid technological change has been a characteristic of British industry for the last two hundred years; automation, micro-processors and information technology are only the most recent stages in a continuum of innovation. The question which has greatly concerned workers ever since the earliest days is whether mechanization destroys jobs. Almost without exception, economists have argued that in the long run mechanization actually increases employment by expanding demand and by creating new types of skilled personnel, but most have acknowledged that in the short term some workers might not be immediately absorbed and some might not or could not ever adapt to new techniques. Issues of this kind were especially prominent in the early stages of industrialization, when 'Luddite' framework-knitters rose in revolt, agricultural labourers destroyed threshing-machines, and handloom-weavers suffered an agonized death at the hands of the new power-looms, but technological unemployment has continued into modern times, albeit masked by euphemisms of 'redundancy' and 'early retirement'.

The progress of the new industrial system was by no means regular, however, but subject to cycles of booms and slumps, identified from at least as early as the 1790s. The new machines could increase output almost infinitely, but their owners could not predict the demand for their products nearly so well, especially when overseas markets were disrupted by wars, revolutions and financial crises. But once production had been geared up it was difficult to slow down quickly: unsold goods therefore glutted the market in the down-swing of the trade cycle, machines were idle and workers unemployed until the surpluses were sold and trade revived. On at least thirteen occasions between 1815 and 1914 slumps threw thousands out of work,[7] presenting poor law administrators and charitable organizations with the unpalatable problem of men and women who desperately wanted to work and for whom a deterrent workhouse was a totally inappropriate remedy.

Fluctuations in the trade cycle were still a major cause of the exceptionally high rates of unemployment between the two world wars. Between 1921 and 1939 the average unemployment rate of insured workers was 14 per cent: it was never less than 10 per cent, and at the worst, in 1932, it reached 22 per cent or 2,828,000 workers.[8] Britain's problems were part of the world depression which affected virtually every country, whether industrialized or not, but Britain, as a trading nation, was among the worst hit: markets for our staple products, coal, iron and steel, ship-building and cotton textiles declined steeply, partly because of lack of demand at home and abroad, partly due to intense competition from more recently industrialized nations like America and Japan. Cyclical movements were violent, but relatively short term, and most of the unemployed were likely to be out of work for less than six months at a time, though that might be a recurrent disaster. But what was new in the 1930s was that even in the best years there remained a hard core of 'out-of-works' of around 10 per cent, and much more in the old staple industries centred in the 'distressed areas': this was structural unemployment, the consequence of a permanent decline in demand for iron and steel, coal, ships and textiles – the very commodities on which Britain's Victorian prosperity had been built. By then long-term unemployment of more than a year had emerged as a new phenomenon, affecting around a quarter of the jobless total, consigning tens of thousands of men in middle life to lengthy, even permanent, unemployment.

In post-1945 years it became customary for economists following John Maynard Keynes to explain the 'Great Depression' as a result of a lack of effective demand, and to believe that any recurrence could be avoided by expansionary financial policies. For almost thirty years after the war unemployment in Britain averaged a mere 2.2 per cent: it began to rise, however, from the early 1970s, averaging 5 per cent over the period 1974–8, and 9.8 per cent over 1979–84.[9] In the year ending mid–1986 unemployed claimants in the UK totalled 3,294,000, higher than in 1932 although representing a somewhat lower rate because of an increased total workforce; the long-term unemployed in July 1986 were 41 per cent of all claimants, the highest proportion ever.[10] Business cycles, of which there were eight between 1945 and 1985, continued to influence unemployment rates, though of shorter duration and less amplitude than formerly. Some observers have blamed the return of mass unemployment on an over-valued exchange rate and the adverse effects of this on Britain's competitiveness in export markets; other economists and politicians have argued excessive wage and price inflation, while others again have seen unemployment as partly benefit-induced, claiming that over-generous welfare systems reduce the need and incentive to work. The debate continues over the causes of recent unemployment, as well as over the real numbers of the unemployed.

This book surveys the changing nature, extent and experience of unemployment in modern Britain over the last two hundred years. From around the late eighteenth century a series of revolutionary changes became evident which were to change profoundly the whole character of British economy and society, creating new occupations and classes, new problems and, ultimately, new remedies. A demographic revolution resulted in a trebling of the population of England and Wales from a mere six million in 1750 to eighteen million by 1850. Although the causes of this 'population explosion' are still a subject of debate, it was in some way associated with the economic changes of the industrial and agrarian revolutions: by the end of the eighteenth century industrialization was an irreversible process, the exploitation of machines, land and human beings for profit having been universally accepted as the road to wealth and power in the modern world. In 1801 almost four out of five people lived in rural areas, most of them working on the land or deriving their livelihoods from it: by 1911 four out of five people lived in towns and cities, the majority of them industrial wage earners. Thus, the nineteenth century witnessed an economic and social transformation of unparalleled speed and scale which changed the life of the worker in almost every way. In the new philosophy of laissez-faire there was no real place for unemployment. Poverty there would always be: it was natural and inherent in society, and the 'iron law of wages' dictated that there must always be many living on the edge of subsistence, but work would always be found in an expanding economy for those who searched hard enough. A poor law which supported – indeed, some believed, encouraged – the idle and shiftless had no place in the new climate of competitive individualism, and from the 1790s onwards it faced a mounting attack from the growing converts to political economy.

The first four chapters of the book follow the changing fortunes of major occupations in the period 1790–1870 – agriculture, the largest occupation of the people in the early nineteenth century (Chapter 1), but thereafter experiencing a long-term erosion in employment as Britain ceased to provide her own basic foods (Chapter 4); handloom weaving, the classic example of technological decline in the face of the new machines (Chapter 2); and the skilled trades which suffered a loss of craft status and increasing irregularity of work due to pressure of numbers and changing consumer demands (Chapter 3). By the closing decades of the nineteenth century unemployment was becoming both more widespread and more recognized as a problem in its own right, distinct from that of poverty: these new trends, and the emergence of unemployment on to the political agenda, are the subject of Chapter 5, 'The Discovery of Unemployment'. In the periods of mass unemployment between the two world wars and since the 1970s, when the effects of depression were not limited to particular groups, the method in Chapters 6 and 7 is to treat the phenomenon as a whole, the shorter time-scales and greater availability of data allowing more detailed consideration both of the nature of recent unemployment and its human consequences. Finally, the Conclusion evaluates the changing responses to unemployment over the period, tests some of the psychological theories about its personal impact against the historical record, and raises some questions about the future of work and employment in post-industrial Britain.

1

UNEMPLOYMENT IN THE COUNTRYSIDE, 1790–1834

WAR AND UNEMPLOYMENT, 1793–1815

In their classic study of the village labourer in the early nineteenth century J. L. and Barbara Hammond wrote that 'This world has no Member of Parliament, no press, it does not make literature, or write history; no diary or memoirs have kept alive for us the thoughts and cares of the passing day'.[1] More recent research suggests that it is possible to penetrate this 'underground world', at least to some extent, from the writings of labourers themselves, a surprising number of whom recorded their experiences of rural life from the late eighteenth century onwards. One of these was Joseph Mayett of Quainton, Buckinghamshire, (1783–1839), who wrote his autobiography between 1828 and 1831, in itself a remarkable achievement for someone whose only formal education was at Sunday school. He was the fourth of ten children of an agricultural labourer who worked for many years for the same farmer at 9s. a week in summer and 6s. in winter, but managed without recourse to poor relief, preferring his respectable poverty. Joseph's own life spanned a very different economic climate – the long succession of French Wars between 1793 and 1815, rapid inflation and famine years of bad harvests, then the post-war depression and widespread unemployment: his history was therefore one of downward social mobility from what was already a miserably low base. His autobiography is the antithesis of a success story: it falls into two distinct periods – youth and early manhood during the war, and adult life from 1815 until his early death in 1839.

> I was deprived of a liberal Education for instead of being Sent to School I was Set to Lace making to provide something toward a livelihood through the narrowness of our Circumstances. However, notwithstanding this my mother being able to read and write a little though in some instances hardly legible yet She taught me to read at a very early age.

He was then seven years old. In 1795, the first of the famine years when wheat rose to double its normal price, he was twelve and strong enough for field labour despite suffering from periodic fits. He now began regular work, at first for the same master as his father, then in a series of yearly hirings during which he lived in with his employers as a farm servant.

> In the year 1798 I left my place on the 11th of October and on the 12th [Michaelmas Day] I went to Aylesbury fair and my father with me and there I was hired servant to another master in our own Parish at a lone farmhouse where there was only one servant man besides myself. . . . My father [a devout Methodist] Requested that my master would employ me in the garden in the spring of the year after I had done my other work while other servants had their liberty to go Cricket playing and other pastimes.

At Michaelmas 1800, now seventeen, he travelled further afield to the fair at Bicester in Oxfordshire and was hired by a farmer at Godington. This was to be his first experience of how precarious employment could be, even in wartime when there was a general scarcity of labour: 'when I had been there just a month he came to me . . . and told me he thought I should not suit him and paid me for my time and told me to take my cloths and go but he never told me the reason nor he and I never disagreed'. By this date the natural recourse of someone 'out of place' was to turn to his parish of settlement for help. Quainton had evidently adopted a 'roundsman' system by which the unemployed were sent to local farmers at wages below the usual rate paid either by the parish or by the employer in lieu of his poor rates.

> So I came away and went to the overseer for work and he sent me one week to a master in the parish to work and gave me eight pence per day [4s. a week] and the next week he sent me to another master at the same price or wages. . . . This was the first time that the Cares of the world laid hold on me and now I began to wonder what I should do for Bread almost all that year untill the next harvest at three shillings and eightpence the half peck loaf [4 lbs. 5¼ ozs.] and I worked for four shillings per week. . . . After I had been there one week my master sent his son to tell me to Come to him again and he would pay me himself. Accordingly I went and when the next week was ended he advanced my wages sixpence per week. . . . During this time through the dearness of provisions I was obliged to live cheifly on barley bread and hog peas except when my master gave me my dinner when I went out with the team. This I was not very fond of but it being winter and provisions dear and many servants out of place I could not extracate myself from it but in about a month or five weeks after Christmass in the begining of the year 1801 I found my master intended to keep me on but in

consequence of the dearness of provision he would not hire me servant so long as he could have me at four shillings and sixpence per week.

At Michaelmas 1802, now nineteen, Mayett obtained another hiring at Waddesdon Hill in Buckinghamshire, with a family who were staunch members of the Calvinist Baptist church there. Mayett was troubled with his conscience at this time, though his sins do not seem to have been more heinous than occasional swearing and a minutely documented theft of apples. When his innocent association with a young woman member of the Baptist church was publicly denounced by the minister, Mayett left this hiring of his own accord. As a farm servant he was required to be under the control of his employers, not only in his working hours but in respect of his social life and moral behaviour, but as a strong-willed youth on the verge of manhood, Mayett was not willing to accept such abuses of authority. After one more employment, making altogether twelve hirings between the ages of thirteen and twenty, in February 1803 he enlisted into the Royal Buckinghamshire Militia, serving with them until the end of the war in 1815. Although Mayett is not specific about his reasons it is not difficult to imagine them. He had had several unhappy hirings, including beatings, abuse, and what he considered unjustified attacks on his character; there had been brief periods of unemployment and poorly paid parish work; above all, the army offered an escape from field drudg-ery and precarious poverty into what he believed was an honourable and glamorous career with hopes of promotion into a non-commissioned rank. In his last hiring at Buckingham he had seen the soldiers at Church service there 'all Serjants and Corporals and musick men and all very Clean. I was much delighted to see them and to hear the musick. This was Congenial with my carnal nature and a great opening for Satan to draw me away from all thoughts about religion'.[2]

In one respect at least Mayett was a typical man of his time. At the first official census of the population in 1801, 80 per cent of the nine million people of England and Wales were rural inhabitants, only 20 per cent town-dwellers: in 1831, when occupations were enumerated in some detail, there were 961,000 families in Britain and 1,243,000 males over twenty engaged in agriculture – by far the largest single occupation and almost three times greater than the next largest, the textile industries.[3] Contrary to what William Cobbett believed, the rural population con-tinued to expand in the first half of the century despite the growing attractions of towns, and no English or Welsh county recorded a decline in numbers until after 1851: even then, agriculture was still the occu-pation of a quarter of all males.

In this vast army of toilers of the fields Mayett was always in the lower ranks, and in later life was to sink to the bottom. By his time there were at least four clear categories of farmworkers with markedly differing wages, security of employment, housing and general standards of comfort. The 'sergeants' he so much admired – the aristocrats of agricultural labour – were skilled workers such as hedgers, thatchers and drainers, some of whom were resident on large estates and some itinerant, working for piece-rates or by contract.[4] Below them were regular labourers who worked for the same master for years or sometimes for life: they usually had responsibility for a department of farming such as plough-teams, wagons or livestock, and had the somewhat doubtful privilege of a tied cottage which rendered them always on call. A third category was the farm servant who was hired for up to a year, was boarded and lodged in the farmhouse or in farm buildings such as the stable, and was paid a small lump sum, usually at the end of the hiring: some had their service renewed for years; others, like Mayett, changed frequently by mutual consent, dismissal or resignation.

By Mayett's time farm service was in decline in the south and east of England, though it persisted throughout the century in many parts of the north and west. As Ann Kussmaul has shown, it was mainly a transitional status between childhood and adulthood, a kind of agricultural apprenticeship usually beginning at around twelve to fourteen and ending at marriage.[5] In past times the majority of English youths had experienced this removal from home and family, which released space in overcrowded cottages and obliged an employer to feed and maintain a growing lad. In Mayett's Buckinghamshire in 1778 there were 1,190 farmers, 1,750 labourers and 1,360 servants,[6] suggesting that most farmers had still found it convenient to keep a supply of living-in labour always on hand. The advantages to the servant were an informal training in many branches of farmwork, fairly high security of employment (though Mayett was twice without a place in seven years) and the rather remote chance of accumulating sufficient savings to rent a small farm after about ten years. But during the French Wars farm service rapidly declined in the arable counties of the south and east for a variety of economic and social reasons. In the years of hyper-inflation it became increasingly costly for employers to board servants: moreover, the more intensive farming methods on enclosed lands required labour which was more seasonal and flexible, much between spring and harvest, but less in winter. In these circumstances it made sense to throw the burden of costs on to the independent day labourer, often subsidized by the poor-rates. At the same time, the high profits of wartime agriculture were creating a wealthier farming class which could aspire to the social refinements of the squirearchy in terms of housing, furnishing, dress and diet: the 'rude manners' of farm servants were no longer welcome at the farmer's mahogany table or even in his wife's tidy kitchen. By 1851 only 277,887 farm servants over the age of twenty remained in England, 74 per cent of them in the north and west where pastoral farming still needed year-round labour.[7]

In the arable counties the result was substantially to change the ratio between servants and day labourers, the lowest category in the hierarchy of farmworkers. Unlike the 'constant men' these had no regular employer but picked up work by the week or the day as they could: they usually rented cottages in 'open' villages and therefore often had to walk miles to and from their work. They were particularly vulnerable to seasonal unemployment and in a hard winter might find little or no work for three or four months, but since they could be laid off at a moment's notice they were also at the mercy of storms, heavy rains or drought at other times of the year: the account books of farmers make it clear that there were many weeks when a man only worked and was therefore only paid for three or four days. On arable farms the trend during the war was to use the day labourers as a reserve army, called in as required to augment the smaller numbers of regular men and living-in servants, and to pay them by the piece for specific tasks rather than on a regular basis. The only time these men might be reasonably sure of constant work was between spring and autumn, and especially during the busy periods between May to June and September to October, when, with extra harvest earnings, they could expect to renew boots and clothes and repay debts. The demand for labour at hay and corn harvests was often so great that casual workers were also brought in – old men, women and children, people from neighbouring towns and specialized gangs of migrant workers from Scotland, Wales and Ireland who followed regular harvest routes through the summer months. This marked irregularity of labour requirements is illustrated by a 1,600-acre farm at Dunton, Norfolk, in the 1780s, where the fourteen servants and twelve day labourers needed sixty-three hands at harvest time, paid from 42 to 45s. for taking the harvest (usually four to five weeks) and supplied with meat and beer three times a day.[8]

Although during the war years farm servants might suffer from breaks in hirings and day labourers from short-time and winter lay-offs, widespread or long-term unemployment were not major problems. More serious were price-rises during which wages tended to lag behind, especially in the frequent years of harvest failure when bread, the staple food, could double or treble in a very short time. Inflation had already been occurring during the second half of the eighteenth century, as the Revd David Davies noted when he surveyed the budgets of his parishioners of Barkham, Berkshire, in 1795: between 1750 and 1795 the cost of a half-peck loaf had risen from 7–8d. to 11d.–1s. 2d., a pound of bacon from 5–6d. to 8–9d., a pound of butter from 5–6d. to 10d.–1s. and a pair of men's shoes from 4s. 6d.–5s. to 6s. 6d.–7s. 6d.: in total, he recorded price-rises in the period from 50 to 100 per cent.[9] Davies concluded that the earnings of a man in regular work (7s. a week plus a further 1s. a week for four months in the year extra task work) together with the occasional earnings of his wife (averaged at 6d. a week over a year) would barely maintain them and two children, whereas in 1750 they would have supported three children 'and in a better manner too'.[10] Unlike many of his contemporaries, Davies did not ascribe the poverty of his parishioners to idleness or extravagance: 'These thrifty people, in assigning the cause of their misery, agreed in ascribing it to the high prices of the necessities of life. Everything, said they, is so dear that we can hardly live'.[11]

It was, wrote Davies, 'The insufficiency of their wages for the supply of their wants': earnings barely covered the basic food items of flour (6s. 3d. out of the weekly earnings of 8s. 6d.), yeast, salt, a pound of bacon, three-quarters of a pound of sugar and one ounce of tea, but when rent, clothing, fuel and medical expenses were added, every one of the Barkham budgets examined was in deficit by amounts ranging up to £7 2s. 9d. a year.

Two years later, in 1797, Sir Frederic Morton Eden's much larger study, *The State of the Poor*, disclosed a similar situation in many parts of the country. Of fifty-two family budgets of labourers examined, forty-four were accumulating debts ranging from a few shillings a year to £18 6s. 1d. at Diss in Norfolk and £25 12s. 2d. at Kegworth in Leicestershire.[12] Here, 'work was very scarce in the beginning of 1795'. Although Eden believed that the main causes of poverty were high prices and large families of children not yet old enough to work, it was noticeable that unemployment now sometimes featured as an independent factor. At Stony Stratford in Buckinghamshire, 'there seems to be a great want of employment: most labourers are (as it is termed) on The Rounds' and wholly paid by the parish. At Yardley Gobion in Northamptonshire, nine or ten men were 'out of employ' in winter and the parish had agreed that every farmer whose rent was £20 a year or more should take a man for a day at 1s., while at Kibworth-Beauchamp, Leicestershire, a recent enclosure had converted arable land to pasture and only one-third of the men employed twenty years ago were now needed. Here the farmer paid 6d. a day to the roundsmen, the parish adding 4d.[13]

In discussing remedies for what was now widely recognized as a critical situation, Davies suggested 'providing additional employment for men and boys in winter, that they may lose no time at that season when they are usually most distressed', regulating the wages of labourers according to the price of wheat, and making specific provision from the poor-rates for families with three or more children too young to earn. The unemployed should be found work on bringing the wastes and commons into cultivation, but if useful work could not be found, 'it would be obviously better policy to set all such persons as cannot otherwise be employed on the useless work of building pyramids than to let them starve in idleness, or become rogues, vagabonds and beggars'.[14]

Contemporary observers like Eden and Davies were at least half-aware that great structural changes were occurring in the agricultural economy. Farming was attempting to meet a growing demand for food from a rapidly increasing population at a time of war when imports were difficult or impossible: given this monopoly of a seller's market farmers and landowners prospered as never before. At least three million acres of common fields and wastes were enclosed by private Act of Parliament during the war, and probably as many again by private agreement: much of this was marginal land, only worth cultivating during the period of high prices. Before the war wheat had usually sold at 40 to 50s. a quarter: in 1795, after a bad harvest, it jumped to 80s., averaged 83s. over the decade 1801–10 and 106s. from 1811 to 1813; at its highest yearly average, in 1812, it was 126s. 6d. and in one month reached 176s. a quarter.[15] With a commodity like wheat, the demand for which was relatively inelastic, quite small failures of the crop could push up prices disproportionately, and of the twenty-two wartime years, fourteen harvests were deficient in some respect. Although over the wartime period it is likely that labourer's wages nearly doubled[16] keeping roughly in line with wholesale prices, they tended to be 'stickier' and to lag behind the sudden and unprecedented rises in retail costs not only of wheat but also of barley, oats, beef and mutton. Given also the facts that work was tending to become more seasonal on the newly-enclosed arable farms[17] and that in some parts of the country labourers' wives were losing their by-employment of domestic spinning and weaving as factories took over, it seems impossible to ignore the contemporary evidence of decline in the labourer's condition.

In the crisis year 1795, and against the background of war and fears of discontent if not of actual revolution, the magistrates of Berkshire assembled at Speenhamland and agreed to supplement the wages of labourers on a fixed scale according to the price of bread and the number of children in the family. Forms of 'Speenhamland' relief quickly spread over the arable counties of the south and east, though in fact a large variety of poor law practices was developed by the virtually autonomous parishes:[18] our concern is only with those which attempted to provide for the unemployed. Under the great Poor Law Statute of 1601 (43rd. Eliz.) was included a somewhat ambiguous requirement that the parish overseers should 'take order for setting to work all such persons as have no means to maintain and use any ordinary or daily trade': over time, this had come to be applied to agricultural labour as well as handicrafts, and by Gilbert's Act of 1782 it was made a requirement for those parishes which adopted the measure to provide work for the able-bodied unemployed, their wages being paid to the parish which would then pay a maintenance to the labourer. The implication of this, confirmed by a further Act of 1796, was that the work and the relief should be outside the workhouse (i.e. outdoor) which in future would be confined to the care of the impotent poor such as orphans, the old, sick and disabled. It was now the duty of the parish to employ the poor, especially during the winter, and to maintain them and their families irrespective of the value of their work.

The most usual remedy was the 'roundsman' system previously mentioned. It could take at least three forms: payment of the labourer by the parish which made a contract with a farmer for certain work to be done at an agreed price; payment partly by the farmer, made up by the parish in accordance with an allowance scale; and finally, an auction of the unemployed who were then knocked down to the highest bidder. A further variant was the labour-rate system, an agreement between the rate-payers that each would employ a certain number, not according to need, but according to the amount of their rates or rent or the acreage of their farms. All these were attempts to allocate the surplus labour of a parish between the employers – motivated partly by the requirement of 'setting to work', partly by the necessity of keeping a large supply of labour locally available against the heavy demands of spring and summer. As Elizabeth Melling has shown in her study of the poor law in Kent, such remedies were piecemeal and owed little or nothing to the initiative of a central government preoccupied with the war and reluctant to interfere in local affairs. In 1803 Kent had a total of 41,632 people receiving poor relief, 14 per cent of the population: of these, 6,337 adults and children were in workhouses, the rest receiving outdoor relief of various kinds – the roundsman system was common here, though the Speenhamland scale only operated in eight of the fifteen divisions of the county. In some parishes farms and workshops were established by the authorities for the employment of the poor, and parish land was allotted for cultivation, though what was described as a parish 'factory' at Staplehurst was not financially successful.[19] These at least were serious attempts at job creation, unlike the roundsman system which too often merely reallocated existing work, sometimes to the detriment of regular labourers who were then forced to become paupers to get employment. At Corsley in Wiltshire, which had the advantage of a long-established cloth industry as well as agriculture, 236 people out of a population of 1,412 were receiving relief in June 1801: here the hiring and boarding of labourers had fallen into disuse and the unemployed were set to work quarrying stones for road-building.[20] In Tysoe, Warwickshire, there were parish purchases of flax, hemp and yarn and of spinning wheels to set women to work for local weavers, and of scythes for men who were going up-country haymaking. There had been a roundsman system here since 1763, and work was also provided on the common lands before the enclosure of

17

1797–1800, and on the parish road which led off the turnpike. In January 1800 there were twenty-one on the round, probably married men who were always given preference for what work was available, but by January 1810 there were only six on the round and forty-six others receiving relief without work. The payments ranged from 1s. 8d. to 18s. per fortnight, being recorded in the accounts as 'lost time'.[21] In 1801, when bread reached 6s. 6d. the peck loaf, more than many men's weekly wage, the parish established a bakehouse, employed a baker and sold bread below cost, but even so it was better to be on the round, with the wage supplemented by the bread scale, than in regular work.[22]

The commonest form of work creation, as opposed to redistribution, was roadwork – usually consisting of the collection and preparation of stones to fill the holes and ruts of parish roads. This was both useful, at a time of increasing wheeled traffic, and was considered by the authorities to be fairly strenuous and therefore deterrent. As the Revd Hugh Wade Gery explained to a House of Lords Committee on the Poor Laws in 1817: 'It would have two good effects; in the first place it would employ those persons who are not wanted by the farmers, and it would make those persons endeavour to look out for work, which they are not desirous of doing'. Although the wage paid was deliberately kept below the local agricultural rates, parishes which operated an allowance system usually supplemented it for the number of children in the family, as they did for roundsmen in the Revd Gery's parish:

> He gets the remainder made up by the parish. They make up the half-crown per week for each individual in the family.
> Q. Then the fact of the allowance of half-a-crown a week to each individual makes it a complete matter of indifference to the workman himself whether he earns ten shillings or five shillings, or what it may be?
> A. It makes no difference to him if his family is large.[23]

Whether parish work and the roundsman system encouraged idleness, improvidence and large families and discouraged the search for work, as some landowners and farmers believed, is open to doubt. There were certainly many complaints about the unwillingness and inefficiency of such forced labour: that one good labourer could do the work of two or three roundsmen, that gangs of men set to roadwork required constant supervision and idled whenever the overseer's back was turned. No doubt the ideal worker was one like Thomas Smart who gave evidence before a Select Committee in 1824, one of the very few labourers to be called before any agricultural enquiry in the first half of the century. At forty-six he had had 'constant work' for the previous twenty-seven years, the last twenty for the same master.

How many children have you had? – Thirteen.

Have you ever received any relief from the parish for the support of any of these children? – For funerals, when any of them died, but not otherwise.

How many children have you alive now? – Seven. I buried six.

What have been your wages for the last five years? – The last two years I have had 8s. and the three years before that we had 10s. They have sunk us now to 8s.

Has your wife been able to earn any thing besides these wages? – She always did as far as she could.

Have your children obtained any thing by their labour for you? – We kept them at work as soon as they were able.

How much have they been earning in a week? – I do not know: the plaiting and lace making is gone, and they cannot earn anything hardly.

What is the food on which you have supported yourself and your family? – Bread and cheese, and what we could get; sometimes we were short, and sometimes we got enough for them.

Do you get meat on Sundays? – I have not had a bit of meat for a month together sometimes.

What do you drink? – Water.[24]

Such was the experience of a 'constant man' who had been fortunate in having regular work, winter and summer, since 1797. His life of plodding toil may be contrasted with that of John Clare, the son of an illegitimate labourer, who was to become an untutored poet compared by some to Keats, Coleridge and Wordsworth. He was born in July 1793 at Helpstone, 'a gloomy village in Northamptonshire', the eldest child of four, two of whom died in infancy. He began work at ten, scaring birds, weeding and tending sheep in the spring and summer, threshing corn in the winter and attending school for about three months in the year (his parents were both illiterate). The family experienced much privation during the dear years, living on barley bread and potatoes, particularly when his father was unable to work regularly: he was 'often crippled for months together with the rumatics for 10 or 12 years past and now totally drove from hard labour by them'.

At twelve, John had a year of hired service, general farm labouring and ploughing, then a spell working in the kitchen garden at Burghley, interrupted by almost a year of illness during which he was unemployed

19

at home while the family fell into debt for bread, shoes and rent. On recovery, he returned to farmwork in the spring and summer, but:

> When I was out of work I went to the woods gathering rotten sticks or picking up the dryd cow dung on the pasture which we call cazons for fireing. . . . I always wrote my poems in the fields, and when I was out of work I used to go out of the village to particular spots which I was fond of from the beauty or secrecy of the scenes.

Clare failed to get a clerk's appointment at Wisbech where, at the interview, he was 'betrayed' by his clothes and general appearance, and failed also to enlist in the Nottinghamshire Militia for which he was rejected as too short. He continued a precarious existence between lime-burning and farm jobs 'as I could catch them'; he eventually published four volumes of poetry, but spent the last twenty-seven years of his life in asylums until his death in 1864.[25]

Unlike Thomas Smart who, it seems, did not question the poor rewards of his labour, or Joseph Mayett who found consolation in religion, Clare bitterly resented the poverty which, he believed, blighted his life and happiness. 'Poverty has made a sad tool of me by times – and broken into that independence which is or ought to belong to every man by birthright. . . . I have been so long a lodger with difficulty and hope, and so often looked on the land of promise without meeting with it'. Clare's escape was into the woods and secret places where he found the inspiration for his rustic poetry. While he believed that poverty restricted his 'independence', it is fair to speculate whether he would have written poetry if, like Smart, he had worked winter and summer, for twenty-seven years, or if he had become a clerk in the lawyer's office in Wisbech. Periodic unemployment at least provided the time to write: poverty and obscurity were perhaps spurs which drove him to seek recognition for what he could do best.

PEACE AND PAUPERISM, 1815–30

As the long French Wars drew to a close the favourable period for agriculture also came to an end. The extensions of the cultivated area had meant a generally heavy demand for labour, at least during the spring, summer and autumn, intensified by the recruitment of so many young men into the services – an estimated 300,000 regular soldiers and embodied militia, plus 130,000 seamen and marines, representing one in every nine or ten men of military age in Great Britain and Ireland.[26] Although farmers had had to meet large rent, rate and tax increases, the high prices of corn and meat had ensured handsome profits averaging between 9 and 14 per cent a year. In fact, the collapse of prosperity began in 1813, two years before the Battle of Waterloo, with a series of good harvests which brought tumbling prices,[27] bankruptcies, the failure of ninety-two country banks, deserted farms and an atmosphere of gloom only briefly relieved by the victory celebrations of 1815. In the words of the celebrated agricultural historian, Lord Ernle, 'Peace and plenty proved a ghastly mockery to all classes of the community. To agriculturalists peace brought only beggary'.

While farmers pleaded for reductions in rents and tithes, they had direct control over their own labour supply, and economies in the numbers as well as cuts in the wages of workers were obvious responses to the depression. There was now a rapid decline in farm service and boarding, with the result that young workers who had formerly had secure employment through yearly hirings now swelled the numbers of day labourers and casual workers. Work became increasingly seasonal, especially in the arable south and east, where an abundance of labour ensured that extra hands could always be found for the busy times. Furthermore, as we shall see, the systems of poor relief which had emerged in wartime as temporary expedients, were now extended and manipulated by farmer rate-payers to ensure an abundant supply of cheap labour, subsidized by the public funding of the poor-rates. A rural population which increased 50 per cent between 1815 and 1851 could not be economically absorbed but was without the means of escape from parish bondage.

Between 1815 and 1830 the state of agriculture was subjected to a series of official investigations unparalleled in scope and intensity. Although much of the emphasis was on the plight of landowners and farmers, the fall in prices and profits and the effects of the Corn Law of 1815 on the grain market, there was also much discussion of the poor laws, wages and the general condition of labour. In 1816 the Board of Agriculture published an enquiry into *The Agricultural State of the Kingdom*, based largely on the replies of landholders to a series of questions sent out in a circular letter.[28] Question 8 asked the Board's respondents, 'What is the state of the Labouring Poor?': 273 replies to this were received from all parts of the country, of which 237 (87 per cent) reported a 'want of employment in terms more or less forcible'.[29] This was remarkable unanimity compared to the diversity of replies received to other questions, and clearly indicated the existence of a major problem causing widespread concern. Of the 237 replies, 101 described 'extreme distress' from unemployment causing 'great misery and wretchedness': only twenty-five letters gave a favourable report on the condition of the labourer, and a further eighteen believed that it was no better or worse than formerly, though in fifteen of these forty-three more favourable replies it was expected that conditions would shortly deteriorate. Reports from the individual counties filled out the overall gloomy picture. In Bedfordshire three out of four parishes reported many unemployed, and the corres-

21

pondent could not refrain from observing that 'the morals as well as the manners of the lower orders of the community have been degenerating since the earliest ages of the French Revolution. The doctrine of equality and the rights of man is not yet forgotten'.[30] At Caversham, Berkshire, the men were 'in great want of employ': of sixteen replies from Cambridgeshire all but two described unemployment 'wretched beyond example', 'dreadful' and 'very deplorable' while in Cumberland there was 'distress beyond all experience'. In Durham 'half [are] out of employment'; in Halstead, Essex, 'four-fifths want employment'; in Lincolnshire men were 'starving for want of employment', and at Brixnorth, Northamptonshire, there were 'four times more unemployed than ever known'.

The reports of 1816 showed little difference between the northern and southern counties, or between Scotland and England – all agricultural areas, whether arable or pastoral, were depressed beyond the recollections of any of the observers. Only in two circumstances were there slightly more optimistic reports – in the few cases where the labourer managed to keep a cow or two on the remaining commons or on holdings granted by the enclosure commissions, or in the neighbourhood of industrial towns where local manufacturers absorbed the 'surplus' labour. This was the case in Yorkshire in the parishes close to Huddersfield, and in Bromsgrove, Worcestershire, where labourers were employed in the nail and iron industry and were said to be 'in a good state'.[31]

These were the conditions to which Joseph Mayett returned in May 1815, one of the 300,000 soldiers and sailors suddenly discharged on to the labour market at the end of the war. At home again in Quainton he quickly got work for the spring and summer, but at Michaelmas 1815 he was unemployed and, as a single man, the parish would not give him work. Mayett's response to this early disaster was twofold: to marry one of the young women who, like him, had joined the Baptist church, and to scratch a living collecting rags and pedling cotton and laces. This precarious existence collapsed in 1816, a particularly bad year when people could not afford his wares, but in 1817 he managed to get agricultural work again at 7s. a week with bread at 3s. a loaf. 'In this Case I was much distressed, but the Summer Coming on I was soon relieved by an advance of wages but the harvest proved very wet so that I met with a disappoint by the great loss of time I sustained.'[32] On Lady Day 1822, 'my master discharged me because the rest of the Parish officers refused to employ their quota of men'.[33] Mayett was now reading Cobbett, Wooller and other radical authors, and was becoming disillusioned with organized religion.

From now until 1830, when his autobiography ended, Mayett could get no regular work and was usually employed by the parish. From 1825 to 1828 he was appointed parish hayward on the open field, but 'I found that the money alowed me for doing the office was less than paupers alowance, and I was Confined and obliged to work the same on the Sabath as on other days and I did not like it'.[34] In 1829 he was again out of work together with many others and was allowed only 4s. a week by the parish for threshing and roadwork. 'So some of us went to the Squire [also the local magistrate] to make our Complaint, but he would not hear a word we had to say, but began to swear and abuse us... he ordered the overseer not to relieve me nor find me a days work So long as I could get 4s. a week.'[35]

Between 1815 and 1828 Mayett worked for at least ten employers, had frequent periods of unemployment and from 1822 onwards was more or less permanently a pauper. Intelligent, perverse and argumentative, he was scarcely 'typical', though his experiences through the depressed years may well make him statistically representative of his class and occupation. His response to unemployment was to stand on his 'right' to relief by the parish, and when he felt ill-treated to go over the heads of the local officials to the county magistrates. As autobiography, Mayett's life is unusual because it ends as it began, as an agricultural labourer in a Buckinghamshire village: in that respect it contrasts with the memoirs of other working men who began life as he did but whose discontent with farmwork led them to other things. Alexander Somerville was born at Springfield, Berwickshire, in 1811, the last of eleven children of a poor agricultural labourer who could not spare a shilling to have his birth registered by the parish clerk. After only a year's schooling he began work at nine herding cows, moving on to hoeing and ploughing and in winter making drains and working on the roads (1s. a day and providing his own hammers): when these ended he went cutting timber, gardening and lime-burning, leaving home soon after 2 a.m. to begin work at 4 a.m. In summer there was harvesting, but at the Martinmas hiring fair at Dunse in 1827 men were more plentiful than masters and no one asked for him. At the Dunbar and Haddington fairs 'Every farmer could get more men than he wanted – men of full growth and good practice, while I was only aged seventeen. I had, however, done the work of a man for two or three years, and being as tall and as strong as most men I was not disposed to return to the pay of a boy'.[36]

In January 1828 he walked twenty-five miles through the snow to Edinburgh and was found work as a sawyer by his brother in a gang of building labourers: for the next few years he dug drains, worked on a new harbour and quarried stone in winter, went mowing hay and harvesting in summer, travelling far afield to get the best wages. 'About this time I began to reflect gravely on the life that was before me. I had learned no trade.... I had not always succeeded in getting hired as a ploughman, and had become a labourer at any kind of work that presented itself. Was I to continue, and do nothing better?'[37] By 1831 he could get no work of any kind. Applying for the position of librarian at a workingmen's reading room, 'I was pronounced to have formed a very absurd opinion of what a librarian should be when I thought that a person of my class could fulfil its duties'.[38] In despair and because 'other work could not be obtained', he and a friend enlisted in the Scots Greys. Somerville's later life took a quite different course. In the army he was court-martialled for radical activities – supporting the Parliamentary reform movement and objecting to the use of soldiers in suppressing popular demonstrations. He subsequently became a successful journalist and publisher, acted as Cobden's adviser on agricultural subjects and wrote an important book on the subject, *The Whistler at the Plough* (1852).

In his *Annals of the British Peasantry* (1895) Russell Garnier extolled the life of Somerville as an example of the superior industry and intelligence of the Scottish over the English labourer:

> The moral of his life's experiences is surely that, amidst the most unfavourable circumstances of an abnormally depressed period, the Scottish labourer was capable, by energy and good conduct, of keeping his head above water until he could better his lot.[39]

Whether this was a 'national character' argument, or whether Somerville's diet of 'hummelled bread' (a mixture of barley and beans) and skimmed milk was supposed to breed fortitude and ambition is not clear. A high proportion of children on both sides of the border necessarily began their working lives as farmboys or female farm servants and continued as such through their teens, but in adult life moved to other occupations more rewarding, secure or socially respectable than agricultural labour. In many autobiographies of the early nineteenth century farmwork is the stand-by, casual occupation of young men on the tramp, mingled at the appropriate seasons with navvying, quarrying, general labouring and pedling, a peripatetic life which usually ended on marriage and the adoption of a settled trade. James Dawson Burn, born about 1802, the illegitimate son of itinerant beggars, spent the first twenty years of his life hawking, begging and agricultural labouring in the north of England, the Scottish lowlands and in Ireland, picking up whatever casual work he could at harvesting, hoeing and shearing interspersed with work as a putter in a coalmine and as an assistant to an Irish cheapjack. His adult life took him first to apprenticeship to a felt hatmaker (1822–9), to business on his own account, and, when this failed, to a series of employments ranging from publican, commercial traveller and warehouseman to clerk, debt collector, journalist and author.[40]

Men like Burn and Somerville believed that they had made something of their lives, overcoming all the disadvantages of parentage, lack of education and poverty. Because they had no settled trade their youth was spent in 'rambling' with relatively short periods of unemployment separating a wide variety of casual work: both rejected farm labour as a permanent employment and had aspirations of social mobility, more or less realized. Joseph Ricketts, born c. 1777 at Castle Eaton, Wiltshire, made a similar transition while remaining in or close to his native village. He writes that 'My spirit of Childhood was buoyant and elastic – I was naturally a wild, roving boy of an Active Unconquerable mind – for Mischief I was superior to other boys of my Age – was stiled their Captain'.[41] After school attendance for two winters, he began farmwork at seven, becoming a living-in farm servant at sixteen and a day labourer on his marriage in 1796. 'Before I was twenty-one years old I took to a Wife, and we scrabled along as well as we could. I received only 8s. a week.'[42] Despite lameness contracted as a child, Ricketts continued at all kinds of farmwork, becoming an expert rickmaker, carpenter and gamekeeper besides developing a useful by-employment as parish doctor and vet. In 1822 he opened a shop at Highworth as a druggist and printer, later adding books and stationery: he was a keen musician, making and selling violins, clarinets and drums, playing the church organ and establishing the first band in the area. 'There was no idle time lost by me night or day'. He retired at eighty-one, leaving a thriving business to a grandson.

For John Blow – born at Ewerby, near Sleaford, Lincolnshire, in 1801 – poverty and unemployment were for many years self-inflicted by 'the drink demon'. He was in farm service until the age of nineteen, when he and his drinking companions gave up regular work and went to Lincoln, where he failed to enlist in the army. From 1820 to 1825 he was on tramp, sometimes working for a spell farming or navvying, sometimes hawking at race meetings, begging and always drinking away what money he could get.

> Sometimes I was a few weeks in service, at other times rambling about, and working with navvies. I was a restless wanderer, I staid nowhere long together in one place, and very seldom carried any money. I mostly left it in care with the first publican I met with. I was not much afraid of being robbed. . . . On the 17th of May 1825 I got married; and all the money I was worth was eightpence after toiling in the labour market for fourteen years.[43]

Although he now returned to agricultural labour, his drinking continued until 1831 when the tragic death of his eldest son by burning led to a conversion to Primitive Methodism and, later, to temperance:

> After signing the pledge [1838] I laboured hard to get the comforts of this life for my family, and to replenish my home with the necessary comforts that makes a working-man's home comfortable, and to redeem my position in life. I sought after employment, such

as working on the rails, or any employment that was the most profitable.[44]

In later life, Blow became a paid temperance speaker, touring eighteen counties and securing 7,500 'conversions' during the winter months, returning to agricultural labour in spring and summer: he therefore neatly overcame the problem of seasonal unemployment while securing an honoured place in the community.

The life histories of such men illustrate the flight from farmwork by many in the depressed years after 1815, and their successful, yet widely different, adaptations to employment opportunities. Those who remained on the land, like Mayett, and those who left it but failed to find a satisfactory alternative, were less likely to write their memoirs. Robert Spurr was born in 1801 at Ossett, near Wakefield, Yorkshire: he worked as an agricultural labourer until 1824, though his brief autobiography gives no details of this stage of his life.

> My wages were very small. I seldom had any money or very little in my pockett – so I went on from year to year until 1824. Then I got married to Miss N. Dewhirst. I then found I had been very foolish for I soon began to learn the cares of the world. My wages been so very small, at Spring I went to work with Brother William out of doors. It was a very rainy, wet summer so we made very little money. So I thought I would try some thing else. I began to be a fancy weaver and, been a new work to me, I missed my way and made no thing of it.[45]

Spurr's life was beset with tragedies. His wife died within a year of the marriage, leaving him a son of a few weeks: in 1825 the Wakefield Bank broke and 'there was a Great fall in the trade'. He and a brother went on tramp for work:

> We walked to Liverpool and back but we never got one bit of work. . . . I soon took the typhus fever and for some weeks was very ill. When just recovering . . . I was seized with another long and bitter complaint which kept me in prison [at home] for 12 months. I could not go in search of work all that 12 months.[46]

He subsequently obtained work as a shoemaker in Leeds, but was so lonely and miserable there that, 'I thought I would end it all by putting myself into the water and there have a watery grave. But I moved off for time to think of it'. He remarried in 1833, eventually having eight children of whom four died: in later life he continued to work as a shoemaker, still plagued by poverty, debt and illnesses, but finding consolation in his religious faith: 'Some has goon into the poor house to live and die there. Some have goon from door to door beggin their bread.

Some has goon out to work and was brought home dead – and many such things. So I have reason to thank God and take courage, for none of these things has yet come upon me'.[47]

In the absence of national statistics of unemployment any general account of its extent and nature can only be pieced together from scattered references drawn principally from the Parliamentary Papers of the period. What can be stated with certainty is that it became much more widespread, more seasonal and of longer duration between 1815 and 1830 than in the war years, and for the first time became the subject of major national concern. Its extent was closely related to the state of harvest and, therefore, the level of prices: it was greatest in the troughs of depression and prices in 1815–16, 1822–3 and the late 1820s; better at the peaks of prices 1818, 1824 and the late 1830s.[48] But the continued population increase easily outstripped the modest rise in demand for labour and meant that even in the best years some men were out of work in winter. A labour surplus, coupled with drastic falls in product prices meant that most farmers economized by cutting their permanent staff to the minimum in the certain knowledge that unemployed, casual and migratory labour could always be found for the busy seasons. Only a few humane landowners deliberately tried to provide alternative winter work such as land-drainage, irrigation schemes and road-making, but employers like Cobbett, who believed that English farm-hands were 'the worst-used labouring people upon the face of the earth. Dogs and hogs and horses are treated with more civility',[49] were rare in the 1820s. On his farm in Hampshire, Cobbett paid his men a constant wage in all seasons and weathers and even when sick, and believed that 'one of my labourers was worth two or three half-famished creatures', but for every generous employer there was probably another like the one an old Suffolk labourer remembered: 'You know what the farmer at Ashfield Hall did one harvest time? He give all his men the sack one day because they had not carried as many loads of corn as he said they might have done. He went down to the Swan and offered one shilling a day extra, and filled their places that evening'.[50]

Some idea of the numbers of the unemployed in these distressed years can be gathered from local reports. In 1818 a House of Lords Committee heard that in Bedfordshire the roundsman system had greatly increased in the last two or three years, and that in some parishes almost half the men were 'on the rounds': several farmers now employed no regular labourers at all, only roundsmen.[51] In 1823 in sixteen Kent parishes, 8,263 out of 21,719 inhabitants were paupers, and 682 men wholly unemployed throughout the year:[52] this would suggest a proportion of adult male unemployment of perhaps one in every six or seven, though the distribution was very uneven, with six parishes having sixty or more men out of work while two had ten or less. Witnesses before the Select Committee on Labourers' Wages (1824) spoke of the 'great superabundance' of labour in winter. James McAdam, the road contractor, reported 'a vast number' of unemployed labourers in the counties around London, mentioning with enthusiasm the case of a man, his wife and eight children who had all been set to roadwork by the parish officers. 'I consider that a very valuable source of employment'.[53] In 1827 the *Chelmsford Chronicle* reported that 634 labourers in thirty-one Essex parishes were unemployed, while in the parish of Ampthill, Bedfordshire, 60 per cent of those who were unemployed in the winter of 1826–7 were still out of work two years later, and 40 per cent three years later.[54] The year 1830 was especially bad, with 1,001 men unemployed out of 2,500 to 3,000 in the Blything Hundred of Suffolk, sixty out of 110 in Baddington, seventy out of 110 in Stradbooke, 110 out of 140 in Frissingfield.[55] Much depended on the time of year the count was taken: also, it is clear that the arable counties of the south and east were much more affected by seasonal unemployment than the more pastoral west and north. Equally, there is no reason to doubt the severity of conditions in a county like Sussex where alternative employment was scarce and mobility difficult before the railway age: overall, the Sussex sample indicates unemployment of up to 60 per cent in winter.[56]

Faced with unemployment – actual or feared – the labourer had several alternatives in this period. He might go on tramp for farmwork or other work elsewhere, particularly if single and unattached, and this period of 'rambling' might precede entry to a new trade, as it did for several of the autobiographers. Entry to skilled crafts was often limited by apprenticeship controls and the high cost of premiums, but some skills like weaving and shoemaking could be acquired quite quickly, and might lead to independence. Otherwise, a healthy agricultural labourer was a natural candidate for any manual work – roadwork, carting, navvying on canals, and later, railways – or for the army. Geographical mobility was, it seems, much greater than has been supposed, even in the early decades of the century, despite the Settlement Laws and the difficulties of travel: men walked great distances, thinking little of twenty miles a day, even covering thirty-four miles[57] and in one case sixty-two miles.[58]

Those who remained in their parish – the overwhelming majority – somehow struggled through the bad times, if they prized their 'independence', by a combination of strategies – picking up odd days of work where they could for themselves or for their wives and children, accepting gifts from relatives, friends, chapel, church, local charity or benevolent squire, ultimately running into debt to shopkeepers and anyone who would lend. In some parts of the country unemployment could be cushioned by concentrating full time on what had always been a family by-employment. The spinning and weaving of wool had formerly existed widely as a paid domestic industry, and was still important in parts of

Scotland, Yorkshire, Norfolk, the Cotswolds and the west of England, though now in decline in face of factory production: in such areas an agricultural labourer might become, for a spell, a wholetime weaver, but his level of skill, and therefore earnings, were unlikely to take him into the 'fancy' trade, as Robert Spurr in Yorkshire discovered to his cost. More often, domestic textile work was the by-employment of women and children, whose other duties or tender age placed obvious limits on expansion: as a small boy Joseph Ricketts in Wiltshire helped his mother and sisters carding and spinning wool, of which they produced 20lbs. of yarn a fortnight at 3d. a pound.[59] Employments such as these, or the straw-plait work of Bedfordshire and Hertfordshire and the lace of Buckinghamshire and Devon, were all 'sweated' and poorly-paid, incapable of supporting a family, but often the mainstay of single women and widows.

For some men, poverty and unemployment almost certainly contributed to crime, the statistics of which showed sharp increases in the period 1815–30. This, at least, was the belief of a Select Committee on Criminal Commitments and Convictions in 1826–7, which ascribed the increase in poaching and vagrancy to the difficulty single men now faced in getting employment, sometimes even in harvest time:[60] a main cause was the 'low rate of wages and want of sufficient employment for the labourer'. Theft was by far the largest category of crime, especially of corn, wood, vegetables, fruit and cheese,[61] which, together with the poaching of game, suggests that hunger may have been a primary cause: in any case, the theft of a few turnips or the snaring of a hare may not have been considered 'criminal' by labourers with a folk memory of open access to common land. The increases in commitments correlate closely with deteriorating social conditions after 1815 – in Suffolk, a rise from fifty-one per 100,000 population in 1801 to ninety-three in 1821 and 136 in 1831, in Norfolk a rise in the total number of commitments from an average of 279 a year in 1800–14 to 558 in 1815–20 and 809 in 1820–30.

Individual discontent periodically coalesced and erupted into collective action, violent and alarming to the authorities who still cherished a picture of a peaceful, deferential peasantry. Riots followed particularly hard winters and high rates of unemployment, the first in May 1816 in Norfolk, Suffolk, Huntingdonshire and Cambridge, where the rioters demanded that the magistrates should fix the price of flour at 2s. 6d. a stone (the traditional price) and wages at 2s. a day. There were burnings of barns and ricks and the destruction of threshing-machines and some rioters carried flags demanding 'Bread or Blood': the main objects of their anger were farmers, shopkeepers, millers and, sometimes, the clergy. The Hammonds estimate that around 1,500 rioters were involved,[62] though this must be speculative. On the suppression of the East Anglian Revolt some 200 prisoners were brought to trial for riot, arson, machine-

breaking and lesser offences: five men were executed and others transported or sentenced to imprisonment. Local disturbances of a less serious
nature were common in the succeeding years, but in February and March
1822 East Anglia was again the scene of serious rioting, particularly
around Diss and Eye: farmers who used threshing-machines received
threatening letters and the firebrand if they continued; there were twenty
arrests by the Suffolk Yeomanry. Significantly, at the close of the disturbances in April, the Suffolk magistrates called upon farmers to give their
'utmost care and attention towards the regular employment of all labourers as much as possible'.[63]

In the years after 1815 unemployment and underemployment emerged
as major concerns of the poor law, and recourse to the parish became
the usual remedy of those who could not find work. The poor law was
therefore faced with two relatively new and highly costly obligations in
addition to its traditional tasks of maintaining the impotent poor – subsid-
izing the wages of those in work to enable them to support their families
and making some provision for those not in work. The former was dealt
with principally by extending 'allowance' systems of various kinds which
broadly related the labourer's relief to the price of bread and the size
and age of his family: ultimately there came to be nineteen 'Speenhamland' counties in the south and east of England, principally in the arable
areas. Although expensive, the allowance in aid of wages, based on some
scale or, at least, on some well-understood local practice, was administra-
tively simple and convenient.

Relief of the unemployed posed more difficult problems. Parliamentary
Committees which continued to investigate the depression in agriculture
had to report that: 'At the present price of corn, the returns to an
occupier of an arable farm, after allowing for the interest on his investment, are by no means adequate to the charges and outgoings, of which
a considerable proportion can be paid only out of the capitals'.[64] In
giving evidence to this Committee in 1821 a witness stated that nine-
tenths of farmers had reduced their scale of labour. In the opinion of
some, this was only a necessary shake-out of the less efficient workers
who had been kept in employment during the prosperous war years: 'The
inferior labourers [are] being turned out of employ, and being obliged
to be employed on the roads and gravel-pits by the overseer. . . . We have
had eight, nine and ten men put on the roads, doing very little good,
but that is better than idleness'.[65] There was, however, general agreement
that there was 'superfluous' population in the countryside which had to
be supported for a mixture of reasons – humanitarian concern, the need
to prevent social unrest and the wish to keep a dependent peasantry on
the land in the hope of better times to come.

The commonest form of provision for the unemployed was the roundsman system. A House of Lords Committee in 1817 heard that this had

grown significantly in the last two or three years: in some Bedfordshire parishes nearly half the men were on the rounds, and some farmers now employed no regular labourers at all, only roundsmen. Wages in Bedfordshire were 10 to 12s. a week: single roundsmen received half of this, but married men with children had it made up to the same by the parish.[66] The roundsman system was a way of apportioning the surplus labour among the farmers of the parish, either by the acreage of their farms, or the amount of their rent or poor-rate: in theory it represented a kind of rough justice by which the wealthier took a larger share in the support of the poor. In some areas the practice was known as 'billeting': in some there were regular 'auctions' of the unemployed, and in others the alternative of a 'labour rate' was adopted, by which rate-payers could opt either to pay a rate or to employ labourers at an agreed wage: in this case, each labourer was assessed for a certain wage according to age and skill. Official opinion gradually turned against these practices, particularly when it became known that farmers were turning off their regular workers in order to get cheaper, subsidized labour from the parish, with the added demoralizing result that sometimes all the men of a parish were becoming technically unemployed and pauperized: 'Thus the evil of this practice augments itself, and the steady, hardworking labourer, employed by agreement with his master, is converted into the degraded and inefficient pensioner of the parish'.[67] But sometimes, especially in winter, it was impossible for the parish overseers to provide any work, and in this case the unemployed had to be paid for no work at all. The Committee of 1824 heard with alarm that 'parishes are burdened with 30, 40 and 50 labourers for whom they can find no employment', and were convinced that the present system, which virtually guaranteed subsistence to all, had the effect of encouraging idleness, profligacy and early, improvident marriage.

> There are but two motives by which men are induced to work; the one, the hope of improving themselves and their families, the other, the fear of punishment.... The great object to be aimed at is, if possible, to separate the maintenance of the unemployed man from the wages of the employed labourer: to divide two classes which have been confounded.[68]

In the face of the rapid increases in the poor-rates, official attitudes towards the unemployed were hardening, as they were towards the payment of allowances to the able-bodied generally. A Committee of 1828 argued that the construction which had been given to the 43rd of Elizabeth as conferring a 'right' to the unemployed to be provided with work was 'erroneous'.[69] Under the present allowance system, 'few care to exert themselves to seek fresh channels of employment'. As an overseer of a Kent parish (Waldershare) reported: 'One man told me the other day, when I offered to give him work at four shillings an acre for hoeing barley, he would not do it because he could get seven shillings and sixpence for doing nothing'.[70] Overseers were sometimes driven to absurd lengths in trying to make the receipt of relief deterrent in some way: thus, in Tysoe, Warwickshire, where the roundsman system had broken down by 1818, the Easter Vestry required that 'all men and boys out of employ shall walk from the Coal Barn to the Red Lion Inn, or stand in the gateway near the Barn the full space of ten hours on each day till Michaelmas next', and would forfeit any relief if they entered any house during this time. There were then in Tysoe forty-five men on relief, plus women and girls: 'the words were a knell tolled after community had died', and the same year the overseers sent a number of small Tysoe children to be apprenticed at a cotton factory at Guyscliffe, twenty miles from home.[71]

However, local poor relief practices before the Poor Law Amendment Act of 1834 varied greatly, and official attitudes were by no means always reflected by what happened on the ground. Some local authorities struggled conscientiously and inventively to deal with the problems of the unemployed, using the large degree of discretion which they still retained while free of central control. What was probably a typical example is illustrated by the proceedings of the Westbourne Select Vestries (Sussex) which had been incorporated under the Sturges Bourne Act of 1819: there were 3,000 such Vestries directing the work of parish overseers by 1828.

10 December, 1819 Thomas King having informed the Vestry on account of the severe frost he cannot work. The overseers are requested to give him 4 shillings.

20 April, 1833 That James Whittington, having a wife and child and out of work, shall have 4/6d. (This man for poaching has been condemned to a month's imprisonment to commence from Monday next).

22 January, 1830 William Stent who has a wife and six children to maintain, and out of work and in want of assistance, the overseers are to give him a sufficient sum of money to purchase 8 gallons of bread weekly. [The gallon loaf was 8 lbs. 11 ozs.]

23 November, 1821 Alexander Stephens, having an opportunity to be employed in excavating the canal, and begging to borrow fourteen shillings to buy him a pair of half boots, Mr. Bowman is to lend him that sum ... he agreeing to pay it by installments of 6d. per week until it is liquidated.

3 March, 1820 Charles Ford, being in receipt of 2s. per week parish allowance, has represented to this Vestry that for forty shillings he can buy a horse which will enable him to get a living, and requested that the 2s. aforesaid may be retained until the 40s. is paid, the overseers are requested to comply.... (In September of the same year his daughter Jane was granted £1 to buy clothes to enable her to go into service at Lyndhurst).

26 May, 1820 John Freeland having applied for twelve shillings to enable him to buy a boat to catch fish to maintain himself and family, the overseers are to comply....

21 December, 1821 James Matthews, a single man and being out of work and being desirous to travel to a manufacturing district to try to get work, the overseers are to comply with his desire and give him six shillings.

1 March, 1822 James Rapkins aged 20 years being offered by James Pidney, a chairmaker in this place, agrees with the overseers to learn him to bottom chairs in six weeks if the parish will pay Pidney two pounds, which the overseers will do.[72]

The overseers here also employed surplus labour on the 'parish farm' – several fields which they rented: single men were paid 4s. a week, married men 7s. plus 1s. for each dependent child. They were also used on roadwork by the Surveyor of Highways, and for hedging and fencing on the common lands which were still being enclosed. A good many payments were made to people unable to support themselves through sickness, rheumatism being particularly common, and one sufferer being sent for treatment as far as Guy's Hospital in London. It appears that, in desperation, the overseers occasionally agreed to 'buy off' a troublesome applicant.

7 June, 1833 It was ordered that Stephen Pearson having 8 children should be assisted with £4 upon the agreement he does not trouble the parish again for one twelve month, at least if able to work.[73]

But the overseers were not indiscriminate in their charity: cases are on record of men refused relief for not seeking work, and of others brought before the magistrates for not working properly and using threatening language on the parish farm. The general impression is that the Vestry dealt justly and humanely with a variety of employment problems – helping some towards independence with equipment or training, aiding migration, 'setting to work' on public improvements and maintaining those unable to work through age or ill-health. How successful the remedies were is impossible to know, but, unlike Tysoe, there is a strong sense of a community under stress but trying hard to cope with its problems in sensible ways and taking some pride in its policies. The cost could be high. The total rateable value of the parish was £5,600, of which approximately half was levied on forty principal rate-payers, each paying on average £70 a year: many found this burdensome, and were regularly in arrears.[74]

Probably most parishes fell somewhere between the extremes of Tysoe and Westbourne. That some parish administration was lax and incompetent and some even corrupt, as the Poor Law Commission in 1832 was quick to point out, is hardly surprising. Amateur officials, often pressed grudgingly into service, faced unprecedented problems in a period of acute agricultural depression – for landowners and farmers falling profits and rent-rolls, for labourers inadequate wages, insecurity and the new phenomenon of structural unemployment. Whether the old poor law, which, with modifications, had served for over 200 years, could have long survived, is uncertain, but by 1830, when a Whig government with a mission to reform came to power, change was imminent.

THE CURE FOR UNEMPLOYMENT?

Unemployment and distress among labourers reached a peak between 1830 and 1834. The Commissioners appointed to investigate the operation of the poor laws in 1832 admitted that winter unemployment was common in Buckinghamshire, Bedfordshire, Cambridgeshire, Kent, Sussex, Essex and Surrey, though this was an optimistic view which minimized what was now widespread over southern and eastern England. A Select Committee on Agriculture the next year heard that in Berkshire and Wiltshire there were 'surplus labourers which are suffering, of which there are many in almost every parish, and these men are very badly off': formerly, labourers were employed for the whole year, now there was no surplus in summer but unemployment 'commences very soon after harvest and they remain in that state till the spring work comes in'.[75] Similar dismal reports came from Hampshire, Sussex, Berkshire and Huntingdonshire, where the vicar of Great Burford believed that the threshing-machine 'throws the labourer out of employment at a season when employment is most wanted': it was, in his opinion, an 'unfortunate invention'. Use of these machines had grown since 1817 when a previous Committee noted that on an arable farm hand-threshing could occupy a quarter of the year's work – and, therefore, demand for labour.[76]

It was also evident that by now social relationships on the land had greatly deteriorated, that many proprietors and farmers had lost the concern, even affection, for their labourers which had once been common, and that labourers had lost much respect for, and deference towards, their employers. Some farms had grown larger and more commercially oriented and, no doubt, labour relations more impersonal, though the emergence of a rural 'proletariat' has been questioned when the average ratio between labouring families and employing families in 1831 was only 2.5 to 1.[77] Some historians have also argued that enclosures had now dispossessed and alienated the peasant from the land over which he once enjoyed common rights, had converted small, independent cultivators into landless labourers, and, since large, enclosed estates could be run more efficiently, required less labour to work them.

All of this is still a subject for debate, though the recent view is that, at least in the short term, enclosures actually created work in fencing, hedging, ditching, the construction of new roads and buildings. This is not necessarily inconsistent with K. D. M. Snell's argument that enclosures increased the seasonality of employment, particularly in the parishes recently enclosed, and also increased the sexual division of labour, providing less winter work for women.[78] Whatever their precise effects, enclosures were often bitterly resented and a major cause of grievance. By 1830 the enclosure of the Midlands and southern England was almost complete, but the remaining late instances appear to have caused particular objection. When the parish of Haddenham, Buckinghamshire, was enclosed in 1831–2 William Plastow records that his grandfather, a commoner, received twenty acres: he kept sixteen and sold the rest to pay the expenses of enclosure but, like many others, failed to make a success of a small farm and later sold out to a London businessman. After the enclosure: 'The place was filled with labourers and they didn't know where to get a job. . . . A good many men, and there were some fine strong men in Haddenham then, left the village: some went to Lancashire and Yorkshire besides other places, and some went abroad'.[79]

The deep discontent which culminated in the serious and widespread riots of 1830–1, known as the Last Labourers' Revolt, was a combination of long-standing grievances – the loss of common land, the growth of seasonal unemployment, the increasing severity of poor law relief and the breakdown of relationships between masters and men – sparked off by particular local circumstances and events. At Corsley, Wiltshire, where many workers had been employed in the cloth industry, a depression in 1827 forced many into agricultural work, so lowering wages and crowding out the regular labourers: one result of this was a large emigration to Canada between 1828 and 1831, partly financed by the parish.[80] At Slapton, on the Buckinghamshire/Bedfordshire border the village was in turmoil because of low wages, unemployment and official opposition to the Methodist sect there.

> Incendiary fires became frequent in the neighbourhood, and this only increased the general discontent, some saying openly that a few more fires would do good. . . . One of the farmers who had emigrated some years ago to America wrote a glowing account of the country and its prospects, urging all who could to come over to Iowa. The letter was read in almost every cottage. It was read at the village inn and at the Methodist chapel every Sunday until it

was nearly worn out. . . . A farewell service was held in the Methodist chapel. . . . The following evening, in the glorious springtime of May, some thirty-three men, women and children knelt down in the street, and after a short prayer-meeting, marched through the village singing hymns. The whole village turned out, and many accompanied them for miles.[81]

Such a loss in a small village was clearly destructive to the community, and Buckinghamshire was to be one of the centres of the 'Swing' riots which swept over much of south and east England in 1830–1. Significantly, they principally affected the counties where 'Speenhamland' forms of poor relief were in operation, and where there had been recent enclosures: wet years and dear bread in 1828 and 1829 were the immediate background. The men's grievances varied in different areas, but generally centred on the deteriorating conditions of poor relief, low wages, the game laws, tithes and the use of threshing-machines: it was the last which sparked the first outbreak at Hardrey in Kent on 29 August when about four hundred labourers destroyed the hated machines which were taking away winter employment. A Scottish invention of the 1780s, the horse-driven thresher had become common in the north of England during the Napoleonic Wars, but was only creeping into use in the cornlands of southern England in the 1820s, where portable machines were moving from farm to farm, completing in a few days what had taken months to do by the hand-flail. Threshing-machines were a principal target of this social war in most of the areas affected – East Anglia, the Home Counties and south-east England – as were demands for constant employment, summer and winter, at wages of 2s. to 2s. 6d. a day. The close connection between the 'Swing' riots and the deteriorating conditions of employment is beyond dispute: as Hobsbawm and Rudé have observed, the labourers' demand for work inevitably became the demand for the destruction of the machines, 'the symbol of their misery'.[82] In some areas farmers and employers did not oppose the smashing of the machines, the economic advantage of which on small farms was doubtful: oats and barley were not suitable for machine-threshing, and even in the case of wheat it was said that the machines damaged the straw which could not then be used for thatching or sold in the metropolitan market. The great advantage of the machine was its speed. Grain prices began to fall quickly after harvest, and especially in a period of depression it was important to get the grain to market as soon as possible.[83] It was usually the larger, profit-oriented farmers who were now employing machines rather than men, a fact which explains why some small farmers actually sided with the labourers in their Luddite attacks. At least 390 threshing-machines were smashed in 1830–1: there were also hundreds of firings of ricks, some destruction of farm buildings and threatened attacks on itinerant Irish workers who were being used as harvest labourers.[84] Altogether, thirty-four English counties experienced some degree of rioting. The newly elected Whig government, anxious to show that the nation had nothing to fear from a party of reform, suppressed the risings swiftly and severely: 1,976 accused rioters were brought to court, 1,176 found guilty of a variety of offences, nineteen executed, 505 transported and 644 sentenced to terms of imprisonment.[85]

The riots had some effect in slowing down the introduction of machinery in following years, but the underlying causes of distress continued unabated. Local disturbances and incendiarism remained prominent features of the English countryside up to 1850 and beyond. In Oturor, Oxfordshire, villagers repossessed the common which had been enclosed some fifteen years previously, and between 1830 and 1835 troops and police were required to prevent the nocturnal destruction of fences and bridges: in East Anglia there were dozens of cases of rick-burning and sheep-stealing in 1832–3 and many of cattle- and horse-maiming, suggesting blind anger rather than theft. In 1830 the farmers of Ely, Cambridgeshire, petitioned Parliament complaining that they were unable to find work for their labourers, 'a circumstance which has been mainly instrumental in reducing them to their present wretched and degrading means of subsistence. . . . [They are] no longer able to maintain themselves by the sweat of their brows'.[86]

It was in 1830 that Thomas Edwards returned to Marsham, Norfolk, after serving ten years in the army: he had previously been a skilled agricultural labourer, but could not now find any work. Between 1830 and 1833 he went on tramp, picking up whatever short-term jobs he could, and in November 1833, he attended a mass meeting of labourers in Marsham demanding work and better wages for those who had it. Edwards moved a resolution that 'the labourer is worthy of his hire', at which a farmer told him to go and pick blackberries or starve, for he should have no work. In December, on the verge of starvation, he went into the workhouse at Buxton, staying there until the following spring when he found work at 8s. a week in a brickfield.[87]

While recognizing 'the distress which unhappily exists', official opinion laid the blame on two things: the low returns of agriculture which, it was claimed, prevented farmers from employing a full quota of labour, and the operation of the poor laws which, many believed, encouraged idleness, improvidence and large families, prevented mobility and kept wage levels low. In 1833 a Select Committee on Agriculture heard with approval of the good effects a stricter system of poor relief was having in some Nottinghamshire parishes under the guidance of Mr Beecher of Southwell. Here 'the principle is simply throwing the men on their own resources': no relief was given without work in return – either heavy labour on the roads, where the men were paid by what they produced, not by a flat rate, or in a strictly run workhouse. As a result, poor-rates had been reduced by a third and the character of the labourers had been much improved. Asked about extending such a system nationally, the witness replied:

When there is a great redundancy of population it may be necessary to find them employment on waste lands at home, or remove them.

Q. Do you mean by emigration?
A. Yes, by emigration if necessary.[88]

Opinions about the unemployed and the able-bodied poor had clearly hardened further after the riots of 1830–1 and the incendiarism which still continued in many areas. In 1832 the Whig government appointed a Royal Commission to enquire into 'the Administration and Practical Operation of the Poor Laws', and, as part of the evidence to be collected, issued a set of questions to magistrates, farmers, clergy and church-wardens in the rural areas, one of which asked whether they could give the Commissioners 'any information regarding the causes and conse-quences of the Agricultural Riots and Burnings of 1830 and 1831'. Many replies attributed the disturbances to the distress of labourers, lack of regular work and a 'prejudice against threshing machines'. Typical replies included:

Generally supposed to originate from the dissatisfaction of able-bodied young labourers being out of regular employment (Capel, Bedfordshire).

During the latter part of the year 1830 only 20 able-bodied labouring men and about as many boys [out of 90] were in regular employ: the rest of the labouring poor were left to themselves, day after day, in idleness (Westoning, Bedfordshire).

The causes – the low rate of wages: the harsh treatment of the labourers: the desire to depress them: the general feeling of distrust and animosity between the agricultural labourers and their employers (Lord Radnor, Coleshill, Berkshire).

I consider the proximate cause of the riots in this county to have been a prejudice against machinery, and the contagious example of neighbouring districts (a JP, Kintbury, Berkshire).

The cause is manifestly the distress which want of employment occasions in an abundant population (Adstock, Buckinghamshire).

The poverty which compelled the farmer to use the threshing-machine bore down the labourer to unprecedented distress, and drove him to desperation (Bourne, Cambridgeshire).[89]

Others, however, took the view that the labourer had been pauperized and demoralized by indiscriminate, over-generous poor relief, a view which accorded with the principal framers of the report, the economist Nassau Senior and Bentham's former secretary, Edwin Chadwick. The report has been described as 'wildly unscientific' in that it selected evidence only which supported the preconceived criticisms of the 'abuses' of the poor law. Particular objects of attack were the allowances to the able-bodied in aid of wages, the labour rate, roundsman and 'auction' systems and the attempts to provide parish work for the unemployed: the last, it was reported, only accounted for one-twentieth of total poor-rate expenditure, and caused so many problems of superintendence that in many places it had been abandoned in favour of payments to the unemployed without work, which often equalled or even exceeded the wages of independent labourers.[90] Some paupers now claimed their 'right' to be exempted from work. At Eastbourne, Sussex, where the average wage was 12s. a week, the unemployed were paid 16s. 'for nominal labour', while in the Isle of Wight, where 240 unemployed men were found work on the parish farm and paid at normal labourers' wages, they twice went on strike and were awarded increases. At Kettering, an overseer reported, the men's attitude was, 'I would not be such a fool as to work – blast work – damn me if I work'.

The present system, it was argued, had obliterated the line between the independent, hard-working labourer and the pauper – indeed, honest men were forced to become paupers in order to support their families. In many southern parishes a majority of the inhabitants were now paupers: they did not try to find work, they had 'all a slave's security for subsistence without his liability to punishment'.[91] This demoralization had now infected his whole family, women, children and succeeding generations: wives had become 'dirty, nasty and insolent' and 'the disease is hereditary'.[92]

Although the authors of the report were obliged to admit to 'a great excess of labourers' in southern, eastern and Midland counties, they believed that this was largely artificial, and that an appropriate reform of the poor law would increase the demand for labour, increase mobility and force wages up: at the same time it would restore independence and responsibility to the labourer and reduce the burden of the poor-rates to his employer. The cure for such a deep-seated disease would necessarily be painful, however. The report recommended, and the Poor Law Amendment Act which embodied it in 1834, that no outdoor relief should be given to the able-bodied, that assistance should only be given to them inside a 'well-regulated workhouse', and that conditions there should be deliberately 'less eligible' than the lowest paid labourer could provide for himself.

The first and most essential of all conditions, a principle which we find universally admitted, even by those whose practice is at variance with it, is that his (the able-bodied person) situation, on the whole, shall not be made really or apparently so eligible as the situation of the independent labourer of the lowest class.... Every penny bestowed that tends to render the condition of the pauper more eligible than that of the independent labourer is a bounty on indolence and vice.[93]

The Act concentrated exclusively on rural pauperism: it had almost nothing to say about destitution, fluctuations in demand or unemployment except in so far as these might be laid at the door of poor law abuses. It took the unit of responsibility as the family, so that outdoor relief would be refused to the wife and children of an able-bodied applicant. The new Boards of Guardians who were to administer the Act were given power to treat any relief to the able-bodied as a loan, recoverable from subsequent wages: on the other hand, they were also given power to pay the expenses of emigrants out of the poor rates since it was accepted that this might be a necessary short-term remedy for the surplus of population.[94]

Between 1790 and 1834 unemployment had emerged as a major problem of the English countryside. In periods before this there had always been occasions when men were out of work through no wish of their own – in especially wet or wintry weather, between hirings or when changing places – but these were brief intervals in what was normally uninterrupted labour from one year to the next. Winter wages had generally been a shilling or two less than in summer since the working day was shorter, but farmers had planned the year so that there was winter ploughing, ditching, draining and threshing in barns and granaries. The new phenomenon was the increasing seasonality of work, especially in the arable areas, where men could now expect regular work for seven or eight months in the year, followed by occasional work for weeks or days, or no work at all. The problem was compounded by the generally depressed state of agriculture after 1814, and by the continued rapid increase in the population which produced a surplus of labour tied by the poor law to the parishes where relief could be obtained. For forty years landowners, farmers and magistrates, many of them retaining a sense of paternalistic responsibility, had been prepared to pay the price of heavy poor-rates for retaining a dependant peasantry on the land against the needs of the busy seasons and in the hopes of agricultural recovery. They had fundamentally changed employment practices, gradually discarding yearly hirings and living-in service, which had given security to the labourer's life, but had then found themselves forced to adapt the poor law to new forms of relief and work creation. Many now believed that the result had been to pauperize and demoralize the labourer, a view which seemed to be confirmed by the revolt of 1830–1 and the continued disaffection of the labourer. By 1834 there was widespread, though not universal, agreement among legislators and administrators that the disease of pauperism had to be cured, that although the cure might be painful it was the only sure way of reviving the agricultural economy and the health of those who laboured on the land. The belief was that, relieved of excessive poor-rates, farmers would take on more regular labour; faced with the option of the workhouse, labourers would stir themselves to find work, and having found it, to keep it: if, at the end, a surplus of labour remained in the countryside, it would migrate to better opportunities at home or overseas, voluntarily or with persuasion. The Benthamite legislators of 1834 were convinced that they had correctly diagnosed the disease and prescribed the appropriate cure.

2

A DYING TRADE: THE CASE OF THE HANDLOOM WEAVERS, 1790–1850

One particular occupation, that of handloom weaving, has attracted major attention from historians, and every account of the Industrial Revolution devotes space to this group of workers whose varying fortunes seem to encapsulate all the problems, all the strains and stresses associated with that great change. The reason for so much attention is not hard to find. Handloom weaving was the largest industry in Britain in the first half of the nineteenth century and the third largest of all occupations after agriculture and domestic service: weaving of cotton, wool, worsted, silk and linen was widely spread over England, Wales, Scotland and Northern Ireland, providing employment for men, women and children on a variety of fabrics at varying levels of skill, while the finished cloth was overwhelmingly Britain's largest export, responsible for more than half the value of our foreign trade. Yet within this great industry the handloom weavers first rose to a brief prosperity, followed by gradual, albeit irregular, decline and ultimate extinction within the space of little more than the two generations covered by the years 1790 to 1850. In the words of a recent historian generally favourable to the consequences of economic change, the handloom weavers are 'the leading example of technological unemployment during English industrialization'.[1] For contemporaries the increasing misery of the weavers, exacerbated by the adoption of power looms and the factory system, produced a series of official investigations and aroused a major public debate about the nature and effects of machinery as Britain entered the 'machine age'. For the first time, the country faced a problem of large-scale redundancy in an age when belief in competition and the efficacy of the free market was becoming paramount. Should workers be protected in some way, should the machine be restrained, or should the members of a doomed craft merely be taught to accept the inevitability of progress, to 'flee from the trade, and to beware of leading their children into it as they would beware the commission of the most atrocious of crimes'.[2]

So much is common ground, but beyond this historians differ widely in their interpretations of the decline and fall of the weavers. The traditional view, well represented by J. L. and Barbara Hammond[3] is that a once proud, skilled craft was gradually reduced by competition to abject misery and pauperdom, the classic case of workers who obstinately clung to an old way of life against all the dictates of economic reason. More recently, Eric Hobsbawm has expressed this view with startling force: 'the weavers were eliminated from it [the cotton industry] by the simple device of starvation, and replaced by women and children in factories'.[4] By contrast, more 'optimistic' historians have tended to minimize the weavers' size and sufferings, and to suggest that contemporary reports misrepresented their real condition by citing extreme rather than typical cases. Thus, Sir John Clapham includes the handloom weavers among 'a few small and [admittedly] specially unhappy sections of the people',[5] F. A. Hayek sees them as 'a small group among a prospering community',[6] while Duncan Bythell contests the view of a painful, long drawn out decline with: 'England's cotton handloom weavers disappeared with remarkable speed and ease . . . [and this] is the really notable feature of their history'.[7]

Much of the writing about the weavers has concentrated on the decline of their earnings and general standard of living – a notoriously thorny debate in which the inadequacy of the available data allows a variety of opinions. The aim of this chapter is to focus on the more specific issue of the extent of unemployment among handloom weavers, their personal experiences of it and reactions to it. That this was regarded as a matter of national concern was evidenced by the appointment in 1837 of a Royal Commission specifically to enquire into the condition of the unemployed handloom weavers – the first time that an official investigation had been set up with such a brief. But official investigations, especially one such as this which was dominated by the leading *laissez-faire* economist of the day, Nassau Senior, may tell a different tale from the actual people under investigation. This chapter therefore uses the autobiographies of hand-loom weavers as a main source, setting them within the changing fortunes of the industry as a whole. Contrary to what has previously been supposed, it is not true that 'the weavers left very few literary remains in the form of letters, diaries, notebooks or memoirs which might give in their own words an indication of their complaints and aspirations'.[8] In fact, hand-loom weavers were, for the early nineteenth century, an unusually literate group, several of whom published poetry or combined journalism and teaching with their main occupation: at least twenty-six autobiographies have been located which span the period and provide first-hand evidence about life, work and unemployment.[9] First, however, it is necessary to outline the structure of the industry on which so many people depended.

SIZE AND STRUCTURE

The manufacture of woollen cloth was Britain's oldest industry, with origins stretching back to Roman times: in the Middle Ages commercial production became organized by craft guilds, while in the sixteenth century the cloth industry was the earliest to experience forms of capitalist organization. Cloth manufacture had always taken two main forms – the weaving of coarser materials for domestic use and the production of finer qualities such as broadcloth and worsted for sale to local markets or for export. By the eighteenth century there must have been few villages in the land where one or other form of weaving was not carried on, and few people who did not have some direct experience of the handloom.

In a predominantly rural society weaving was a cottage industry which combined neatly with agriculture, the farmer-weaver dividing his time between work on the land in the spring and summer and returning to his loom in winter. Since many types of weaving could also be done by women and older children, this gave further stability to the family economy. Several autobiographers experienced this duality of occupation, which in later times tended to be remembered with nostalgia. Bob Stewart (b. Eassie, Scotland, 1877) recalled that his father worked the farm while his mother worked the loom: 'Handlooms were in all the houses', providing for the families' own needs and for the merchants at Forfar.[10] John Wood (b. Allerton, near Bradford, 1802) recalls that in his youth, 'All the handloom weavers did their work in their own homes, many of which were cottages connected with the farm building',[11] Ben Turner (b. Holmfirth, near Huddersfield, 1863) writes that his grandparents were 'small farmers and weavers',[12] while around Joseph Livesey's village of Walton, near Preston, Lancashire, the countryside was all 'weaving farms' with an attached 'shop' containing a number of looms.[13]

By the late eighteenth century the number of independent, self-employed farmer-weavers who sold their cloth direct to the market was beginning to decline, and more were now dealing through agents or were employed by them on piece-work wages. At least three further types of weaver were distinguishable by this time. One was the 'customer-weaver', typified by Silas Marner, who dealt directly with the orders of people in local villages and small towns. Not very different was the 'artisan-weaver', a skilled man who generally worked on fine fabrics for a variety of masters: he at least had more independence than the 'journeyman-weaver' who was employed by a single master clothier, either in his own home or on the employer's premises. In the woollen industry all four types survived into the middle of the nineteenth century, though there was a gradual merging towards the common journeyman wage-earner who worked to the orders and specifications of the 'gentleman-clothier'. This had long been the form of organization in the West

Country, but less so in Yorkshire where independent weavers had formerly prevailed and small capitalists continued to survive.[14]

An important branch of the woollen industry, namely worsted, developed along different lines. Woollen cloth was made from short fibres which had first been 'carded' before spinning, while worsted was made from long fibres which were combed. Worsted weaving had been centred in East Anglia, especially in the villages around Norwich, but by the late eighteenth century it was migrating to the West Riding of Yorkshire, where good supplies of raw material and sources of water power existed. In Bradford, Halifax and the surrounding villages it became organized on a large-scale, capitalist basis, though still mainly on a domestic, 'putting-out' system: John Foster, the founder of Black Dyke Mills, for example, put out work to some seven hundred weavers.

As an old-established industry, woollen manufacture was conservative and resistant to innovation, and the adoption of power-loom weaving in factories was a very gradual process, not significant on any scale in the worsted branch until the 1830s, and not in wool until the 1840s: even after that some handloom weavers could still compete successfully in periods of good trade.

The manufacture of cotton goods, which was quickly to become Britain's major textile industry, had a rather different history. Dependent on imported raw materials, it only came into existence in the mid-eighteenth century, concentrated in north-east Lancashire and in parts of Scotland, especially around Glasgow and Paisley: at this time 'cotton' goods in fact consisted of a cotton weft and a linen warp since the spinning-wheel did not produce thread sufficiently strong for both. Unlike the woollen industry, the very rapid expansion of cotton in the late eighteenth century depended critically on mechanical inventions and organizational developments. Handloom weaving was a much quicker process than hand-spinning, requiring six to eight spinners to keep a loom employed, and after the adoption of Kay's 'flying shuttle' in the 1770s the balance was further upset. The incentive to mechanize spinning resulted in a series of inventions by Hargreaves (1767), Arkwright (1768) and Crompton (1775): Arkwright's 'water frame' was a factory machine, while Compton's 'mule' was originally hand-driven but later converted to power.

By the 1790s vast quantities of cotton yarn were available to handloom weavers who, now in short supply, entered on their period of greatest prosperity. Attempts to mechanize weaving proved far more difficult, and early power-looms such as that of Cartwright (1784) were unsatisfactory in many respects. A successful power-loom was invented by Horrocks in 1813 and began to be widely used in the cotton industry in the mid-1820s. By 1835 factory weaving of cotton was well advanced, with 96,679 power-looms in England and 17,531 in Scotland, but there were still firms which continued to employ large numbers of handloom weavers on the domestic system – the Fieldens of Todmorden with 1,000 out-workers, Massey's of Manchester with 1,200, Dixons of Carlisle with 3,500 scattered over the Border country and Northern Ireland, while in 1816 Horrockses of Preston employed 7,000 workers, the great majority being handloom weavers.[15] In the woollen industry by this time there were only 5,105 power-looms in England and a mere twenty-two in Scotland.[16]

A much smaller, though significant, number of handloom weavers worked in the silk industry which, since Tudor times, had been centred in the Spitalfields district of East London. By the late eighteenth century there were still some independent weavers who bought their own raw material and sold their fabrics to warehousemen, but most now worked for small masters or mistresses who typically employed between ten and forty hands on an outwork system.[17] The workers here had a trade club of some power, and the Spitalfields Act of 1773 established a joint committee of masters and employees to agree rates of pay which were then ratified by a Justice of the Peace. This lasted until its repeal in 1823, by which time branches of the silk industry had moved out of London to Manchester, Coventry (for ribbons) and Macclesfield (for handkerchiefs). As with wool, the adoption of power-looms was slow – a mere 309 in 1835 and still only 1,141 in 1850.[18]

The total number of handloom weavers in all fabrics must be uncertain, partly because no census was ever taken and partly because there were significant numbers of part-time and occasional weavers, including women and children, who defy enumeration. Sir John Clapham believed that at their height in the 1820s 'there cannot have been fewer than 500,000, and there may have been very many more',[19] while Select Committees in the early 1830s placed the total between 240,000 and 280,000, with 200,000 to 250,000 in cotton alone.[20] Other official estimates at this time somewhat vaguely cited the numbers 'dependent on the handloom' as 500,000 for cotton alone and 840,000 for all fabrics. Scotland contributed around 50,000 to the total, three-quarters or more in cotton. What seems clear at least is the pattern of growth and decline – a surge of expansion from the 1780s onwards reaching a peak in the late 1820s, followed by a decline to the 1850s, rapid in the case of Lancashire cotton, less so in Scottish cotton and slowest in the case of wool. In Scotland the number of handloom weavers did not peak until around 1840, when it is estimated to have stood at 84,500, but within ten years it had fallen to 25,000, and by 1860 to 10,000.[21] In Lancashire, cotton handloom weaving was practically dead by 1850, and a total of 40,000 to 50,000 for the whole of Britain seems likely by this time. Meanwhile, the numbers employed in cotton factories had grown from 90,000 in 1806 to 313,000 in 1849, exceeding the handloom weavers for the first time in 1834.[22] The virtual extinction of the handloom weaver was therefore the first major instance of technological displacement in Britain, yet almost nothing has been written about the weavers' experiences of unemployment. To this we now turn.

ACT 1: 'THE GOLDEN AGE', 1780–1800

They [the handloom weavers] brought home their work in top boots and ruffled shirts, carried a cane and in some instances took a coach. Many weavers at that time [1793] used to walk about the streets with a £5 Bank of England note spread out under their hat bands.

G. J. French, *Life and Times of Samuel Crompton*,
Simpkin, Marshall and Co., 1859

The operative weavers ... might truly be said to be placed in a higher state of wealth, peace and godliness by the great demand for, and high price of, their labour than they had ever before experienced, their dwellings and small gardens clean and neat, all the family well clad, the men with each a watch in his pocket and the women dressed to their own fancy, the Church crowded to excess every Sunday, every house well furnished with a clock in elegant mahogany or fancy case, handsome tea services in Stafford-shire ware with silver or plated sugar tongs and spoons.

W. Radcliffe, *Origin of the New System of Manufacture, commonly called Power-Loom Weaving*, James Lomax, Stockport, 1828

If the history of the handloom weavers is viewed as a drama in four Acts, then Act 1 opens in lightness and festivity, a time which later generations were to look back on as a 'Golden Age' unparalleled before or since. It is not difficult to pile quotation upon quotation which all attest to the weavers' prosperity and contentment in the closing years of the century. In Gloucestershire, 'Their little cottages seemed happy and contented. ... it was seldom that a weaver appealed to the parish for relief ... Peace and content sat upon the weaver's brow',[23] while in the Pennines, such was the demand for more weavers and more accommodation as a result of the mechanization of spinning that 'the old loom-shops being insufficient, every lumber-room, even old barns, cart-houses and outbuildings of any description were repaired ... and all were fitted up for loom-shops. This source of making room being at length exhausted, new weavers' cottages with loom-shops rose up in every direction'.[24]

Idyllic pictures were painted of the family life and economy under the domestic system, the father weaving, mother spinning, children helping with the preliminary processes, all happily united under one roof with time for education, for leisure or for work in the garden or small-holding. Peter Gaskell believed that a family of four adults and two children could comfortably earn £4 a week when working for ten hours a day,[25] while some employers complained that weavers were so well paid that they worked only three or four days a week, always observing 'Saint Monday' and sometimes Tuesday also as days of rest or enjoyment. Writers often went on to contrast this with the horrors of the subsequent factory system where the family was broken up, where adults and children worked for unlimited hours to the tireless rhythm of the machine under the discipline of harsh overseers. The domestic handloom weaver was pictured as a proud, independent gentleman who controlled his own destiny, the factory worker as a wage slave, a mere 'hand' at the mercy of an employer who regarded him as no more than one of the costs of production.

In fact, any idea that there was ever an extended 'Golden Age' of prosperity for the handloom weaver is a myth created by later generations who, understandably, compared their own miseries with what had been comparatively better times. The economic position of weavers had always been subject to fluctuations in demand, to changes in fashion and to booms and slumps in the trade cycle: during the years of the French and Napoleonic Wars (1793–1815) there were added to these insecurities a series of exceptionally bad harvests and high prices, and interruptions of overseas trade caused by the French conquest of much of Europe and the closure of markets to British exports. If the 'Golden Age' ever existed, it was a relatively brief one – from the 1780s to the late 1790s, when wages already began to turn down. During this short period weavers were in great demand as a result of the large quantities of yarn now available, and because after 1793 men were beginning to join the army and navy in large numbers: the result was that many women and children transferred from spinning to weaving and some men from other occupations such as farm labouring. Weaving on coarser fabrics like fustian could be learned in a matter of weeks, and apprenticeship had largely broken down except in some branches of silk and luxury cloths. According to the inventor and manufacturer, William Radcliffe, 'we employed every person in cotton weaving who could be induced to learn the trade',[26] and the number of weavers increased rapidly from 108,000 in 1788 to 164,000 in 1801, 200,000 in 1810 and 220,000 by 1815.[27]

Actual earnings in this prosperous period were probably hardly ever as high as memory recalled, but nevertheless substantially better than farm-work and comparable with those in skilled trades. Since earnings were on a piece-work basis, they varied greatly with the hours worked, the degrees of strength and skill, and the quality of cloth woven: most wages were also subject to deductions for preparatory processes such as bobbin-winding, quilling and sizing, for setting up the loom for complicated patterns, for candles, heating and general wear and tear, all of which could amount to a quarter of the wages. Some exceptionally high earnings were reported to a Select Committee in 1802–3, including £2 10s. 3d. for a piece of nankeen woven in five days by a woman who worked from 5 a.m. until 11 p.m.: the employer reckoned that two guineas of that would be 'clear money'.[28] More typically, Joseph Foster of Glasgow reckoned his wages as averaging £1 a week between 1800 and 1803,[29] while Richard Needham placed his at £1 6s. 8d. between 1797 and 1804.[30] These figures accord fairly well with G. H. Wood's calculation of average wages of handloom weavers, which suggest 18s. 9d. from 1797 to 1801, rising to 21s. in 1802 and 23s. in 1805 before beginning a long decline to 6s. 3d. in the 1830s.[31] Where several members of a family worked together – adult sons, wives, daughters, and younger children contributing part-time labour – such wages could produce very substantial combined earnings, sufficient to support a comfortable standard of living without excessive labour.

The autobiographies of weavers confirm and illuminate this generally optimistic account of the brief 'Golden Age'. William Thom, a Scottish weaver, described the 1780s as 'The daisy portion of weaving. . . . Four days did the weaver work – for then four days was a week as far as weaving went – and such a week to a skilfull workman brought forty shillings. . . . Sunday, Monday and Tuesday were, of course, jubilee'.[32] Similarly, in the village of Birch, between Heywood and Manchester, where the Marcroft family lived,

> The silk trade at this period [1800] was very good, and large wages were earned; the working week commencing about Tuesday or Wednesday and ending late on Saturday, and bearing home [i.e. collecting fresh supplies of yarn] on Monday. One of the happiest sights in Lancashire life was the home of a family of silk weavers; there could be heard the merry song to the tune of the clacking shuttles and the bumping of the lathe, the cottage surrounded with a garden filled with flowers and situated in the midst of green fields where the lark sang and the thrushes whistled their morning's adoration to the rising sun.[33]

Not surprisingly, parents did not hesitate to put their children to a remunerative and well-respected trade, and in 1807 at thirteen Benjamin Marcroft, the eldest son of the family, was formally bound apprentice to silk-weaving for three years. William Hanson's father, a farmer-weaver of Soyland, West Riding and 'considered well-to-do', set every one of his ten children to handloom weaving.[34]

The life of a farmer-weaver in the 1780s is well described in the diary of Cornelius Ashworth of Waltroyd, Wheatley, near Halifax.[35] He divided his time between the two occupations depending on the season and the state of the weather. He wove for some time every day, but the amount varied from less than a yard up to ten yards: over a year he completed thirty pieces, usually of thirty yards each but a few of sixty yards, and around every ten days carried the completed cloth for sale in Halifax. Ashworth does not tell us the size of his farm or small-holding: it was laid to grass and corn, but his diary refers to ploughing, manuring, haymaking, threshing, foddering cows and churning butter. He was evidently regarded as a man of some standing, being appointed Overseer of the Poor for the township of Ovenden in 1780: at busy times like harvest he employed six or seven men, and though not one of the 'gentry' he rated as a thoroughly respectable gentleman.

ACT 2: 'THE DEPLORABLE CHANGE', 1800–15

Within a remarkably brief period during the wars the formerly bright picture suddenly darkened: weavers' wages began a long downward spiral, while a series of depressions in trade brought poverty and unemployment which culminated in an outbreak of Luddism and attacks on machinery. In William Thom's words, the 'daisy portion of weaving' had already passed, and when he began work in 1814 he experienced 'the deplorable change that had overtaken our helpless calling' for the 'tenpence a day weaver'.[36] In fact, the decline of weavers' wages began well before the competition of power-looms became significant, and was initially caused by an over-supply of labour as workers continued to be drawn into what had once been an attractive occupation. The average weekly wage, which peaked in 1805 at 23s., had already fallen by almost half to 13s. 6d. in 1815,[37] though there were significant variations between different fabrics, wages for cotton weaving falling earlier and more rapidly while worsted wages in Yorkshire continued to rise until the end of the Wars. Again, the average statistics illustrate the overall downward trend but not the variations from year to year which became a marked characteristic of this period: thus, James Smith, a 'fancy' weaver of Paisley who stood nearly at the top of the weaving hierarchy, earned £70 8s. 8d. in 1810 (his peak) but £54 6s. 0½d. in 1811 and £40 7s. 5d. in 1812, recovering to £56 13s. 4d. in 1815.[38]

Even if money wages had remained constant through the war years, the real income of weavers would have deteriorated sharply and irregularly due to the rapid price inflation of the period. On the Silberling index of prices which takes its base as 100 in 1790, they rose to 130 in 1795, 170 in 1800, 154 in 1805, 176 in 1810 and 187 in 1813. Wheat, the staple of English diet, rose from 56s. a quarter in 1790 to an average of 83s. over the decade 1801–10 and to 106s. in 1810–13: at its highest yearly average, in 1812, it was 126s. 6d., while during one month it reached 176s.[39] A subsequent Parliamentary Committee estimated that while in the period 1797–1804 the average wage had bought 281 lbs. of food, in 1804–18 it bought only 131 lbs.[40]

In these circumstances the handloom weavers believed that they had a right to protection – that as an ancient, honourable industry which contributed importantly to the wealth of the nation they were part of a moral economy which was regulated by traditional values rather than purely market forces. Since 1773 the silk weavers of Spitalfields had worked under the terms of an Act of Parliament which established a joint committee of masters and men to agree piece-rates, ratified by a Justice of the Peace:[41] faced with a drastic decline in their own wages, the much larger body of cotton weavers pressed for some similar form of public control from 1799 onwards. In that year a committee of thirty members, representing all the major Lancashire cotton towns, presented a petition to Parliament complaining of their distress and asking for the establishment of minimum wages. Concerned to allay popular discontent in wartime, the government responded with an unsatisfactory Cotton Arbitration Act in 1800 which merely allowed individual complaints about piece-rates to be adjudicated. Neither weavers nor employers found the measure workable, and it was amended by a new Act in 1804 which proved equally inoperative. The weavers subsequently kept up their demands for an effective minimum wage bill, presenting another petition in 1807 which allegedly contained 130,000 signatures, but this time a Select Committee made its objection to any such measure abundantly clear: 'Fixing a minimum for the price of labour in the cotton manufacture is wholly inadmissible in principle, incapable of being reduced to practice by any means which can possibly be devised and, if practicable, would be productive of the most fatal consequences'. Yet another petition in 1810 produced an even more perfunctory Parliamentary enquiry in 1811 which confirmed the new political philosophy of *laissez-faire* even more forcibly, and rejected 'any interference of the legislature with the freedom of trade'.[42] Although this was by no means the last time that the weavers looked to Parliament for protection, it was, or should have been, clear that no help could be expected from this quarter. Even the long-standing Spitalfields Act was repealed in 1823.

Two other main factors account for the deterioration in the weavers' status during the war years. One was the increasing size of the labour force, especially in cotton handloom weaving where numbers grew from 164,000 in 1801 to 220,000 in 1815, and the increasing casualization of the trade as more unskilled labour was drawn in. Plain weaving of calicoes and fustians was easily learned and could be done by women and by children of nine or ten if their legs were long enough to reach the treadle. Machine-spun yarn made weaving easier and simpler, and although some branches of the 'fancy' trade required considerable physical strength this was not true of the coarser cloth trade to which most women went. In 1799 it was said that 'If a Man enlists, his Wife turns Weaver ... and instructs her children in the art of weaving'.[43] The result was that the labour market became geared to the demand in good years, when there was work for all, but over-stocked in the bad years and, increasingly, even in normal years. Over-supply gradually became a permanent feature of the industry, with consequent pressure on piece-rates and employment.

The other, and related, problem was the uneven progress of the industry, which, although moving forward, did so jerkily, by booms and slumps. The timing and duration of these fluctuations varied somewhat between England and Scotland, and local factors such as the failure of a bank or changes in fashion for a particular fabric could alter the general pattern, but in most branches of weaving there were booms in demand in 1782–6, 1790–2, 1793–6, 1801–2, 1805, 1810 and 1813–14, with slumps in 1787, 1792–3, 1797, 1798–1800, 1807–8 and 1811–12. From the outbreak of war in 1793 trade was dislocated, and the cotton industry, which was critically dependent on imports of raw material and exports of finished cloth, was especially vulnerable. To the underlying problems of an over-supply of labour except at the peaks of demand, sudden changes of fashion which killed the market for particular fabrics, and the general inflation which periodically drove the prices of necessities up to famine heights, the war added a serious interruption of normal trade and, in its later years, a scarcity both of suppliers and customers. In his attempt to force the nation of shopkeepers into economic collapse, Napoleon's Berlin Decree of 1806 closed a number of European ports to British trade with limited success: Britain's reply, the Orders in Council of 1808, blockaded French trade so successfully that it irritated the United States, who closed her ports to British ships in 1809 and followed this the next year with a general ban on British trade. This was especially disastrous for the cotton industry since America was the main supplier of its raw material.

During these periods of depression the handloom weavers suffered, at best, cuts in their wage rates and, at worst, severe distress and unemployment while the masters watched for signs of recovery and sought new orders against which they could again give out work. Total unemployment before 1815 was rarely long-continued – usually a matter of days or weeks rather than months – but even brief periods of 'play' as it was euphemistically called could be calamitous to families which had no reserves, especially when they coincided with high food prices as was often the case. This combination of factors largely explains the frequent, but unsuccessful, petitions to Parliament for the fixing of minimum wages. It also explains the increasing frustration and anger of workers who were normally regarded as respectable, law-abiding citizens, which now began to erupt into strikes, riots and attacks on machinery.

As early as 1780 weavers' clubs around Glasgow united to form a trade union to try to secure uniform wages, and in 1787 many workers in the west of Scotland went on strike against proposed cuts in their rates. Negotiations with the employers having failed, there were attacks on 'blacklegs' and a serious riot in Calton during which three weavers were killed by the military. The two months' stoppage and self-imposed unemployment did not prevent a reduction in wage rates.[44] A few years later occurred the first attack on power-looms, twenty-four of which had been installed at Grimshaw's factory in Manchester in 1790: in 1792 the premises and its contents were burnt down by irate handloom weavers in the first outbreak of Luddism.[45] Both these events occurred in years of economic slump. In another bad year, 1801, it was reported that unemployment was causing 'famine and scarcity' in Glasgow such that an extensive system of soup kitchens was organized by public subscription under the direction of the Lord Provost.

The depressions of 1808 and 1811–12 produced more serious and widespread outbreaks. In 1808 the Lancashire weavers attempted to defend their economic position by a large-scale strike following the rejection of their petition for a minimum wage. After a demonstration of 10,000 to 15,000 weavers in St George's Fields, Manchester, in which one man was killed, the strike spread to surrounding towns such as Rochdale, Preston, Bolton and Stockport accompanied by food riots and attacks on strike-breakers. After a month's well-organized campaign the weavers won a wage advance of 20 per cent, which proved to be short lived, but they had brought their case to public notice and had won a good deal of local sympathy: the Mayor of Wigan, for example, told the Home Office that 'the present distresses of the weavers and their families are such as were never before experienced'.[46]

That was to be even more true in 1811–12 when handloom weaving experienced its first major crisis. With flour at 8s. a stone in 1812 prices had never been so high, while as a result of Napoleon's Berlin and Milan Decrees foreign trade was at its lowest point in the century: 'In the great towns of Yorkshire, Lancashire, Cheshire and Nottinghamshire the poor were seeking for work or, failing to obtain it, were parading through the streets in gaunt, famine-stricken crowds, headed by men with bloody loaves mounted on spears, crying in plaintive, wailing chorus for bread'.[47] The Luddite risings in Nottinghamshire and Derbyshire against the stocking-frames easily spread to distressed cloth finishers and croppers in Yorkshire, where they were joined by weavers, tailors, shoemakers and 'almost every handicraft ... on the brink of starvation'. In fact, power-looms were still in their infancy in 1812 – probably less than 2,000 in total – and had as yet a minimal effect on employment, though they were beginning to have a symbolic hold on weavers' aspirations: the main causes were the general depression in trade during which 'few masters could give employment, and none could give good wages'[48] and the unequivocal rejection of the petition for a minimum wage in 1811. Committees of handloom weavers which had existed in at least sixteen Lancashire towns for the purpose of peaceful petitioning, now broke up into more direct action – raids for arms and money, food riots to force down the price of bread and potatoes and mass demonstrations for reform which turned into ugly revolts. Luddism was only a minor part of this deep discontent, but it involved unprecedented violence which indicated a new degree of bitterness among the weavers. At Stockport the warehouse of William Ratcliffe, one of the first manufacturers to use power-looms, was burnt to the ground; at Middleton, where a power-loom mill was attacked by a huge crowd, three men were killed by the defenders and seven more by the military when the attackers fired the millowner's house, and at Westhoughton another power-loom factory was destroyed by fire. Lancashire Luddism was on a smaller scale than that in the Midlands, did not have the same degree of discipline and organization, and was not confined to weavers, but it marked a crisis in their condition from which they never fully recovered.[49] 'There was . . . a violent prejudice against machinery', wrote a contemporary observer of the riots,[50] though as yet it was only a minority who could foresee the ultimate death of their craft.

In Scotland, where a higher proportion of weavers were skilled and where the general level of education was higher than in England, events in 1812 took a more constitutional course. Here the union pressed for the maintenance of seven-year apprenticeship in order to control entry to the craft, and called on the magistrates to fix reasonable wage rates. The Justices of Glasgow declared that the rates proposed by the weavers were 'moderate and reasonable', and when the employers refused to observe them the union called a strike, believing their action to be legal. It was estimated that some 40,000 looms were idle for three months towards the end of 1812, but early in 1813 and without financial resources the strike broke down: seven leaders of the local union committees received sentences of imprisonment. The Scottish weavers had to return to work at the old rates and had failed to prevent dilution of their trade by controlling entry: it must have seemed to them that their peaceful campaign had been no more successful than the violence of the Lancashire Luddites.[51] Although the long years of war ended with a brief recovery in 1813–14 the crisis of 1812 was the first decisive turning-point in the fortunes of the weavers.

ACT 3: 'BITTER DISTRESS', 1815–30

If the weavers had expected that their prosperity would return with the return of peace they were quickly disappointed. Act 3 of their tragedy was marked by a general stagnation of trade with particularly severe slumps in 1816–17 and 1819, by a continuous decline in wage rates for those who managed to stay in work, and by the appearance for the first time of extensive unemployment. In retrospect, it becomes clear that the brief revival of 1813–14 was the last of the good times for many handloom weavers, though for at least a decade-and-a-half after 1815 people continued to crowd into what they refused to recognize as a doomed occupation. After farmwork, weaving was a natural outlet for many of the half-million demobilized soldiers and sailors, while with declining male earnings more women and children also turned full time or part time to the loom: immigrants from Ireland into Lancashire and Scotland added a further large element of unskilled labour, already accustomed to low wages and poor living standards. The precise total size of an industry which included these casual elements as well as workers who combined weaving with farming or small-holding must be uncertain: Dr Bythell suggests a figure of between 200,000 and 250,000 at its peak around 1830,[52] though this probably underestimates the Scottish component which did not reach its maximum of 84,500 until 1840,[53] partly due to heavy Irish immigration and partly because of the better survival of some of the finer cottons and silks woven there.

Average wages can also be misleading since there were major differences between the rates for different fabrics. That said, the trend was clear and depressing enough – from a rise to 18s. 6d. a week in the good year 1814, to 10s. 3d. in 1816, 8s. 3d. in 1819, 7s. 9d. in 1826 and 6s. 3d. in 1830.[54] The worst sufferers were the less skilled weavers who worked on coarse fabrics such as calicoes where the labour market was most glutted, and linen also fared badly, while wages in woollens, worsteds and the 'fancy' trades held up better. The rate paid by employers for weaving a piece of the same fabric over time therefore gives a more accurate indication of the fall. Thus, the piece-rate for fine muslin weaving at Bolton, which had been 34s. in 1795, stood at 23s. in 1814 (the last good year) and then fell drastically to 10s. by 1820: the rates for plain calico – the easiest, least skilled type of weaving, fell from 6s. 9d. in 1814 to 2s. 10¾d. in 1816 and 1s. 5½d. in 1830.[55]

Not surprisingly, weaver-autobiographers who lived through these years frequently refer to the misery and privation which had overtaken them. Alexander Bain was one of eight children of an Aberdeen weaver:

> It was the sad experience of our family that the remuneration of piece-work steadily fell from year to year [after 1815]; and my earliest feelings of bitter distress were due to my father's announcing, time after time, the reduction of the rate per piece of the fabrics that he wove. As the increase of his family was steady at the same time, the result was that he increased his amount of production until, I may say, for a number of years his working day ranged from thirteen to fifteen hours.[56]

At least the Bains apparently kept in work through these years and were more fortunate than some. William Farish's parents had been handloom weavers in Armagh and had first moved to Scotland, then to Carlisle where, at the beginning of the century, weaving had been 'a thriving and profitable industry'. Between 1814 and 1820 the family experienced a period of calamity when 'work and wages became reduced to the lowest point'. During the depression of 1819 the eldest son died, his mother fell ill and his father and another brother were unable to get weaving work: they eventually got temporary employment as canal navvies and as summer harvesters.[57] Yet despite the evident deterioration in weavers' standards, weaving was still the natural – almost inevitable – occupation in certain areas and in traditional weaving families. When William Thom began work in an Aberdeen weaving shop in 1814 as a 'tenpence a day weaver' (he was then fifteen and not on adult wages) he already noticed 'the deplorable change that had overtaken our helpless calling': neverthe-less he stayed there for the next seventeen years, during which the wages of first-rate hands varied from 9s. to 6s. a week, and of second-rate hands from 5s. down to 3s. This was in a large weaving 'factory' which employed between 300 and 400 people on handlooms, but from the employer's viewpoint this had the advantage that his workers were under direct control. Despite the very low wages, 'Vacancies daily made were daily filled, often by queer enough people and from all parts, none too coarse for using. . . . He trained to the loom six months in Bridewell came forth a journeyman weaver'.[58]

Since little or no training was needed for coarse work, weaving was easy to enter but difficult to leave since it gave little opportunity for acquiring any other skills. Nevertheless, from the post-war period onwards some men of exceptional talents and perseverance were able to make the transition into the worlds of business, literature and scholarship. Joseph Livesey, who was born at Walton, Lancashire, in 1794, began winding bobbins as a child and at fourteen started weaving in his grandfather's damp cellar into which the River Ribble sometimes overflowed. Despite little formal education he craved for books and deeply regretted that there was no Sunday school, no public library or cheap publications: when he could obtain a book he learned to read and weave at the same time – the only man he ever knew who managed this feat. 'I never regretted that poverty was my early lot. . . . It is a question whether poverty or plenty makes the most sterling character.' Livesey married in 1815 but because weaving was then so depressed he began selling cheeses at the weekend in Preston Market: this quickly became more remunerative than weaving and he moved successfully into cheese wholesaling, printing and property-owning: he was later a leading Temperance reformer and spokesman for the Anti-Corn Law League.[59]

Within the general depression of trade after 1815 caused by the sudden ending of wartime demands and the dislocation of foreign markets after twenty years of conflict, there were particularly severe slumps in 1816–17 and 1819. Although there had been many times in the past when weavers had waited a few days for work from the employers or warehousemen, or had been 'stinted' to one or two pieces when a normal week's work was three or four, these had been periods of underemployment rather than total unemployment, and when wages had been reasonably good such periods could usually be survived. But in June 1816 60 per cent of the looms in the Stockport district were said to be idle[60] and 'scarcity of employment' was reported from many of the manufacturing districts of Lancashire: in the Scottish weaving trade there was unemployment and severe distress in Glasgow, Paisley, Hamilton, Strathaven and Avondale, when public subscriptions were opened and relief works for the unemployed were organized. The depression continued into 1817 and returned even more severely in 1819: in Gorbals in the summer of that year 167 looms out of 645 were without work, there were public subscriptions for the unemployed in Irvine and elsewhere, while it was claimed that even those who had work were reduced to between £12 and £14 a year. Unemployment was both more widespread and longer lasting than previously, extending into April 1820 before the Edinburgh silk-weavers returned to work.[61] In the absence of any general relief to the able-bodied under the Scottish poor law, the main remedy in these periods of distress lay with local charities, the kirk sessions and *ad hoc* subscriptions opened under the aegis of town officials. The commonest provision for the destitute was soup-kitchens, where a meagre allowance of six quarts weekly for a family of husband, wife and two children was given on payment of 1s. Proud weavers felt considerable antipathy towards soup-kitchens, and in both 1816 and 1819 make-work schemes for the unemployed were organized – in Glasgow building and turfing walks, and improvements to Glasgow Green, at Hamilton roadworks and in Paisley cultivating waste ground. Several hundreds of unemployed were so occupied at a weekly wage of 7s. 6d. for families with three children, deliberately kept at mere subsistence level. Very few weavers held deposits in savings banks, and although in better days many had been members of Friendly Societies these did not usually provide unemployment relief. One further possibility – to aid the emigration of what was coming to be recognized as a surplus of weavers – was attempted briefly in 1818 when government aid was made available for 2,000 Scottish weavers' families to settle in North America: although there was considerable support for such schemes from numerous weavers' emigration societies, this was apparently the only direct government contribution.

A response of the weavers themselves to their deteriorating conditions was to become heavily involved in the Radical political activity which characterized the period from 1815 to 1820. Many were, for example, involved in the Hampden Clubs which were pressing for Parliamentary and Constitutional reform, and as Samuel Bamford noted when acting as Secretary of the Middleton Club in 1816, seven of the seventeen principal leaders of the movement in Lancashire were weavers.[62] This activity culminated in 1817 in the March of the Blanketeers to petition Parliament for reform. Handloom weavers were a large element of those who set off from Manchester – possibly, as E. P. Thompson argues, the majority[63] – and a large proportion of the vast crowd which demonstrated on St Peter's Fields two years later and were wounded in the ensuing 'Massacre'. Traditionally docile and long suffering, many weavers became politicized in the years of depression, and while most advocated only peaceful agitation, some were driven to more direct action. In the summer of 1818 the rejection of the weavers' demand for a 7s. in the pound advance in wages was followed by a strike in Manchester and adjacent towns which showed an unusual degree of organization: an increase of 4s. was won, though lost again in the slump of 1819. In 1820 there was an attempted armed rising in the West Riding whose object was apparently to capture Huddersfield: its leader Comstive, a weaver, and some twenty others were sentenced to transportation or imprisonment.[64] The same year another abortive armed rising occurred – the so-called 'Scottish Insurrection' – during which a body of handloom weavers attempted to seize the Carron Ironworks at Falkirk: they were prevented by the military and two ringleaders were later executed.[65]

As trade began to revive somewhat after 1820 the deep distress and agitation declined for the next few years. But the insecurity and resentment of weavers at this time is well represented by the diary of William Varley of Higham, near Burnley, which covers the critical period 1820–30.[66] As a domestic weaver, Varley was constantly subject to alterations in the rates paid by his employers, particularly William Hargreaves of Burnley who reduced and, less often, restored rates at least thirty times during the ten years, frequently 'stinted' the amount of work he gave out and sometimes put out none at all.

> **Jan. 1st, 1820** The poor weaver is now very hard put to it, what [with] the rigour of the weather and the unrelenting hearts of our masters, whose avarice will not allow us above half wage; their money must be spent in other ways. They have about 200 soldiers of Infantry and Cavalry at their grand and populous but infamous town of Burnley. These soldiers must be maintained [even] if the poor weaver die at the looms.
>
> **Jan. 8th** A great talk of an advance of wages which was to take place this day, but all is a mistake. Alas, poor weaver, thy fond hopes of better days always proves abortive.
>
> **April 7th** The country is all in an uproar; some say that Huddersfield Castle is pulled down. There is great disturbance in Scotland . . . and well there may be because there is no trade to be

had. . . . It is reported that the Scots will shortly invade England and join the English Radicals.

Feb. 6th, 1821 Wm. Hargreaves lowers wages 3d. per cut, and most of Burnley masters has lowered wages.

July 7th This day John Moore lowers 74's 3d. a cut. I hope that other masters will not follow the example of this wicked man who delights in distressing the poor.

Oct. 23rd This day Wm. Hargreaves lowers wages 3d. per cut. The masters is now very bad to please, and some of them is scant of work.

April 28th, 1824 There is now a very great uproar at Burnley, for John Moore, Holgate, Cook and Masseys are made bankrupt. [The bankruptcy of these large Burnley firms was caused by the failure of Holgate's Bank.]

August 23rd Work is now very plentiful, for there is two new masters coming . . . and there is great talk that wages will advance.

1826 There are many without work, and what must become of them? They must lie down and die for anything that I know, for if they would beg, I know of none that will give anything.

Feb. 11th No better, but worse; more short of work; this day I got none at all.

April 18th There is a great disturbance at Accrington; they break the windows where the steam looms are; the country is all of an uproar for the poor weaver has neither work nor bread.

May 23rd This day I received 9lb of meal of the donation from government, that is 3lb a head.

June 6th This day I got 6lb of meal of the donation . . . that is 2lbs per head.

July 1st This day Mr. Corlass stints his weavers to half work.

July 5th This day I got 7½lbs of dole meal.

Aug. 12th This day I got work of Roger Hartley.

Nov. 11th This day there is a general lowering of wages by 3d. a cut.

1827 Sickness and disease prevails very much, and well it may.

Feb. The pox and measles takes off the children by two or three a house, and well may they die for there is no aid. . . . The times is no better for the poor.

May 5th, 1829 Very rough work at Manchester; they are breaking the power looms and the country is in an uproar, for the weavers are almost starved to death for want of bread.

July 2nd This day there is a dole of 3d. each a week at Higham for weavers. [The dole continued until February, 1830.]

Varley's diary makes clear the misery of 1826, the next deep cyclical depression in the textile industry, and the inadequate measures of relief available to the poor and unemployed. In normal times his family had bought 27lbs. of oatmeal a week, the main constituent of Lancashire diet at this time, and it is not clear how they existed on the 'donation' of 9lbs., later reduced to 7½lbs., and the parish 'dole' or allowance of 3d. each a week. His bitter resentment is directed mainly against particularly low-paying employers rather than against the system, though other entries show that he was well aware of local radical activity. The crisis of 1826 features in most of the autobiographies of this period. William Thom in Paisley reported that 'Banks were falling like meteors, but rather oftener. The world seemed hurrying to ruin'.[67] For William Farish's parents in Carlisle the winter of 1826 was particularly bad, relieved only when the local gentry subscribed to set the unemployed weavers on roadwork,[68] and at Heywood, Lancashire, in 'the bad trade of 1826' weavers who were waiting weeks for work were helped by a Relief Committee which distributed blankets and clothing: here, nettles and dock leaves were boiled with oatmeal for dinner, and the Marcrofts survived on credit from the village grocer, as many other families must have done.[69] However, it was common in the weaving districts for employers to keep a shop and 'we must spend that money at their shop or we must have no work',[70] a practice which lent itself to obvious abuses.

Added to the cyclical downturn was the fact that by 1826 the power-loom, and the factory system which it implied, had for the first time become a serious competitor. In 1817 it is estimated that there were a mere 2,000 power-looms in Lancashire, but in the relatively good years 1820–5 there was a rapid adoption of the unproved machines of Horrocks (1813) and Roberts (1822): in 1820 there were 14,150 power-looms in England and Scotland, by 1829 69,127 and by 1833 100,000.[71] There was little direct transference of adult handloom weaving to the new factories, in which it was estimated that a girl operating two power-looms could weave at least as much as six handlooms, while later improvements increased productivity still further. From around 1830 handloom weavers in cotton – by far the largest part of the labour force – were no longer competitive and increasingly formed a 'reserve army' only likely to be in regular employment at times of upswing in the trade cycle, and even then only at subsistence wages or less.

The distress in 1826 was of a greater scale and intensity than anything previously – a 'state of distress bordering upon actual famine' in 'a large portion of the county of Lancaster, together with parts of Cheshire, of the West Riding of Yorkshire and of Cumberland, and in Scotland principally the counties of Renfrew and Lanark', according to a Parliamentary report.[72] The same enquiry found that in the weaving town of Westhoughton half of the 5,000 inhabitants were 'totally destitute of bedding, and nearly so of clothes'. In April 1826 3,000 Glasgow weavers were out of work, while 4,000 who had employment earned less than 8d. a day: in Paisley and the surrounding district 12,899 were unemployed in May, amounting to 20 per cent of the population, the same proportion as in Hamilton.[73] In Darwen, Lancashire, 897 weavers were in work and 1,985 unemployed out of the total population of 7,283.[74] Again, in the village of Lowertown 148 of the 177 looms were idle, while in the Blackburn district at the end of 1826, 10,682 were unemployed out of the population of 73,000.[75] Other reports testified to the scarcity of food, the forced sale of furniture and bedding and the lack of decent clothes which made weavers ashamed to attend Church or send their children to school.

A direct result of the distress and frustration was the most serious and widespread attack on power-looms yet experienced. The 'admirable spirit of resignation and patience' which earlier reports had noted now gave way to rage against an object which seemed to represent the cause of their misery, and in April a series of organized attacks on power-loom factories occurred in Accrington, Blackburn, Darwen, Rawtenstall, Chadderton, Helmshore and Gargrave in Lancashire, and even spread into Yorkshire where Bradford woollen weavers attacked Horsfall's mill. Major Eckersley, the military commander at Manchester, reported that 'the obstinacy and determination of the rioters was most extraordinary'. Compensation of £16,000 was later paid to millowners: the sixty-six accused rioters were treated, for the time, with comparative leniency, ten being transported and thirty-three imprisoned for periods of up to eighteen months.

The growth of mechanization in the textile industries and its effects on communities such as the handloom weavers precipitated the first major debate on the economic and social consequences of technological change. Most political economists saw the machine as a benign wealth-creator in which, ultimately, all would share, and in a Parliamentary debate in 1823 which considered public support for the weavers the leading economist, Ricardo, while admitting that machinery must 'in great degree, operate prejudicially to the working classes', argued that they must learn to adapt to it with 'a little foresight, a little prudence'. His colleague, McCulloch, believed that labour-saving machinery did not put men out of work but that they would be absorbed into making more labour-saving machinery and be released for more leisure and education.[76] In an address to the unemployed workmen of Yorkshire and Lancashire in 1826, Edward Baines who was then touring the textile districts of France, warned his readers that the French were formidable rivals, doing all they could to promote machinery, and it would be fatal for Britain to lose its competitive advantage. 'It is a very great mistake to attribute your distress to machinery, and a fatal error to think the destruction of that machinery would be a remedy. The fact is just the contrary.... Machinery almost always increases the demand for labour.'[77] He believed that with 'patience and good conduct we shall get through this difficulty'. Similarly, Dr J. P. Kay admitted that the power-loom had caused 'temporary embarrassment by diminishing the demand for certain kinds of labour', but believed that it was 'ultimately destined to be productive of the greatest general benefits'.[78]

The alternative view – that machinery was disastrous for the working classes – was put forward most forcibly by traditionalists, of whom Peter Gaskell was representative. They saw the family unit – the basis of a moral society – being broken up and ultimately destroyed by the factory system, which separated the fathers, mothers and children who had formerly worked together in the home. The power-loom was, therefore, the enemy of society, the great 'screw' both to handloom employers and workers who could not compete on equal terms with the factory.[79] Somewhat similar views were expressed by Cobbett, who looked back nostalgically to independent craftsmen and peasant proprietors, by Owenite co-operators with visions of building self-supporting communities, and by early Socialists such as Engels who wrote of 'the degeneration into which the worker sinks owing to the introduction of steam power, machinery and the division of labour'.[80] Now there was competition of all against all – of power-loom weavers against handloom weavers, of employed handloom weavers against the unemployed or poorly paid willing to undercut, of women and children against men and of the Irish against the English and Scots.

Since industry always passed through a continuous series of booms and slumps, each cycle lasting about five or six years, industry must always have a reserve of unemployed labour except for the brief periods when the boom was at its height: even when trade was moderately active between booms and slumps there would be unemployed people – the 'surplus population'.[81] Official concern about a 'surplus' or 'redundant' population, which extended to the rural labourer as well as to the handloom weaver, has to be seen in the context of the Malthusian anxiety that the rapid growth in numbers would soon outstrip the resources necessary to sustain it. It resulted in the appointment, appropriately in 1826, of the Select Committee on Emigration from the United Kingdom, which had hitherto been of negligible size.[82] The report concluded that: 'There are extensive districts in Ireland, and districts in England and Scotland, where the population is at the present moment redundant. . . . There exists a very considerable proportion of able-bodied and active labourers beyond that number to which any existing demand for labour can afford employment'.[83] Much of the report, and of its two sequels in 1827, was concerned with the plight of the weavers who, it argued, were the victims of double misfortune – the general downturn in trade and 'the transition from handloom to powerloom weaving'.[84] Evidence was given by weavers that even in full work their wages had been reduced to 4–7s. a week, and that numerous emigration societies had been formed by unemployed or partially employed weavers who saw no prospect of improvement in their condition. 'If there were no increased demand [for labour]' said one witness, 'the people would starve to death', and he went on to cite the case of a woman who had had no food, only water, for two days.[85] Another pointed out that some unemployed weavers were turning to farm labouring and causing unemployment there.[86] A Manufacturers' Relief Committee had agreed to put up £25,000 to aid emigration, provided a further £50,000 was contributed from 'other sources', presumably from government: it was estimated that £75,000 would be sufficient to remove and relocate 1,200 families, amounting to between 6,000 and 7,000 people, in Canada. The final, third report in 1827, however, recommended voluntary emigration only in the case of Ireland and, hesitantly, for England but not Scotland.[87] It is extremely unlikely that an emigration of this scale could have helped the condition of the handloom weavers: it was not put to the test since the report was not accepted by Parliament.

ACT 4: 'FLEE THE TRADE', 1830–50

Ordinary handloom weaving is, perhaps, the lowest grade of manufacturing industry. . . . The powerloom is invading – successfully invading – their territory. They cannot stand against it. . . . I do not think that better advice can be given to the handloom weavers than to seek all fair occasions of abandoning a trade which must be more and more invaded, and in which the average rate of wages will necessarily be lower than in almost any other handicraft labour.[88]

In Act 4 of the drama handloom weaving died, not with 'remarkable speed and ease'[89] but slowly and infinitely painfully, clinging to life with a stubbornness which defied reason but excited widespread sympathy. Through the 1830s and 1840s the plight of the handloom weavers was investigated by surveys and Parliamentary enquiries which piled up evidence of almost unimaginable poverty and distress, more acute than in any other large occupation including that of agricultural labour. Descriptions of a scanty diet of potatoes and oatmeal, of all clothes and bedding pawned but for a few rags, of dark, damp cellars where emaciated figures toiled at their looms – when work was to be had – for up to eighteen hours a day for a less-than-subsistence wage, horrified contemporaries as they have subsequent readers. A recent historian has estimated that already by 1834 half of all weavers were in a state of 'primary poverty', defined as a diet insufficient for merely physical efficiency, with a further 20 per cent in 'secondary poverty', and that by the 1840s almost all handloom weavers were in the former category.[90] Moreover, 'unemployment' had not only entered into the vocabulary, but for the first time was specifically the subject of a Royal Commission of Enquiry.[91] For the first time also, observers began to discuss not only the incidence, but the personal effects of unemployment in terms which would be reproduced for the next hundred years. Visiting Burnley, Lancashire, in 1842 William Cooke Taylor noted that:

> Groups of idlers stood in the midst of the street; their faces haggard with famine and their eyes rolling with that fierce and uneasy expression which I have often noticed in maniacs. I went up to some of them, and entered into conversation. . . . Each man had his own tale of sorrow to tell; their stories were not 'the short and simple annals of the poor'; they were complicated details of misery and suffering, gradual in their approach and grinding in their result, borne, however, with an iron endurance. . . . 'We want not charity, but employment', was their unanimous declaration.[92]

Between 1820 and 1830 the total number of cotton handloom weavers in Britain, after growing rapidly in previous decades, stabilized at around 240,000. Thereafter, the decline began – to an estimated 200,000 in 1834, 160,000 in 1837, and 123,000 by 1840[93] – a reduction of half within ten years. Already an endangered species, they were virtually extinct by the end of the next decade – an estimated 43,000 in 1850 and a mere 10,000 by 1860.[94] The much smaller numbers in wool, silk and linen showed a similar, though later, decline, and in Scotland, where these other fabrics were strongly established, the total of all weavers continued to grow until 1840, when it peaked at 84,500: subsequently, the decline was very rapid – to 25,000 by 1850 and 10,000 in 1860.[95] Hand-weaving of wool persisted longest in both Scotland and England, late survivals in the 1870s being reported by several autobiographers. At Eassie, Glen Ogilvie, Bob Stewart's mother worked in the fields and as a weaver, 'doing two jobs and rearing a family at the same time': 'handlooms were in all the homes', weaving for the families' own use and for sale to the merchants in Forfar and Glamis.[96] And at Holmfirth, six miles from Huddersfield, Ben Turner at the age of nine in 1872, began to work for his Aunt Alice who had two broad handlooms in her weaving chamber.[97] Significantly, both boys at ten went to work in steam-powered mills.

Until the late 1820s the main causes of the weavers' growing distress had been the overcrowding of the labour market and the succession of cyclical depressions due to financial crises and fluctuations in demand. From then on, however, the power-loom was added as an effective competitor, worked in steam-driven factories by girls and young women, producing evenly woven cloth at a fraction of handloom costs.[98] The number of power-looms in England and Scotland now grew rapidly, from an estimated 69,000 in 1829 to 100,000 in 1833, 225,000 in 1844–6 and 247,200 by 1850.[99] At first, power-looms were used mainly for weaving the coarser fabrics such as calicoes, and for a time optimists believed that the handloom would remain supreme for finer materials and complicated patterns. The enlightened employer of Todmorden, John Fielden, believed that 'Each loom has its distinct province' and that there was room for both.[100] But by the later thirties improved power-looms were conquering the field in fustians and cambrics, leaving only the specialized markets for fancier grades and Jacquard silks still in competition in the forties.

Handloom weavers attempted to meet the growing competition of power by working longer and harder – in some cases up to eighteen hours a day and occasionally through the night – by accepting lower and lower piece-rates, and, if they had sufficient skill, by transferring from coarser to finer grades until these branches became over-stocked. On G. H. Wood's estimate of average weekly earnings of cotton handloom weavers earnings had fallen to between 6s. and 7s. through the 1830s, compared with 8s. 3d. in 1820, 13s. 6d. in 1815 and 18s. 9d. in 1800. The general price index had fallen somewhat since the end of the war, but in 1840 stood at eighty-one on the Silberling Scale compared with 100 in 1815[101] and therefore went little way towards compensating for the drastic fall in earnings. Through the 1840s wages of 1d. an hour (5s. a week for sixty hours or 6s. for seventy-two) were widely reported, as low or lower than many agricultural wages, but for underemployed weavers who were 'stinted' to a less-than-full week's work earnings could be even lower still. Fines for real or alleged faulty work, deductions for warp-dressing, for new shuttles and other equipment and for setting up complicated patterns could reduce real earnings further. For all these reasons, precise earnings in the thirties and forties are difficult to assess, but some evidence appears particularly convincing. In 1834 Sir John Maxwell, the MP for Lanarkshire, produced accounts from Scottish weaving agents showing that in the first quarter of 1833 average wages were 3s. 10½d. from which 1s. was deducted for loom rent and candles; another agent, Alexander Abercrombie, attested that he paid 2s. 11½d. after deductions; a manufacturer, William Gray, deposed that he paid 4s. 6d. to his steady weavers, less 1s. deductions, while at Bedworth, Warwickshire, ribbon-weavers earned 3s. a week.[102] Individual examples of this kind can be supplemented by some widescale statistical surveys, unusual at this period. In 1833 John Fielden directed a survey into the extent of poverty in thirty-five smaller Lancashire and Yorkshire townships, the main occupation of which was handloom weaving: the survey covered 49,294 persons, of whom 23,947 were workers. Their average weekly wage was 3s. 8⅝d. and the average income per person 1s. 9⅝d., from which rent of 6½d. per person was to be deducted.[103] The area covered by the survey was principally the cotton districts of Lancashire where wages were now lowest, and in areas which specialized in other fabrics earnings were notably higher, when in full work. The Royal Commission of 1841 quoted numerous examples of these: for stripes, checks and muslins a skilled Glasgow weaver might earn 7s. to 7s. 6d., Barnsley linen weavers averaged 7s. 8½d., 'first hand' Jacquard silk-weavers in Coventry might make 15s. 6d. though the lowest grade of ribbon-weavers only 5s.: in Norwich, where the power-loom had not yet penetrated, fancy stuff weavers averaged 14s. 5d., while Scottish carpet-weavers went up to a maximum of 18s.[104] But by the 1840s these were the fortunate minorities of men of great skill or strength or both, who worked on materials or designs which the machine could not yet reproduce: at least two-thirds of all weavers were in plain cottons, where wages were now at starvation levels.

Although poverty and distress in varying degrees were now the normal lot of most handloom weavers, their extremes of misery were concentrated in the years of cyclical slump when unemployment became widespread and persistent. While occasional days of 'play' and underemployment in the form of 'stinting' had long been normal in the trade, whole weeks and even months without work were characteristic of the dying days of handloom weaving when deep trade depressions were added to the competition of the power-loom. These occurred in 1831–2, 1837, 1841–42 – the worst of the half-century – and 1847–8, in at least seven years of the twenty and following quickly on the severe slumps of 1826 and 1829 which had already exhausted what reserves weavers might have had. Between these years trade and employment recovered somewhat, though even in a better year like 1833 Fielden's survey of Lancashire townships found 2,287 (10 per cent of the workforce) unemployed. In particular areas and sections of the trade things were much worse. In 1832 in the Warwickshire ribbon-weaving districts of Nuneaton, Poleshill, Bedworth and Coton eighty out of every hundred workers were unemployed: 'They pray for adequate wages and employment, or means to emigrate'.[105] In June 1832, 1,000 Paisley weavers were without work, and the following month almost half the weavers of Kilbarchan were unemployed, while in the next depression of 1837 the percentage of unemployment among Scottish weavers ranged from 10 per cent in Paisley to 18.9 per cent in Kilmarnock, 23.5 per cent in Airdrie, 33.8 per cent in Dunfermline and 43.1 per cent in Lanark.[106]

Confirmatory evidence about unemployment was collected in 1834–5 by a Select Committee appointed to consider petitions from handloom weavers seeking Parliamentary intervention on their behalf. 'If I could get anything else to do, I would quit it immediately, and never place a child at it – it is the general opinion of everyone', reported a distressed weaver of Preston,[107] while another suggested that a pension should be paid to the unemployed, derived from a tax on power-looms.[108] Richard Oastler, the champion of factory reform, reported 'a great many out of work' in the Huddersfield fancy trade, and that those who had work, at

4s. 6d.–5s. 0d. a week after deductions, were existing on a diet of porridge and potatoes.[109] Edward Baines MP testified that in Leeds weavers of the first class got work only for ten months in the year while those of the second class worked only for six,[110] while many witnesses argued that the weavers had become demoralized by poverty and unemployment. 'The energy of mind they were formerly possessed of is broken'; 'I am a loyal man . . . but I cannot think I have a right tamely to submit to perish without a struggle'; 'I think that the state of society is unsafe without some mode of relief being devised'.[111]

Individual experiences of unemployment in the 1830s illuminate the general statements and illustrate the variety of its causes. Joseph Gutteridge's autobiography chronicles the changing fortunes of the Coventry silk-ribbon trade from 1829 when he began as an apprentice to his father at the age of thirteen: 'About this time we had long intervals without employment, and some of our experiences were bitter indeed, particularly in the severe winter'. For sixteen weeks his father was unemployed and the family survived on credit from a friendly shopkeeper, but in 1832 the anger of the men culminated in a riot and destruction of the factory of Josiah Beck who was introducing power-looms to be worked by women, against local custom: the riot was suppressed by the cavalry and three of the leaders transported. Married in 1835 and still on apprentice's wages of two-thirds, Gutteridge now experienced spells of unemployment: 'When work was short, which was only too often the case, I turned my hands to other means of earning money such as odd jobs of carpentering, wood carving, etc. . . . . Scarcity of work afforded opportunities for pursuing botanical studies'. But at the end of his apprenticeship in 1836 his employer refused to keep him on at journeyman's wages, and he was again without work.

> How the life of my wife and children were preserved under these trying circumstances I cannot, nay, dare not, think, and feel thankful that the harrowing details have passed from memory. . . . I tried many times to get back to my old place of work, but could not succeed, and my health would not permit me to follow any very laborious occupation. The mode of life and thought I had adopted were also a hindrance rather than a benefit to me; I began to be known as a very 'Free thinker'. . . . It was a long time before permanent employment came.[112]

William Thom's life took a tragic turn in the 1830s: 'Weaving, as year after year it dwindled, became at length an evendown waste of life – a mere permission to breathe. Sickened at the very sameness in this mode of dying, I resolved to vary the method'. In a commercial crisis in 1837, 6,000 looms in Dundee stopped work, and now 'stinted' to one piece of cloth a week at a wage of 5s. he decided to go on tramp with his wife and children, selling the few books that he had collected in better times:

[My thoughts] partook less of sorrow than of indignation, and it seemed to me that this same world was a thing very much to be hated, and on the whole, the sooner that one like me could get out of it, the better for its sake and my own. I felt myself, as it were, shut out from mankind.

One child died from exposure after sleeping out, and the family was reduced to begging in the streets – 'but for the poor, the poorer would perish'. In 1839 he obtained work from a customary weaver, which gave him employment for the 'season' of seven or eight months in the year: his young wife died shortly afterwards in 1841.[113]

The vulnerability of weavers both to changes in fashion and to the solvency of their employers is illustrated by the autobiography of John Castle, a silk-weaver of Coggeshall, Essex. At seventeen he was working for Messrs Beckwiths when they suddenly failed, throwing a hundred out of work: 'I was out some months, sometimes tramping to Halstead, then to Colchester to seek for employment. . . . I returned home to Coggeshall penniless'. Applying to the Guardians for relief in 1837, he, his brother and his brother's young wife and child were sent to the Union Workhouse at Witham, where they met several families of their former shopmates: a fortnight later they were removed to their 'settlement' at Soulbury, in Buckinghamshire, a hundred miles away. From the workhouse at Leighton Buzzard Castle was shortly expelled for alleged insolence to a visiting magistrate, given 4s. and recommended to enlist in the army. He made his way to London, and although the silk trade there was also very depressed, with 8,000 unemployed in Spitalfields, found work with a friend of a relative. Here he prospered for a while until his employers, Ratcliffe and Dicking, failed, 'and my prosperity failed with them'. Castle was again unemployed, trying to get work as a dock labourer where 'I found the [East India] dockyard full of labourers, and nothing to do': he eventually found employment as a satin-weaver back in Colchester.[114]

The condition of the weavers – as of many other industrial workers – sank to its lowest point in the worst of the cyclical depressions of 1841–2. In many towns where handloom weaving was still a major occupation unemployment reached new and alarming levels – in Stockport 4,145, in Colne 2,355 – numbers which represented half or more of the employable population: in Paisley 33 per cent of the population were existing on charity, in Clitheroe 2,300 were paupers and in the Brontes' Haworth (population 2,400) 308.[115] In 1840, before the slump had reached its worst, a detailed investigation was carried out into the circumstances of 50,000 of the poorer inhabitants, or one-third of the population of Manchester township. Manchester itself was not a principal centre of handloom weaving, but of 10,132 families who received charitable relief in that year, more than one in seven were weavers, and of the Irish population of the city almost one half. In the Ancoats and Newtown districts the average earnings per person per week ranged from 1½d. to 1s. 7½d.: these 2,000 families held 22,417 pawn tickets, totalling £2,780 14s. 4d. Actual cases indicated the depths of poverty to which weavers had sunk:

J. C.   A weaver, wife and child. When employed earned 4s., now out of work. Never had parish relief, but received 2 quarts of soup from a charity. 'Have pawned every stitch I had' – including a shawl, petticoat, shirt, apron. No bedding, chair or table.

D. D.   Weaver, partly employed at 4–5s. week. Cellar-dwelling. Holds 12 pawn-tickets (blanket, shawl, quilt, petticoat, a handkerchief). No chair. Nearly destitute.

Butterworth.   Weaver, wife and 9 children. When in work earns 4s., now unemployed, as are the children. 'They are in a most wretched state, literally starving.'

A Town Missionary reported on two young weavers, aged twenty-five and twenty-seven, out of work for several weeks, members of temperance societies,

Reduced and broken-hearted by the impossibility of obtaining work: they and their families are sinking in the midst of misery which they can neither remove nor flee from. . . . It is vain to think of private charity [as a remedy] – it is spread far beyond the reach of the most extensive charity.

The poor law in fact relieved an aggregate of 130,156 cases in the years 1841–2, 1,080 in the workhouse.[116]

National concern over the plight of this large and formerly important industry resulted in the appointment of a Royal Commission in 1839 under the direction of the leading economist of the day, Nassau Senior. A mass of evidence was collected by Assistant Commissioners in that year and in 1840, before the crisis of 1841–2, the main conclusion being low wages and irregularity of employment. Assistant Commissioner Symons reported that, 'There is no constancy of employment in any branch of Scottish handloom weaving: all are liable to periodic stagnation'.[117] In Glasgow some of the unemployed were put to work breaking stones and widening the Clyde at 1s. to 1s. 4d. per day,[118] but in Govan, where similar outdoor work was provided, it was noted that this unfitted the weavers from returning to their former occupation because of injury to their hands.[119] The report on Scotland gloomily concluded, 'Thus, weaving has become, as it were, the common sewer of all unemployed labour'.[120] From

Spitalfields, the centre of the silk industry, Thomas Heath, regarded as one of the most skilful weavers, reported that 'I have had a great deal of play, as others have', that he had just taken in one piece of silk, which he had woven in six days, but, 'it will probably be a week of play before I am set to work again'.

Q. Have you any children?
A. No. I had two, but they are both dead, thanks be to God!
Q. Do you express satisfaction at the death of your children?
A. I do. I thank God for it. I am relieved from the burden of maintaining them and they, poor dear creatures, are relieved from the troubles of this mortal life.[121]

Parish relief was offered in stoneyards and oakum rooms, but the men preferred to go begging in the streets rather than accept it. And of the ribbon trade there, weavers said, 'Nothing can save this trade from total annihilation. . . . There is no relief but getting out of the trade to something else'. In Colchester another silk-weaver, now in the workhouse, testified that his last piece of work had taken five weeks instead of three because he had had to wait for his employer to distribute the weft.[122] Norwich weavers were reported as unemployed for a third of the year;[123] in Bradford-on-Avon 49.6 per cent of looms were unemployed;[124] J. M., a weaver of Trowbridge, attested that he sometimes 'played' three weeks, sometimes four weeks, sometimes seven;[125] and only one employer in Leeds had been able to give regular employment during the last four years.[126]

By this time the response of many weavers was, if possible, to leave what had become a doomed trade. Older men clung on in the hopes of better days, and because work under the domestic system – when it could be had – gave a sense of independence and preserved family life in the old tradition. In any case, it was often difficult for weavers to find employment in other occupations, which were likely to be depressed at the same time as their own, and especially hard to gain entry to skilled trades dominated by apprenticeship and craft unions. Nevertheless, substantial numbers of younger weavers made successful escapes into better employments, attaining respectability and sometimes even wealth. Ben Brierley dragged coal wagons when unemployed in 1840 and had taken part in the Plug Plot riots of 1842 when he had suffered 'a month of Sundays': he subsequently became a journalist on the *Oldham Times*, the editor of *Ben Brierley's Journal* (1869–91) and the author of forty-nine books.[127] As a boy, Thomas Wood wanted to be a handloom weaver like his parents: fortunately for him, they would not hear of it, and somehow managed to apprentice him in 1836, ironically to a local power-loom engineer. He later obtained work at Platt's of Oldham at a wage of 32s. a week, and was able to help his parents to pay off their debts. On a visit home in

1846, 'I found father and mother suffering great want from the scarcity of work and the high price of the absolute necessities of life [potatoes 2s. a stone, flour 4s. 6d. a stone]. Father would have died and seen his children die before he would have paraded his wants or, I believe, asked for help. . . . His independence was equal to a lord's'.[128] For William Heaton, born at Luddenden, near Halifax, in 1805, the life of a handloom weaver in an upland village acted as a spur to his poetic imagination, and when he was later forced to work at Crossley's Carpet Manufactory he hated the regular hours and the 'clatter' of the machinery; previously he had loved to ramble in the countryside, collecting eggs, fossils and natural history specimens: 'I frequently wish now for my churchyard cot and my busy loom, that I could walk in the fields at the close of the day'.[129] Joseph Greenwood's father, a worsted weaver of Hebden Bridge, experienced much irregularity of work in the forties and 'had frequently to play': in the summer he went to farmwork at 1s. a day, and for a while got work on the railway building between Leeds and Lancaster. Many men at this time left Hebden Bridge to work for Crossleys or Akroyds in Halifax. Joseph became a fustian cutter, an active trade unionist and co-operator, founder of the local Mechanics Institute, a Councillor and a JP.[130] William Farish abandoned weaving in the 1840s and had a varied career as a schoolteacher, commercial traveller, insurance clerk and temperance reformer: active in local politics, he ultimately became Mayor of Chester.[131] Another self-taught poet, William M'Gonagall, gave up the handloom and supported himself by his writing and dramatic recitals,[132] and Abraham Holroyd abandoned weaving in 1830, served in the army in Canada, worked in the United States and in 1851 returned to Bradford, opening a bookshop and publishing his own poetry and that of others, including the Revd Patrick Bronte.[133]

The number of weavers who became poets, journalists, authors and schoolteachers, usually on the slenderest foundations of formal education, is remarkable: many others became active in self-help organizations, co-operation, mutual improvement societies and temperance movements. At least two achieved extraordinary success in very different careers. Alexander Bain, born in Aberdeen in 1818, one of eight children of a weaver, had more advantages than some by attending school to the age of eleven: imbued with a thirst for self-education, he studied mathematics, Latin and other subjects while working at the loom so successfully that at eighteen he gained admission to Marschal College at the University of Aberdeen. In 1860 he was appointed Professor of Logic and English, and in 1881 Rector of the University.[134] A career of a very different kind was that of Andrew Carnegie, born in Dunfermline in 1835, the son of a damask weaver.

The change from handloom to steam-loom weaving was disastrous to our family. My father did not recognise the impending revolution, and was struggling under the old system. . . . Shortly after this [1842] I began to learn what poverty meant. Dreadful days came when my father took the last of his webs to the great manufacturer, and I saw my mother anxiously awaiting his return to know whether a new web was to be obtained or that a period of idleness was upon us.[135]

Two aunts had previously emigrated to America, and in 1848 the family joined them in Pittsburgh, borrowing money from a friend for their passage. Beginning work there in a cotton factory, Carnegie had a spectacular career, becoming America's foremost ironmaster by 1880, a multimillionaire, philanthropist and founder of many public libraries.

Few weavers, of course, attained such heights as these. Most who left the dying trade went into semi-skilled or unskilled occupations – children and youths into factory work, fit young men into building, general labouring and navvying on the railways, where the great period of construction in the 1840s fortunately coincided with the grimmest years of weaving. Some emigrated, some joined the army, tried shopkeeping or went on tramp with a pack of books or household goods: some transferred from weaving the cheaper cottons to finer fabrics or to carpets when these were eventually mechanized. Single women were less resistant to millwork than married men with families, and could often find work in factory spinning or weaving. By the thirties and forties, therefore, the age and sex structure of handloom weaving was changing, and was increasingly composed of older, married men who would not or could not move, many still living in remote villages which lacked other employments, too old and settled to risk uprooting into a foreign land.

Collectively, weavers were too scattered, and latterly too depressed and apathetic, to put up any effective concerted defence of their position. Although there was a tradition of craft societies in towns such as Preston and in the Spitalfields silk industry, and local strikes in the earlier part of the century had sometimes been temporarily successful in maintaining or even increasing piece-rates, no more widely based trade union endured, and in the period of their greatest need the weavers had no bargaining power left. Chartism understandably attracted many weavers between 1838 and 1842, and some historians have claimed that they formed a backbone of Northern Chartism, particularly of the 'physical force' wing led by O'Connor. Some took part in the plug-drawing riots of 1842 but by that time few had the spirit for revolution and Chartism effectively died in that year though it lingered on until 1848.

Until then, the weavers had always hoped and believed that they were a special case deserving of public protection – that they were such a large and economically important group with a tradition reaching back for centuries that Parliament would assign them a privileged status not subject to the normal laws of supply and demand and inexorable market forces. In doing so, they looked back to a 'moral economy' of pre-industrial times when a sense of justice and fair play had regulated wages, conditions of employment and relations between masters and men, based upon custom and precedent rather than the market-place ethics of the political economists. They were encouraged by the fact that a few employers still accepted such views, headed by the influential manufacturer John Fielden MP, and also by the fact that while the Corn Laws still remained on the statute book there was a precedent for the legislative protection of a specific class of society. As another friend of the weavers, Richard Oastler, argued, 'Capital and property are protected, but labour is left to chance'. Fielden was principally responsible for the appointment in 1834 of the Select Committee which recommended the establishment of local Wages Boards which he believed would prevent the undercutting of wage rates by 'slaughter-house' employers. The Bill was rejected by 129 votes to forty-one, and the succeeding Royal Commission of 1839–41 emphatically rejected any idea of special assistance to the handloom weavers. Despite a mass of evidence to the contrary, collected by the Assistant Commissioners, the report did not accept that unemployment was a widespread or serious problem. The gloomy and seemingly sarcastic conclusion was that 'All that remains, therefore, is to enlighten the handloom weavers as to their real situation, warn them to flee from the trade, and to beware of leading their children into it as they would beware the commission of the most atrocious of crimes'.[136]

Constructive advice was limited to recommendations for more education (presumably in the principles of political economy) and emigration (unaided by the state). The unemployed were to be left to their own resources, the support of friends, relatives, shopkeepers and pawnbrokers, the soup-kitchens of local charities and the tender mercies of the poor law. There is much evidence that handloom weavers, still conscious of prouder days, spurned the charity soup and demeaning make-work schemes which coarsened their hands for future employment, and that they feared and hated the new poor law of 1834 with its threat of the 'Bastilles'. Under the previous poor law there had been extensive outdoor relief to the urban unemployed, as the Royal Commission of 1832 discovered: of the parishes which replied to the Town Queries 68 per cent admitted money payments to the unemployed and 60 per cent provided forms of paid work, while 55 per cent gave child allowances.[137] The Amendment Act of 1834 was designed to end these costly and demoralizing subsidies to the able-bodied poor and to offer only a deterrent form of relief in workhouses where conditions would be deliberately 'less eligible' than even the worst outside. But most historians have argued that the 'workhouse test' was not applied stringently in the industrial north of England (as it was in the rural south), partly because of the strength of local opposition, partly because of the humanity of Boards of Guardians who understood that in periods of cyclical depression widespread unemployment was not the fault of individuals needing to be punished. When the Assistant Commissioners attempted to enforce the new Act in the textile districts in 1837 they found existing workhouse accommodation totally inadequate for the numbers seeking relief, and usually allowed existing practices of outdoor maintenance to continue. Subsequently they compromised by issuing a Labour Test Order requiring some form of task work such as stone-breaking as a test of the genuine need of the applicant: this practice was codified by the Outdoor Labour Test Order of 1842, which gave Boards of Guardians in these areas a good deal of discretion to support the unemployed provided half the relief was given in the form of goods and not wholly in cash. In some unions workhouses were certainly used for single men and for married men with small families, as the autobiographies have shown, but it was both cheaper and more humane to support large families with an allowance of a few shillings and loaves of bread than to accommodate them all in the 'House'. Thus in the Bradford Union in July 1848 13,521 persons were relieved, of whom 1,391 were adult, able-bodied men, but the workhouse had accommodation for only 260.[138] Some weavers undoubtedly received outdoor relief in times of unemployment, but as Williams has recently shown, the total numbers of able-bodied men relieved outdoors was small – a mere 21,000 in 1842 – and declined even further in the later forties.[139] In this respect the New Poor Law largely achieved its objective, by making outdoor relief subject to a 'less eligible' work test and, perhaps more importantly, always holding over the applicant the threat of the workhouse or of removal to his parish of settlement – quite likely to a distant rural area where he would have little or no prospect of employment.[140] It should be added that the new poor law did not apply to Scotland, where there was no statutory form of relief to the able-bodied poor.

CONCLUSION

The handloom weavers did not disappear 'with remarkable speed and ease': their death was slow and painful, not the result of an acute illness but of a chronic disease which, over at least thirty years, gradually undermined their strength until, at the end, they gave up the unequal struggle with resignation, perhaps even thankfully. Since around 1800 they had had to become used to fluctuating, but always declining, wages which drastically lowered their standards of living, while since the end of the war in 1815 they had also suffered periodic unemployment which left them workless for weeks or months. Their condition has been described as one of 'underemployment' in the sense that their work tended to be irregular – that although periods of unemployment were frequent, they were generally not continuous and at their end the weaver resumed his former occupation. As we have seen, weavers often had to 'play' for a few days while waiting for their employer to give out more orders, or to spin out what should have taken a week into ten days or a fortnight, as well as being totally without work for several months during cyclical depressions or in the closed season for fashion garments. These forms of unemployment were certainly different in degree from that caused by the sudden shut-down of an industry, the permanent closure of a coalmine or shipyard, but so far as the effects on individuals were concerned, hardly different in kind. Between the 1820s and the 1840s, when many weavers were always living on the margin of existence, even a few days of enforced 'play' could be catastrophic, tipping the balance from poverty to total destitution.

Governments of the day had no solution to propose for this first example of widespread industrial unemployment. They recognized that there was a 'surplus' or 'redundancy' of labour except in the boom periods of trade and that the greater efficiency of the power-loom must ultimately triumph over hand-weaving in every branch of the trade. The law of progress demanded that the weavers should accept this inevitability, should respond like sentient beings and 'flee the trade' while they still had strength. Parliament rejected proposals to fix minimum wages, to aid emigration, to tax machinery or provide pensions for those displaced by it: it merely recommended that weavers should be educated that they might understand the new rules of the game and act accordingly.

Public provision for the unemployed was therefore limited to charity and the poor law, neither of which had the resources or experience to cope with a problem of such dimensions. Local charities opened soup-kitchens in times of depression, sometimes gave out small doles of money or oatmeal, or organized work-creation schemes, usually on roads or other public improvements, for which they paid a less-than-market wage. Before the reform of the poor law in 1834 some parishes had paid Speenhamland-type allowances to both employed and unemployed, a practice increasingly disapproved in the new climate of opinion. After the Amendment Act most of the new Boards of Guardians sought to apply the 'less eligibility' test by refusing relief to applicants who would not enter the workhouse, perform menial tasks in the labour yard, or agree to be 'removed' to their parishes of settlement. Practices varied, and some Boards took advantage of the loop-holes in the Outdoor Relief Prohibiting Orders which permitted some financial assistance in cases of temporary unemployment or sickness, even of an applicant's children. Others insisted on admission to the dreaded 'House', where oakum-picking or stone-breaking were the usual tasks for men, though some Lancashire workhouses rather oddly provided weaving shops and required a set number of hours at the loom each day, the cloth then being sold to local manufacturers at bargain prices.[141] Since such work was mostly done at times of depression it had the unfortunate effect of still further reducing the demand for weavers outside the workhouse.

But after 1834 weavers generally only applied for poor relief when in the last extremities of hunger and destitution. Despite their poverty they were a proud people with a strong folk memory of better days when, as one witness to the Royal Commission reported, a weaver was regarded as 'a precious jewel'. Much evidence was produced claiming that the growth of poverty had now greatly demoralized the weavers, and that although some older men still retained 'no inconsiderable portion of that high mental and moral merit which so long and signally distinguished them among the artisans of the Empire', many, particularly younger weavers, had ceased to attend public worship, to educate their children or retain their membership of libraries and Friendly Societies with the single exception of burial clubs.

> Poverty is a great barrier to enlightenment . . . for, in the degree in which extreme privation bars out civilization and refinement, is scope given to each brutalising impulse and debasing passion . . . It is perhaps more probable that pecuniary distress or, what is more mischievous, great and sudden alterations of prosperity and adversity, will produce a low moral condition than that a low moral condition will occasion pecuniary distress.[142]

The decline of Church-going – ascribed to the lack of decent clothes and the inability to pay pew rents – was not in itself evidence of moral decline, and, hardly surprisingly, the Royal Commission was unable to confirm allegations of increased drunkenness among distressed weavers. Deterioration of physical standards was more readily provable, and there was abundant evidence of the forced sale of the furniture, clocks and household goods of which the weavers had formerly been so proud, of the pawning of bedding and clothes, and of the reduction of dietary standards to levels of semi-starvation and beyond. A Manchester doctor who had much direct experience of the poor, Dr R. Baron Howard, began also to penetrate the psychological effects of unemployment and destitution in terms which were to become familiar to much later observers:

> His energies naturally give way under the repetition of fruitless efforts to improve his condition; his spirits are broken, and finding that he has no domestic comforts to lose – that he cannot descend lower in the scale of social existence – that his degradation can scarcely be increased – his wretchedness drives him to despair, and he sinks at last into a state of mental apathy or plunges into reckless improvidence. . . . The sight of his house without furniture, without

food, without fire, and his children perhaps crying for bread, will probably have the effect of impelling him to crime or depriving him of reason.[143]

In only somewhat different language, the same comments were to be made in the 1930s and the 1980s.

3

UNEMPLOYMENT AMONG
SKILLED WORKERS, 1815–70

Unlike the occupations so far considered – agricultural labourers who represented the lowest paid group of any regularly employed workers, and the handloom weavers who gradually sank from relative prosperity to abject poverty – skilled workers were the elite of nineteenth-century labour. Their expectations, if not always their achievements, were of respectable, honourable lives and a comfortable standard of living derived from regular work in a trade which required skill and experience. Although only a declining minority were still independent, a strong sense of pride and possession characterized the craftsman – possession of his knowledge and of the tools of his trade, pride in his relations not only with fellow workers but also with the master with whom he felt on terms of near equality. In all probability formally uneducated, he was not illiterate: his children would have at least some schooling, his home was modestly comfortable, his food plain but ample and his domestic life managed by a wife who was not expected to contribute to the family earnings.

In centuries before the nineteenth, the distinction between the skilled and the unskilled was a fairly easy one since, with few exceptions, it rested on apprenticeship: the skilled man was one who had 'served his time' in an organized craft, proceeding from apprentice to journeyman and, perhaps, to small master, while the unskilled had no formal training, no 'calling' and no association for his protection. Although some occupations were traditionally associated with skill, and others with the absence of it (wheelwrights' work, for example, was predominantly skilled while agricultural labour was considered unskilled) many occupations contained a hierarchy where labourers worked alongside the craftsmen, fetching and carrying and doing rough, preparatory jobs for which muscle rather than skill was the main requirement. It was a well-understood relationship, which defined not only role and status but also earnings, and just as the medieval mason had received a wage twice that of his assistant his modern counterpart still expected a similar differential to be maintained. Well into the nineteenth century many artisan trades per-

78

sisted in maintaining customary rates of wages and price-lists for goods which preserved a sense of status and independence of purely market forces: hence, piece-rates and 'task' work were generally opposed as disturbing traditional practices and subordinating skill to economy. Writing to his American readers in 1848, William Dodd found it necessary to explain the divisions of English Society: immediately below the professional classes and above the general labourers he placed

> **5th** The higher order of Mechanics, known as 'skilled laborers' (from their being obliged to pay large fees, and to serve an apprenticeship of seven years, to the trade which they follow). Generally speaking, they are an industrious and intelligent class, and are sufficiently remunerated for their services to enable them to bring up their families in a respectable manner, and to lay by something for the comforts of old age.[1]

Dodd was right to select apprenticeship as the distinguishing characteristic of the artisan. Apprenticeship had originally been controlled by the statute of 1563 which made it compulsory for artisans, and even when this was abolished for particular trades such as the hatters in 1771, the trade clubs of the journeymen succeeded in enforcing it by custom. During the Napoleonic Wars, when rapid inflation threatened to erode standards of living, apprenticeship was still generally well observed, and even after 1814, when Parliament, now strongly persuaded of a *laissez-faire* economic philosophy, repealed the 1563 statute, the men's unions continued to try to enforce it, though their success varied. While the London printers had a long struggle down to 1850 to try to prevent the influx of newcomers, the 'New Model' unions of the mid-century such as the Amalgamated Society of Engineers and the Amalgamated Society of Carpenters and Joiners admitted only apprenticed men to membership and regarded it as the chief means of controlling entry to privileged trades. As John Rule has pointed out, in many trades apprenticeship was primarily a means of limiting numbers in trades which could be learned in less than seven years – 'the object was to prevent "overstocking" '.[2]

By the end of the eighteenth century only a small minority of artisans were self-employed – even in London, the largest centre of artisanal labour, probably only 5 or 6 per cent of the working class. Men who had 'served their time' could now generally expect a lifetime of waged work, and it was natural that they should look increasingly to means of self-protection. As apprentices they had invested in the trade: their parents had normally had to pay a premium of several pounds for admission, while during their five to seven years of learning they had received much less than full wages although, by the later years, they had been doing men's work. It was for these reasons that artisans believed that they owned a 'property of skill' for which they had paid, an exclusive property against the unskilled and also against women workers. The ownership of skill conferred an 'honour' which was exclusively male, and was represented by the traditional customs of the trade and the collective rituals of the 'Society' to which only skilled men belonged: hence it was usual in the nineteenth century to speak of 'honourable' and 'dishonourable' trades or of 'honourable' and 'dishonourable' sections of the same trade depending on whether or not men were 'in Society'. 'Honourable' men were not supposed to work for less than the customary rates on price-lists; their workshop practices remained a closed, secret world only slowly divulged to the apprentice through rites of initiation;[3] the men's trade clubs (and later unions) were also Friendly Societies which provided forms of relief in times of sickness or unemployment and might extend to death grants and widows' pensions. Protection was the underlying ideology of the skilled worker – protection against the invasion of his craft by outsiders, protection against a master who wished to impose detrimental practices, protection against the natural vicissitudes of life which might bring poverty or dishonour to the worker or his family.

E. J. Hobsbawm has estimated that these 'aristocrats' of labour consti-tuted around 15 per cent of the adult male working class in the middle of the nineteenth century, while in 1867 the contemporary statistician, Dudley Baxter, placed the higher skilled labour class at 1,123,000 out of the total manual labour classes of England and Wales of 7,785,000, or 14 per cent.[4] Both figures are almost certainly underestimates because they rested on narrow definitions of the traditional crafts and took little account of new skills which industrialization was creating but which did not necessarily require formal apprenticeship. Baxter's list included car-penters (136,000), ironworkers (92,000), masons (69,000), bricklayers (65,000), printers (57,000), cutlers and toolmakers (44,000), cabinet-makers (39,000), shipbuilders and shipwrights (35,000) and watch- and instrument-makers (33,000) as well as smaller numbers of painters, earth-enware workers, sawyers, coopers, plasterers and glass-workers. For all these he estimated men's weekly wages at between 28s. and 35s., and for this reason relegated two other large groups of skilled workers, tailors and shoemakers, whose earnings he placed at 21s. to 25s., into his category of lower skilled labour. Furthermore, an industrializing economy was creating new skills which did not require formal apprenticeship and did not qualify as crafts though they needed acquired expertise which was rewarded as well or better than some traditional skills. In the new factories machines provided much of the skill formerly supplied by the hand, eye and judgement of the worker: they made mass production and the mass market possible, and in the hierarchy of labour they interposed a new class between the artisan and the labourer, variously described by contem-poraries as lower skilled, lesser skilled or semi-skilled labour. Frequently the term 'factory operative' was also used since these workers were primarily the tenders of powered machines in factories, especially in the textile mills which were the prototype of the new form of production. Here most of the requisite skills could be learned in weeks rather than years, and much machine-minding could be entrusted to low-paid women and children: 'apprenticeship' survived only in the slavery by which pauper children were sometimes bound to millowners by poor law officials anxious to dispose of unwanted burdens.

But the cotton mill offered its own kind of progression in skill to those who survived its rigours – from child scavenger to piecer or doffer to adult spinner or weaver in charge of two, three or four machines and a team of young assistants. A male mule-spinner on 'fine counts' (top quality yarn) and earning up to 42s. a week in the mid-century was an 'aristocrat' in every sense except for the lack of formal apprenticeship, and a woman power-loom weaver with four looms in her charge stood very near the top of female occupations. Similarly, there were many gradations within the expanding mining industry, and the coal-hewer was more akin to the craftsman than the labourer in earnings and in strong independence of thought and action. He, too, had had a kind of apprenticeship, moving up from boy trapper to putter to helper: now, usually alone in the 'stall', he had a good deal of discretion in how to 'get' or 'win' the coal and could regulate his wages by the amount produced. In the Census of 1851 coalminers at 216,000 stood ninth in the occupational order. In the same year women milliners and dressmakers numbered 340,000, the largest female category after domestic service. Many of these were 'sweated' workers, performing repetitive stitching jobs for very low pay, but a proportion were highly skilled women who had served an apprenticeship requiring a £30 to £50 premium in a fashionable West End house. An employer told a House of Lords Committee in 1854 that her 'improvers' were, 'very respectable young people [who] would not like to mix with common young people. They are the daughters of clergymen and half-pay officers and of first-rate professions'.[5] Many girls served an apprenticeship in the country and came up to London as 'improvers' for one or two years, paying £10 to £15 for this experience of à la mode fashions, and others had begun as 'out-door apprentices' living at home, paying no premium but receiving no wages.

Skilled workers in the mid-nineteenth century extended well beyond the men 'in Society', and even beyond formal apprenticeship. Marx correctly observed that 'The distinction between skilled and unskilled labour rests in part on pure illusion, or, to say the least, on distinctions which have long since ceased to be real, and that survive only by virtue of a traditional convention'.[6] Equally, it is not very helpful to rest the distinction primarily on wages, as Baxter did and some subsequent historians have done. Hobsbawm regarded a weekly wage of 35s. as the base for his 'aristocrats', which would broadly include the 'Society' men in traditional occupations such as the building trades, cabinet-making, printing, high-class tailoring and shoemaking and would extend to the new skills in iron and steel and engineering, assuming in all cases that the men were in full-time work. But at Ashton-under-Lyme in 1849 fine spinners who were not 'skilled' in the traditional sense, were earning 42s. a week[7] and a Scottish or Lancashire miner at 5s. a day[8] could approach an 'aristocrat's' pay in good times, especially if allowance is made for a free cottage and coal. And skilled women's wages were dramatically lower than almost any male occupation – 6s. to 8s. a week in the 'better-class' London dress houses[9] and up to 16s. a week for a power-loom weaver minding four looms,[10] the female equivalent of an 'aristocrat'. The discussions of skilled workers which follow therefore include these wider categories which were well recognized within the contemporary working class.

THE EROSION OF SKILL

This picture of the skilled worker, master of his craft and of his own destiny, secure in the possession of a scarce commodity which ensured good wages and regular employment, had ceased to reflect the experience of many in the middle of the century. The crafts were undergoing a transformation by the erosion of skill which was leaving the traditional craft societies as islands of privilege under increasing threat from outside. Through the French Wars from 1793 to 1815 the skilled trades had generally flourished with strong demands for specialist labour, and despite the Combination Acts against unions their trade clubs had continued to exist as Friendly Societies. The beginnings of their decline date from the post-war years of depression and the surplus of labour which introduced competition into the trades and broke the monopoly of the skilled. In many trades by mid-century the 'honourable' men were swamped and outnumbered by the 'dishonourable': wages were falling, former trade practices being abandoned and the intensity of work increasing; above all work itself was no longer regular or certain and the worker, whether 'in society' or not, was having painfully to adjust to frequent periods of unemployment. These secular trends, apparent in many trades since the end of the Wars, were further exacerbated by the economic crisis of 1826, the widespread collapse of unions in 1833–5 and the depression of 1841–2, the most severe of the century.

The deteriorated condition of the trades in London, the largest centre of artisanal occupations in the country, was well described in the series of reports by Henry Mayhew to the *Morning Chronicle* in 1848–9. Boot and shoemakers, numbering 28,570, were the largest handicraft and the third largest occupation (after domestic servants and labourers) in the metropolis as a whole. The trade was now divided into 'legal' and 'scab' shops, equivalent to the 'honourable' and 'dishonourable' branches of other trades, and only 820 men were now in union – the West End Body of Associated Shoemakers. Their highest earnings had been back in 1812 at 35s. a week, placing them firmly in the aristocratic ranks: now a very skilful worker might make 27s. a week by increasing his hours to fourteen a day, and only during the busy 'season', April to July: his average for the year would be more like 15s.[11] One witness told Mayhew that when he began work in 1815 for Mr Hoby he made just under £3 a week and soon had £100 invested:

> The bootmen then at Mr. Hoby's were all respectable men; they were like gentlemen, smoking their pipes, in their frilled shirts, like gentlemen – all but the drunkards. At the trade meetings Hoby's best men used to have one corner of the room to themselves, and were called the House of Lords. There were more than 100 of us when I became one.[12]

Since those palmy days there had been a great increase of hands, competition from French imports and from factory-made shoes from Northampton, and intense competition between the masters in London, especially between the 'honourable' West End trade and the East End 'slop' employers. Here, undercutting and low prices were maintained by the cheap labour of boys and women and by 'apprentices' who were paid no wages: whole families now had to work for fifteen or more hours a day in order merely to survive in poverty. In Stepney the bootmen 'will not be more than half employed during five months in the year', and even in the 'honourable' branch work was no longer certain or regular. A West End 'Society' man, chosen by his workmates to represent them, told Mayhew that he owed £10 rent and was planning to emigrate if he could raise the funds: 'I should be the happiest mortal alive and be contented if I could be certain of a fair quantity of employment and a fair rate of wages for it, but it's vexatious in the extreme to an industriously inclined working man to go to seek work and be unable to get it'.[13]

Tailors, at 23,500, were the second largest skilled trade and the fourth largest occupation of London in mid-century. Although by now there were only around 3,000 'honourable' men in union, half the number of thirty years ago, the tailors had retained their artisan status longer than many other crafts, aided by a powerful society which had pushed up wages during the French Wars to 36s. a week by 1813. According to Francis Place the aristocrats or 'Flint' tailors had their own 'houses of call' (public houses which operated as meeting places and labour exchanges) and 'no man is allowed to ask for employment' – the masters must apply to the union. But by the 1820s the trade was divided into the 'Flints' and the 'Dungs', the latter forming about a third of the total, but 'the Dungs work a great many hours, and their families assist them'. These were the originators of cheap and ready-made clothes whose numbers increased rapidly after the economic crisis of 1826 and an unsuccessful strike of the 'Flints' in 1834.[14] By the time Mayhew wrote his letters to the *Morning Chronicle* the tailoring trade was one of the worst for 'cheap and shoddy'. The small minority of West End bespoke tailors had still been able to earn 6d. an hour, but in 1834 the masters had changed from daywork, under which a man was paid for every hour he was on the premises, to piece-work by which he was only paid for the work produced: employers now often kept men for days without work or wages in the slack times in order to meet demand in the busy seasons.[15] Work was usually plentiful for three months between May and July, followed by a slack period from August to October: it then picked up for the Christmas trade, but was slack again from January to March.[16] Much more work was now put out to homeworkers where many women and children were employed, and outside the few busy months of the London season even some of the 'honourable' men were reduced to this sweated 'sank work' for as little as 4s. to 6s. a week. The East End trade was dominated by small masters and middlemen 'sweaters' who put out work to the lowest bidders, subdivided the processes and sold shoddy goods to the warehouses and ready-made 'show houses'. A skilled tailor reported:

> Four years come this winter was the last time that I had employment at the honourable part of the trade. But before that I used to work for the sweaters when the regular business was slack. I did this unknown to the society of which I was a member. If it had been known to them I should have had to pay a certain penalty, or else my name would have been scratched off the books, and I should have no more chance of work at the honourable trade. When working for the honourable trade I was employed about one-third of my time. . . . I was out of work two thirds of my time. . . . I could get no employment at my regular trade, and a sweater came down to the house and proposed to me privately to go and work for him. . . . I kept on the four years secretly working for the sweaters during vacation, and after that I got so reduced in circumstances that I could not appear respectable and so get work amongst the honourable trade.[17]

Many casual workers were only taken on for two or three days or even two or three hours at a time in busy periods, while another tailor affirmed that from 20 to 25 per cent of union members (600 or 700 men) were unemployed (his word) for ten months in the year.[18]

At 20,780, dressmakers and milliners were next in order, and by far the largest women's skilled trade. In these trades too, although there were no unions or societies as such, there were 'honourable' and 'dishonourable' or 'slop' branches with very different wages and conditions. There was, however, a Dressmakers' and Milliners' Association which operated as an employment agency for the respectable houses: this had 7,500 names on its books, which led Mayhew to believe that there were around 10,000 in the 'slop' trade, a much smaller proportion than in the male trades.[19] Work was extremely subject to the 'season' for ladies' fashions from February to July, and many hands were hired only for this period, or only by the month, even in the 'honourable' branch: some houses were also busy for a few weeks before and after Christmas for the winter fashions, but at best there was always a slack time of three or four months in the summer when dayworkers, if they had any employment at all, could barely average 1s. 6d. a week.[20]

By mid-century all the skilled trades were suffering in greater or lesser degree from the same problems of over-stocking of the labour market and undermining of traditional customs and wages. The 1,770 carpenters and joiners 'in Society' were struggling hard to maintain their 5s. a day against more than 15,000 'dishonourable' men prepared to work for two-thirds or less of standard rates. Large numbers of apprentices and 'improvers' were doing men's work for less pay, while many men now came up to London after serving their time in the country in the mistaken belief that their prospects would be better: they usually had to work for speculative builders and 'strapping' (over-working) employers at 'scamp' (inferior quality) work.[21] One such man told Mayhew his sad story. He had worked for a speculative builder at £1 a week until he caught cholera, but since he was not 'in Society' he had no support from the union:

> I am a jobbing carpenter, and in very great distress. All my tools are gone – sold or pawned. I have no means of living but by parish relief, and picking up what I can in little odd jobs. . . . And when I can't find any other employment I go to the workhouse yard and get a job there wheeling the barrows and breaking stones. Sometimes I go to the yard four days in the week, sometimes only one day, and sometimes the whole of the week, according as I can get work. I have got a wife and three children to keep out of my earnings, such as they are. . . . In the winter we all of us goes into the house (the Union workhouse) because we can't afford to pay for firing.[22]

Cabinet-makers were regarded as considerably superior to the carpenter – woodworkers 'of the very highest order'. The 642 'Society men' out of the total of 8,580 still worked to a Book of Prices agreed with the masters in 1810, which gave them a minimum wage of 32s. for a sixty-hour week: they contributed 6d. a week to their Society, which provided them with 10s. a week in periods of unemployment. This was an increasingly necessary security since cabinet-making also had its busy season in spring and summer and a slack time in autumn and winter. In the previous twelve years (1836–48) the West End Society had paid out £11,000 to its unemployed members, and its Secretary supplied Mayhew with a detailed table showing the number of members out of work and the number of days lost in each year from 1831. Between 1834 and 1840 an average of sixty-two members had been unemployed for twenty-two days, and between 1840 and 1849 eighty-one members for fourteen days: the cyclical pattern of unemployment was very noticeable, with 110 members out of work for an average of thirty-five days in the depressed year 1842, and 125 unemployed for thirty-three-and-a-half days in the next worst year of the decade, 1848.[23] A very skilful Scottish cabinet-maker who had tramped to London a dozen years ago after his apprenticeship reported, 'I have been very fortunate, never having been out of work more than a month or six weeks at a time – but that's great good fortune'.[24] These 'Society men' were the fortunate few. Below them was the much greater number of 'dishonourable' or 'slop' workers whose wages were determined by competition rather than by custom, and who had only irregular employment with a variety of masters. Many of these were 'garret-masters' who were reported to have increased enormously in recent years: they were independent men who usually worked at home with the assistance of one or two sweated employees and, often, their wives and children. Many had set up on their own account as a way of avoiding unemployment: provided a man had his own tools he could start on small pieces such as tea-caddies or work-boxes with a couple of shillings, and by working himself and his family seven days a week could sell very cheaply to 'slaughterhouse' warehouses or middlemen. Mayhew was told that the wages of these non-society men had declined 400 per cent in the last twenty years – that for what they used to receive £1 they now had only 5s.[25]

As the largest centre of the old hand-crafts London was suffering particularly in mid-century from a surplus of labour, intense competition and underselling. The best-protected trades were those whose skill was still scarce and strongly in demand such as coach-builders, engineers and, as yet, shipwrights. In the provinces, the semi-independent Sheffield cutlers were still strong enough to hold back the tide, but the same problems of over-supply of labour and irregularity of demand for the finished articles were reproduced in the old crafts everywhere in the country. In Oldham in 1849 'I observed as I walked up from the railway station melancholy clusters of gaunt, dirty, unshorn men lounging on the pavement. These, I heard, were principally hatters, a vast number of whom are out of employment'.[26] London still had 'fair' and 'foul' branches of the trade at this time, and outside the busy seven months of the year the 'honourable' masters divided the reduced amount of work equally between the men who then earned £1 a week rather than 32s.: in the 'slop' trade there was no such protection. The silk industry, which included some very skilled weavers on complicated designs as well as many who worked on plain and coarse fabrics, was now in terminal decline in its old London centre, Spitalfields. Much of the industry had previously moved to Macclesfield, where for a time it was prosperous, but now, Mayhew heard from a domestic weaver, that 'the work was terribly irregular. . . . He had been three months "playing" '.[27] The women and girls who worked as throwsters and spinners in the Macclesfield mills had more regular employment.

In this respect factory workers were the beneficiaries of the new machines and mass production, where the overheads were so great that it was good sense to keep the wheels turning as long as there was the smallest profit to be made. Domestic workers with others employed in small workshops not using expensive plant were the first to suffer in slack seasons and periods of cyclical depression unless they were so skilled as to be indispensable. While most of the old crafts suffered erosion of skill and loss of status, the new 'aristocrats' of the post–1850 period were predominantly those who worked in metals and with machines – engineers, iron-founders, steam-engine makers, steel-workers and (iron) ship-builders. In these and similar technologically-based industries effective trade unions developed which controlled membership, apprenticeship, working conditions and wages: they fought hard to preserve the distinction between skilled men and labourers, to prevent or, at least, control overtime and piece-work. In these ways 'New Model' unions were generally able to prevent the permanent gluts of labour and cut-throat competition which befell the old crafts, though they were no more able to control the cyclical fluctuations of the economy and the swings of boom and slump. For different reasons and in different degrees unemployment affected the new skills as well as the old, and to its variety and incidence we now turn.

THE EXPERIENCE OF UNEMPLOYMENT

The position of a working man is at all times an exceedingly precarious one, and is more readily and seriously influenced by circumstances beyond his own control than the position of almost any other class of men. . . . I have heard and read a great deal to the effect that a man with an ordinary share of intelligence and a willing pair of hands need never want for work . . . and those who cannot find employment nowadays must be idlers or dolts . . . [but] I say that there are very few men who do not occasionally suffer from want of employment . . . and the frequency with which they are out of work makes the average of the actual earnings of many working men disagreeably small as compared with the wages at which they are rated when they are in employment.[28]

So wrote Thomas Wright, an engineer, in 1868, one of the new 'aristocrats' at the top of the hierarchy of labour. He was offering a personal perspective from direct knowledge of his trade at the same time as two leading statisticians, Leone Levi and Dudley Baxter, were conducting a debate about the average time lost from work and its effects on wages. Professor Levi had estimated this to average only four weeks out of the fifty-two (7.7 per cent), to which Baxter rejoined,

> If this were the real state of things England would be a perfect Paradise for working men! . . . Far different is the real state of affairs, and a very different tale would be told by scores and even hundreds of thousands congregated in our large cities, and seeking in vain for sufficient work.

Citing examples from the building trades, cabinet-makers, coalminers, ironworkers and the cotton industry, Baxter concluded that for loss of work from every cause 'we ought to deduct fully 20 per cent from the nominal full-time wages'.[29]

Other contemporary observers believed that even this was a gross underestimate. The indefatigable Mayhew made what must be the first attempt to categorize the chief causes of unemployment as follows:

1 Owing to a glut or stagnation in business, as among the cotton-spinners, the iron workers, the railway navigators and the like.
2 Owing to a change in fashion.
3 Owing to the introduction of machinery, as among the sawyers, the handloom weavers, pillow-lace makers and others.
4 Owing to the advent of the slack season, as among the tailors and mantua-makers and bonnet-makers.
5 Owing to the continuance of unfavourable weather [rain and winds].
6 Owing to the approach of winter, as among the builders, brickmakers, market gardeners.
7 Owing to the loss of character . . . culpably or accidentally.[30]

Mayhew later added other predisposing factors to this list, including panics in the money markets with failures of banks, merchants and manufacturers (as in 1825–6 and 1846), foreign wars and revolutions which interrupt trade, and political disorders at home (Chartism is mentioned) which destroy confidence and reduce employment.[31] And, in addition to these specific causes, he believed that there existed a 'general superfluity of labour' which greatly increased the amount of casual, irregular work, an over-stocking of the labour market caused by increasing the amount of work demanded from men, increasing mechanization, and increases in the supply of labour as more apprentices, women and children were taken on at low wages to replace men.

> On a careful revision of the whole of the circumstances before detailed, I am led to believe that there is considerable truth in the statement lately put forward by the working classes that only one-third of the operatives of the country are fully employed, while another third are partially employed and the remaining third wholly unemployed; that is to say, estimating the working classes as being between four and five millions in number, I think we may safely assert that... only 1,500,000 are fully and constantly employed, while 1,500,000 more are employed only half their time, and the remaining 1,500,000 wholly unemployed, obtaining a day's work occasionally by the displacement of some of the others.[32]

There can be no precise count of unemployment at this period, or at any point in the nineteenth century, since there was no national collection of the relevant statistics. One set of data, the poor law returns of the numbers of paupers relieved, can be quickly discounted, even if limited to the minority classified as 'able-bodied' and, therefore, available for work. Resort to the deterrent poor law was the last refuge of the destitute, particularly abhorrent to the pride of the skilled man: the records refer mainly to casual and unskilled groups, and in any case not all those receiving relief were necessarily unemployed. The statistics which have been most used for this period are the returns made by some trade unions of the relief given to their unemployed members, either in the form of donations or tramping allowances: these records were kept with considerable care and accuracy in an attempt to prevent fraudulent claims on limited funds. The objection to them as general measures of unemployment is that before the 1880s trade unions covered only a very small and selective segment of the working class – engineers, metal-workers and shipbuilders from 1851 onwards, and printing, woodworking and some building trades from 1860:[33] only one small union, the Steam Engine Makers, which was founded in 1824 and had a limited national coverage by the 1830s, has records of its unemployed members from 1835.[34] Although such unions were clearly very unrepresentative of the working class as a whole, they are valuable for our purpose since they refer only to skilled men, the aristocrats 'in Society'. A detailed examination of the Steam Engine Makers' records between 1835 and 1846 shows that the proportion of members receiving unemployment relief varied between 1.5 per cent in the good year 1835–6 and 24.1 per cent in the deep depression of 1842–3: over the eleven-year period it averaged 10.8 per cent. Unemployment relief, which in this period meant an allowance for tramping in order to seek work, varied directly with the state of trade, as did the distances tramped. The statistics do not tell us the duration of unemployment, but the number of miles travelled gives some indication of this: over the period the mean distance tramped was 129.4 miles, but in the bad year 1841–2 it rose to 333.8 miles,[35] suggesting a minimum of perhaps twenty days of continuous tramping, not allowing for what must have been frequent stops in towns to look for work. Tramping was somewhat more common among younger members of the union, though by no means confined to them: in 1842–3, 32 per cent of the men under thirty were on tramp, but a surprisingly high figure, 23 per cent, of those over sixty.[36]

A similar cyclical pattern of unemployment is noticeable in other skilled trade unions. From its formation in 1851 the Amalgamated Society of Engineers was the largest of the 'New Model' unions, and the first to begin to provide its members with 'static' unemployment benefit (the 'donation'). Since the Society published monthly returns of the number of its members receiving relief, it is possible to plot with some accuracy the proportions and regional distribution of unemployment in particular years of depression, 1858, 1862, 1868 and 1879. In July 1858 the Society relieved 12.5 per cent of its members, but 24.7 per cent in York, Humberside and Yorkshire towns compared with 8.5 per cent in London: in October 1862 and in April 1868 the national average was 8.8 per cent and in July 1879 11.3 per cent. In these later depressed years Greater Manchester and the north-west usually had the highest rates of unemployment while London, the south and east of England were consistently lower.[37] As a major export industry, engineering suffered considerably from instability of foreign demand, and experienced repeated periods of unemployment within an overall pattern of growth. The Amalgamated Society of Carpenters and Joiners, whose members worked principally on domestic building, suffered less, with a highest annual average rate in the sixties of 3.6 per cent in 1869 and, in the next decade, 8.2 per cent in 1879: these statistics, however, are averages over the year and do not reflect the considerable seasonal and monthly variations.[38] Similarly, the average annual rates for printing and bookbinding unions are well below those for the metal trades – a mere 2.5 per cent over the decade 1860–9. It should be emphasized, however, that as measures of unemployment these are very blunt indeed since they average out the very variable monthly rates over the year. While employment in the metal trades was particularly influenced by the trade cycle, levels of investment and exports, the woodworking and printing trades were primarily influenced by seasonal patterns.

One general factor, however, underlay any particular causes of unemployment in the skilled trades in the middle of the century. Contemporaries were convinced that the supply of labour had over-stocked the market, so that even in good times there were always more workers available than could be kept in steady employment. The unprecedented increase in population, which doubled between 1801 and 1851 from nine to eighteen million, could not always be absorbed by an economy which, though growing overall, was growing by fits and starts. Industrialization was still immature and unadjusted to the complexities of supply and demand: Malthusian fears of over-population had not yet been replaced by the optimism of the 'Golden Age' when increasing numbers came to be viewed as a necessary, desirable asset for a firmly-established expanding economy. The pressure from cheap labour, most of it unapprenticed men and large numbers of women and children, meant that there was now insufficient work for 'Society' men except in the busiest seasons. A tailor told Mayhew that 20 to 25 per cent of the men in union were 'off work' for ten months in the year,[39] while a carpenter stated that there was only regular work for two-thirds of the hands: 'It is one of the chief evils of the carpenter's trade that as soon as a man turns of forty, masters won't keep him on'.[40]

By the 1830s the London printing trade was also suffering from persistent unemployment of compositors and pressmen. A report by the London Union of Compositors in 1835 stated that, 'All employment has become uncertain – no situation is permanent'[41] and in 1837 apprentices made up 40 per cent of the labour force. Charles Manby Smith ended his apprenticeship to a Bristol printer in 1826 and, now unemployed, moved to London in search of work. He found hundreds unemployed and notices on the doors of printing houses, 'Compositors and pressmen need not apply'; an older unemployed man told him, 'There's three times the number of boys brought up to this trade that there's any occasion for.... If the trade suffers a general depression, as is the case just now, full half or even two-thirds of the workmen are turned adrift'.[42]

A constant flow of new recruits from the country and small market-towns flooded the labour market in London and other large cities, willing to work, when they could get it, at less than 'stab' wages in order to gain experience of the latest techniques. They were augmented in other trades by considerable numbers of foreign workers who came to England for similar reasons, or to escape persecution or military service. By mid-century the London tailoring trade already had large numbers of Jewish workers who, it was complained, depressed wages and caused unemployment: there were four 'houses of call' specifically for foreigners.[43] Many Germans moved into the baking trade, where it was said that 'a lad can learn to be a tolerably good hand in a year or two.... Of the estimated number of 13,000 journeymen bakers in London, many hundreds are continually without regular work ... [they] may get one or two days employment at the latter end of the week'.[44] Germans came over on a four-year passport and were prepared to work for low wages to learn the language, but did not return in order to avoid conscription: a master baker who employed six in his three shops thought that they were 'fast superseding the English workmen' because the latter were 'so unsteady and so given to drink'.[45]

Trade depressions

Charles Smith had arrived in London in 1826, searching for work at a particularly bad time of cyclical depression and financial panic: one of the largest publishers, Hurst, Robinson & Co. had failed due to over-speculation, and several other firms had suspended operations. On his second day in London he called at a dozen of the largest printing houses without success: the state of trade was as bad, or worse, than in Bristol which he had left in high hopes of finding work. In the cotton-town of Blackburn, Lancashire, the crisis of 1826 was the worst to date, with 6,412 of the 10,686 people dependent on the industry laid off and another 1,467 on half-time.[46] There were further trade depressions here in 1829, 1832, 1837, 1841, 1842–3 (a time of 'extreme distress') and 1847–8. Over the whole period from 1815 to 1870 W. W. Rostow has identified eleven trade cycles, with troughs in 1816, 1819, 1826, 1829, 1832, 1837, 1842, 1848, 1855, 1858, 1862 and 1868: conversely, the peak years of economic expansion, when virtually full employment was assured, were 1818, 1825, 1836, 1845, 1854 and 1866. Between 1816 and 1848, 64 per cent of the years are described as 'prosperity periods', and between 1848 and 1868, 67 per cent.[47] Thus, up to 1870 approximately one-third of the time was characterized by declining prosperity, more or less intense cyclical depression and unemployment: in a wide range of occupations regular work was only available at particular points in the trade cycle.

The severity of depressions in the late 1830s and 1840s caused much public concern and sympathy as well as an unprecedented extent of social investigation by individuals and statistical societies. From these it is clear that the timing and extent of depressions varied between different towns and industries, so that in Nottingham, the centre of the hosiery and lace trades, prosperous years 1836 and 1837 were followed by a slump early in 1838 when 5,850 people – one-ninth of the total population – were receiving poor relief: over 1,100 houses were uninhabited, and pawn-brokers had to refuse the quantity of goods offered.[48] But the years 1841–2 saw the deepest and most widespread depression of the period, affecting almost all industries in all parts of the country. In Bolton in 1842, 36 per cent of ironworkers were unemployed, 84 per cent of carpenters, 87 per cent of bricklayers, 66 per cent of stonemasons, and 50 per cent of tailors and shoemakers.[49] In Dundee half the mechanics and shipbuilders were out of work and only five out of 160 tailors had full employment, according to the report of an Anti-Corn Law Conference, which also stated that two-thirds of London tailors and three-quarters of carpenters and plumbers in Dundee were unemployed.[50]

Members of Parliament described the depression of that year as unprecedented in their experience. In July Stockport had 50 per cent of unemployment, Greenock 60 per cent, and in Newcastle 12,000 of the adult population of 29,000 were out of work. In Sheffield, where highly skilled workers were much valued by the employers, one response to the depression was to spread the available work on a part-time basis: hence in 1842 19 per cent were in full employment, 63 per cent partly employed, but only 18 per cent wholly without work.[51] A detailed survey of conditions in the Vauxhall Ward, Liverpool, is particularly useful since the population of 24,000 contained a high proportion of 'superior mechanics', and it was believed that conditions here were better than in the borough as a whole: there was an unusually high proportion of 'mechanics and artisan families' at 1,621 compared with 2,628 families of labourers. Table 1 shows that of men engaged in skilled trades 592 out of 1,621 (36 per cent) were fully employed, 423 (26 per cent) wholly unemployed, and the remaining 38 per cent partly employed.[52]

Although the depression of 1841–2 has generally been regarded as the worst in the century, that of 1847–8 also caused exceptional distress and unemployment, especially in the Lancashire cotton towns. In Manchester in November 1847 of a total of 28,000 cotton workers, 13,400 were fully employed, 7,400 unemployed and 7,200 partly employed: engineers fared even worse, with only 2,800 of the 6,000 fully employed, 1,600 unemployed and 1,600 partly employed.[53] Of the total of 41,300 workers in all Manchester textile factories (including silk, worsted and dye-works) only 19,100 were fully employed. As the crisis receded after November, unemployment began to fall down to February 1848, but rose again in March and April as revolutions in Europe interrupted exports: most mills had returned to full work by the summer. The crisis of 1847–8 illustrated clearly how violently employment could fluctuate over a short period, with disastrous consequences to workers – at its worst 9,400 Manchester families, accounting for 23,742 people, were receiving poor relief, approximately one-tenth of the whole population.[54] It also illustrated the fact that in the early stages of the depression the reaction of factory owners was to put workers on short time, since because of their high fixed costs it was preferable to keep production going even in the face of losses, but as the depression worsened production was stopped completely.

It was previously noticed that the employment experience of different regions varied widely. A study of the Black Country, a major centre of heavy industry, has shown that over the period from 1839 to 1875, sixteen years were characterized by depression and only twelve by good trade:[55] there were only three sustained spells of reasonably full employment – 1834–7, 1845–55 and 1870–4 – and even these were interrupted by some brief slumps. The evidence from the Black Country confirms that the

Table 1 Extent of employment in Vauxhall Ward, Liverpool 1842

	Not employed	Fully employed	Employed five days per week	Employed four days per week	Employed three days per week	Employed two days per week	Employed one day per week	Not ascertained	Total
Labourers	855	807	17	206	344	271	113	15	2628
Widows, and other females	459	91	2	8	63	56	3	101	783
Coopers and brushmakers	11	31	1	7	9	6	4	–	69
Smiths and engineers	35	89	1	8	14	2	3	5	157
Slaters and plasterers	20	2	1	5	3	5	3	1	40
Painters, plumbers and glaziers	28	12	–	6	7	5	6	–	64
Joiners and cabinet-makers	54	48	–	9	5	10	2	26	154
Shoe and bootmakers	50	49	1	23	56	44	18	8	249
Tailors	40	24	–	8	30	26	6	4	138
Bakers and millers	10	22	1	–	1	1	–	2	37
Bricklayers and stonemasons	35	11	1	7	9	5	6	1	75
Sailors, fishermen and pilots	28	120	–	5	7	3	–	31	194
Millwrights and wheelwrights	5	19	–	2	1	1	1	3	32
Engravers and watchmakers	7	5	–	2	2	4	2	–	22
Sawyers	7	8	–	4	6	3	3	6	37
Sailmakers, riggers, and block-makers	13	12	–	5	10	5	2	–	47
Shipwrights and ropers	16	11	1	10	15	5	2	1	61
Printers and bookbinders	2	8	–	–	1	1	1	11	24
Tinmen and braziers	9	22	–	–	3	1	–	1	36
Iron boilermakers	6	27	–	3	–	–	–	1	37
Iron moulders	8	12	–	2	–	–	–	–	22
Nail-makers	10	16	1	3	2	4	–	–	36
Sundry other trades	29	44	–	1	7	7	1	1	90
	1737	1490	27	324	595	465	176	218	5032

Not employed		1737
Fully employed		1490
Employed five days per week	27	
Employed four days per week	324	
Employed three days per week	595	
Employed two days per week	465	
Employed one day per week	176	
		1587
		4814
Not ascertained	218	
Not described	60	278
Total		5092

trade union statistics of unemployment are very inadequate for this period since they covered so few trades and, in any case, took no account of short-time working which was common here among iron-puddlers and coalminers, as also among Lancashire cotton workers. When reduced to two or three days a week a worker was effectively unemployed half the time.

The autobiographies of skilled workers clearly testify to the nature and frequency of periods of unemployment. Of twenty-five relevant memoirs covering representative trades such as stonemasons, printers, tailors, shoe-makers, engineers and woodworkers, depressions in trade emerge as the major cause of unemployment, given by a third of the authors as the reason for their dismissal. After failing as a fancy weaver in 1825 when the Wakefield Bank broke and 'there was a great fall in the trade', Robert Spurr was helped by one of his brothers to find work in 'snob' shoemaking near Leeds. 'My Master was very poor, and liked his drop of ale, and he had very little money and little work, so when I had been there 18 months I had to leave 50s. of my wages in his hands.'[56] His next employer's business also failed in 1831, and Spurr did not find regular employment until he went to work for a Methodist shoemaker where the six men sang psalms and hymns and 'every Saturday morning I got my wage – this was what I never had in my life before'. Charles Manby Smith served a seven-year apprenticeship as a printer in Bristol, where his father and brother were cabinet-makers. Unhappily, the end of his apprentice-ship in 1826 coincided with deep depression and the 'dreadful money panic': his master's business had greatly declined in the previous four months and he now had no work for men at journeyman's wages. Smith left for London, where he found trade equally depressed with 'many hundreds of hands . . . out of employ and thrown either upon the trade fund or their own wretched resources. . . . "We are doing nothing, and have not work for our old hands", was the stereotyped form of the reply I received at almost every house'.[57]

After failing to find any work in London, Smith was advised by a fellow compositor to try prospects in Paris, where pirated editions of Scott, Byron and other authors were being printed and English hands were preferred: he spent the next four years there until the revolution of 1830 when all the presses were closed and he returned to England. Equally unfortunate was Thomas Wallis, whose apprenticeship to a carver and gilder in Hull ended in the notoriously depressed year 1842, though he had been exceptionally farsighted in preparing himself for such misfor-tunes. 'I very early thought that my future life would include much tramping. I decided to prepare myself for it [at fourteen] by severity of living, exercise, learning my trade and improving my education.'[58] Wallis was unemployed for twelve weeks in 1842 and had 'very little work to do' in 1843 despite tramping in Yorkshire and Lincolnshire. Thomas Wood's apprenticeship as an engineer in Bingley, Yorkshire, also ended in 1843. His parents, poor handloom weavers, 'doomed to be crushed out by remorseless machinery', had made great sacrifices to apprentice Thomas, the eldest of their ten children, to the local power-loom mechanic – an 'anomaly' which he did not understand at the time. After only two months as a journeyman with his former master, Wood was dismissed: 'Trade was bad in the extreme . . . the road swarmed with beggars. Families of six or eight persons were on the road together, and esteemed themselves fortunate if they could obtain the shelter of an outhouse or a hayrick'.[59] Wood tramped for a month through Lancashire, eventually getting well-paid work at the great engineering firm of Platts Bros., in Oldham, but in 1846, 'I, along with 50 others, got stopped. I was told to come again in a few weeks and see if anything turned up'.[60]

For two autobiographers, J. H. Powell and W. E. Adams, the years of the Crimean War (1854–6) were a period of trade depression and unemployment. Powell ended his apprenticeship as an engineer in 1853, followed by a long tramp through the 'principal towns of Middlesex, Lancashire and Yorkshire': trade was 'at a low ebb', and during sixteen months he only had work for four, for brief periods in a dozen different shops. When he eventually found regular work on the construction of a flour-mill at Watford, he married and joined the Amalgamated Society of Engineers. 'Thus, by wise forethought, I secured ourselves against absolute want' – a fortunate decision since shortly afterwards his employer went bankrupt and he had to move to London, where 'For many weeks I sought employment and found it not'.[61] Adams served his time as a printer on the *Cheltenham Journal*, also ending his apprenticeship in 1853, when he went to work at Brantwood on Lake Coniston (Ruskin's later house) on a Socialist weekly, the *English Republic*. This failed after a year, and Adams set out to tramp the 274 miles to London in 1855:

> Not an odd job anywhere, nor any relief either except a shilling at Birmingham. . . . The times were out of joint. It was the winter of the Crimean War – the severest as regards weather, the dreariest as regards depression, the direst as regards distress that we had had for years. . . . I find in my old diary a note on the state of the country – 'Everywhere the cry is want of work. In Macclesfield . . . the weavers "play" nearly as often as they work. Some of them oftener. "I have never known such a winter", has been the expression of all with whom I talked'.[62]

Another printer, W. J. Francis, had a series of temporary jobs in London after his apprenticeship in 1865, until in 1868 'trade became very slack, and I, with others, was "stood off" for a while, so I thought it a good opportunity to take a holiday'.[63] This was quite different from the euphemistic 'play' of the unemployed, however. Francis made an enjoyable sightseeing tour of Kent on foot until offered work by his father, a printer on his own account.

One of the fullest accounts of the effects of a trade depression is contained in the journals of a Lancashire power-loom weaver, John O'Neil, which cover the years 1856–75, and therefore include the period of the 'Cotton Famine' when supplies of raw cotton from the southern states of America were interrupted by the Civil War. O'Neil had been a handloom weaver in Carlisle, but had turned to the power-loom in 1833 and moved to Low Moor, Clitheroe in 1855 where he and his daughter worked at Garrett and Horsfall's large factory. Here, nearly 700 workers produced 5,000 pieces of cotton cloth each week, and for a few years O'Neil, who worked three looms, enjoyed reasonable prosperity, buying new furniture for the house and new clothes which included a velveteen shooting-jacket. Early in 1861 there was a six-week strike at Low Moor for increased rates in common with many other Lancashire towns, and O'Neil, now President of the Clitheroe Weavers' Union, had been a principal negotiator of the compromise which ended the dispute. Shortly afterwards, the first effects of the Cotton Famine began to be felt. The workers at Clitheroe were in favour of accepting short time (i.e. work-sharing) rather than reduced staff or wages, and a four-day week began in September 1861. As supplies worsened in 1862 Garrett's turned off 400 of their employees, more than half the workforce: there was no possibility of alternative employment as three other mills in the district were stopped and four more on short time. When H. B. Farnall, the government's special Poor Law Commissioner, visited the town in November 1862 he found that of the 2,739 people normally employed in the cotton industry 1,051 were out of work, 1,138 on short time and only 500 fully employed.

O'Neil was an intelligent man, who followed the gathering crisis with great interest and concern from the newspapers in the Clitheroe Reading Room. The first mention in his journal was:

Jan. 20, 1861   There is great excitement in the United States upon account of electing Mr Lincoln President. All the slave states are talking of seceding.

Jan. 24   Thawing all day, and we have got a notice put up in our mill today giving us notice of a reduction in wages.

April 27   Civil War has broke out in the United States and Fort Sumter has been captured by the secessionists.

May 11   President Lincoln has blocaded all the ports in the south, and the rebels are sending out letters of marque for privateering.

Jan. 1, 1862   We are beginning the New Year under very poor prospects. Bad trade, short time, and a prospect of a war with

America which, if it should take place, will be worse than ever, as we shall get no cotton.

Jan. 8   Another wet, cold day, and owing to the scarcity of cotton we are working such rubbish as I never saw in my life. We cannot do the half work that we used to do.

Jan. 15   We commenced running short time . . .

Mar. 19   Another fine day. We have stopped today for all week.

May 2   A cold, windy day. We stopped at noon and won't start untill Monday morning . . .

May 22   Another fine day, and we stopped this forenoon for all week.

June 8   [the Journal breaks off here and resumes on 10 April 1864]

April 10, 1864   It is nearly two years since I wrote anything in the way of a diary. . . . It has been a very poor time for me all the time owing to the American war, which seems as far off being settled as ever. The Mill I work in was stopped all last winter, during which time I had three shillings per week allowed by the relief committee, which barely kept me alive. When we started work again it was with Surat cotton. . . . We can earn very little. . . . The principal reason why I did not take any notes these last two years is because I was sad and weary. One half of the time I was out of work, and the other I had to work as hard as I wrought ever in my life and can hardly keep myself living. If things do not mend this summer I will try somewhere else or something else, for I can't go much further with what I am at.

Oct. 30   We commenced work last Thursday and started full time, as our Masters have bought a large supply of cotton. . . . The cloth market is a trifle better this last week, and it is thought that it has got a turn for the better.[64]

The end of apprenticeship

Several autobiographers cite the end of apprenticeship as the reason for their initial unemployment. The reason was obvious enough. For five or, often, seven years, the master had had the benefit of increasingly skilled labour at a fraction of a journeyman's wage, quite apart from the premium for the indentures which had brought him anything from £10 to £50 as his fee for instructing the youth in the mysteries of the trade. In practice, such instruction as there was was usually given by journeymen, and cost the employer nothing. Apprentices started at a purely nominal wage of 1–2s. a week, progressing by small annual increments until in their last year, aged between eighteen and twenty-one, they would normally receive half an adult wage. Small shops often had three or four apprentices and only two or three journeymen, making them a very useful source of cheap labour for routine work which was learned long before their time expired. Having served their time, however, it was frequently made clear that there was no place for them at a qualified man's wage, regulated in most skilled trades by the 'stab' (established rate maintained by the unions). Inevitably, this meant a search for work, either in the same town or further afield 'on tramp', a period of unemployment which might extend for weeks or months, especially when termination of apprenticeship coincided with a trade depression.

This, as we have seen, happened to the printer Charles Smith in 1826 and to the engineer, Thomas Wood, in 1843, but other autobiographers record their unemployment at the end of apprenticeship almost as a natural, expected event. Thus, William Fairbairn ended his time as a millwright in a North Shields colliery in 1810 to find he was no longer required: 'I left reluctantly the scene of my trials and many friendships, and went in search of other employment. Some of the other young men did the same.'[65] For the next five years he had a series of temporary jobs in Newcastle, Bedlington, Hertford, Cheshunt, London, Bath, Bristol, Cardiff, Dublin, Liverpool and Manchester, before setting up in business with a partner. James Burn ended his seven-year apprenticeship as a hatter in Otley, Yorkshire, in 1829, moved immediately to Edinburgh where he found work for a few months, then to Glasgow, 'in consequence of the slackness of trade': after three months' work there from August to October 1830, this came to an end and Burn, now married, set out on a long tramp leaving his wife and young child behind.[66] The same year John Bray ended his apprenticeship to a printer in Selby, Yorkshire, and failing to get employment there, went on tramp. Bray, who later became a Utopian Socialist and the author of *Labour's Wrongs and Labour's Remedy*, left a third-person account of his experiences on the road:

> He conceived the idea of the necessity for industrial reforms while wearily plodding from town to town in search of work as a 'tramp'. He constantly met the tailor, the shoemaker, the weaver and other workmen, all 'tramps' looking for employment and all in need of the things which his fellow tramps could produce. Walks of twenty or thirty miles a day, half-fed and a shelter in some low lodging-house where vermin prevented sleep, was enough to set any man thinking about the causes of these miseries.[67]

Business failures

Once established in what seemed to be regular employment, there was no certainty that this would continue. The frequency of job changes, punctuated by spells of unemployment, is partly to be explained by the high mortality rate of businesses, with the inevitable discharge of hands. Firms in the craft industries were typically small-scale and under-capitalized, consisting of a master who worked alongside two or three apprentices and journeymen: only in engineering and shipbuilding, and to a lesser extent in printing and building, were there some larger units of production which could count their employees in scores or occasionally even in hundreds, and could expect to survive temporary crises by short time or lay-offs. But the small firms were especially vulnerable to the state of the market, to bad debts, changes of fashion and to the personal failings of proprietors which ranged from simple business incompetence to drunkenness and crime. The extreme precariousness of these small employers, who lacked any reserves to tide them over setbacks, is illustrated by their frequent inability to pay their workers' wages and the suddenness of their collapse into bankruptcy. William Lovett, apprenticed to a ropemaker in Newlyn, Cornwall, had already had to bring his master before the magistrates to recover the wages due to him. On qualifying in 1819 he could find no work locally and was advised to try his luck in London: despite letters of recommendation he could get no work in his trade in 1821, and turned to cabinet-making in which he had acquired some amateur skill. Since he was not qualified he had to work for a 'trade-working' (slop) master who soon owed him £6 to £7 in wages and was taken into the Fleet prison for debt: 'I had wasted the prime of my life in learning a trade which I found comparatively useless'.[68] Similarly, Francis Place completed his apprenticeship as a leather breeches-maker in London in 1789 to find that his master was in debt and his business ruined: unemployed for a while, he 'now got a job where I could, first at one place and then at another'.[69]

J. D. Burn's first master became bankrupt, obliging him to have his indentures transferred to another: he had been 'frequently without food, or the means of obtaining any'.[70] W. E. Adams became unemployed when the weekly *English Republic* failed and he went on tramp with a bundle of unsold tracts, while another printer, John Bedford Leno, having served his apprenticeship in Uxbridge in 1847, found that his employer was in debt and the firm on the verge of bankruptcy. 'Eventually I was forced to leave in search of work ... I had not a penny piece, mother had sixpence. This she gave me, supplemented by her blessings and tears.'[71] Bankruptcies in these small provincial printing firms were especially common, but could occur in firms of any size or description. The anonymous 'Colin' became unemployed in 1815 when his employer, a master shipbuilder of Leith, went bankrupt,[72] while the failure of J. H. Powell's millwright employer in Watford has previously been noted (see p. 96).

Technological changes

In his analysis of the causes of unemployment Mayhew included the effects of machinery, or what would now be called 'technological unemployment'. In a general sense much of the unemployment described above might be considered technological in that periods of depression in trade heightened the competition between the newer, more efficient firms which used the latest machinery and older, high-cost firms which were then forced to go on to short-time working or to close down completely. Over the longer term it is debatable whether mechanization reduces the total demand for labour since it also creates new, different demands, but there were many instances from the 1820s onwards of the displacement of workers by specific mechanical inventions. Many of these occurred in textile factories, the heartland of the Industrial Revolution, where a simple adaptation of spinning-machines was to enlarge the number of wheels in order to do with fewer hands. William Dodd wrote in 1842:

> This will account for the many cotton spinners I have met with out of employment. . . . I was not surprised to see scores walking about the streets with nothing to do; employed in going errands, waiting upon the market people, selling pins and needles, ballads, tapes and laces, oranges, gingerbread, etc., etc., while those who are in work are killing themselves by over-exertion.[73]

The particular cause, he believed, was the 'double-decking' of spinning-mules, so increasing the output of one man: in one factory 'they have actually coupled five pairs of spinning mules together, and these are worked by one man instead of five as formerly . . . [until lately] a pair of mules was thought as much as a man could manage'. Dodd also noted that there had been a great increase in self-acting mules, which did not require any adult spinners but were operated by child 'scavengers'.[74] In Yorkshire he found wool-croppers in very distressed circumstances. They had formerly served five- or seven-year apprenticeships and earned 36s. to 40s. a week, but since the introduction of machinery the cloth was dressed by boys at 5s. to 8s. a week and a few men at 10s. to 14s. At Leeds:

> I met about 20 men sweeping the streets, and on enquiring found they were mostly men who had served a legal time to some trade such as croppers, flax-dressers and others connected with the [woollen] manufactures. They generally affirm that the introduction of machinery is the chief cause of their misery: they are employed by the parish at 1s. a day.[75]

The introduction of machinery for planing wood, tonguing and grooving and preparing mouldings was claimed to have taken over at least one-sixth of joiners' work by mid-century,[76] but the sawyers were affected even worse by the introduction of steam sawmills: Mayhew was told that only one-third of sawyers now had full employment, a second third three or four days' work a week and the remainder one or two days or none at all. Veneer sawyers used to be the best paid of all for their very fine work, but now not one was left in London: machines could cut fourteen veneers to the inch, while the best a man could do was eight, more usually six. 'We look upon it [machinery] as a curse', said one sawyer, who added that it was no use emigrating because it was used as much, or more, in America.[77]

In engineering, the adoption of the slide-rest on the lathe led to a considerable influx of youths and unskilled labour: ropemakers suffered from the introduction of the 'Devil' by which nine men could make a ship's cable formerly requiring over eighty:[78] the sewing-machine, first exhibited at the Crystal Palace in 1851, had the effect of greatly increasing the cheap, sweated sectors in tailoring, dressmaking and shoemaking at the expense of the traditional crafts. Mechanization in these and other trades often met with the sort of resistance which handloom weavers put up against the power-loom, and as early as 1826–7 there were campaigns organized by pressmen and sawyers calling for a tax on machinery to slow down its adoption and compensate workers displaced,[79] though this refined version of Luddism had no more success than its predecessor. A different type of innovation which had disastrous effects on another old skill was the gradual replacement of timber by iron for shipbuilding, which began to affect the London shipbuilding trade from the late 1860s onwards as the iron-based industry shifted to Tyneside, Clydeside and elsewhere. The once powerful Thames Shipwrights' Provident Union, founded in 1824, was in rapid decline by the 1860s[80] and its members increasingly thrown into casual, repair work. A similar fate overtook sailmakers in the next decade as steam gradually superseded sail, leaving these skilled workers also to irregular repair work or tramping to sea.[81]

As William Lovett found, it was quite possible to spend seven years training for a craft whose products had been largely superseded – in his case rope was increasingly being replaced by chain, and 'Thus it was very difficult to obtain employment at my trade, unless for a few weeks in the winter when vessels came into the bay disabled and wanting ropes'.[82] Qualified as a leather breeches-maker, Francis Place found that the trade was 'rapidly declining' because of the growth of the cotton trade: 'Corduroys and velveteens were now worn by working men instead of leather. . . . Scarcely anyone was fully employed'.[83] Similarly, James Burn complained that his skill as a felt hatmaker was increasingly redundant as the fashion changed in the 1830s to silk hats, requiring quite different materials and processes, and manufactured in different locations. The classic instance of decline of an old craft was, of course, that of handloom weaving, which was the subject of Chapter 2. Although there was a tradition of children following their parents in the industry, wise parents by the 1830s were insisting that their sons should not join a doomed trade. Thomas Wood had wanted to be either a weaver, like his father, or a wool-comber, 'the two occupations which at that time employed nine-tenths of the population about here . . . (Bingley). Father would not hear of it, so I was put to be a mechanic. Perhaps it caused as much remark among our neighbours as it would now if I put a son to be a doctor. My parents must have made a costly effort to get me a trade',[84] but in later life and earning good wages in Oldham he was able to send money home and help to pay off family debts, accumulated now that handloom weaving was in terminal decline.

Seasonality

Skilled workers were subject to cyclical fluctuations in demand and to the effects of technological innovations, but many were also exposed to shorter-time, seasonal fluctuations occurring at fairly regular intervals each year in response to weather conditions or the dictates of fashion. As early as 1747, Campbell, the author of *The London Tradesman*, estimated that the working year of a bricklayer was six or seven months, and in 1830 the 3,000 to 4,000 regular London painters were supplemented by a further 6,000 to 8,000 employed for about seven months of the year.[85] The state of the weather was a major factor influencing employment in all outdoor trades, especially affecting bricklayers, masons, painters, glaziers, carpenters, plumbers and slaters, who could not work in heavy rain, frost or snow. A few large building contractors like Thomas Cubitt were less affected since they kept a permanent staff of carpenters and joiners working indoors, preparing materials for the next busy season; but most workers were employed by small speculative or jobbing builders who had to stand men off when bad weather interrupted work. The amount of time lost through bad weather obviously varied from year to year, but Charles Booth in the 1880s estimated that in a slack week only 30 to 35 per cent of bricklayers were employed compared to a busy one.[86] Hard winters were particularly prevalent in Victorian England – in the thirty years between 1865 and 1895 there were fifteen winter months with a recorded average temperature of 34°F or less, compared with none in the next thirty years, 1895–1925, and Mayhew believed that weather was the most significant barometer of employment in London.

London skilled trades were also especially affected by 'the season' when fashionable society paid its annual visit to the capital and made heavy demands on a variety of articles of conspicuous consumption. This derived originally from the Parliamentary season when leading families began to return to London in February or March from their country seats: the fashionable 'season' began in mid-April and lasted until mid-July when the rich migrated to spas and resorts at home or abroad. Mayhew listed the following trades directly affected by this brief seasonal surge: West End bespoke tailors, shoemakers, cabinet-makers, milliners and dressmakers, also coachbuilders, saddlers and farriers, cooks, confectioners, bakers, artificial flower-makers, and all the trades concerned with the renovation of property – plasterers, painters, plumbers, upholsterers, carvers and gilders. There were also extra demands for jewellery and silverware, though in these particularly highly skilled crafts employers usually tried to keep a permanent staff throughout the year, not least in case trade secrets were poached by other firms. But apart from these special cases, all the other trades tended to have a peak of employment in June, a trough in August, a minor peak in October/November when Parliament re-opened and winter fashions and Christmas presents were in demand, followed by a trough until next spring.[87] A few trades experienced the reverse of the usual winter slackness, such as piano-makers, indoor games and toymakers, while undertakers were also busiest at this season. Printers who worked in the large firms specializing in government work, such as Hansards and Spottiswoodes, were critically dependent on Parliamentary sittings, and hundreds of compositors were dismissed during the long recesses.[88]

Employers generally coped with seasonal fluctuations in demand by retaining a nucleus of their best workers and taking on extra hands for 'the season' or whenever weather permitted outdoor work: such an arrangement presented few problems since there was always a reservoir of available labour. From the worker's point of view, however, it inevitably meant periods of total or partial unemployment for up to half the year and, all too often, a descent into permanently casual labour. Given the fact that the seasons of heavy demand did not correspond in all trades, it was sometimes possible for a worker to 'dovetail' employments if his skill was transferable, so that a piano-maker who was busy in winter but slack in summer might move to cabinet-making at this time. 'Dovetailing' could only happen on a limited scale, however, and as Booth pointed out it was usually from a more skilled trade to a less skilled one, which only increased the pressure on the lower strata of the labour market. Much more often, the skilled man who could not find alternative work at his usual level had to go into the already over-stocked 'slop' trades out of season, or set up on his own account as a 'chamber-master', exploiting his family to earn a bare subsistence. This process was accelerated when a seasonal trough coincided with a general depression, as in 1847 when Mayhew noted a rapid proliferation of small masters in the East End furniture trades.

Outside London, the effects of the fashionable 'season' were less, though still significant in county and resort towns: the effects of weather on employment were, however, universal, and greater in the more severe climate of the north and Scotland. One of the few attempts to survey the irregularity of employment outside the capital was made by a Statistical Committee of the Town Council of Leeds in 1838–9. It found that the trades which had regular employment for only nine months in the year included painters, plasterers, bricklayers and woodsawyers, but also some indoor trades such as cloth-pressers, dyers and paper-stainers: those which had ten months work were shoemakers, plumbers, masons, wood turners, wheelwrights, hatters and wool-combers, while trades which normally had employment throughout the year included millwrights, smiths, printers, mechanics, gunsmiths, iron moulders and turners.[89] The preponderance of the metal trades among the best employed is notable. Nevertheless, millwrights working outdoors could be subject to the seasons, as William Fairbairn found. Having spent the summer working at Bedlington 'very agreeably', 'The Works were finished, and as was frequently the case in the North, I was thrown out of employment, with a very distant hope of obtaining another situation during the winter. Business was slack, and work scarce . . .' After failing to get work in London, he walked to Hertford through rain and sleet and applied to a millwright to be told that there was no prospect of work until 'the days were a little longer'.[90] In the winter of 1858–9 the stonemason, Henry Broadhurst, undertook a 'disastrous journey' of four months during which he tramped 'about twelve hundred miles without succeeding in finding a single day's work'.[91] And almost twenty years later another stonemason, Alfred Ireson, suffered similarly in the winter of 1876: 'Bitter snows and hard weather put work out of the question', and from earning good wages he was reduced to selling coal at 5s. a week and commission: he got mason's work again the following spring, on a new chapel.[92]

Of indoor trades, those associated with clothing and footwear were particularly subject to seasonality. Hatting, for example, was a notoriously seasonal trade, and at Hexham, where James Burn served his apprenticeship, the sixteen master-hatters employed thirty-five to forty hands in summer but only around twenty in winter. The hatters' union had developed one of the most elaborate systems of tramping in response to this situation, and Burn found himself being 'continually whirled along from one eddy to another. . . . I was both temperate and industrious, and I can say with the confidence of truth that I never lost half a day from my employment through drink'.[93] By contrast, shoemaking had its slack period in the summer months, especially in London and county towns after 'the season' closed, but an unusual instance was reported by George Herbert, a Banbury shoemaker, whose shop in the 1840s was making top-quality boots for the local 'noblemen and clergy'. The trade had a local Society providing lodging and an allowance, and tramping shoemakers found it a convenient first stop from Oxford when unemployed during university vacations. Herbert employed them casually, sometimes as many as a dozen at a time. 'By this means I had at one time or the other the best workmen in England.'[94]

The London tailoring trade experienced similar seasonality. Moving there from Colchester in 1810, Thomas Carter quickly got employment by using the call-book of the tailors' club, but at the end of July 'I fell out of work'. Returning to Colchester he found no prospects there either: 'I tried to procure work at . . . shops in the town. I succeeded, however, but very indifferently, because it was then the season of the year in which cucumbers are said to be vended at the rate of two for a penny, when, according to the averment of the Covent Garden Market ladies, "tailors, twice as many" may be had for the like sum'.[95] Back in London in the autumn, 'Trade continued to be very dull, so that I could not procure employment except a few trifling jobs on my own account'. His meals at this time consisted of a penny roll and half a pint of porter taken at a public house so that he could read any job advertisements in the newspapers. 'I found employment sooner than I should have done in consequence of a death in the Royal Family':[96] this created a sudden demand for mourning clothes, lasting two or three weeks, but followed by further stagnation as people adapted these to ordinary wear and did not buy any new: 'The tenure by which journeymen tailors hold their employment is more than ordinarily slight. No workman of this craft can be sure of remaining in his present master's service after he has finished the garment he has in hand'.[97]

The insecurity of London compositors, as noted by Charles Manby Smith, was partly due to the general over-stocking of the labour market and partly to the seasonal nature of employment, particularly in the large firms which specialized in government work, when hundreds were dismissed during the long Parliamentary recesses. Smith was told by an unemployed compositor that, 'fathers and mothers, all of 'em, think that printing is a light and genteel business. . . . There's three times the number of boys brought up to this trade that there's occasion for'.[98] After a succession of short-term jobs in London, on a provincial newspaper and, changing occupations completely, as an usher in a grammar school, Smith eventually found more regular employment in a large firm (probably Hansards) printing government papers. The office took on many extra printers in January in preparation for the new season of government work:

> As usual in the month of January, the overseer was now daily and hourly besieged by applications for employment from hands out of work. As a matter of policy, old faces were preferred to new, but old and new together soon filled the house until every available

frame was occupied. The Queen opened Parliament to the great satisfaction of crowds of hungry and thirsty typographers. Colonial papers, reports of committees, election returns, prison statistics, accounts, and fifty things besides, poured in upon us thick and fast.[99]

But only for a while. The 'season' ended at the end of August, when scores were turned away to search for casual work for the next four months.

Few autobiographies of skilled women workers have survived, but the dressmaking and millinery trades in which most of them were employed were particularly subject to seasonality. One exception is the memoir of Lucy Luck, born at Tring, Hertfordshire, in 1848, and brought up in the union workhouse there when her drunken father, 'an experienced bricklayer', deserted his family of four children and was never heard of again. At nine, Lucy was put to work in the local silk-mill, and at thirteen into service in a public house. At fifteen she managed to get herself apprenticed for six months, without wages, to a straw-plaiter, one of the principal domestic industries of Luton, though soon found that this was very irregular work as she was dismissed at the end of the season: 'The season was over, and I was homeless, penniless, and with only the clothes I walked in'. Later she became an 'improver' in a workroom, and, after her marriage to a farm labourer in 1867, an out-worker, becoming a highly skilled straw hatmaker, working for over thirty years for two leading London stores. 'The straw-work is very bad, as a rule, from July up to about Christmas', so at these times she went charring, washing and did needlework. She had at one time seven children too young to work, and described her hatmaking as her 'fortune'.[100]

Dismissal for personal reasons

The circumstances of unemployment so far illustrated – trade depressions, seasonality, the decline of old crafts and the business failure of employers – were external to the individual, caused by circumstances beyond his control. However, a number of autobiographers record unemployment arising from quarrels or disputes with their employer which were more personal than economic. Occasionally, though rarely, the fault lay clearly with the worker rather than his employer, as in the case of the drunkard, 'Colin', who, until his conversion to temperance at the age of forty-five, could never hold a regular job. Generally, however, the blame lay with the employer, for failure to pay agreed wages, demanding excessive work or acting unreasonably. James Burn quarrelled with his master's son who was an 'ignorant, presuming, petty tyrant': 'Having been put on my defence by his unmanly treatment, I returned him payment in kind such as he had not anticipated', and left before he could be sacked.[101] John Bezer was dismissed for singing hymns at work (he had been a Head Teacher in a Sunday school), but in the following six months of unemployment supported himself, his wife and child by singing hymns and begging in the streets. 'I began to think that, by perseverance, I could get any day enough food and something to spare – in other words, could live much more comfortably by begging than by hard work.'[102] And John Buckmaster, a carpenter, was dismissed for trying to invent a mortising machine, his employer assaulting, kicking and abusing him.[103]

But the most common cause of disputes and dismissals by employers was the participation of workers in trade unions, radical or other political activities. Many of the skilled workers who wrote autobiographies were actively involved in movements for the betterment of their fellow men: for some, this meant through the agency of religion, working as Sunday school teachers or lay preachers, often allied with temperance reform, but for others the progress of the working class was seen as coming through organizations which would give power to the people in this world rather than salvation in the next. Many authors were imbued with the spirit of self-help which took many forms ranging from mutual improvement societies, reading rooms and mechanics institutes, to more radical activities such as trade unionism, Chartism, co-operation and Socialism, some of which could easily conflict with an employer's perception of his right to control the labour, and even the opinions, of his workers. Those who took part in organizing labour disputes or spoke out too freely about their 'rights', could find themselves not only dismissed but victimized by other employers in the trade, 'black-listed' as agitators who would disrupt the authority of masters over their men. In 1793 Francis Place, a member of the Breeches Makers' Benefit Society, was discharged with others who had struck for higher wages, and he proposed that the unemployed members should be put to work in a co-operative shop under his management. When the strike failed through lack of funds, the masters agreed that no striker should be taken back as long as any other man was unemployed, and that Place should never again be given work by any master breeches-maker. 'A dreadful state of poverty followed. . . . During the next eight months I could obtain no sort of employment, either in my own trade or in any other way.'[104] Later, Chartism absorbed the hopes of many working people, its converts including the printer John Leno. After the failure of his employer in Uxbridge, Leno got work in the printing office of Eton College where, in this unpromising situation, 'I managed to convert the whole of the printers, with the exception of the foreman, to my way of thinking'. It is not too surprising that he was sacked after a year: 'Perhaps my most serious offence was my starting in the royal town of Windsor a branch of the Chartist organisation'.[105]

Some men experienced victimization over long periods of their working lives. Edward Rymer, born at Boldon, Durham, in 1835, started pit work at nine as a trapper, moving through the ranks of driver and putter before becoming a hewer. Objecting to the yearly bond system of hiring which operated in the Durham coalfield, he broke his contract after an illness in 1857 and was sentenced to fourteen days' imprisonment: two years later he had a fight with an overseer who had insulted him because of his lameness, and was sentenced to a month's hard labour. From that time, Rymer claims he was a 'marked man', and at the next annual hiring in 1860 he and several leaders of the local miners' union were refused employment. Altogether, Rymer was victimized thirteen times during twenty-six years of mining, frequently being told 'Agitators not wanted': he subsequently became a paid union agent in Lancashire.[106] J. H. Powell, a member of the Amalgamated Society of Engineers, also suffered long-term victimization after taking part in the strike and lockout of 1851–2. He refused to accept the 'Document', by which employers were requiring workers to give up their union membership or lose their jobs: 'I had decided to suffer death before dishonour: consequently, for a long time I was barred out from the workshop'.[107] Later, in London, 'there seemed to be a charmed circle in possession of the work-field. I was not in possession of the password of admission to it'.[108] Will Crooks, born in Poplar in 1852, was brought up in a poor law school since his crippled father was unable to support the six children: by sweated labour making oilskin coats, his mother managed to have him apprenticed as a cooper as she was determined that he should have a trade. Out of his time at nineteen, Crooks objected to the excessive overtime and to the inferior timber he was made to use, and was dismissed as an agitator. 'Every shop and yard in London was closed to him. Word had gone round that he was an agitator. Try as he did, he could not break through the barrier that had been raised against him.'[109] After a tramp and casual work in Liverpool, Crooks found regular employment in an east London brewery where he worked for ten years: he subsequently had a remarkable career as a Labour leader, becoming a Poor Law Guardian, a London County Councillor and the Member of Parliament for Woolwich.

RESPONSES AND REACTIONS

The response of skilled workers to periods of unemployment depended crucially on its duration, and also on a variety of individual circumstances. Nevertheless, it is clear from the writers of autobiographies that there was a normal pattern or sequence of events which usually began with a reduction of expenditure so that existing resources could be stretched over as long a time as possible. Since in working-class families food often took two-thirds or three-quarters of income, a cut in food expenditure was the almost inevitable reaction to loss of income. In a paper to the

Statistical Society William Neild compared the budgets of cotton workers in Dukinfield, Lancashire, in the good year 1836 with the depressed one of 1841 when workers were on short time and suffering a loss of normal earnings of around a third. Their reaction was to increase the proportion (but not the amount) of income devoted to food, to increase particularly the proportion spent on bread and flour and to reduce that on meat and other more expensive foods. Nevertheless, six out of seven of these families found it impossible to adjust their expenditure satisfactorily to their reduced circumstances, and were accumulating debts to local shopkeepers of from 3s. to 5s. a week.[110] When wages stopped completely the result was far more drastic, and usually meant a total dependence on bread and potatoes, if possible made more palatable by scraps of bacon or other 'relish'. Even to provide this depended either on some savings or on the willingness of shopkeepers to give credit to known customers who could be expected to repay their debts in better times.

Despite volumes of middle-class advice about the virtues of thrift, working-class families rarely saved habitually and were ill-prepared for any lengthy period of unemployment. The exception to this was membership of a Friendly Society, substantially more common among skilled workers than unskilled, but benefits were payable for funeral expenses, sickness and, sometimes, old age pensions, not for unemployment. In Bristol in 1839, of 9,861 heads of households or married to heads of households, only 15.7 per cent had deposits in savings banks or were members of benefit societies or trade clubs,[111] and as late as 1911 Lloyd George believed that 'not a tenth of the working classes have made any provision at all' for insurance against unemployment.[112] In such circumstances, what little savings working-class families possessed were quickly exhausted, and the unemployed had to turn to other remedies. The family was clearly a primary source of support, a wife or children sometimes finding casual work easier to obtain than a husband: this might be 'sweated' domestic industry, washing or charring, though in an area or period of general depression even such opportunities were limited. Several autobiographies mention small amounts of financial support from relatives, particularly from brothers or from sons who had regular work in another town or occupation, though immediate kin often worked in the same industry, such as cotton or mining, and were themselves unemployed. Beyond this, the principal sources of immediate relief were the credit institutions which existed in all working-class districts, ranging from the corner shop and the Scotch draper to the unlicensed street-lender and the licensed pawnshop. Pawning was the major life-support system at such times of crisis. National statistics for the mid-century are not available, but in 1914 no fewer than 230 million pledges were made, equivalent to six for every man, woman and child in the country, or one a fortnight for every working-class family: in that year

5,087 pawnbrokers' licences were issued in Great Britain, compared with 3,390 in 1870.[113] The enormous extent of pawning in a period of unemployment can be detailed from a survey of Vauxhall Ward, Liverpool, in 1842, a manufacturing district which contained a high proportion of mechanics and artisans. Of 4,814 families surveyed, 1,737 heads of households were unemployed and a further 1,587 partially employed: 2,126 families were described as indigent and requiring support. It was found that 1,052 were being maintained by pawning, charity or crime, 1,017 by savings, credit, relatives or casual employment, and only fifty-seven by parish relief: 1,236 families were lodgers, owning no furniture.[114] From the detailed reports of the six investigators who surveyed the Vauxhall Ward, house by house and family by family, one extract must serve as typical:

> With regard to the class altogether unemployed, it is more than I can comprehend how they really exist, not only of labourers but tradesmen (artisans). I visited many families of this description in houses, rooms and cellars, the children almost in a state of nudity. . . . sleeping on shavings or straw, covered with an old wrapper or a couple of sacks cut open and then stitched together. . . . I met with several cases of extreme distress, where their neighbours declared to me that they knew them to be often twenty-four hours without food or fire; yet the husband, they would say, is an honest and sober man, and out from morning till night seeking employment.[115]

Borrowing, pawning and reducing expenditure were only immediate, temporary expedients, and, as the above quotation states, they were almost always coupled with a search for work. This was often based on local or familial contacts, several autobiographers using an informal network of former workmates, relatives and previous employers for their initial searches: in this connection, it was common practice to carry letters of introduction or recommendation from a well-wishing employer to his friends in the trade. But local searches were unlikely to be successful in a period of depression, and most unemployed men knew that they would have to look for work further afield: in fact, no fewer than sixteen of the twenty-five autobiographers went on tramp for work, often over long distances. Tramping systems were the major response of skilled unions to the problem of unemployment, at least until the 1860s and, in some trades, much later. The rationale was twofold: to aid their members to look for work in other parts of the country by providing them with a regular route and 'houses of call' where they could obtain lodging and job information, and at the same time remove surplus labour from the place of origin where, through competition, it could reduce the amount of full-time work and wages available. This kind of tramping, on foot and carrying the tools of one's trade, was a respectable, even honourable status, not to be confused with the vagrant pauper or professional beggar. It was especially common among single men without family responsibilities, and it is clear from the accounts that it was sometimes partly regarded as a pleasurable, sight-seeing experience; it also provided an opportunity to see new processes, new machines or merely new faces. Alfred Ireson, apprenticed to his stonemason father, had an 'intense desire to get free. I wanted to see and to find a fuller life'.[116] After a tramp from Market Harborough to Cambridge, and a short stay there, 'London became the object of my ambition', then a long tramp from the south coast through the west country and the Midlands to Glasgow and ultimately back to Birmingham and marriage. 'The days of careless rambling were now at an end. To have a home, and enjoy its comfort, was my ambition and desire.'[117] Thomas Wood, the engineer, left his old master in Bingley in 1845 to find work in Oldham:

> I thought I was deficient in my trade.... I heard about new tools, new machines and new ways of working. I could never hope to see them in our shop, and if I was to learn, and improve, I would do so now before I either married or thought of it.[118]

And the anonymous 'Colin', a leather-tanner, was as confirmed a traveller as he was a drunkard, having picaresque adventures in France, the Netherlands, the Mediterranean and the East Indies before returning to England and 'genuinely seeking work', supported by his trade union.

With these exceptions, the rest of the autobiographers tramped, not from choice, but because they were impelled by economic forces. Although tramping was obviously easier for single men, it was not restricted to them, and two of the writers (James Burn and Will Crooks) tramped when married, leaving their wives behind and sending for them later when they found work. Others, though single, did not accept tramping readily, resenting the necessity for it and criticizing those who abused the system. Thomas Carter wrote:

> I have long felt a great repugnance against what is called 'tramping' in quest of work, as I had seen much of the misery consequent thereon in the wretchedly-clad and half-starved persons of many among the numerous 'trampers' who had ... visited my first master's workshop for the purpose of getting pecuniary relief from the journeymen,[119]

though he had to accept it when he himself became unemployed. Charles Manby Smith, the compositor, was even more condemnatory, strangely because he associated tramping with lack of unionization, when the reverse was the case and the printing unions had well-organized tramping systems.

Owing to the want of any efficient system of union among the members of the trade, the practice of tramping had, at the time I speak of [1820s], risen to a most disgraceful climax. A regular tide of lazy and filthy vagabonds, professedly of various trades, but virtually living without work or the intention of working, flowed lazily through the kingdom.[120]

Although there was doubtless some abuse of the system, Smith was wrongly equating the highly organized tramping systems of the craft unions with vagrancy and professional begging. As R. A. Leeson has shown, systems of relief for travelling craftsmen had developed at least as early as 1800 in a wide variety of crafts, including carpenters, hatters, curriers, cordwainers, wool-combers, calico-printers, cabinet-makers, joiners, printers and brushmakers: they were later joined by boilermakers, coachmakers and others, so that by the 1820s virtually all crafts were so organized.[121] With two major exceptions – cotton-spinning and coalmining, where because of the localized nature of the industries tramping was less appropriate – the system was the main response of trade unions to periodic unemployment and the need to encourage mobility of labour from over-supplied to under-supplied regions. The system operated by providing accredited members of the union with tickets or 'blanks' which entitled them to a daily allowance and a night's lodging at the club's 'house of call' (almost always a public house) at intervals along an established route. The total route might be a thousand miles or more, and could extend to Scotland and even Ireland. The daily allowance of a shilling or two depended on the 'grade' (length of service) of the member and the distance travelled, typically between twenty and twenty-five miles a day, but more in areas where the club houses were widely spaced. The member's 'blank' was stamped by each local secretary in an attempt to prevent fraud: the tramp was given an evening meal and beer, a bed for the night (sometimes shared) and information about local jobs from the 'call-book' which kept an up-to-date list of vacancies, local unemployed members having first 'call', followed by travellers. The system was widely regarded as fair, popular and effective except in periods of total prostration of trade throughout the country: thus, the Leeds masons in 1837 described it as 'our main support', and the iron-moulders in 1846 as 'our greatest bulwark', while the tailors thought that a man was 'not considered a good tailor until he had done his turn on the road'.[122] During the depressions of the 1840s, however, the system came under great pressure as the numbers of men on the road threatened to exhaust the funds of the unions – in the winter of 1847–8, for example, it was reported that all the Reading iron-moulders were on tramp, and that of the national membership of 4,000, 1,200 were on the road. At such times tramping was all but useless, and from as early as the 1830s the Steam Engine

Makers introduced a 'donation' of home aliment, or 'static pay' as an alternative form of relief. This was adopted in 1851 by the Amalgamated Society of Engineers (ASE), and other unions followed since by now, more travellers were heading for the large towns by railway than keeping to the route. The moulders now offered a 'donation' to their unemployed of 8s. a week for thirteen weeks, followed by 4s. for the next thirteen: the boilermakers allowed static pay to those with twenty years' membership, while others were required to tramp with an allowance of 1s. 6d. a day. By the 1860s tramping was clearly in decline. Of the ASE's 30,000 members, 3,000 were unemployed, but only 300 were on the road: tramping was coming to be regarded as somewhat unrespectable, especially for married men, and some unions renamed tramps as 'travellers' and offered it only as an option. Tramping survived into the 1870s and 1880s, especially in years of depression such as 1879 when the Ironfounders Union issued 2,000 'cards' to 16 per cent of its membership, and in the same year half the engineers who took out cards were over thirty, many of whom must have been married.

Some authors provide an idealized account of the tramping system which almost certainly belies the reality of long, footsore marches with few prospects at the end. For example, Thomas Wright, the engineer, describes the conviviality of the club house, where the refreshed traveller is invited to join the circle of regulars, swap reminiscences of former workmates and learn of job prospects in the district.[123] There is no doubt that many of the autobiographers used the system, sometimes successfully, sometimes not. In 1830 the hatter, James Burn, undertook a tramp of 1,400 miles from Glasgow 'ere I could obtain work' in Sherborne, Dorset, which lasted two months.[124] The printer, Leno, undertook two long tramps, one of over 1,000 miles in 1848, recalling that while resting his aching feet on a grassy bank outside Rugely, 'I remembered that it was my 23rd birthday. The outcome of the fairy palaces I had built during my apprenticeship was to find myself an outcast ... with not so much as a penny in my pocket'.[125] And during a series of tramps in the late 1850s Henry Broadhurst, the stonemason, described himself as 'a hobbledehoy – out of employment. For five years I was like Cain, a wanderer on the face of the earth',[126] although his wanderings were interrupted by short periods of employment:

> During a period of terrible depression in trade – I think it must have been the winter of 1858/9 – I left the city of Norwich in search of work on what proved to be a disastrous journey. . . . My tramp had lasted nearly four months, a time of much suffering and considerable privations, and totally unrewarded by any work. . . . Before I started on this unfortunate journey I had been out of work for a week or two, so that my entire capital amounted to less than ten

shillings, and I finished the tour with the sum of sixpence in my pocket.... On many occasions I was without even a penny. My trades-union had relieving stations in nearly every town, generally situated in one of the smaller public-houses.... [I] was entitled to receive a relief allowance of one shilling for twenty miles, and threepence for every additional ten miles traversed since the last receipt of relief money.[127]

Yet for other writers the organized tramping system was evidently their avenue of mobility which brought them employment, if only after privations. Powell was helped by 'donations' from the ASE to find work in a variety of different towns: Buckmaster used Rechabite Lodges to tramp from Uxbridge to Salisbury where he found work: Crooks got employment in Liverpool after his tramp from London supported by the Coopers' Union. But the changing attitude towards tramping in the later years was well expressed by Henry Broadhurst when he was elected to the TUC in 1872:

My experience of the tramping system led me to the conclusion that the search for employment on foot, from county to county, often continued over a long period, was liable to develop in men of weak character permanent demoralisation, and to instil a distaste of settled life. While not desirous of putting hindrances in the way of a man's leaving his home to find fresh employment elsewhere, I was convinced that he ought not to be compelled to go on the tramp in order to make himself eligible for relief. I therefore advocated a system of small weekly allowances for a limited period to men out of employment, payable in the town where the applicant resided.[128]

'Static pay' increasingly replaced tramping from the 1860s onwards, its generosity depending on the size and wealth of the union and the length of the depression for which members needed to be funded. The Amalgamated Society of Engineers, the most powerful of the 'New Model' unions, normally paid 10s. a week for fourteen weeks, 7s. a week for the next thirty and 6s. indefinitely thereafter,[129] but in periods of high unemployment some unions had to raise their contribution rates to meet demand. Thus, in the bad year 1849 the Sheffield table-blade forgers had to increase their normal weekly subscription of 1s. to between 2s. and 5s.[130] Other Sheffield cutlery unions devised different remedies for their unemployed. One society put its unemployed members to stone-breaking, all too reminiscent of poor law relief: another purchased a farm to employ its surplus labour on food-production, while both the filesmiths and the spring-knife makers established co-operative production societies in the 1860s to give work to the unemployed in their own trades: these were fairly successful for about ten years, showing considerable profits in prosperous times.[131] By then, the idea of co-operative employment as an alternative to capitalism already had a long history, Francis Place having established a co-operative workshop for breeches-makers during a strike in 1793.[132] Under the influence of Robert Owen, co-operative production gained considerable working-class support in the 1820s, William Lovett giving up cabinet-making in 1829 to become storekeeper of the First London Co-operative Trading Association:[133] the provision of work for the unemployed remained an objective, though the ultimate aims of these schemes were considerably wider.

Not surprisingly, skilled workers made little use of charity, either private or institutional, except in extreme distress. As 'respectable' citizens they wished to avoid any taint of pauperism: membership of the trade club or union normally provided a safety net against destitution, and even those who had not qualified for membership could often expect some informal aid from workmates or fellow craftsmen in other towns. Only two autobiographers mention begging – 'Colin', the confirmed drunkard, and Bezer, who was a 'snob' shoemaker, not a unionized tradesman: the typical attitude towards charity was that of Fairbairn who refused to accept half-a-crown from a millwright who could not offer him or his tramping companion work: 'At this kind offer, my pride took alarm, and though without money and almost fainting for want of food . . . I peremptorily refused the half-crown'.[134]

In the troughs of depressions, however, even skilled workers might be driven to accept support from local charities opened to meet such particular crises, usually by providing food and sometimes clothing and fuel. Publically subscribed soup-kitchens were the commonest form of relief, especially, though not exclusively, in the Lancashire towns. Thus in the crises of 1826, 1842–3 and 1847–8 Blackburn charities opened soup-kitchens feeding some 12,000 people and organized work on new roads for the men.[135] The great extent of charity during the Cotton Famine ultimately totalled £1,800,000 from national sources. Even in Sheffield, with its high proportion of artisans and ten local trade unions, soup-kitchens had to be opened by public subscription in the slumps of 1862 and 1866–7.[136] Even such forms of relief were preferable to dependence on the stigmatizing poor law, though, as is well known, outdoor relief generally continued to be given in the manufacturing districts in times of depression despite the intention of the Poor Law Amendment Act of 1834. In Nottingham in the depression of 1838 only twenty-eight of the 1,000 inmates of the Union workhouse were able-bodied unemployed men, but 450 were employed on works of public utility and paid allowances intended to be sufficient to support 1,800 people.[137] Outdoor relief to the unemployed – usually in return for work in the stoneyard or on the roads so that the principle of 'less eligibility' was not openly flouted

– was, in any case, forced on Boards of Guardians in times of depression by the limited accommodation available in workhouses. In July, 1847, when almost 24,000 people were being relieved by the Manchester Union, the workhouse premises, including the hospital, stoneyard and farm, could accommodate only 2,400.[138] Nevertheless, the threat of indoor relief, or of removal to an applicant's settlement if he could not prove five years' residence, must have discouraged significant numbers of those in need, especially among the artisans. Nevertheless, outdoor relief in Manchester rose and fell more or less in line with the level of unemployment, but with a 'lag' averaging six weeks between becoming unemployed and applying for poor relief, suggesting that private and communal relief was always the first recourse.[139]

Two more radical alternatives to unemployment remained. One, particularly attractive to artisans, was to leave the labour market and become self-employed by setting up one's own business. In crafts like shoemaking and cabinet-making the capital costs were very small, while even in printing and engineering autobiographers sometimes succeeded by borrowing the initial outlay. Thus Spurr, Leno, Herbert, Francis, Wallis, Carter and Fairbairn established businesses in their own trades, sometimes precariously and interrupted by bankruptcies, sometimes, as in Fairbairn's case, with extraordinary success. Another group of writers changed from their original crafts to different occupations. Adams and Bray became journalists and professional authors: Buckmaster became a teacher and School Inspector, Ireson a City Missionary and Powell a bookshop manager, poet and lecturer. Five more – Place, Lovett, Rymer, Broadhurst and Crooks – became professionally active in political and labour movements, taking leading parts in the emancipation and elevation of the working class: Place's autobiography, sub-titled the 'Pursuit of Bread, Knowledge and Freedom', perfectly sums up their aspirations. In total, therefore, seventeen of the twenty-five autobiographers moved away from waged work in the crafts for which they had been trained. It is not suggested that escape from unemployment was their only, or primary, motive, though all had suffered from it and written bitterly of their experiences. Most were highly intelligent men who were naturally ambitious for themselves and their class: self-employment, or involvement in radical movements, offered opportunities of progress impossible while working for another.

Finally, for some skilled workers the ultimate escape was by emigration to a country which seemed to offer permanent prospects of employment and advancement, economic, social and political. In this context, the United States was overwhelmingly preferred to Australia or other British Colonies, where the limited extent of industrial development at this time was generally unattractive to craftsmen. Thus, during the Cotton Famine of the early 1860s, despite aid from the Mansion House Fund and free passages offered by the Australian governments, only 2,000 Lancashire spinners and weavers had availed themselves of the offer by June 1863.[140] Skilled unions had already been encouraging emigration since the 1830s as a means of alleviating distress from industrial depression, reducing the over-supply of labour and thereby leaving a larger share of the Wages Fund for those who remained. By mid-century brushmakers, printers, cotton-spinners, carpenters, flint glassmakers, engineers, potters, moulders and others had adopted emigration schemes, ranging from an allowance of four guineas passage money up to grants of £30.[141] The carpenters' union specifically limited their grant of £6 to five-year members and to times when unemployment reached 7.5 per cent, while iron-workers adopted emigration policies during the strike and lockout of 1865. Emigration grew rapidly in popularity in the 1860s and 1870s, an official total of 506,244 skilled workers leaving British shores between 1862 and 1885, predominantly for the United States.[142] It is impossible to know how much of this was trade-union sponsored, though possibly not more than a few thousand,[143] nor how much of it was motivated by unemployment: it is, however, significant that there were peaks of English emigration in 1819, 1827, the early 1830s and 1842, corresponding closely with periods of acute industrial depression,[144] and there was considerable return migration of skilled workers back to England during the American depression of 1874–8. Of the twenty-five skilled workers who experienced unemployment and wrote autobiographies, only one, John Bezer, emigrated, to Australia in 1852. Charles Manby Smith lived and worked as a printer in Paris after the depression of 1826, and 'Colin' spent five years (1815–20) drinking and occasionally working in northern Europe and at sea in the navy. J. H. Powell wrote that he would have emigrated in the 1850s 'if I had had the means', but instead opened a small grocery shop, and when unemployed Thomas Carter amused himself with 'some day-dreams' about emigrating to the United States. It is clear from the very extensive internal migration which many skilled workers undertook, usually through the tramping system, that this was both more attractive and convenient, and offered similar possibilities of employment combined with an element of adventure.

The reactions of autobiographers to unemployment must be judged primarily by their actions rather than by any extended accounts of their feelings and emotions. Francis Place is one of the few to enter this difficult territory, impelled by a period of eight months' unemployment in 1793 during which his child died of smallpox.

> At the commencement of this state of things I contrived so to conduct myself as to keep away anyone who was likely to visit us, and no-one excepting my brother ever called upon us, and thus none knew how poor we really were. We visited no where except now and then our parents. . . . This is the only period of my life on

which I look back with shame.... My temper was bad, and instead of doing everything in my power to sooth and comfort and support my wife in her miserable condition... I used at times to give way to passion and increase her and my own misery. It is but too common for a man and his wife whose circumstances compel them to be almost constantly together in the same room to live in great discomfort.

Our sufferings were great indeed. As long as we had anything which could be pawned, we did not suffer much from actual hunger, but after everything had been pawned but 'what we stood upright in', we suffered much from actual hunger.... After about two months privation I became somewhat more reconciled to my condition, hopeless as it at times seemed, and at length I obtained such a perfect command of myself that, excepting commiseration for my wife and actual hunger, I suffered but little, and bore my lot without much repining.[145]

Place's account already seems to display the syndrome observed by psychologists in the 1930s, of an initial reaction of anger followed by resignation, even apathy. In fact, Place used his enforced idleness to study, reading widely in history, law, politics and philosophy, re-reading Adam Smith, Locke and Hume several times. 'This reading was of great service to me: it caused me to turn in upon myself and examine myself in a way which I should not otherwise have done. It was this which laid the solid foundation of my future prosperity, and completed the desire I had always had to acquire knowledge.'[146]

Most authors did not get beyond their sense of anger and resentment to reach Place's second stage. Powell bitterly resented 'the factory gate being slammed in my face, or the most uncivil words employed against me' and the fact that he was 'not in possession of the password',[147] and Bezer recalls his bitter disappointment when he saw

what I looked out for every day in my travels – a bill up in a window for 'A Man Wanted', and I lost three parts of the day before I could get an answer. And the anxiety I felt – the war between hope and fear all those hours – was very severe. 'Call again in an hour', then 'another hour', and so on. At last the lottery turned up a blank. He couldn't take me because I'd been out of work so long, 'six months and above, oh dear, no'.... Once an outcast, mind what you're at; if you are only hungry six hours, why, they'll give you to eat, but if hungry for six months, O, starve away, or beg or steal, there's plenty of workhouses and jails for such obstinate burdens.[148]

When giving up his work as a stonemason to become a City Missionary, Alfred Ireson commented, 'To thousands of workers the dreadful, bitter, haunting experience that eats the soul away is the lack of security. . . . How thankful I was to see the last of a stonemason's life.'[149]

How deep and lasting the experience of unemployment was on the attitudes and character of people is impossible to generalize or to separate from the host of influences which affect and mould individuals from childhood onwards. Like poverty, it could all too easily blunt natural feelings and emotions, could sour relationships within the circle of family and friends. An unemployed printer told Smith that he now had only four children, having 'planted' one last week. Asked what he meant, he replied:

> I mean buried, to be sure – a good job too, hoping its no harm to say so. Children are all very well when there's plenty for 'em, and a good trade to look to: but 'tis the devil and all to have half a dozen hungry mouths to feed and never even a shirt left to sport.[150]

Yet, for others, unemployment strengthened their resolve to try to change the order of things. Again, to argue that unemployment itself made men into radicals would be to grossly over-simplify complex processes, but it is clear that it was an important, formative element in the political education of a number of autobiographers. John Bray 'conceived the idea of the necessity for industrial reforms' while tramping as an itinerant printer:[151] Bezer, like Leno, became an active Chartist: 'When you are out of a place, you are about the first one to say there's something wrong'.[152] Place and Lovett, Broadhurst and Crooks, all moved on to the stage of national politics, variously advocating co-operation, Socialism, Chartism, trade unionism and education as the salvation of the working class from poverty and insecurity. The experience of unemployment entered like iron into the souls of these men, so that long afterwards they recalled the bitterness and sense of rejection.

> It is a weird experience, this, of wandering through England in search of a job. You keep your heart up as long as you have something in your stomach, but when hunger steals upon you, then you despair. Footsore and listless at the same time you simply lose all interest in the future. . . . Nothing wearies one more than walking about hunting for employment which is not to be had. It is far harder than real work. The uncertainty, the despair when you reach a place only to discover that your journey is fruitless, are frightful. . . . You can imagine the feeling when, after walking your boots off, a man says to you, as he jingles sovereigns in his pocket, 'Why don't you work?' That is what happened to me as I scoured the country between London and Liverpool, asking all the way for any kind of work to help me along.[153]

For Crooks, work came eventually and unexpectedly, from a chance word dropped by a stranger: he does not record whether, on receiving his first wage packet, he threw it on the ground and rolled over it, as Thomas Wright saw men do who had been out of work for a long time.[154] But Crooks was among the earliest to argue that long-term unemployment could so degenerate a man that he became unemployable, a burden to society and the state:

> There are few things more demoralising to a man than to have a long spell of unemployment. . . . A man who is out of work for long nearly always degenerates. For example, if a decent fellow falls out in October and fails to get a job say by March, he loses his anxiety to work. The exposure, the insufficient food, his half-starved condition, have such a deteriorating effect upon him that he becomes indifferent whether he gets work or no. He thus passes from the unemployed state to the unemployable state. It ought to be a duty of the nation to see that a man does not become degenerate.[155]

Such views were becoming current in some circles by the 1880s. They marked a new stage in the understanding of unemployment and in the demand that the state had a responsibility for remedying or, at least, alleviating it in some more humane way than the humiliating poor law.

4

UNEMPLOYMENT ON THE LAND, 1834–1914

THE NEW POOR LAW

In 1835 George Pulham, a twenty-two-year-old agricultural labourer, was executed at Bury St Edmunds for arson. On the scaffold, he was reported as saying:

> Good bye, good bye, and God bless you all. I hope my fate will be a warning to you all, and I hope you gentlemen farmers will give the young men work; it was the want of work that brought me to this.[1]

Although there was no more concerted revolt of farmworkers on the scale of the 'Swing' Riots of 1830–1, local discontent constantly flared into acts of violence in the decades following the introduction of the new poor law in 1834. Machine-breaking and rick-burning, sheep-stealing, cattle-maiming and poor law rioting continued to be common forms of protest, almost everyday occurrences in some parts of southern England and especially in East Anglia, where a strong radical spirit and bitter resentment survived the death of 'Captain Swing'. Serious disturbances at Ampthill, Great Bircham and elsewhere in 1835 were direct responses to the new poor law, which aimed to substitute a 'well-regulated' work-house for the doles of money previously given to the unemployed and to underpaid heads of large families.[2] Sheep-stealing was especially common in East Anglia, no doubt often to provide meat for a family who rarely tasted it, but the fact that slaughtered animals were sometimes left on the farms, and cattle and horses maimed but not removed, suggests merely blind resentment directed at farmers who paid starvation wages and dismissed men on the first approach of slack times or bad weather. 'Every parish in this neighbourhood is . . . ripe for any outbreak', reported a Member of Parliament for Cambridgeshire in 1846.

The causes of discontent were the continuation of low wages and unemployment, compounded now by the dread of the 'Bastilles'. The poor had lost what they had come to regard as their right to a minimum standard of living maintained by their parish, in work or out of it; now their cases would go before a distant Board of Guardians where no sympathetic treatment could be expected, and the relief for an able-bodied man and his family would be an order to the 'House'. Many men convicted of arson and other offences said that they were prompted by poverty – wages as little as 8d. a day in one case – and that they sought transportation as better than the lives they lived. As in the riots of 1830, offenders were often young men, who were now at a disadvantage in the labour market: after 1834, employers tended to give preference to married men since the cost of maintaining them and their families in the workhouse was considerably greater, and as rate-payers they had a strong interest in economy. Wages, employment and the lack of it were at the heart of the discontent, starkly (and ungrammatically) expressed in 1842 in a threatening letter to a Huntingdonshire farmer who employed Irish labourers and machinery:

Warning – to those that imply the Irish and use machines while our countrymen and neibours are starving for food, we do assure the farmer we as Labourers cannot bear it no longer, as we would as willing die to live this oppress conditions; therefore, if the farmers do not act defernt they may expect the town [Godmanchester] to be very hot soon, with many other calamities.

John True Blue[3]

Official opinion, however, was at variance with the evidence of continued distress. The Assistant Commissioners who were busy imposing the new poor law congratulated themselves that more men were at work, the number of paupers was declining, and attitudes were changing for the better. Referring back to the Ampthill (Bedfordshire) riot of 1835, Assistant Commissioner Adey remarked that 'The only cry was, "We want nothing but work" '. Now, in 1838, he saw 'more people in the fields, and more people employed generally, and I hear no complaint': when he stops his carriage and walks into the fields the men touch their hats to him, whereas 'four years back, if you passed them they were generally sulky-looking people, and now they are civil and polite: I can perceive that difference'.[4] The new Act was evidently doing its work: in the previous winter in Bedfordshire outdoor relief had been refused to unemployed men.

The state of agriculture continued to cause concern, however, and in 1836 a Select Committee was appointed to enquire into Agricultural Distress. A Buckinghamshire farmer testified that things were now worse than in 1833, that because of low wheat prices farms had gone out of cultivation, others had reduced rents by a quarter, and farmers could not afford to employ so many men as formerly. There were no able-bodied men in the workhouse because they had preferred to leave the parish and find work on the railway or elsewhere.[5] The Chairman of a Board of Guardians in Sussex also believed that there were now fewer unemployed: 'In consequence of finding that it is not quite so pleasant a task to work for the parish as it was, they have many of them got work, perhaps half of them'.[6] He also believed that, 'We have made friends of our best labourers and put the others at defiance, and that is as the thing should be'.[7] A widespread view was that if the labourer's own parish could not provide him with regular work, he now looked elsewhere instead of sliding into pauperism. The Duke of Bedford's steward at Woburn reported that some labourers had found work on the Birmingham Railway then being built, 'and are very much pleased with the result of their going', while 'others now come and ask for a job instead of refusing it when it was offered'.[8]

Attitudes had clearly hardened, and few voices were now to be heard which spoke sympathetically of the labourer. One of these few was a farmer and miller of Wickham Market, Suffolk, who testified in 1837 to 'a great number . . . out of employ. . . . One good labourer whom I have known for years . . . said he was discharged last April and had but two weeks' employment since [now the following February]'. This witness believed that the new poor law was affecting the labourers 'dreadfully': he could get on his horse and find a hundred men at 1s. a day. 'I consider that the Poor Law Bill deprives a man of any resource but the prison, as they call it; they say that if they are to be sent to a prison they will do something to be sent to a prison for.'[9] Other witnesses spoke of widespread unemployment in Norfolk, Kent, Berkshire and Somerset. No great, immediate improvement in the labourer's condition had followed from the 'reform' of the poor law in 1834: the harsh conditions of relief, coupled with the growth of employment on the railways or in towns, was beginning the long migration of workers off the land, but the resentment of those, the great majority, who remained, still flared up in strange outbreaks like the Courtenay affair in Kent in 1838,[10] in 302 reported cases of arson in Norfolk and Suffolk in 1843, and in another serious wave of incendiarism in 1849–51 when the collapse of corn prices led to further wage reductions and unemployment.[11]

'LIFE UNDER THE BREAD TAX'

This general account of unemployment and distress in the mid-century can be illuminated by the life histories of people who lived through these years. One such was J. T. Burgess, a Warwickshire labourer, who remembered the times before the new poor law with some regret:

At that time [the early 1830s] there were big lads and great lungeous fellows, able and willing to work, where there was no work for them. . . . A man was like tied to the ground. He belonged to his parish, and if he strayed from it the overseers of other parishes sent him back. . . . A man had a reet to two shillings and sixpence a week if he had more nor two children. . . . There was a good kind o' homely feeling about it, which made us think we were o' the same family.[12]

Autobiographers do not always explain the causes of their unemployment beyond the general fact of a surplus of labour, but it is clear that there were often particular reasons why some men in a village would be kept in work while others were refused it. The preference to employ married men with families has already been noted. Regular workers with responsibilities for horses, cattle, sheep or wagons were much more secure than day labourers who could be stood off on the spot in rain, snow, drought or frost. Some men were simply better workers than others – stronger, more reliable, sober and uncomplaining. Some had suffered illness or lameness from childhood, or had subsequently been injured by accidents at work – it was noticed that many of those convicted for the Swing riots had been maimed by threshing-machines – and by the time a man reached fifty he was often 'crippled up' with rheumatism from long exposure to wet and cold, and unable to keep up with fitter men. All such considerations entered into the hiring of labour at a time when the market was glutted.

Illness and accidents plagued the life of James Bowd, born at Swavesey, Cambridgeshire, in 1823. At the age of seven he suffered illnesses which left him permanently lame, but shortly afterwards he was at work, leading horses and ploughing: in his teens he went to yearly hirings until his marriage in 1849, by which time he had amassed a bed, a family Bible and three shillings: 'I was as fond of my wife Has a Cat is of New Milk. . . . I Dare not tell her how much I Loved her because I thought she Would be trespising on were I should be, and that would be the Head of the house'. As a married man, he now worked as a day labourer. 'Sometimes, after a Long Days' work Drilling I did not know how to get my Lame Leg of the ground to put it forward to take a step', and possibly because of his infirmity he fell off a ladder in 1855, breaking his collar-bone, missing six weeks' work and the extra earnings from harvesting that year: 'My old master did not care for having me much more, but however gave me a little work but not Regular. I had to Graple along with the Winter in my front as well as I could, sometimes work and sometimes none, and that ment not much for a man and two Children to live upon'. Soon after this his cottage burned down and he lost everything except his bed: he ran into debt for £4, was sued in the county court at Ely and ordered to repay four shillings a month, which his wife met by charring. Bowd's short autobiography ends in the 1860s, when he was again working for his former employer but often stood off after harvest and picking up odd jobs through the winter as he could.[13]

Help from other members of the family was the most immediate recourse of unemployed men. Wives, and children of both sexes from the age of six or seven, could often find poorly paid field work at from 2d. to 6d. a day, especially between spring and autumn. From the 1830s agricultural gangs of women and children were being organized by gang-masters in East Anglia and the Midlands for intensive cultivation such as weeding, hoeing, bean-setting and stone-picking, often under conditions which outraged humanitarians and moralists. As a child of eight, Mrs Burrows had worked in such a gang at Croyland, Lincolnshire, for four-teen hours a day under the control of a master armed with a long whip: she was the oldest of forty or fifty children, some of whom were only five years old. The reason in her case was that her father was unable to work at all for sixteen years owing to 'a tumour in the head'.

> My mother worked like a slave to keep a home over our heads. Not once to my knowledge did she ever ask or receive charity, and never did she run into debt. Scores of times I have seen her sit down to a meal of dry bread so that we might have a tiny mite of butter to our bread, and yet she never complained. . . . [Four years later] it felt like Heaven to me when I was taken to the town of Leeds and put to work in the factory. Talk about White Slaves; the Fen districts at that time was the place to look for them.[14]

In the close village societies of the time men of strong opinion and outspoken words could also find themselves without employment. What passed for 'radical' opinions could mean anything not in conformity with the predominantly Tory views of the landed interest and the Established Church, and could therefore include membership of dissenting sects and support for Parliamentary reform or free trade as well as more overtly radical movements such as Chartism or trade unionism. The fate of the Tolpuddle Martyrs in 1834 for merely joining a union was to be denied employment in their own country by the sentence of transportation to Van Diemen's Land. The previous year, Thomas Edwards was blacklisted and refused work by local farmers for having moved a resolution at a public meeting that 'The labourer is worthy of his hire': destitute and unemployed, he had to spend the winter of 1833–4 in the workhouse. By the 1850s, now married with a family of seven, they were living in 'abject poverty' on a wage of 7s. a week, and when bread rose to 1s. the 4lb. loaf during the Crimean War (1854–6) he took five turnips from a field to help feed his starving family. His sentence of fourteen days' hard labour broke the frail economy of the family, who had to spend the winter of 1854–5 in the workhouse. Now branded a thief, Edwards could not get work locally until taken on next spring in a brickfield seven miles away.[15]

Joseph Arch's father suffered similar victimization when in 1835 he refused to sign a petition in favour of maintaining the Corn Laws which the local landowners were circulating, and consequently became 'a marked man for the rest of his life'. He could get no work for eighteen weeks in the winter of 1835, and the family survived on barley bread ('and even barley loaves were all too scarce') and his wife's laundry work. The Arch family was unusually fortunate in owning their cottage, which their grandfather had bought for £30 in palmier days, and its good-sized garden at least provided them with vegetables. Although when in work Arch's father never earned more than 8–10s. a week, the family was proudly independent: their mother would never accept charity or 'sink to the level of the pauper', at a time when most labourers' wives were 'tamed by poverty, cowed by it [into] spiritless submission'.[16]

Contemporary accounts of this kind make it clear that dread of the new poor law deterred the unemployed from seeking relief, and made the workhouse the final resort of the destitute after all else had failed. It is also likely that, once experienced, its rigours had the desired effect of encouraging people never to use it again. By mid-century agricultural labourers were becoming considerably more mobile, partly because new work opportunities for unskilled labour were opening up in the rapidly growing towns and on the railways, partly because the conditions of life and public relief were becoming unacceptable to many. In the very hard winter of 1840, Isaac Anderson's father could get no work: he and four young sons had to go into the workhouse at Rochford, his wife and three smaller children remaining at home and 'supported by several kind friends'. Isaac began work the following spring at the age of seven, remaining with the same farmer for sixteen years until 1856:

> Not long after this, the London, Tilbury and Southend Railway was opened, and most of the young men left Prittlewell, going into the towns. I was tired of my work, and gave Mr. Kilworth a week's notice. . . . He was astonished and said, 'Where are you going, Isaac?' I answered, 'I do not know. I can't stand this work any longer'. I left him . . . and fell down on my knees under a bush and prayed to the Lord to guide me.[17]

He obtained work as a navvy, but later took a variety of jobs carting, gardening, roadwork and laying sewers in Southend, eventually becoming the foreman of a gang of eleven men.

Railway navvying had appeal for strong young men who wanted to see something of the world and a wage better than 8s. a week. It was often temporary work which ended on the completion of a line, but it could be combined with harvesting – the most lucrative part of agricultural work – with general labouring and tramping – a way of life which had attractions for single men though it inevitably involved periods of unemployment. Thus the anonymous 'Working Man', one of a family of eleven children which 'died down to six', decided to go on tramp in 1836 after a quarrel with his farmer-employer. For the next twenty-three years he was 'rambling about the country', picking up casual work as a navvy interspersed with poaching and harvesting, when he sometimes earned £10, enough to take him through the winter. One year when there was 'bad harvesting' and no work he tramped 400 miles in a month, but even in the worst times he scorned to beg or seek poor relief:

> It is not our way, don't you see, to ask any one to help us, unless its one of we're own sort. We don't mind taking a few shillings from people like ourselves, so as we can do the same for them another time, but we never begs of anyone else; its against our rules.[18]

This kind of existence was not an avoidance of work or a 'dropping-out' of society so much as a search for adventure, variety and experience by men escaping from the boredom and bondage of village life. It also strongly appealed to Bettesworth, who described his life as 'a roamin' commission': he spent forty years travelling the country after a boyhood as a living-in farm servant. He worked at harvesting, road-building, carting, brick-burning and building, always enjoying new jobs and new places:

> A man's never so happy, to my way o' thinkin', as when he's goin' to his day's work reglar. That *is* enjoyment, sir, I've always found in my life. . . . When you be at work there's always something to interest ye.[19]

But 'reglar work' continued to be the major problem for those labourers – the great majority – who remained in their villages through the depressed years of the 1840s. In retrospect, the decade earned the reputation of the 'Hungry Forties', but although there were six particularly bad years the decade was probably not consistently 'hungrier' than those which preceded or succeeded it. In 1905, when free trade was under attack from protectionists, Mrs Cobden Unwin collected the reminiscences of old people about 'Life under the Bread Tax' with the object of reminding voters what conditions had been like before the repeal of the Corn Laws in 1846. Many witnesses spoke of unemployment and of the inhumanity of farmers towards their men. David Miles, a labourer of Heyshott, recalled:

> It woz awful bad for the low class: many on 'em were nigh starvin'. If 'ee complained to the masters they on'y said, quite indiff'rent, 'Eee can go: we don't want 'ee'. An' if 'ee went to the vestry, which they woz every blessed one on 'em farmers, and said as 'ow 'ee

wanted work, they'd ask 'Who've 'ee bin a-working for?', an when 'ee answered, 'Mr. So-an-So', up the farmer 'd get an declare 'ee was dissatisfied, and then ne'er a one 'ud have anythin' more to do with 'ee. . . . Them that cud'nt get work 'ud sometimes fire the barn. I got a job once six an' a 'alf mile away, and that seemed a fair step I can tell 'ee when I come 'ome tired of an evenin'.[20]

Aged twenty-four in 1850, Joseph Boddington of Northamptonshire was told by his employer that he could not keep a single man on, 'so I went the next day and put the banns up in church': the farmer then took him back at 8s. a week, but two years later 'he gave me the sack because I asked the servant girl to go to chapel'.[21]

Writing on the condition of the agricultural labourer in 1846, George Nicholls who had been instrumental in framing the new poor law, regretted the discontinuance in many parts of the country of the yearly hirings of young men which had formerly provided employment throughout the year and had made them feel 'part of the family' of the farmer. A return to this practice would 'restore a very important link in the social chain', would help to prevent 'improvident marriages' and 'those breaks in his engagement to which the labourer is now often subjected'.[22] There was, of course, no sign of a return to the old ways. While the new poor law itself extolled the values of market forces and supply and demand, farmers increasingly hired labour only when it was needed, and this casualization of adult males was exaggerated by an increased employment of women and children for certain repetitive jobs at busy seasons. The range of women's employment was now extended to weeding, hoeing and pulling turnips, planting and digging potatoes, planting beans, picking stones, filling carts, spreading manure and tending threshing-machines, as well as their traditional work at hay and corn harvest. At wages averaging 8d. a day, this was very cheap labour, particularly suitable for the intensive 'high farming' of the south and east. Boys and girls from seven or eight upwards were also useful at many of these tasks at wages which began at 1s. or 1s. 6d. a week. Commissioners who investigated the subject in 1843 believed that children were now employed more widely since the new poor law, and were able to spend less time in school.[23] The Revd S. J. Howman of Bexwell, Norfolk, found that 'the schooling is almost universally sacrificed to earning. . . . This is one of the few evils arising out of the operation of the New Poor Law'.[24] There was particular criticism of the gang system, which had apparently originated at Castle Acre in Norfolk about 1831, and was now widely used in East Anglia, the Fens and parts of the Midlands: it was said to overtax the strength of young children, to prevent their education, and to expose older boys and girls to immorality, especially when they had to stay overnight on distant farms and were accommodated in barns. A gang-master reported:

> I believe that owing to ganging seventy out of a hundred girls are very imprudent girls – prostitutes. They get working along with the lads in the daytime, and make appointments at night. I should not like myself to take a wife out of the gang.[25]

This increased use of women and children clearly had adverse effects on the employment opportunities of men. Samuel Peeling, one of the few labourers to give evidence in 1843, complained that 'the gang system prevents one getting regular work', a view supported by the Commissioner for Kent, Surrey and Sussex.[26] After 1834, and the ending of allowances in aid of wages, heads of households had to try to sell more labour in order to bring earnings up to a living standard, and this usually meant more of the labour of their dependents. As early as 1838 Dr Kay reported that such employment had 'wonderfully increased since the Poor Law came into operation. It has had that effect by rendering it necessary that the children should be so employed in order to adjust the wages to the wants of the family'.[27]

THE FLIGHT FROM THE LAND

The great issue of the repeal of the Corn Laws which inflamed passions and divided the nation in the 1840s was a matter of indifference to most labourers, whose wages generally rose or fell according to the price of wheat, whether home-grown or imported. 'The one thing that did concern him was the number of workless days he had in the year – the great question was whether Protection or Free Trade provided more or less employment.'[28] The effects of the repeal in 1846 were only felt gradually as farmers adjusted to the expected flood of cheap, imported grain, a flood which did not fully materialize for another quarter of a century. Those who could afford to invest began to look for protection in more intensive methods of cultivation, exploiting new machinery, fertilizers, land drainage and so on, or by moving away from arable towards mixed farming. Such changes did not increase the overall demand for workers – rather the reverse – and on farms where capital was not forthcoming for improvements, a natural response to fears of falling prices and profits was to economise further on labour.

The wide gap between the conditions of labourers in north and south, which Frederic Eden had noted half a century before, was still very evident in 1850 when James Caird surveyed the state of English agriculture. Wages in south Wiltshire were as low as 6s. or 7s. a week because of the continued over-supply of labour: here he found a general desire to emigrate, as the only way of helping 'those who go and those who remain behind'.[29] Similarly, in Suffolk where wages were 7s. or 8s. a week, 'the supply of labour is redundant',[30] but in parts of Cumberland and Lancashire wages rose to as much as 15s. a week due, he believed, to the sparser population and the competition of industry and mining. It was no coincidence that pauperism followed the north–south divide: in the northern counties the percentage of paupers to the whole population in 1848 was 6.2 per cent (the lowest Derbyshire at 4.2 per cent), while in the southern counties it averaged 12.1 per cent, rising to 15.7 per cent in Dorset and 16.1 per cent in Wiltshire.[31] The remedy, he believed, was to abolish the law of settlement and allow the free movement of labour, because the present law 'binds the labourer to a parish in which his labour is not required'.[32]

Another observer of the agricultural scene, Alexander Somerville, found much distress even in one of the most prosperous parts of southern England, where the Great Marlow workhouse in Buckinghamshire was crowded with the unemployed, and 'the half-employed, and less than half-fed, labourers were crawling about', complaining that 'times be so terrible bad that they couldn't get half enough of work to do'.[33] One labourer referred to the practice of some farmers of treating their labourers like 'pitting potatoes'. Somerville explained:

> I found this to refer to a farmer who had said that he did with his labourers as he did with his potatoes; he did not keep all the potatoes out for use every day, and he did not, like some farmers, try to find work for the men all the year round. When he did not need them he put them in the workhouse until they were needed.[34]

In fact, workhouse inmates were always only a small minority of all paupers, averaging between 14 per cent and 16 per cent between 1840 and 1847,[35] and only a minority of these were able-bodied men since the workhouse was the refuge of all those who could not care for themselves – children, the chronically sick, the old, feeble-minded and disabled. In any case, Poor Law Guardians quickly found that it was much cheaper to help a temporarily unemployed man in his home with 2s. or 3s. a week than to maintain the whole family in the workhouse where he would have little opportunity of seeking employment. Prohibitory Orders, designed to prevent these evasions of the Act, were issued in 1842, 1844 and 1852, but they allowed so many exceptions that they became, in effect, licences for the continuation of outdoor relief. Under the 1842 Order the able-bodied could be relieved outside the workhouse in return for a specified task (the 'Labour Test'), under that of 1844 in cases of accident or 'sudden and urgent necessity', while under the 1852 Order outdoor relief was specifically allowed to a man 'working for wages on one day and being without work the next, or working half the week and being unemployed during the remainder'.[36] Thus, rural Guardians, who usually included a majority of farmers and local tradesmen, were armed with considerable discretion in treating problems with which they had long familiarity – the surplus of labour in many parts of southern England and the inevitably seasonal nature of farming operations.

There was, therefore, a conflict between the policy of the central Poor Law Commission in Whitehall, whose Secretary Edwin Chadwick, struggled to enforce the 'less eligibility' principle based on the workhouse test, and the local administration where many rural Guardians deliberately evaded the principle for reasons (either or both) of economy and humanity. When the Commissioners proudly announced in 1840 that allowances were 'almost totally extinguished' in the rural areas they cannot have known what was happening, and when they claimed that employment was now more regular, they were contradicted by two of their own Assistant Commissioners who reported that in Cambridgeshire, Hertfordshire, Essex and Wiltshire employment was irregular for two-thirds of the year.[37] As well as keeping down costs, rural Guardians also had an interest in keeping an adequate labour supply on the land against the needs of the busy seasons. They therefore adopted a variety of expedients to help their unemployed, often using the deterrent workhouse only as a last resort for the more difficult, recalcitrant or shiftless cases: so successful were these expedients that in the 1850s and 1860s 87 per cent of adult, able-bodied paupers were receiving relief outside the workhouse,[38] allowances being given for temporary or partial unemployment, accident or sickness – this, a broadly interpreted exception which extended also to the labourer's wife or children – provided that part of the payment was in food or fuel and not wholly in cash.

Employment schemes were also set up by many rural Boards, usually for work on the roads, financed by the highway rate or by voluntary subscriptions so that costs were concealed from the poor rate. There were many similarities here with pre–1834 practices, and even more so with the 'ticket' system which developed in East Anglia from the 1840s, and was barely distinguishable from the much-criticized 'roundsman' system of the old poor law. Under its new form, unions acted in effect as labour exchanges, allocating as far as possible the surplus workers: the unemployed were issued with a ticket to take round to employers, requesting work and reminding them of the costs of poor relief. The applicant might then be offered employment at a wage below the prevailing rate, or, if no work was available, each farmer signed the ticket to that effect: only then did the applicant become eligible for poor relief, having provided the evidence that he was 'genuinely seeking work'. The practice was strongly criticized by some contemporaries for keeping the labour market over-stocked and depressing wages, but some 25 per cent of unions between the Thames and the Wash adopted the 'ticket' system as a persuasive form of 'job creation' which kept families out of expensive workhouse accommodation.[39]

Workhouses proved to be not only expensive (an average cost of 3s. 6d. per inmate per week in the eastern counties) but generally inefficient ways of employing the poor, as it was often difficult to provide the ten hours of labour a day which the rules prescribed for the able-bodied. Tasks for men included grinding corn by handmill, pumping water, picking oakum, and spade cultivation of workhouse land, while women inmates were given domestic duties such as cleaning, washing and nursing. The dread and stigma of the 'House' lay more in the prison-like discipline, the low diet and pauper dress, than in the work required, though in the Andover workhouse the daily task of crushing a hundredweight of decayed animal bones to powder drove numbers out of the 'House' to escape the heavy labour and sickening smell.[40] In general, however, rural Guardians preferred to help the genuinely unemployed out of the workhouse, using their discretionary powers under the Prohibitory Orders to tide families over difficult times with small allowances. In this respect there was an unexpected continuity of social policy after 1834, despite the radical intentions of the new poor law.

The fundamental problem remained – a surplus of labour on the land except during the busiest four or five months of the year when there might be an actual shortage. It seemed obvious that some should leave the land, seeking work wherever youth and strength were in demand. The 1830s coincided with the first great surge of railway-building, and strong labourers, used to outdoor work, made natural navvies for digging, excavating, carting and plate-laying. An estimate by the Assistant Engineer of the London and Birmingham line that 15,000 to 20,000 men had been drawn from the surrounding rural population during its construction from 1835 to 1838 must have relieved pressure on employment, and by 1850 6,000 miles of track had been laid in Britain. Even so, the opinion of one Poor Law Commissioner in 1836 that railways would absorb 'all surplus labour . . . at no distant date' was over-optimistic, partly because of the strength of local ties and because a migratory existence was not appealing to many married men.

Migration to the towns had long held attractions for labourers' sons and daughters, offering prospects of higher wages, a more exciting social life and a wider choice of marriage partners. Before the railways, it had usually been a short-distance, centripetal movement from neighbouring rural areas,[41] but after 1834 the new poor law adopted a deliberate policy of encouraging mobility, both by migration to manufacturing towns and by emigration overseas: the policy coincided with a recovery of the textile industry after a long depression, and an estimate that 90,000 extra hands would be needed in Lancashire. In December 1834, a pathetic letter from thirty-two poor labourers in Great Bledlow, Buckinghamshire, begging for work or relief, was published in *The Times*, and after much difficulty a few families were persuaded by the Poor Law Commissioners to remove, by canal, to the mills of Messrs Greg at Styal and Ashworth at Egerton, near Bolton. This was the beginning of a regular scheme under which migration agents were established in Lancashire and the West Riding to negotiate three-year contracts of employment between northern mill-owners and 'surplus' families of southern labourers. Between 1835 and 1837, when the scheme ended because of the return of depression in the textile industry, 4,684 migrants were removed, almost half from Suffolk, followed, in order, by Norfolk, Buckinghamshire, Bedfordshire, Kent, Cambridgeshire and Essex.[42]

It was a remarkable experiment in social engineering, which aroused heated controversy, complaints of 'transportation' and of driving the labourer into 'factory slavery': it seems that in some cases millowners wished to use the imported labour to break the power of trade unions or to force down wages, while on the other hand there were suspicions that poor law officials used the scheme to rid themselves of troublesome paupers. Emigration overseas to British colonies, especially Canada, was also encouraged and subsidized by the poor law, and between 1835 and 1837, 6,400 aided paupers left the English shores: the fact that the great majority of them came from eastern and south-eastern counties – two-thirds of the total from Norfolk and Suffolk – indicates that they were predominantly agricultural workers escaping from the 'superfluity' of labour in these counties. The emigration scheme continued after 1837, though at a much slower pace, and poor law emigrants formed only a small proportion of the total after that date. Between 1835 and 1846 the average annual migration from the United Kingdom was 84,700, of which poor law emigrants averaged only 1,400 a year.[43] Although they undoubt-edly had a dramatic, even traumatic, impact on particular village com-munities, neither migration nor emigration did much to relieve the surplus of labour before 1850.

Despite the ending of tariff protection in 1846, the expected collapse of British agriculture did not occur: on the contrary, farming was probably never more profitable than in the so-called 'Golden Age' of the third quarter of the century. Contemporaries believed that this prosperity was even beginning to extend to the labourer – though, ironically, not so much because farming had absorbed the pools of idle labour but because it was driving them away. An agricultural expert in 1871 wrote: 'Perhaps nothing has done more for the agricultural labourer than the opening out of the country by railway enterprise, and the facilities thereby afforded for the movement of superfluous labour from one district to another.'[44] By then, many men had begun to move to better-paid jobs in the towns, on the railways, in police forces and the army, and those who remained were receiving somewhat better wages, ranging from 9s. a week in the south up to 18s. in parts of the north. Mechanization had much increased recently, twenty-seven counties now reported to be using machines for mowing, threshing and steam-ploughing: there was even a new class of 'engine-men' who could earn as much as £1 a week. Although it was admitted that winter unemployment 'may still be the case to a limited extent', in some areas and at some seasons there was now a scarcity of labour, and 'the only way to retain good men upon farms is by improving their houses, and making their wives reluctant to leave a comfortable home'.[45] Poor law administrators were also optimistic that the proportion, if not the actual numbers, of paupers to the total population had fallen substantially since the middle of the century: in 1871 Yorkshire, with only 2.9 per cent of paupers, was the best, while Norfolk with 6.8 per cent, Dorset with 7.1 per cent and Wiltshire with 7.3 per cent were, as previously, still the highest.[46]

The prosperity of 'high farming' in this period implied that agriculture be treated like any other commercial enterprise, that all the factors of production be operated with strict attention to the laws of supply and demand. Writing on the subject of 'The Rural Exodus', the author quoted a large landowner in Cheshire, 'The secret of farming profitably is to keep down the labour bill. Our work is done with the fewest possible hands. Not a man or woman or child more than is absolutely necessary is employed'. The author continued: 'He gives the youths to understand that the majority of them, as they grow up, must find employment elsewhere'.[47] The youths were taking his advice. Between 1841 and 1911 it is estimated that the rural areas of England and Wales lost four-and-a-half million migrants, either internally or overseas: put another way, while the whole population of the country more than doubled between these years, the countryside grew by only 13 per cent.[48] Between 1851 and 1911 the labour force in agriculture fell by 708,000, the majority of them young men between fifteen and twenty-four. While the reasons for this mass desertion from the land depended ultimately on individual circumstances and on local networks of information from previous migrants, it was the case that young, single labourers were more likely to be casualties of unemployment than others, and that the counties of greatest emigration were those where wages were lowest and work least regular – the West of England (Dorset, Somerset, Devon), followed by the eastern counties (Norfolk, Suffolk, Lincolnshire, Cambridgeshire).

Two examples indicate the impact which migration had on village communities at this time. At Corsley, Wiltshire, the population halved from 1,621 in 1841 to 824 in 1901: emigration to Canada had begun as early as 1828 here, but increased in the 1840s and 1850s with agricultural distress and the decay of the local weaving industry. Poor law officials apportioned the unemployed among the rate-payers and set others to work on the roads rather than send them to the union workhouse at

Warminster. Further depression in agriculture occurred in the 1870s, when imports of cheap American wheat forced farmers to turn from arable to pasture and dairying, greatly reducing the demand for labour. The 1870s witnessed particularly rapid migration from Corsley – of young men to the colonies and of girls to domestic service in towns.[49] There was a similar story at Tysoe in Warwickshire. Here, emigration began in the 1830s, but jumped to new heights in the 1870s when farm prices tumbled and there was a succession of bad seasons in 1874–6: in the wet weather many men who were not paid 'wet or fine' were taking home only 5s. or 6s. a week. A few years before two Mormon missionaries had visited the village, trying to gain converts and immigrants to Utah, and many men now left for the United States, or for Canada and New Zealand on assisted passages.

> The men and boys who left tended to be the more forceful and bright characters, the darlings of the family. For the village to say goodbye to the twenty, thirty good fellows seemed a calamity: it would never be the same again.[50]

By the 1870s emigration schemes were beginning to be organized by the newly established agricultural trade unions, but before that, one remarkable experiment had been made at Halberton, north Devon, where Canon Girdlestone had been appointed to the living in 1866. He was outraged by the conditions of labour there – wages for those in full work of 7s. or 8s. a week, and nothing at all when a man was sick or injured – and while a cattle plague was raging in 1866 he preached a pointed sermon from the text, 'Behold, the hand of the Lord is upon thy cattle': 'He plainly asked those who were assembled in the church whether they did not think that God had sent the plague as a judgment upon farmers for the manner in which they treated their human labourers.'[51] Ostracized by the local farmers, Girdlestone wrote letters to *The Times* which produced many offers of employment at good wages from different parts of the country. He then set up his own migration scheme, which between 1866 and 1872 settled 4–500 men, many with families, in Lancashire, Yorkshire, Durham and Sussex at wages between 13s. and 22s. a week.

'Low wages and irregular employment of the agricultural labourer were the chief causes of the depopulation of the rural districts', wrote the General Secretary of the Land Restoration League. 'In winter they are so often "rained off", or kept from work by frost or snow, that they frequently place their meagre earnings during the winter season at something like three days a week.'[52] 'Short time' was now the major cause of unemployment in the later nineteenth century. The flight from the land had reduced the 'superfluity' of labour which had so concerned poor law administrators, but the nature of agricultural work, and the failure of workers to secure 'wet and dry' wage agreements, still meant a precarious standard of living for many in which even a few days of unemployment could be disastrous to budgets which rarely showed a surplus even in the best times. A Somersetshire labourer who kept an exact account of his earnings and expenditure in 1872 found that he lost twenty-one days for bad weather, the equivalent of three-and-a-half weeks, in what was a year of good seasons. He earned £19 16s. 6d. from piece-work and £12 from day work at 10s. a week, a total of £31 16s. 6d. to feed two adults and four young children: this included nothing for meat, clothes or other necessities, but his employer, a Guardian of the Poor, had promised to try to get them a shilling a week from the union provided the doctor would put some of the family on the sick list.[53] Piece-work paid better than day work, but was even more dependent on the weather: the wife of a piece-worker who could earn 2s. a day told Francis Heath that in the present week her husband had lost one day and in the previous week two days, reducing his fortnight's earnings from 24s. to 18s.[54]

A Royal Commission in 1867 heard that in the eastern counties about half the men on a farm, those employed about horses and stock, were paid 'wet and dry':[55] the other half, known as 'catch-work men' or 'shifty labourers' had only precarious employment, and could not survive without the labour of their children. In the east Midlands the Hon. E. Stanhope reported that these 'catch-work' or 'running' men lived mostly in the 'open' villages and often worked several miles from home: they are 'always in an unsettled state, living from hand to mouth, and their children must work at the earliest age they can'.[56] Reformers like H. S. Tremenheere, who wanted to prohibit the employment in agriculture of children under ten, had to admit that the problem was these men 'who only work occasionally, or who are thrown out of work in winter', who were forced to rely on the shilling or two which their young children could bring home.[57]

Odd days of unemployment were bad enough, but could often be overcome by extra work of the family, by help from friends or relatives, or by credit from village shopkeepers: longer spells of bad weather, either in summer or winter, were a different matter. A bad harvest – the result of either too much rain or too little – could mean only a few days' work instead of a month, and the loss of 'harvest money' of between £5 and £10, the labourer's chief contingency fund against the rent, boots and clothes for the family, or any sudden emergency. In winter, hard frosts or deep snow could prevent work for long periods, especially in the cold lands of East Anglia and the Fens. Here in the 1860s Arthur Randell's father experienced winters when no work was possible for nearly four months, and again in the great freeze of 1875 when the Great Ouse was frozen for several weeks: the farmers thoughtfully organized skating matches for the unemployed with prizes of flour and bacon, a charity which ensured that food went to the best athletes rather than the most needy.[58]

Poaching features so frequently in the autobiographies of this period as to suggest that it was a widespread response to the poverty, unemployment and boredom of rural life: for some it was no more than an occasional nocturnal adventure which brought a rare treat of meat to the bread-and-potato diet, but for a few it was a wholetime occupation, described by 'The King of the Norfolk Poachers' as his 'profession'. Born in 1860, he early rebelled against the life which his father had endured, working for forty years for one farmer. 'When he could work no more, he was not wanted any more.... By all his honesty and hard work he died a Pauper, and was Buried in a Pauper grave.'[59]

> In winter when work was slack I have seen twenty or thirty young men standing about. Lots of the farmers would have the married men working three days a week to help them along. I am not dispurging the Farmer of them days, some were human, some did not care.... There was plenty of Poaching and fowl Stealing goen on wen they were driven to it.[60]

The Poacher concluded his life story:

> Well, so I have riten it as best I could, but I am no scoller. Not that I count myself any the worse for that, it may be verry well for the Upper Classes, or the Middle Classes, but for working people lerning is a hinderence and they are best with out it.[61]

In fact, it was through education, and the opportunities it afforded for mobility into better-paid, higher status employment, that some men were able to quit farmwork. This was especially so in Scotland, where education was more widespread and more valued than in England before the 1870s. Thus William Milne, born at Greyrigg, near Forfar, in 1828, did not begin to herd cattle until he was twelve, twice the age at which George Edwards started work: by then he had had seven years of schooling – the equivalent at that time of a middle-class education south of the border. From 1840 to 1855 Milne worked as a living-in farm servant, offering himself at the annual feeing (hiring) fairs for a few pounds a year plus oatmeal, milk and a bothy lodging shared with six others. Despite these social disadvantages, he joined a mutual improvement society, the only farm labourer member, and attended summer evening schools. Increasingly disgusted with hiring fairs and bothy life, he gave up farmwork for good in 1855, and for the next forty-four years had a successful career in railway service, as a steamboat agent and commercial traveller – all occupations which required literacy and numeracy. The last twenty-seven pages of his autobiography consist of his own Poems and Lyrics.[62]

THE REVOLT OF THE FIELD

The so-called 'Golden Age' of agriculture which lay between the repeal of the Corn Laws and the onset of depression in the seventies had brought substantial profits to farmers and landowners, and some indications of dawning improvement to the labourer which was beginning to raise his expectations to something above a subsistence wage of 1s. 6d. or 2s. a day. The year 1872 saw the first major attempt to form an agricultural labourers' trade union and to strike for improved conditions.

The history of this remarkable 'Revolt of the Field' has been documented[63] and need not be detailed: our main concern is with its effects on employment. There had been earlier, isolated attempts at union – the martyrs of Tolpuddle in 1834, short-lived associations in Wiltshire and Somerset in 1852 and a strike at Gawcott, Buckinghamshire, in 1867, but the widespread activity of 1872 was of a quite different scale. The necessary conditions for a national union now seemed to exist – a prospering agricultural industry, railways to carry speakers and a penny post to carry literature, above all, Acts of Parliament passed in 1869 and 1871 which legalized trade unions. Unemployment was not a specific cause. Joseph Arch, the founder of the union, said in 1873 that he remembered the time when ten or a dozen men were out of work in the villages, but that had not been the case for the last three or four years. Arch was driven by ambition, initially for himself and his family, subsequently for his fellow workers: as a young man 'I was determined to take up everything which would further the one aim and object I had in life then, *ie* the bettering of my own position by every honest means in my power.'[64] This desire for better conditions and better life chances underlaid the Agricultural Labourers' Union which he founded at Wellesbourne, Warwickshire, in February 1872, with a demand for 16s. a week instead of the local rates of 9s. to 12s. It was significant that the 200 men who struck work when this was refused included no shepherds or wagoners – men who had regular employment and 1s. a week above day labourers.[65] Here, then, was a new source of self-inflicted unemployment. Without reserves or strike pay, many of the first strikers had to look for work in Birmingham or Liverpool or to emigrate to Canada, but by the summer the farmers had given way and agreed to wages of 14s. to 16s. a week: by 1874 a membership of 86,214, organized into thirty-seven districts, was claimed for the union.[66]

Retaliation and victimization soon followed, however. Farmers in East Anglia, Essex and Suffolk formed defence associations, agreeing not to recognize the union, nor to pay more than 2s. a day, and to discharge members of the union after giving a week's notice. In the spring of 1873 men began to be locked out and evicted from tied cottages on the ground that accommodation only went with work: a year later a much larger lockout occurred in East Anglia and continued until August, 1874. With many men without work and threatened without homes, the union collapsed: its official organ estimated that £24,432 had been paid out in strike and sick pay, and that of 3,116 men locked out, 694 had migrated, 429 emigrated, 415 were still unemployed, 402 had left the union and 1,176 had returned to work.[67] Of the separate Lincolnshire and Suffolk Federal Union it was claimed that 2,500 had been locked out. The strikes and lockouts had covered much of the east and south of England and the west as far as Dorset: the numbers affected must be uncertain, but F. E. Green estimated that at its height 10,000 men were out of work.[68]

In fact, the strikes and lockouts demonstrated the continued existence of a substantial surplus of labour, especially in the eastern counties. Although the strikes began in the busy springtime and continued through the hay and corn harvests, farmers generally had little difficulty in finding local labour, supplemented in some cases by casual workers from neighbouring towns or by itinerant Irish harvesters. According to a contemporary observer, the strike taught farmers to be even more economical with 'much useless labour': one farmer was reported as saying that instead of employing twenty-six men he now did the work with seventeen, and it was never more forward.[69] It was also observed that during and after the strike farmers made greater use of machinery, which had been making slow progress in many areas when labour was cheap. Another contemporary believed that the conditions under which labour was hired had greatly changed: formerly, the labour supply was fixed and permanent, now it was mobile and fluctuating. Only married men and old men were now stable: the young men were wandering from farm to farm, picking up the best wages they could, not only in harvest but for eight or nine months in the year, and the old stability of village communities was being destroyed.[70]

Increased social mobility of men who began life as farm labourers was also characteristic of the later decades of the century, the chief agents in the change being the spread of village schools and education which opened up new career prospects. Literacy, allied as it often was with religious conviction, enabled John Kemp (b. 1850, Flattenden, Sussex) to progress from labourer to preacher (1879) and subsequently, minister of a Strict Baptist Chapel in Kent.[71] His career paralleled that of John Hockley (b. 1861, Wickford, Essex), one of thirteen children of a farm labourer. John had the advantage of five years in the village school, not beginning farmwork until he was eleven. In 1887 he started a general store and coal business: meanwhile, he had been converted to the Peculiar People, for whom he later became a pastor and missionary in Chelmsford and Southend.[72] Personal ambition and intelligence were the keys to Isaac Mead's success (b. 1859, near Dunmow, Essex). As a young man he became an expert hand-thresher, working out a 'time-and-motion' scheme which greatly increased his production and earnings, but becoming dissatisfied with prospects as a farm labourer, he became an 'improver' to a miller, progressing to foreman and, ultimately, master miller, farmer and landowner. He ascribed his success as due to education, hard work and effort.[73] Mark Thurston (b. 1861, Larkfield, borders of Suffolk) experienced unemployment during the depression of the late seventies and eighties when 'the young and unmarried men hung about the village and learned . . . the habit of idleness'. Resentment turned to anger when he was wrongfully dismissed for the alleged offence of stealing straw: he moved to London, where he worked as a carter, and later to America as a nurseryman, joining his son who had previously emigrated.[74]

For a few men the emergence of trade unionism offered a route into professional organizing and to a career in politics. Joseph Arch became a County Councillor (1888–92) and a Liberal MP for north-west Norfolk (1885–6, 1892–1902). George Edwards took part in the strikes and lockout in Norfolk in 1872–4, and like many others, suffered victimization afterwards: 'No one in the district would employ me. . . . I was a horrible Radical, setting class against class.'[75] In 1889 he attempted to found a new union in Norfolk at a time of renewed depression when 'thousands of labourers were discharged' and wages were again driven down to 10s. or 11s. a week:[76] in later life he became a Councillor, a member of the Board of Guardians, and Labour MP for south Norfolk (1920–2, 1923–4). Like Arch, he was a staunch Primitive Methodist and a preacher for sixty years.

Arch was one of the few working men to give evidence before a Royal Commission on the Depressed Condition of Agriculture in 1881–2, strongly contesting the view that the agricultural labourer had suffered least of the farming classes. Not surprisingly, farmers and landowners complained that the events of the seventies had greatly damaged relations:

> There is not the same sympathy. There is not the same inclination on the part of the labourer to do anything that he is not obliged to do for his employer. . . . The labourers' unions, or the delegates who represent them, have not only succeeded in disturbing, but have to a great extent destroyed, the good feeling which once existed.[77]

Witnesses also complained about the effects of the Education Acts of 1870 and 1880, which now required young children to attend school. 'We get no boys now', testified one farmer. 'This last winter I may state that I have had three men employed doing work that used to be done by boys. I could only get one boy.'[78]

Arch explained to the Commission that, reluctantly, his union had taken up sponsoring emigration to Canada, and estimated that between 1873 and 1882 it had been responsible for emigrating 700,000 men, women and children from agricultural districts.[79] By this time it had become impossible to ignore the scale and the consequences of the rural exodus, which by 1881 had reduced the numbers of agricultural labourers in England and Wales to 830,452: by 1901 they had fallen by another 27 per cent to 609,105.[80] The concern was not only about numbers, but about quality – that it was 'the cream of the rural population', 'the most stalwart of the natives of the country', who were deserting for the towns and colonies. In the short term, these strong young countrymen enriched the poor physique of the town-bred populations – it was observed that in 1906 out of 5,657 men in the Inner Division of the Metropolitan Police Force, 66 per cent were country-born, and of the Glasgow Police 91 per cent[81] – but where would the next fit generations come from for industry, the army and the Empire? The campaign for National Efficiency was closely linked with concerns about the flight from the land and the decline of what many nostalgically regarded as the natural occupation of Englishmen.

There was little doubt that the root cause of the mass desertion was the labourer's dissatisfaction with his conditions of employment. Much information on the subject was collected in the early nineties by the English Land Restoration League, whose 'Red Vans' carried speakers into many parts of the countryside, gathering details of life and work in over 1,000 villages. Their study concluded that 'the low wages and irregular employment . . . are the chief causes of the depopulation of the rural districts'.[82] Even experts like William Bear, who were generally optimistic about improvements in the labourer's condition, had to admit in 1893 that in this 'terrible depression' arable land had been converted to pasture, with a consequent reduction of labour, piece-work and harvest earnings.[83]

In the late nineteenth century social investigators like Charles Booth and Seebohm Rowntree were beginning to map the extent of poverty in English cities, but no comparable attention was given to the village until 1904, when P. H. Mann surveyed Ridgmount, adjoining the Duke of Bedford's estate at Woburn. Of the working-class population of 390, seventy-five, or one in five, were receiving poor relief, but on Rowntree's scale of primary poverty 41 per cent were below the poverty line: irregularity of work was the third largest cause after lowness of earnings and largeness of family, accounting for 16.9 per cent of the poverty.[84] He concluded: 'The standard of life on the land is lower than in the cities; the chances of success are less and of poverty are greater; life is less interesting, and the likelihood of the workhouse as the place of residence in old age the greater'.[85] The continuation of low wages – still as little as 10s. or 12s. a week in Oxfordshire and Northamptonshire in 1912, and only 8s. in winter – meant that for a family of two adults and three children there was an average of precisely ¾d. per person per meal,[86] and when Rowntree and Kendall investigated labourers in all parts of England in 1913 they found that a minimum diet for 'merely physical efficiency' was attained only in five northern counties – Northumberland, Durham, Westmorland, Lancashire and Derbyshire.[87]

By the end of the century the practice of yearly hiring, which had given a measure of security to many young labourers, was practically extinct, surviving mainly on some small, pastoral farms in the north and west – Cumberland, Westmorland, parts of Yorkshire, Devon and Cornwall.[88] Fred Kitchen (b. 1891, Edwinstowe, Sherwood Forest) was a late survivor of the dying system, being hired at the age of fourteen for 2s. 6d. a week plus board and lodging, and attending 'stattis' (statute fairs) at Doncaster until 1910 when he left farmwork.[89] Security of employment hinged on whether a man worked with animals – 260,785 such men in 1901 – or was an ordinary labourer paid by the week, day or piece – 347,535 of these.[90] These were the men still at risk from seasonal unemployment – possibly more so now than formerly, since piece-work had increased, and the greater use of machinery had tended to concentrate and shorten the demand for labour. A most detailed enquiry, covering 1,992 English parishes, was carried out by the Board of Trade into the question of loss of time in bad weather. It found that time and earnings were lost in wet or frosty weather in 47 per cent of all parishes, the greatest loss – 67.5 per cent in eastern and south Midland counties, low-paid areas, while the least loss (18.7 per cent) was in the mainly pastoral northern counties. A Lincolnshire farmer reported that the men often lost two days a week through the autumn and winter, while a former Norfolk labourer testified that he had often had only 7s. to 8s. a week in winter, 'as its very rare that they would give you a job under cover'.[91]

The ultimate recourse of the unemployed, when all else had failed, was still the poor law, largely unchanged in 1900 since its 'reform' in 1834. Outdoor relief in the form of small doles of money and food was still given by most rural unions in cases of temporary accident or ill-health of the husband or his family, but attitudes hardened in the late nineteenth century under the influence of the Charity Organisation Society and the Campaign against Out-Relief. As a result, the proportion of all adult male paupers obliged to accept relief in the workhouse increased dramatically from 20.7 per cent in 1865 to 62.1 per cent in 1905.[92] Not all of these were cases of 'normal unemployment', since the statistics included vagrants, who were very temporary inmates of any one workhouse before moving on to the next. Their numbers must be uncertain, but S. and B. Webb estimated them at 30,000 to 40,000 in good times, rising to some 80,000 in periods of depression:[93] a Departmental Committee on Vagrancy in 1906 put the number of professional tramps at 20,000 to 30,000 which, the Webbs infer, suggests that the remainder – perhaps 50,000 in depressed years, were genuinely 'unemployed'. Those

143

who sought public relief in the casual wards of workhouses were typically required to perform a task of three hours' stone-breaking in return for a meal and a night's lodging.

By 1914 the permanent 'surplus' of agricultural labour had been dispersed. Men could still be seasonally unemployed for longer or shorter periods, could be unable to work through sickness or accident – both common to employment on the land. Walter Barrett (b. 1891, the Fens) contracted tuberculosis from inhaling the dust of mouldy hay and straw used in the chaff-cutting machine: he spent six months in a sanatorium and was never fully fit afterwards, but the two men who had worked with him on the machine both died of 'farmer's lung'.[94] But apart from dramatic occurrences of this kind, agricultural labourers rarely wrote in detail about periods of unemployment which they doubtless regarded as natural hazards of life on the land. One of the few exceptions was Henry Snell (b. 1865, Sutton-on-Trent, Nottinghamshire), who began field work at eight, attending school only when there was no seasonal work. As a young man in the early eighties he was unable to get regular employment and existed on casual jobs in great poverty until he decided to leave farmwork:

> That was for me a most miserable and demoralizing period, and I have never since needed textbooks on economics or the descriptions of social workers to teach me what unemployment means. . . . Unemployment, which involves physical degeneration and the sense that a man is superfluous, is dismissed, unused and unwanted, is not ennobling; it is entirely debasing. It is more likely to turn a man into a loafer, a criminal or a revolutionist than into a balanced and creative citizen. It warps both body and mind. . . . I sometimes think that to a sensitive and alert-minded man long-continued unemployment is the major curse of life: it is psychologically disastrous, because its effects are permanent: it leaves its sinister mark upon both mind and character, and it may so take the light out of a man's life that he lives thereafter in a darkened world.[95]

Fortunately for Snell, his unemployment was not sufficiently long-continued to become disabling, and he put it to good use by self-education at the Nottingham Mechanics Institute. He became Secretary to the first Director of the London School of Economics in 1895, an LCC Councillor, Labour MP for East Woolwich in 1922, was created Lord Snell in 1931 and became Deputy Leader of the House of Lords in 1940. His was the most outstanding example of an agricultural labourer who rose to public eminence.

5

THE 'DISCOVERY' OF
UNEMPLOYMENT, 1870–1914

'THE FUNDAMENTAL PROBLEM OF MODERN SOCIETY'
(*THE TIMES*, 1888)

In the summer of 1887 Britain and the Empire celebrated the Queen's Golden Jubilee with due pride, pomp and pageantry. To the crowds who cheered the processions of visiting European monarchs, Indian princes and African chiefs it seemed that the world paid homage to the richest and most powerful nation on earth, the leader in industry and trade and the centre of the greatest Empire the world had ever seen. The Jubilee celebrated half a century of astonishing progress, not only in material things but in the arts and sciences, in education and democracy – in short, in civilization. Yet painful and disturbing contrasts were all too close at hand for those who dared to penetrate 'Darkest England'. Along the Victoria Embankment one of 'General' Booth's officers counted 270 homeless persons sleeping out and a further ninety-eight in and around Covent Garden Market.[1] In the same year as the Jubilee the unemployed paraded their plight in marches to St Paul's and Westminster Abbey, pitched ragged bivouacs in Trafalgar Square and cheered Socialist propagandists under their banners, 'Work, Not Charity'. To a contemporary observer, the heart of the Empire had become 'a dreadful place, a civic quagmire. . . . Instead of a mere place of nightly shelter, the lodgers made it their home all day. It was a convenient central position for displaying their bitter lot, and exceptionally well situated as a rallying ground for begging forays'.[2]

The unemployed demonstrations of 1886–7 marked a new phase in working-class militancy and caused near panic in London, but although they caught the authorities unawares they were not without precedent or prior warning. The unemployed had demonstrated in Trafalgar Square in 1870 when the Land and Labour League demanded nationalization of the land and the establishment of 'home colonies' for the workless:[3] the number of strikes grew from a mere thirty in that year to around 350 a year in 1872 and 1873, probably the first major explosion of union

145

militancy which was to become characteristic of British industrial relations in the years up to 1914.[4] Further unemployed agitation occurred during the severe depression of 1879 and each winter from 1883 to 1887, coinciding with the worst sequence of years of economic distress so far experienced. But the events of 1886-7 were different in scale and character from anything before. For the first time unemployment became a political issue, perceived as a problem distinct from poverty, caused by factors other than moral failings, deserving of public sympathy and remedial action by the state. The impetus for changes in policy came from the more radical trade unionists and members of the recently formed Social Democratic Federation (SDF), Hyndman, Burns and Mann who were organizing meetings of the unemployed from 1884 onwards. Serious rioting first began in February 1886 during the worst winter for thirty years which had virtually stopped all work in building and at the docks. A meeting of around 20,000 unemployed men in Trafalgar Square was being addressed by the Fair Trade League advocating protective tariffs and relief works when it was interrupted by the SDF demanding more revolutionary Socialist measures. After scuffles between the two groups, rioting occurred in Pall Mall and Piccadilly, with looting of shops and damage to the Carlton and other clubs: in Hyde Park carriages were overturned and their wealthy occupants robbed before the rioters returned to the East End. *The Times* reported that 'the West End was for a couple of hours in the hands of the mob', believing that the danger had been greater than the Chartist demonstration of 1848 when the young Queen and her husband had fled the capital. For two more days of dense fog there were reports and rumours of thousands of 'roughs' from east and south London preparing to invade the West End: shops and banks were closed and shuttered, hundreds of police were assembled at trouble spots and soldiers at nearby barracks put on alert: for the Socialist William Morris, the February riot was 'the first skirmish of the Revolution'. Although no more serious incidents followed immediately, tension continued throughout 1886 and into the Jubilee Year 1887, with the unemployed camping out in Trafalgar Square and St James's Park. After more threatening demonstrations, the government was eventually prodded into action by pressure from the propertied classes, and on 13 November, 'Bloody Sunday', the Square was cleared by a strong police force and two squadrons of Life Guards.[5] Alfred Linnell, an innocent radical bystander, was killed, his subsequent funeral receiving maximum publicity when the route was lined by tens of thousands in a defiant protest which mocked the recent celebrations of the Jubilee.

The events of 1886-7 had profound effects for both government and governed – or, as some preferred to see it, for both capital and labour. Although trade unionists, still mainly of the skilled 'New Model' type, had not been involved, and Fabians and other middle-class Socialists had denounced the riots, the revolutionary Social Democrats emerged with a greatly heightened profile as potential leaders of the unskilled, the unemployed and the outcast 'residuum' who, it seemed, had found a voice and a champion. In that sense, the formation of trade unions among gasworkers, dockers, match-girls and others in 1888–9 was an immediate result of SDF agitation and organization while, in the longer term, campaigns for the eight-hour day, the Right to Work and state responsibility for the unemployed were initiated mainly by the radical and Socialist wings of the labour movement. 'The unemployed laborer today is not a replica of the out-of-work of a few years back', wrote John Burns in 1893.

> His predecessor was a patient, long-suffering animal, accepting his position as beast of burden with a fatalistic taciturnity, looking upon his enforced idleness as inevitable, and with blind submission enduring his lot. . . . Mute, inarticulate, unenfranchised, he escaped observation because he had no vote, no political, no municipal influence. The extension of the franchise, education, trade unionism, socialist propaganda, the broad and rising Labor Movement, have altered all this. The unemployed worker of today is of different stuff. He has a grievance, and thinks he has a remedy.[6]

Burns was writing in the year the Independent Labour Party was born and not too many years before he was to find himself President of the Local Government Board in the Liberal government, responsible both for the poor law and for new policies towards the unemployed which removed many from the stigma of pauperism.

Even more significant were the effects of the crisis of the 1880s on public attitudes towards what was now widely recognized as 'the problem of the unemployed'. These were compounded by a mixture of fear and sympathy. As early as 1882, *The Times* was warning that unemployment was 'a social problem always pressing in this country, and liable at times to become dangerous', while by 1888 it believed that unemployment was 'the fundamental problem of modern society, in comparison with which almost every question in politics seems diminutive'.[7] The same year Canon Barnett, whose intimate knowledge of the poor no one could doubt, was writing:

> The existence of the unemployed is something more than even a disgrace: it is a danger to the well-being of society. . . . Because, too, the unemployed live a low life, the selfish are encouraged to go on saying 'Nothing can be done' till their hearts are hardened. A degraded class creates an oppressive class, and the end is a revolution. If their [the unemployed] ignorance and their sense of injus-

tice are allowed to increase they may some day appear to overturn ... the very foundations of our trade and greatness.[8]

Actual revolution in the 1880s was a highly remote possibility given the tiny numerical strength of Socialist organizations and the continued attachment of most working-class voters to Gladstonian Liberalism, but a threat to the stability of class relationships was widely feared. As Sir John Gorst put it, 'If the number of unemployed and unemployable should increase beyond a certain limit, if hunger, cold and nakedness should overwhelm our temporary expedients for their relief, society might be in imminent danger'.[9]

Differing views of what this 'threat' might be abounded in the closing decades of the century. Socialist theories, either of the Henry George or Karl Marx school, had not struck deeply into an unintellectual English working class, but Socialist sympathizers might quickly gain ground by the parade of hunger and squalor. Whether from genuine, humanitarian concern or from a desire to head off further agitation and destruction of property, the Lord Mayor's Mansion House Fund for the relief of the unemployed rose from £19,000 to £72,000 in two days immediately following the demonstration of 1886.[10] A widespread fear was that the genuine unemployed, who at times of economic downturn included 'respectable' artisans and trade unionists, would sympathize and identify with the 'residuum' of idlers and loafers who congregated in London and other major cities because of the availability of charitable handouts: in this way, moral 'infection' would spread, undermining existing social relationships based on clearly defined divisions within the working classes and spreading Socialism like a disease.

The social crisis of the eighties therefore steered official opinion towards more interventionist policies in place of former beliefs in individualism, self-help and personal responsibility. Charity relief became increasingly discredited when the Mansion House Fund was frittered away in small, indiscriminate doles averaging 13s. 1d. to 40,950 families, predominantly the chronically poor rather than the exceptionally unemployed, who did not apply: according to C. S. Loch, the Secretary of the Charity Organisation Society, the Fund became merely 'a panic-stricken pauperiser'.[11] Much attention was subsequently focused on the need to separate the 'efficient' unemployed, who could and should be helped into the labour market, from the 'unemployables' or 'inefficients' who should be removed from it. The residuum constituted too great a threat to be left to the operation either of natural forces or the poor law, which had no powers of coercion, and there was general agreement among the Liberal reformers that the only solution was to draft them into strictly administered labour or farm colonies. These views fitted comfortably with Social Imperialists such as Lord Brabazon and Arnold White who were deeply concerned about the apparent physical and moral deterioration of the citizens at the heart of the Empire. If Britain was to retain her leadership as the foremost industrial nation and a great military and naval power, 'national efficiency' required improved physical fitness, higher standards of education and technical development. 'Distress in London', believed White, 'is not the distress of a great city – it is the distress of a great empire'.[12] Such views also accorded well with fears about 'urban degeneration' – that the town-bred worker after two or three generations grew smaller and physically and morally weaker, a prime candidate for the unemployable residuum. 'The child of the townsman', wrote Dr Freeman-Williams, 'is ... painfully precocious in its childhood, neurotic, pale, dyspeptic and undersized in its adult state, if it ever reaches it'.[13] If few contemporaries went so far as the neo-Darwinians and eugenicists there seemed to be visible evidence of poor stature, physical disabilities and low morals in the slums of east London and every other great city. *The Bitter Cry of Outcast London*, Andrew Mearns' scathing attack on the slums in 1883, had forced the problem of working-class housing on to the public agenda: the demonstrations and riots of 1886–7 had now done the same for unemployment.

It was symptomatic of the 'discovery' of the problem that the words 'unemployed' and 'unemployment' only came into general usage in the 1880s – indeed, some contemporaries as well as subsequent historians believed that they were only coined at this time and continued always to insert inverted commas. Thus, Sidney and Beatrice Webb could write in 1929 that ' "Unemployment", as we know it, is comparatively speaking a new phenomenon ... the word "unemployment" seems to have been first used in 1888, and to have become common only in the following decade',[14] while Sir John Clapham noted that 'unemployed' was first recorded in the *New English Dictionary* in 1882 and 'unemployment' in 1888.[15] It has also been claimed that 'the word was not introduced into the language of political economists until it was used by Alfred Marshall in 1888'.[16] In fact, as we have seen earlier, the words had been in occasional use for at least half a century, and a Royal Commission had enquired into unemployed handloom weavers in 1841, but the belief that a new problem and a new terminology had appeared only in the 1880s indicated an anxiety not previously experienced. So too did the number of articles in leading periodicals and *The Times* editorials on the 'Labour Problem' which appeared between 1880 and 1893, ranging from a minimum of twenty-two to 104 a year, and reaching a remarkable total of 920 over fourteen years.[17]

The anxieties about unemployment which these publications reflected, not to mention a huge literature on poverty, housing and other related social issues, occurred at a time when the almost monopolistic industrial and commercial prosperity which Britain had enjoyed in the third quarter of the century came under serious challenge. A boom in the early 1870s was broken in 1874, and was followed by a period of deflation and recession in a number of industries which contemporaries designated the 'Great Depression'. A 'great downward sweep of prices' brought with it, as was said in 1888, 'a depression of interest . . . a depression of profits',[18] especially in such leading industries as agriculture, shipbuilding and iron and steel trades where competition from Germany and the United States had a serious impact. Whether the Great Depression merited its title has been much debated,[19] especially by comparison with what was to happen between the two world wars, but those alive at the time saw it as the first major setback to Britain's industrial predominance, shaking Victorian optimism about continued progress and prosperity. These concerns were evidenced by the appointment of a Royal Commission on the Depression of Trade and Industry in 1884 which gloomily reported that German competition and enterprise was making headway in the markets of the world and that British industry now possessed few, if any, advantages over her. There was little doubt that Britain's rate of growth of manufactured exports had declined sharply, due partly to import substitution and tariffs imposed by overseas customers and partly to a sharp fall in the growth of world trade in manufactures as a whole. It was, therefore, British export industries such as shipbuilding, engineering, metal trades and textiles which suffered particularly, but building and construction also experienced a serious downturn and the arable sector of agriculture was badly hit by mass imports of American wheat. In the worst years, 1884–7, industrial output fell by 10 per cent,[20] and growth rates remained consistently lower than in the third quarter throughout the rest of the period.

Table 2 Average annual real growth rates of British industrial production (excluding building)[21]

	Total %	*Per head %*
1861–5 to 1866–74	3.6	2.4
1866–74 to 1875–83	2.1	0.9
1875–83 to 1884–9	1.6	0.2
1884–9 to 1890–9	1.8	0.4
1890–9 to 1900–7	1.8	0.2
1900–7 to 1908–13	1.5	–0.2

The verdict of a relative decline – though not an absolute one – seems inescapable, and as we will see, the available statistics also confirm a worsening of employment prospects in the 1880s and 1890s. While the period of the Great Depression marked a substantial rise in living standards for those in regular work because of lower food prices, a wider gap opened up between them and the unemployed and casually employed.

However, neither the period of the Great Depression (usually dated 1873–96) nor the years which followed it were times of unrelieved gloom. The British economy continued to experience cycles of boom and slump averaging around nine years' duration, which affected an increasing proportion of people as Britain became more highly industrialized. W. W. Rostow has distinguished the following peaks and troughs of the cycles (see Table 3), and has further computed the duration of periods of rising and declining prosperity: for the period 1879–94 the 'prosperity proportion' was only 50 per cent, compared with 67 per cent in 1848–68 and 73 per cent in 1904–14. 'One might firmly draw the conclusion that in the seventies the relative periods of prosperity fell away, and rose again after the middle nineties.'[22]

Table 3 Annual turning-points in British trade cycles[23]

Trough	Peak
1868	1873
1879	1883
1886	1890
1894	1900
1904	1907
1908	1913

The extent of unemployment followed more or less closely these alternations of boom and slump, though other, local factors also greatly influenced the fortunes of particular occupations. Already in 1909 William Beveridge had identified the most important cause of unemployment as 'the requirement in each trade of reserves of labour to meet the fluctuations of work incidental even to years of prosperity. The men forming these reserves are constantly passing into and out of employment. They tend, moreover, to be always more numerous than can find employment together at any one time'.[24] What this number of unemployed people was at any given time is, however, impossible to know, even within broad limits. George Barnes, who had wide practical experience of the problem, believed in 1907 that, 'There are at the best of times half a million of men for whose labour there is no demand, and the numbers of these increase in times of depression to a million or more',[25] but provided no evidence for what may well have been a reasonable 'guesstimate'. The statistics always quoted, for want of anything better, are the returns made by trade unions to the Board of Trade of their members receiving unemployment benefit (either 'static' or 'travelling' allowances), but, as is well known, trade unions covered only a small portion of the labour force, predominantly skilled workers in craft industries. Not until 1872 did total trade union membership covered by the returns reach 100,000, and

although the basis grew somewhat wider after the late 1880s the membership of participating unions still only reached 993,000 in 1914 – about a
quarter of total trade union membership[26] and a mere one-twentieth of
the whole labour force. Furthermore, the returns are very unrepresentative even of trade unions, since engineering, shipbuilding and the metal
industries account for 40 per cent of the total, and as industries heavily
dependent on exports, these were particularly subject to cyclical fluctuations: in times of depression they therefore tend to indicate an unemployment rate probably higher than that which prevailed generally. On
the other hand, the returns take no account of short-time working, which
was the normal response to depression in coalmining and the textile
industries (34 per cent of the total returns), and obviously do not include
unskilled and casual labourers who were notoriously subject to seasonal
unemployment.[27]

Figure 1 indicates the extent of unemployment in the trade unions
making returns between 1885 and 1915.[28]

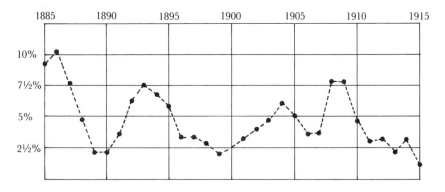

Figure 1 Annual percentage unemployed among members of certain
trade unions

Clearly, the average proportion fluctuated widely, and violently, from a
peak of 10.2 per cent in 1886 down to 2.1 per cent in 1889–90 and 1913:
the even higher figure of 11.4 per cent had been recorded in the black
year, 1879.[29] But the averages conceal much wider variations in particular
trades. In 1879 the metal and shipbuilding unions experienced 15.3 per
cent unemployment: between 1884 and 1886 the Boilermakers and Iron
Shipbuilders had three successive years when the average rate was above
20 per cent: in 1893, the worst year of the nineties, when the average
rate for all unions was 7.5 per cent, the shipbuilders and boilermakers
reached 14.3 per cent compared with only 3.1 per cent among carpenters

and joiners and 4.1 per cent among printers and bookbinders. At the start of the South African War in 1899 a general boom brought very low rates of 1.8 per cent among engineers and 1.2 per cent for carpenters and joiners, but a subsequent stagnation in building and construction brought the carpenters up to 8 per cent in 1905 and almost 12 per cent in 1908 and 1909, while the boilermakers reached 21.4 per cent unemployment in the latter year during a depression in shipbuilding. Trade revived after 1910, with unemployment rates averaging only 2 or 3 per cent up to 1914.[30]

Another possible measure of unemployment, the poor law statistics of able-bodied persons receiving indoor (workhouse) or outdoor (home) relief, can be easily dismissed. In view of its deliberately deterrent policy and a tightening-up of the eligibility for outdoor relief after 1871, very few able-bodied people were likely to apply for its tender mercies unless in ultimate distress. Furthermore, the statistical data published by the Local Government Board's Poor Law Division is very inadequate for distinguishing the genuinely unemployed from other classes of pauper.[31] In England and Wales in 1907, 20,000 able-bodied adults received indoor relief, less than half of whom were males: 16,000 able-bodied males drew outdoor relief, but only 2,200 of these for reasons of unemployment or of sickness in the family.[32] Similarly, Beveridge believed that not more than 3 per cent of the destitute travellers and tramps who used the casual wards of workhouses for nightly lodgings were the genuinely unemployed seeking work.[33]

An indication of the growing public concern for the problem was the appointment in February 1895 of a Select Committee of the House of Commons on Distress from Want of Employment, the first time that an official general enquiry into the subject had been commissioned. It followed a particularly severe winter which had stopped much outdoor work, and the Committee was anxious to discover how much unemployment was due primarily to climatic factors as opposed to general economic conditions: its method was to circulate enquiries to all Mayors of Towns and Chairmen of District Councils in England and Wales requesting information on the extent of 'exceptional distress' in their areas and its causes. It received 1,574 replies, representing a population of 26,591,000 persons: of these, districts representing 10,292,000 reported no exceptional distress, those representing 11,793,000 reported exceptional distress 'due solely to the severity of the winter', and in districts representing 4,507,000 people there was, apart from the effects of weather, 'an exceptional want of employment owing to slackness of trade, depression of agriculture, or to particular local or industrial causes'.[34] The Committee believed that

It is abundantly clear that ... there is and has been during the present severe winter, much grave distress affecting workmen ordinarily in regular work, as well as those whose employment is always liable to be intermittent, and that much suffering has been caused by this distress in many parts of the country: and there are, without doubt, many places where, underlying the distress due to weather, there exists a want of employment of labour which will remain in force after milder weather has opened the outdoor trades.[35]

This public recognition of widespread distress due to unemployment, whether temporary or prolonged, was to have an important impact on future attitudes and policies. Alarming as the official record was, some members of the Committee believed that it had under-represented the real extent under the influence of the Local Government Board which had an interest in minimizing the seriousness of the issue. Keir Hardie, the founder of the Independent Labour Party (ILP), reported that local unemployment committees had been established in every major industrial town, consisting of representatives of trade unions, Socialist organizations and branches of the ILP with the object of collecting accurate information on labour conditions. He reported that in Leeds there were at least 8,000 people unemployed and absolutely destitute, in Liverpool 18,000, in Glasgow 8,000, while in West Ham, London, of 44,700 wage earners, 10,000 were out of work and another 6,100 only casually employed.[36]

One other source gives some indication of the extent of unemployment towards the end of the period. Under the Unemployed Workmen Act of 1905 Distress Committees were to be established in all the chief industrial centres whose first task was to register and investigate the unemployed persons applying for assistance outside the poor law. Some Committees took little or no action, many only operated during severe winter months, and it was found that most of those who applied for the relief work offered – almost always rough labouring – were unskilled and casual workers who stood somewhere between the skilled craftsman who looked to his union for assistance and the vagrants and 'unemployables' who were the concern of the poor law. In their first year of partial operation in 1905–6, 110,835 persons applied for relief and in 1908–9 196,757, approximately a quarter from London and three-quarters from the provinces.[37] Taking one local area, Lancashire, where sixteen Committees covering most, but not all, principal towns had been established, Chapman and Hallsworth calculated that in November 1908 approximately 6 per cent of non-unionist adult male wage earners were unemployed.[38] An independent census made by Manchester City Council in March 1909 found 16,100 males out of work, or 9 per cent of the normally occupied men over eighteen,[39] while a careful enquiry by Rowntree and Lasker in York in June 1910 found 1,278 people unemployed in this normally prosperous city which was just recovering from a depression: this figure represented approximately 7 per cent of the wage-earning population.[40]

The difficulty of arriving at any national statistics of unemployment before 1914 is obvious. One could hardly do better than to quote Beveridge:

> The first question asked with regard to the unemployed is generally as to their number. It should by now be clear that this is about the last question to which any scientific answer can be given.... Even if it were possible to determine for any particular moment how many persons were standing idle though able and willing to work at something, the result from either a scientific or a practical point of view, would be all but worthless. The difficulty is fundamental – that there is no homogeneous unit which can be numbered. The hand bootmaker who has been permanently superceded by a new machine and will never be wanted again; the compositor out of work in the August holidays and certain to be in demand in the November publishing season; and the casual labourer on one of his off days but likely to be in demand the day after tomorrow, are not really in the same case at all, and cannot be added together as if they were. Yet these are only some of many types of unemployment.[41]

From the 1880s onwards much attention was focused on classifying and categorizing unemployment as a first step towards understanding its causes. Writing in 1885 Arnold White was typical of those observers who still associated the unemployed primarily with the 'roughs' and vagrants who slept out or walked the streets at night. He believed that these 'nomad poor' could be divided into three groups: 40 per cent were 'physically, mentally and morally unfit', and 'there is nothing that the nation can do for these men, except to let them die out by leaving them alone'; another 40 per cent were 'poor, weakly, feckless creatures', capable of three or four hours' work a day but 'unfit for the stress of competition'; while the remaining 20 per cent were capable and anxious to work and contained 'many fine characters . . . whose repugnance to the degradation of a dole is only one degree less than their loathing of workhouse relief'.[42] Not surprisingly, moral overtones were even more audible in a Charity Organisation Society Paper of 1886 which also divided the unemployed into three groups: 1. 'Thrifty and careful men'; 2. 'Men of different grades of respectability, with a decent home'; 3. 'The idle, loafing class, or those brought low by drink or vice': this latter class should be left to the poor law, while in the intermediate class the husband should be taken into the workhouse and his wife and children supported by charitable relief.[43] The same year, however, the Fabian Society suggested a more scientific, dispassionate classification which began to consider causation by distinguishing between seasonal, cyclical and casual employment.[44]

Thereafter, most students of the subject concentrated on elaborating these basic categories, but usually emphasized the importance of separating the genuinely unemployed from the 'unemployables' who should be removed from the labour market in some way. Thus, although Charles Booth concluded in his great study, *Life and Labour of the People in London*, that 'loafers' only constituted 4 per cent of those in 'great poverty' and that 52 per cent of all poverty was due to casual and irregular work, he felt moved to write:

> I do not doubt that many good enough men are now walking about idle; but it must be said that those of their number who drop low enough to ask charitable aid rarely stand the test of work. Such usually cannot keep work when they get it; lack of work is not really the disease with them, and the mere provision of it is therefore useless as a cure. The unemployed are, as a class, a selection of the unfit.[45]

What seemed agreed by the end of the century was that the pool of casual workers lay at the heart of the problem, and that this was primarily due to fluctuations in demand for labour. Llewellyn Smith, the civil servant responsible for the Board of Trade's unemployment statistics, distinguished various types of fluctuation – those due to changes of season, regular fluctuations within the year, those dependent on seasonal changes abroad, cyclical fluctuations more or less regular over a series of years, irregular fluctuations due to changes of fashion or caused by the reorganization or migration of trades.[46] Such an analysis had moved well away from a simple distinction between the 'blameable' and the 'genuine' unemployed, and from a predominantly moral to an economic explanation of its causes. Until at least the 1870s the classical, *laissez-faire* theory of a natural balance between the supply of and demand for labour had held sway: such unemployment as existed was merely a temporary, self-correcting condition, and a willing worker could always find employment. During the mid-Victorian boom such views had general approval, but the onset of depression after 1874 began to shatter confidence in continued progress and a self-adjusting economy; it was, for instance, difficult to believe in 1879 that more than 10 per cent of skilled craftsmen were choosing to be out of work. By then, theories rejecting competition were beginning to have credence among some workers and middle-class propagandists. Henry George was arguing that speculation in land was the main cause of industrial depression, and that the remedy was to take it into public ownership. For Marx the problem was that the capitalist system inevitably caused a succession of booms and slumps and required a 'reserve army' of labour which was only employable at the peaks of demand. Without accepting his critique of capitalism, Liberals like Charles Booth and Beveridge came to acknowledge the inevitability of a 'reserve army' consisting not only of a 'residuum' of casual workers but even including artisans whose unemployment rate never fell below 2 per cent at the best of times.

The diversity of views about the causes of unemployment was well represented at a conference of the Sociological Society held at the London School of Economics in 1907. Beveridge argued that it was an industrial problem caused by economic cycles, by changes in the structure or location of industries, by personal factors which determined who would be unemployed in times of depression, and by the 'standing reserve' which was always necessary to meet sudden variations in demand: these were the 'chronically unemployed' or 'underemployed' who included the physically or morally 'inefficients' as well as those who had been degraded by the industrial system. The Socialist economist, J. A. Hobson, argued that the root cause was the unemployment of all the factors of production, and under-consumption. Industry tended to produce more than could be consumed by the wage earners: the solution was therefore to increase the proportion of income that went to labour and reduce that going to rent and profits by taxation and redistribution to increase consumption. H. Rider Haggard believed that the problem of unemployment had been caused by the continued flight of workers from the land, and that this could be cured by encouraging home resettlement and emigration to the uncultivated lands of the Empire, while Robert Fels argued that 'Emigration only means that you squeeze the best blood out of your own country into another', and that the only solution was ownership by the state of all natural monopolies.[47]

The debate over the causes of unemployment now rested essentially at this point up to 1914. A minority view, even among organized labour and trade union leaders, was that the only remedy lay in revolutionary transformation of the economy and society to public ownership and control of the means of production and exchange, a solution far too radical for the Labour Party itself to adopt in its formative years after 1906. At the other end of the political spectrum, represented by such influential bodies as the Charity Organisation Society, some continued to see unemployment as primarily due to personal failings and argued that public support, whether in the form of make-work schemes or indiscriminate almsgiving, only demoralized character and multiplied the unemployables. Thus, J. S. Davy, Assistant Secretary of the Local Government Board which administered the poor law, opined in 1906 that 'the unemployed man must stand by his accidents: he must suffer for the general good of the body politic'. Such extreme views now commanded little informed support, and were to decline further as the Royal Commission on the Poor Laws absorbed a mass of expert evidence about all aspects of poverty between 1905 and 1909. Middle opinion was now preeminently represented by William Beveridge, whose significantly titled book,

Unemployment. A Problem of Industry (1909), was widely accepted as the best-informed, scientific and liberal approach to the subject. Beveridge accepted that 'the simple faith that at all times any man who really wants work can obtain it' could not be justified:[48] the root cause of unemployment was the imperfections of adjustment between the supply of and the demand for labour, and the fact that it appeared to be a normal condition of the labour market that there were always more sellers than buyers.[49] There was, therefore, no ultimate cure possible, but there were palliatives which would improve the adjustments between demand and supply – particularly labour exchanges which would gradually substitute a single pool of labour for the thousands of separate pools which presently existed, each larger than required. With a national system of exchanges it would be possible to keep unemployment to an irreducible minimum: efficient workers would be given priority for jobs, the inefficients retrained for new industries or for emigration. Cyclical fluctuations would remain a problem, but their effects could be reduced by shortening hours and spreading the available work, and by a system of unemployment insurance which would provide subsistence benefits for those not found work by the exchanges. There could be no 'right to work', and in this respect Beveridge's message was more realistic than idealist. He concluded:

> Unemployment . . . is to some extent at least, part of the price of industrial competition – part of the waste without which there could be no competition at all. Socialistic criticism of the existing order has, therefore, on this side much justification. The theoretic reply to that criticism must take the form not of a denial, but of a gloss – that there may be worse things in a community than unemployment. The practical reply is to be found in reducing the pain of unemployment to relative insignificance. In this there seems to be no impossibility.[50]

UNSKILLED LABOURERS

In categorizing unemployment and analysing its causes, contemporaries were sure that it was most widespread among general labourers who had no particular skills and no support from a trade union in times of need. This appeared to be true in all parts of the country, in Lancashire,[51] in York,[52] and most of all in London, where unskilled labour was sustained by a wide variety of casual work and supported by the multiplicity of charities. Charles Booth calculated that in his Classes A and B, living in 'great poverty', 43 per cent was due to casual work and a further 9 per cent to irregular work, while only 4 per cent were 'loafers': in Classes C and D, the 'poor', 43 per cent were again irregular earners.[53] In all four groups, poverty was overwhelmingly due to 'questions of employment', or, rather, the lack of it, while 'the demon drink' which Victorian moralists loved to hate, accounted for a significantly smaller proportion of poverty at 13 per cent.

Much of the concern of reformers was directed at the casual class, which many believed was at the heart of the unemployment problem. The difficulty was that there was no general casual labour market or 'typical' casual labourer. The characteristics were that he had no security of employment, being hired by the day or even by the hour for a specific task: he competed in a large pool of unskilled and semi-skilled labour which, even in periods of peak demand, was surplus to requirements and in times of depression, grossly so: moreover, many of the occupations which required casual labour – dockwork, portering, daily markets, small factories and sweatshops and the unskilled sectors of building work – were subject to seasonal fluctuations caused by the weather and social habits of the consuming classes. But while acknowledging these external constraints on employment, it was difficult for commentators not to include personal faults of character as important elements of the casual class, especially at the lower end where it merged into the 'residuum' and the 'unemployables'. Thus, Booth described the lowest Class A as consisting of 'occasional labourers, loafers and semi-criminals. . . . Their life is the life of savages, with vicissitudes of extreme hardship and occasional excess. . . . It is not easy to say how they live; the living is picked up, and what is got is frequently shared'. He estimated them at $1\frac{1}{4}$ per cent of East London's population as a rough estimate, but thought that they were really 'beyond enumeration'.[54] Class B, at $11\frac{1}{4}$ per cent, were also 'casual, very poor', constituting 100,000 of east Londoners. Their main employments, when they had work, were in the docks and about the wharves, canals and markets, but 'they do not get as much, on average, as three days' work a week, but it is doubtful if many of them could or would work full time for long together if they had the opportunity. . . . There will be found many of them who from shiftlessness, helplessness, idleness or drink, are inevitably poor'.[55] Class C – 75,000, and 8 per cent of east Londoners – also suffered from 'intermittent earnings'. They too were dockers, building and general labourers and street-sellers, but even included some artisans and small shopkeepers. They were 'more than any others, the victims of competition, and on them falls with particular severity the weight of recurrent depressions of trade'. Many are 'in or out of work according to the season or the nature of their employment . . . stevedores and waterside porters may secure only one or two days' work in a week, whereas labourers in the building trades may get only eight or nine months in the year'.[56] These three groups, Booth calculated, made up a fifth of the population of east London and almost 200,000 people: for the whole of London, Stedman Jones has estimated casual labourers at 10 per cent in the 1890s or 400,000 people,[57] but in other towns, especially those without docks, the proportion may have been somewhat lower.

Other commentators adopted rather more elaborate classifications while not departing basically from Booth's analysis. Alden and Hayward in 1909 produced one of the most detailed breakdowns:[58]

1 The unemployable
  (a) The vagrant
  (b) The incapable
      (i) 'Inefficients'
      (ii) The physically unfit
      (iii) The mentally deficient
2 The underemployed
3 The unemployed
  (a) Lower types
  (b) Higher types

They believed that the unemployables were at least 30 per cent of all the unemployed, who could not or would not do regular work if supplied. Their 'underemployed' were Booth's Class B, the casual 'sediment of labour', never wholly unemployed but rarely fully employed, while Category 3 were the 'genuinely unemployed', normally regular workers displaced by economic circumstances over which they had no control. Beveridge added more explanation of the types of casual worker – they were either 'casuals by necessity who could and would work regularly if they got the chance'; 'casuals by inclination', who once had good employment but now through long experience of insufficient work had become unfit for anything else; or, 'some, perhaps, were born with an invincible distaste or incapacity for regular exertion'.[59]

This last group included the vagrants who, by common agreement, stood at the base of the rank order of the unemployed. In a sense, they were outside the labour market altogether, as they had either chosen or been forced by circumstances to live wandering lives, supporting themselves primarily by begging supplemented by an occasional day's work at harvesting or fruit-picking, by hawking, poaching or theft. Some were mainly summer vagrants, spending the winter in towns or workhouses: many used the casual wards of these institutions for a night's lodging in return for a prescribed work-task, usually breaking a certain quantity of stones for men or cleaning and washing for women, before following an established route to the next. Salvation Army hostels and soup-kitchens might also be available, and it was said that much of the money collected for the Mansion House Funds for the unemployed went to vagrants, loafers and even petty criminals who had congregated in London in the expectation of easy pickings. Most charities, however, especially those which adopted the Charity Organisation Society's philosophy, refused to support the vagrant as 'undeserving', believing that indiscriminate almsgiving only encouraged idleness and dependency. This was the view of a Departmental Committee on Vagrancy, appointed by the Local Government Board in 1904 in response to public anxiety about an increase in numbers and the failure of the poor law to develop appropriate remedies.[60] 'Were it not for the indiscriminate dole-giving which prevails, idle vagrancy, ceasing to be a profitable profession, would come to an end.' But the difficulty was, as the Committee recognized, that there were at least four different types of vagrant who required different treatment: 1. The *bona fide* working man travelling in search of work (the Committee thought normally rare); 2. Men who are willing to undertake casual labour for a short time, but object to or are unfit for 'any continued work'; 3. 'The habitual vagrant . . . who certainly has no desire to find it'; and 4. 'Old and infirm persons who wander about to their own hurt'. The total size of the vagrant class was a matter of anxious speculation. The Committee thought 'there are no trustworthy statistics of vagrancy in general', but went on to estimate that, excluding licensed hawkers, pedlars and gipsies, there was an 'irreducible minimum' of between 20,000 and 30,000, and that in times of industrial depression it could run up to 70,000 or 80,000.[61] In bad times perhaps two-thirds of these were not professional vagrants but fell into the first category of mainly unskilled men moving from job to job – navvies, harvest labourers, discharged soldiers and seamen and even some tramping artisans.[62] It was further estimated that around 3 per cent of vagrants were children, and that women formed 9 per cent of the inmates of casual wards and were 'on the road',[63] further disquieting revelations to those who cherished the innocence and frailty of these groups.[64]

In fact, many unskilled workers took to the road who were neither vagrants or professional tramps simply because this was the most obvious way of looking for work when local contacts had failed: for young, single men there was also a sense of adventure and even enjoyment, at least until spirits were dampened by a fruitless search. Will Thorne, born in Birmingham in 1857, had already been working since the age of six, turning the wheel for a ropemaker for twelve hours a day for 2s. 6d. a week: his father had died and his mother worked at a sweated trade, sewing hooks and eyes on cards, twelve to a card, at 1½d. a gross. In 1875, at eighteen, he and a companion set off on tramp:

Tramping is not as romantic as it is supposed to be. . . . Mile after mile we went along the country roads, inquiring in villages and towns for work as we went, but we had no luck. At Burton we slept in a common lodging-house for 4d. a night. It was a very rough place. Most of the lodgers were navvies, and the language they used in their arguments and quarrels would make the famous 'blue' talk of Billingsgate sound like refined and cultured conversation.

However, one old navvy told them that they might get work on the Burton and Derby Railway, then building:

> Father Fairbanks, as he was called, was the contractor, and we started work for him for 2s. 6d. per day. A new shovel was supplied to us, for which we had to pay 2s. 6d out of the first week's earnings. My companion was not used to this class of work, and the first day of handling the shovel brought big blisters up on his hands, so he gave it up. . . . The shovel and I were old friends, but the work was hard and heavy. I had to fill so many waggons of muck a day. . . . I held this job down for some time, lodging at one of the huts near to the work. It was kept by a very respectable navvy ganger who was working on the same job as myself. . . . The food was both good and plentiful, and we were charged 12s. a week for board and lodgings. This did not leave me much out of my earnings of 15s. per week.[65]

Railway navvying still offered opportunities for a strong, unskilled labourer in the late nineteenth century on the smaller branch lines still being built, though there was often keen competition for such jobs despite the small wages. Albert Pugh spent many years in the late eighties and nineties as a navvy, tramping from one new line to another, with spells of unemployment between: as Thorne had found, the main means of getting jobs was through the 'grapevine' which operated within the community of navvies staying at the 4d. lodging-houses. On tramp with his brother in 1892 they failed to find work in Lancashire, so walked on into Derbyshire.

> We were early astir the next morning and away along the road towards Sheffield. That night we stayed at Castleton, the next day we passed through Sheffield, and by nightfall we had reached the outskirts of Chesterfield and put up in a common lodging-house – in navvy parlance a 'Pudding Can'. . . . The place was full of men on tramp, navvies tramping from job to job, tramps who never worked, hawkers who tramped from town to town selling their wares on the way.

Failing to get work on a new railway at Tibshelf they tramped on to the Bourn and Saxbey Railway in Lincolnshire, also unsuccessfully. Reduced to one shilling, they decided to walk to London, completing the ninety-four miles in four days, sleeping in ditches and barns which they found occupied by other tramps.[66]

Pugh was evidently an intelligent man who followed a peripatetic life-style at least partly from choice, rarely staying long at any job and turning his hand to other casual work when navvying failed. Others, like Joseph Stamper, were forced on to the road unwillingly and resentfully. In 1906 at the age of twenty-one a strike occurred at his foundry works: 'After certain vicissitudes and a long period of unemployment, despairing of ever getting work again, I went "on the road" and obtained a first-hand and intimate knowledge of the highways and doss-houses of England'. Unused to the life, it was for him a bitter experience: 'Constant failure to get decent employment crushed my spirits ... I became as my associates, listless, apathetic, slouching aimlessly along without definite objective, living from hand to mouth, from day to day. Ambition ceased to exist'. Jobs came 'fitfully and spasmodically' – cleaning old bricks, unloading timber, shifting offal in a slaughter-house. One of the worst was at a chemical works, cleaning out retorts, where the method of selection of the casual labour rivalled that at the docks.

> Just outside the time office on a piece of waste land adjoining the road, the day workers congregated each morning. The first time I saw it crowded with casuals it made me think of a slave market, but I found that the workers themselves called this plot of land the 'scrap heap', which was even more vividly descriptive than my thought of a slave market. For the men there were the broken scrap of the district, dreary and abject creatures. When a foreman came into the doorway of the time office there was a momentary eager rush and push to get into the front line of the chorus; human mongrels scrambling to get nearest to a thrown-out bone. From a foreman's point of view this would be an excellent proceeding; he was out to buy brute strength and, naturally, the strongest would get into the front row, the rows would graduate to the weakest and oldest and lamest at the extreme rear. An aspect of drawn, haggard anxiousness would appear for a few moments on the erst vacant faces. The foreman would look us over appraisingly, jab a forefinger here and there. 'You and you and you and you' he would say, and a few of us would follow in a straggling line into the passage by the time office.[67]

Experiences of this kind, which might have seemed unremarkable to an earlier generation, had a profound influence on some men in the period before 1914. Stamper became an active trade unionist and transposed some of his own experiences into novels. Patrick MacGill, born in Donegal, Ireland, in 1890, one of thirteen surviving children, had been a farm-boy from the age of ten and had stood at the hiring fairs at Strabane waiting to be employed. At sixteen he joined a gang to go potato-harvesting in Scotland, following this with seven years navvying and tramping around Kinlochleven: his experiences were like those of many others 'on the road':

It was hard to obtain constant employment; a farmer kept me a fortnight, a drainer a week, a roadmender a day, and after that it was the road, the eternal, soul-killing road again. When I had money I spent it easily; spending was my nearest approach to pleasure.... Always, however, I sought for work; I wanted something to do. My desire to labour became a craze, an obsession, and nothing else mattered if I got plenty of work to do.

MacGill's resentment turned to anger at his parents and the world, and later, to Socialism.

Why had my parents brought me into the world, I asked myself. Did they look to the future? At home I heard them say when a child was born to such and such a person that it was the will of God, just as if man and woman had nothing to do with the affair. I wished that I had never been born.... My parents had sinned against me in bringing me into the world in which I had to fight for crumbs with the dogs of the gutter. And now they wanted money when I was hardly able to keep myself alive....

Later, in Glasgow:

When I heard the words spoken by the socialists at the street corner a fire of enthusiasm seized me, and I knew that the world was moving and that the men and women of the country were waking from the torpor of poverty, full of faith for a new cause. I joined the socialist party.[68]

Vagrants merged into tramps, and tramps into casuals. Every town had its fringe of casual labourers whose employment was more or less irregular, perhaps two or three days a week, perhaps six or eight months a year. Some preferred to describe this as 'underemployment' rather than unemployment, arguing that some wage was being earned and that, in some trades at least, the slack periods were predictable and could be provided for. This implied either that earnings were sufficient to allow saving – which in the nature of casual work was highly unlikely – or that one casual job could be 'dovetailed' with another, so minimizing the gaps between. This was sometimes, but not generally, possible because the majority of casual trades had their slackest periods at the same time, from November to February, when most men would be searching for the few available jobs, and when living costs were at their highest. In any case, the budgets of casual workers were generally so frail that there was never any margin to tide over an unusually severe winter,[69] an illness or the death of a child. In Lambeth just before the First World War, Mrs Pember Reeves found families of unemployed casual labourers existing on 5s. 5d. and even 2s. 6d. a week, averaging 1¼d. per person a day for food: all had some support from neighbours and the children had free school dinners.[70] Family life was not sustainable for any length of time at this level without credit from shopkeepers, pawnshops, friends, relations and petty money-lenders, or without occasional earnings from wives and children at sweated trades, charring, washing, pre-school milk rounds and after-school errand jobs. When all else failed, single men and women slipped into the vagrant, homeless class, like the unemployed docker, tailor, builder's labourer, sawyer, waterside labourer and confectioner discovered sleeping-out on the Embankment in 1890 – all former casual workers:[71] 'I'm a tailor: have slept here four nights running. Can't get work. Have been out of a job three weeks'; 'I've slept here two nights. I'm a confectioner by trade. I came here from Dartford. I got turned off because I'm getting elderly. They can get young men cheaper . . .'; 'No. 8. Slept here four nights running. Is a builder's labourer by trade, that is, a handyman. Had a settled job for a few weeks which expired three weeks since. Has earned nothing for nine days. . . . Does anything he can get. Is 46 years old. Earns about 2d. or 3d. a day at horse minding'.

Some of them had probably reached the point of no return to regular work and settled habits, and were fast becoming unemployable. But most casual workers tried to live something like normal family lives despite precarious earnings and pitifully low standards of living. One such family were the Nevinsons – husband, wife and three children renting a small four-roomed house in York in 1910. Nevinson had regular employment as a labourer until three years ago when the works closed because of slackness in trade, and he and many others were discharged: before that, he had an excellent 'character' for twenty years with one employer, is sober and has never been known to refuse work. He now exists by very irregular labour, 'catch' jobs, mostly at the waterside. The following diary entries represent a typical week.

> **Thursday, July 7** Went to work at Messrs. L's, 6 a.m., carrying sacks of wheat. Breakfast 8 to 8.30 – one kipper and bread; dinner 12 to 1 – bread and margarine; left at 6 p.m.; tea – bread and margarine; got a bit of twist [tobacco] given. Earned 4s.
> **Friday, July 8** Up at 6 a.m. No breakfast. Went round to L's and W's wharves, stayed out until 12, came home, had dinner – kipper and bread; walked round and round until tired, came home at 4.30; tea – bread and cup of tea.
> **Saturday, July 9** Up at 6 a.m., waited at L's until 9, no chance; went round to W's wharf, nothing doing; home at 11, bit of bread and margarine for dinner; walked round to see if I could pick any work up, home at 7 p.m.; no supper.
> **Sunday, July 10** Up at 4 a.m. and went round the town to see if I could find anything that had been lost, could not see anything so

came home at 7 a.m.; had breakfast, consisting of jam and bread, went to bed until 1 p.m., had dinner – stew, and cup of tea; to bed at 9 p.m.

Monday, July 11 Got up at 5.30; got a job at L's, earning 4s.; took it for rent. Meals: breakfast – butter and bread; dinner – nothing; tea – hot cakes and bacon, – got a pound of bacon given, also some tea and ¼ stone of flour.

Tuesday, July 12 Earned a shilling at wharf for working three hours. Breakfast – bacon and bread; dinner – bacon and bread; tea – margarine and bread.

Wednesday, July 13 Went out at 5.30 a.m.; walked round to several different jobs until 10, cut some old boots up to mend the little boy's boots, went out again until 4, got nothing. Breakfast – margarine and bread; dinner – dripping and bread; tea – kipper and bread, and not much of that.

Over a four-week period Nevinson earned a total of 7s. 0d. and his wife, by charring, 6s. 9d.: their budget had a deficit of £1 6s. 9d., consisting of £1 unpaid rent and the rest food on credit.[72]

Beveridge believed that casual labour was 'a modern evil'. Earlier chapters have shown that it was by no means new, but casuality increased in the later nineteenth century, especially in London and some other large cities where old-established hand crafts were declining in the face of factory-made goods in new centres of production. London trades suffered acutely from the 1870s onwards with the virtual destruction of the silk industry, the wooden shipbuilding industry of the Thames and the formerly important engineering trades, while bespoke tailoring, boot and shoemaking and cabinet-making all continued their long-term decline in competition with ready-made, factory products from outside the capital.[73] Workers who remained in these trades experienced reductions in earnings and increasing seasonality of employment, while others left to swell the ranks of the already over-stocked casual labour market. The classic casual occupation was dock-work, which, in many branches (stevedores, wharfingers and lightermen excepted) required little more than muscular strength and a certain agility: in the late 1880s Llewellyn Smith found that few men had begun their working lives in the docks but included former shipwrights, clerks and soldiers, while he was told by dock officials of a clergyman, a baronet and the son of a general who picked up livings in this way.[74] Dockwork was invariably casual because of the uncertain arrival time of ships and the need to unload cargoes at great speed, especially if perishable but in any case to minimize dock charges. The dock companies kept three types of labour: 'permanent' men, who had secure employment; 'preference' men, who were next to be called on but had no guarantee of work; and casuals who were only needed at peak times. Charles Booth estimated in 1892 that there was more or less regular employment in the London Docks for 14,500 to 15,000 men out of a total labour force of 22,000:[75] the 'superfluous' struggled and fought at the dock gates for a day's or half-day's work now and then, hoping to catch the eye of the foreman or, according to Beatrice Webb, bribing him with drinks in exchange for a job. They were part of what Beveridge described as the 'inner ring' of 'chronically unemployed': 'All could get occasional shillings, few a decent living'.[76] Following the great London Dock Strike of 1889 there was an attempt in 1891 to reorganize dockwork by 'decasualization', further categorizing the men into 'permanent' and 'A' classes with regular work at weekly wages, 'B', 'C' and 'casual' who would be taken on in order and paid by the day. The effect was to concentrate employment to some extent, giving a minority more regular work, but actually increasing unemployment for the lowest casuals: in any case, the scheme only applied to the London and India Docks Company, which employed about one-fifth of the workforce, and for the rest the old evils remained. 'In waterside labour as a whole', wrote Beveridge in 1909, 'the methods of the past continue: the same economic forces are at work and produce the same consequences'.[77] Divided and still largely casualized, dockwork remained a major occupation up to, and well beyond, 1914, the numbers increasing (England and Wales) to 102,639 in 1911, not including 295,343 'general labourers', some of whom added to the census classification from time to time: London and Liverpool made up half the total, the rest being distributed over more than twenty smaller ports.[78] The casual system survived partly because some dockers themselves favoured it: hourly rates of pay were relatively high for unskilled labour, and a few fortunate men could make good money when employed regularly. In the Liverpool docks in 1913, 21 per cent of men were earning over 30s. a week (a few over 40s.) while 43 per cent earned less than 15s., including two lower strata who could make only 5s. and 5s. to 10s. a week.[79]

What casual labour in the London docks was like around 1880 was ably described by Ben Tillett, later to become the dockers' leader in the strike of 1889. After four years in the Navy and Merchant Marine he returned to London to look for work:

> I was fated to tramp footsore, for many miles, through many docks in London. The joy of my home-coming soon faded away. . . . The callers-on, the foremen and the contractors were all of Pharoah's kind, and hardened their hearts against me. I was scorned and rejected. . . . As a child I had tasted of the squalor of a tramp's life, but the infernal, terrible degradation of London slums, the life of the out-of-work casuals, the tigerishness of dock jobbing contractors, the hideousness of the doss house, revolted my soul.

At the docks Tillett discovered the 'cage', 'so termed because of the stout iron bars made to protect the "caller-on" '.

> In a building that would hold very few in comfort men were packed tightly into suffocation, like the Black Hole of Calcutta, and this struggling mass fought desperately and tigerishly, elbowing each other, punching each other, using their last remnants of strength to get work for an hour or half-hour for a few pence. Such struggling, shouting, cursing, when one man younger than the rest would throw himself bodily on to the heads of the close-packed, struggling mass! For what? The possession of a ticket which, at the best, would afford four hours' labour, for a wage at its highest of no more than sixpence per hour. . . . Coats, flesh, even ears were torn off. Men were crushed to death in the struggle. The strong literally threw themselves over the heads of their fellows, and battled with the milling crowds to get near to the rails of the 'cage' which held them like rats – human rats – who saw food in the ticket.[80]

Tillett eventually 'became learned in the methods of obtaining employment' – knowing the call places and times, reading the shipping papers to watch for arrival times. But 'we who picked up a livelihood at the docks lived more by accident than design. How others lived I never could guess. To me it sometimes seemed impossible to tolerate life at all'.[81]

The other great employer of casual labour was the building trade, though it differed from dockwork in having a substantial proportion of skilled workers and in having no fixed centres of employment. As Beveridge pointed out,

> By the nature of things, no two pieces of work follow closely on one another in the same spot. The foremen, to whom the whole business of engaging men is entrusted, move continually from one job to another, from one end of a town to the other, or even from town to town. . . . He starts on a job with a few leading hands. The rest are taken on as they come – guided by recommendations from their mates or stray hints in public-houses, following up a load of builder's materials . . . obviously such a system, or want of system, could not work unless there was an army of men always on the tramp, a reserve of labour drifting perpetually about the streets.[82]

These 'first comers', once taken on, had to prove themselves against later arrivals, so a process of 'weeding-out' of the less efficient or more troublesome began until the foreman had selected a satisfactory gang. Those rejected might get occasional work, insufficient for a decent living, but were free to go and repeat the process elsewhere. 'The obvious result is to maintain in a state of permanent demoralisation a mass of low grade casuals.'

This was a vastly larger industry than dockwork, totalling 938,747 workers in England and Wales in 1900.[83] Each of its branches – carpenters and joiners, bricklayers, painters and decorators, masons and plumbers – had its skilled craftsmen and its unskilled labourers, the latter most numerous in bricklaying but very common also in painting where, it was said, many 'come to earn a drink' by a few hours' work.[84] In London (LCC area) the building trades were the largest single employers, a total of 143,000 in 1900 having increased from 129,400 ten years earlier. As well as experiencing the cyclical fluctuations common to other industries, usually a year or so later, the building trades in the later nineteenth and early twentieth centuries were generally suffering a long-term decline with only occasional periods of prosperity. A decade of boom collapsed in 1878 and was followed by a long depression in the 1880s: good years from 1895 to 1900 resulted in over-stocking the market, and a high bank rate during and after the South African War reduced building activity to another depression in 1903–8. In many places the rapid growth of towns and suburbs was now slackening, and as Robert Noonan (Tressell) found in Hastings, the building boom of the second half of the century was over, and work was now mainly maintenance and renovation: during his stay there, from 1902 to 1910, there was a general slump in the trade, with much unemployment.[85] The trade was also suffering from the adoption of some new building techniques such as the use of ferro-concrete in large-scale construction which reduced the work of stonemasons and brick-layers, and the introduction of specialized manufactured materials for flooring, tiling and metalwork which saved labour.[86]

Added to these problems was the fact that a good deal of the trade was seasonal as well as casual. Much building work was necessarily outdoor – bricklaying, masons' work, a good deal of carpentry and painting – and directly affected by weather conditions, especially frost, but also heavy rain, damp and fog. A great deal of time was lost at such jobs, especially but not only during November to February. It was said of painters that 'even in the best of years, there are some bad months', and Dearle was told by one man that, 'We are lucky if we do six months work in the year'.[87] Indoor joiners, plumbers and decorators were better placed in this respect, though equally subject to frequent failures of employers, the small, jobbing builders who made up a large part of the trade having a notoriously high rate of bankruptcies. The trade was also affected by social factors, particularly in London but also in other fashionable provincial centres and resort towns: the winter months were always a slack time, March to May a brisk period, June and July slack, August to October busy again, repairs and decorating being fitted around the gaps in the 'season' when town houses were least occupied. In Rowntree and Lasker's survey of those unemployed in York on a single day, 7 June 1910, the building trades numbered 173 out of the total unemployed of 1,278 (13.5 per cent), while of the 441 casual workers out of work (34 per cent) a number had normally worked as rough painters, whitewashers, plumbers, glaziers and bricklayers' labourers.[88]

A series of particularly severe winters in the 1880s contributed to the explosion of working-class discontent in that decade. Mrs Yearn's father, a brick-setter, was unemployed at this time. 'We had the terrible winters of frost and snow, and for six or seven months in the year father was unable to work, so mother had to go to the mill': her mother had fourteen children, eight of whom died very young, 'six of us left, and too many even then to feed and clothe'.[89] Louise Santer, born at Ore, near Hastings, in 1894, had similar early memories of privation. Her father, a scaffolder by trade, was often unemployed:

> I can remember my father walking to Crowhurst in the snow drifts trying to get work. There was nothing in them days. . . . If you hadn't got work you got nothing. Us children, we often got no bread. . . . Sometimes we couldn't go to school because if it was wet we got no shoes. We must have owed the baker and the grocer some money. They used to let us have credit, but we never could pay them.

He later got work as a platelayer on the railway, but was killed taking the lamps into a tunnel early one morning.[90] At eighteen, Jack Lanigan was sacked as a grocer's assistant in 1908 for allegedly spending too much time at his hobby, amateur dramatics, though he had always been punctual and hardworking. At that time in Manchester:

> At the factory and workshop gates you would find dozens of men waiting for a door to open and someone to step outside and shout, 'One man'. There would be such a scramble, worse than any rugby match, to get to that door. It reminded me of the jungle – the survival of the fittest. It was a wonder the people did not revolt. I suppose revolt was not thought of. Men were kept too busy trying to find work. . . . What was I going to do now, become a grocer again? Not on your life. I would try and find a labouring job with a building contractor and I did. Fortunately it was a contractor engaged in conversions, replacing the old type of toilets to water closets, and I became a bricklayer's labourer, five pence an hour, and you were paid only for the hours you worked. The hours were from 8.0 a.m. to 6.0 p.m. Monday to Friday, 8.0 a.m. – 12.0 noon Saturday. In a full week my pay packet was £1 0s. 5d. When the weather was fine it was not too bad, but by the end of September the weather broke and it was lousy until Christmas. Many were the days you would commence at 8.0 a.m. and at about 9.0 or 10.0 it would commence raining, but the bricky would continue working until lunchtime. By then you would be soaked to the skin. After

lunch if the rain had not eased off the bricky would look at the clouds and shout, 'Knock off', and that meant no more money for that day. This happened week after week and my wage would perhaps be ten shillings, sometimes less.[91]

And in neighbouring Salford, Robert Roberts observed a similar scramble for work by casual labourers in the building trade.

Building labourers I have seen as a child follow a wagon laden with bricks from the kilns, hoping to find a job where the load was tipped. For the same reason, too, they would send a wife or child trailing behind a lime cart. On some building sites a foreman might find fifty labourers pleading for a mere half-dozen jobs. It was not unknown for him to place six spades against a wall at one hundred yards' distance. A wild, humiliating race followed; work went to those who succeeded in grabbing a spade.[92]

Many other occupations besides building and dockwork were subject to seasonality and its consequence of periodic unemployment. In the majority of trades the slack season was the three or four winter months, sometimes interrupted by a Christmas consumer boom which was then followed by a depression until activity resumed in the spring: this was the pattern in most outdoor trades, but also in some indoor occupations affected by the social 'season' – cleaners, laundry-workers, bakers, cooks, barbers and waiters as well as women's work in millinery, dressmaking, artificial flower-making and luxury trades generally. A few trades, however, experienced their peak demand in winter and suffered from summer slackness, especially the coal and gas industries. Working at the gasworks Will Thorne found that 'About February of each year some of the retort houses would be shut down; the days would be growing longer and not so much gas would be consumed as in the winter. This meant unemployment for many. As a junior and a late-comer to the works, I was one of the first to go'.[93] Thorne found work in a brickfield for the summer, illustrating the possibility for some of 'dovetailing' casual jobs which had their peak demands at different seasons. Haymaking, harvesting, fruit- and hop-picking provided other casual summer work, but the slack winter period common to most trades was much more difficult to fill. Stedman Jones estimated that at least twenty-seven major occupations experienced seasonal slackness in January: in total, these amounted to 285,000 male workers in London in 1891, or one-third of the male working-class labour force.[94]

BOY LABOUR AND WOMEN'S LABOUR

Two particular aspects of the labour market were much discussed in the late nineteenth century, partly because both were known to be subject to unemployment but, more importantly, because they were seen as competitors to adult male labour and, therefore, a cause of unemployment among the supposed chief breadwinners of families. There was, of course, nothing new about child labour, and until elementary education became (theoretically) compulsory in 1880 boys in poor families were still able to start work in uncontrolled trades as early as in medieval times. Will Thorne started at six in 1863, working twelve hours a day for a ropemaker: at eight he was in the brickfields, at nine a plumber's mate, then a lath-splitter, at thirteen collecting cow- and pig-hair, at fourteen in a metal-rolling works, at sixteen in a wagon works, then a builder's labourer, all before he was eighteen. This pattern of a wide variety of unskilled jobs, each usually held only for a few months or weeks, remained common among youths up to 1914, work often having begun part time while still at school. Wal Hannington's father, 'a first-class bricklayer', experienced long periods of unemployment between 1901 and 1911, and with seven living children all had to contribute as soon as they were able: Walter worked as an errand-boy from the age of ten, and on leaving school in 1910 had ten different jobs in the next eighteen months. 'Jobs for boys seemed to be plentiful', and he tried his hand in a vinegar brewery, an ironworks, several printing works, a wheelwright's shop, dental mechanic's and an organ-builder.[95] Although the legal minimum for part-time work was ten, enforcement was all but impossible and many began as errand-boys, lather-boys and newspaper-boys well below this. But the principal objections to boy labour were that youths at low wages 'crowded out' adult workers and that they themselves after a succession of casual, unskilled jobs often joined the ranks of the unemployed when at eighteen or nineteen they required adult wages. 'At a time when a man could earn 12s. 6d. for a 60-hour week, employers found it more economical to employ two boys part-time at an individual wage of 2s. 6d. per week.'[96] In poor families the pressure was always for the boy to be bringing home a wage as soon as possible, a fact which strongly militated against post-elementary education and apprenticeship.

> To return to my schooldays, in this elementary school in Bethnal Green only one pupil in 400 each year passed to a foundation or a grammar school.... For the unlucky 399 it was just a free-for-all on leaving school at 14. There was the search for work, and it largely depended on chance whether a boy became an apprentice for a skilled job or an errand boy, a can carrier for workmen or a van boy on the back of a horse and cart. Mostly they were blind alley jobs; the boy was sacked as soon as he reached an age to justify

paying him higher wages. Many finished up as labourers, more often out of work, or as dockers standing idly at the dock gates. . . . What was I going to do then? 'Anything you like', my father said when I appealed to him for guidance, 'so long as you bring some money home to keep yourself'. Father had long lost any ambition by following his dying trade of cutting quill pens.[97]

According to an ex-elementary schoolteacher and Probation Officer with wide experience of the youth of south London,

The boy, as a rule, does not keep his first place for very long. The reasons for his leaving are put in many different ways, but commonly amount to the simple fact that the work he does is only worth a boy's wage, and that he must leave it as soon as he shows signs of becoming a man. A firm of carriers may employ a thousand drivers and a like number of van-boys. But the career of a driver is forty years, that of a van-boy only four, so that a driver will outlive ten van-boys in the service of the firm. In other words, of every ten boys who dangle their legs over the tailboard of a van, only one can reasonably hope to stay on and become a driver. Another of the ten may aspire to a permanent position as stable-hand or checker, but there will still be eight boys thrown out of work at seventeen or eighteen.[98]

Of the 1,278 people unemployed in York on 7 June 1910, 129 were youths aged fourteen to nineteen, two-thirds of them sixteen to eighteen: seven had been out of work for over a year, sixteen for more than six months, and 'not a few' for more than three months. According to the authors of the survey, 'about 80 per cent of the lads found unemployed have begun badly . . . primarily due to their home conditions': the largest first employment was as errand boys, followed by factory work, but only two of the unemployed had been apprenticed.[99] National statistics collected by the Royal Commission on the Poor Laws, 1905–9, showed that boys who started in factory work on leaving school had, on average, three different jobs by the age of nineteen, while messenger-boys changed jobs four times: one boy had thirty-eight jobs between fourteen and seventeen, another twenty-two by the time he was twenty.[100] By the end of the century the issues of boy labour were widely debated in government circles and by trade unions concerned by both aspects of the problem – the displacement of adult labour by youths and the subsequent unemployment of such youths themselves, adding to the existing surplus of labour and competition for jobs. Remedies advocated by the Trades Union Congress included raising the school leaving age to fifteen, followed by further trade and technical instruction at work, and pressure on employers to take more apprentices. In 1909 the Poor Law Commission was alarmed to discover that between 70 and 80 per cent of boys leaving elementary school entered unskilled occupations, and the Minority Report went further than the TUC in advocating a limit of thirty hours of work a week for youths under eighteen, the released time being devoted to continued education and technical instruction.[101]

Women's labour similarly presented a dual problem of unemployment among women themselves and its tendency to replace men in certain trades. This was particularly noticeable in tailoring and the boot and shoe industries, where traditional male trades based on hand crafts were being transformed into factory industries for a cheaper, ready-made market. From the 1860s onwards the sewing-machine increased the 'sweated' outwork trades in tailoring and dressmaking in London, but at the same time stimulated competitive factory production in Leeds and other northern towns, while by the 1890s adaptations of the sewing-machine to leather were concentrating boot and shoe manufacture into factories in and around Northampton. The bespoke tailoring trade, predominantly male, had always suffered a seasonal trough in demand from Christmas to March and, often, again in the summer holiday period, but cheap, 'slop' ready-mades, whether from sweatshops or factories, now reduced demand still further. By the end of the century a trade union official of the Boot and Shoe Operatives believed that 'there is absolutely no doubt that machinery has displaced one-third of the men'.[102] This was scarcely an exaggeration, since English males in the London footwear trades declined from 33,435 in 1861 to 24,004 in 1901, a reduction of 28 per cent, considerably greater than the fall of 8 per cent in the numbers of English males in the London clothing trades over the same period.[103] Technical changes undoubtedly provided work for some men, but left more unemployed or underemployed. The sewing-machine allowed unskilled labour, mainly female, to take their places at greatly reduced wages, and many skilled men were driven to casual work, either in their own trade or elsewhere – Ben Tillett, the dockers' leader, believed that a quarter of London dockworkers were former tailors and shoemakers.

These concerns about the 'crowding out' of skilled men by unskilled women and boys coincided in the 1880s with the beginning of a wave of Jewish immigrants from Poland and Russia, many of whom gravitated to the East End tailoring, shoemaking and cabinet-making trades and, to a less extent, to similar work in Leeds, Manchester, Glasgow and other towns. The total of 120,000 Jewish immigrants to England between 1870 and 1914[104] was not vast, though its concentration into particular areas and occupations, and its apparent willingness to work at sub-standard wages for unlimited hours, heightened fears about unfair competition and led to trade union demands for restriction and protection. Keir Hardie told a Select Committee on Emigration and Immigration in 1889 that 'every foreigner throws one British workman out of employment',[105] and TUC resolutions against alien immigration were frequently passed from 1888 until the mid-nineties, when anti-Semitism seems to have abated. Early fears about widespread undercutting and job replacement had no doubt been exaggerated, but in the London tailoring trade coat-making, vestmaking and trousermaking were largely in the hands of Jewish entrepreneurs and workers by 1900: foreign-born Jews then made up 36 per cent of the male labour force in London tailoring and 12.3 per cent in the boot and shoe trade.[106] In these, the statement made by the statistician Llewellyn Smith to the Royal Commission on Alien Immigration in 1903 that he could find no evidence of displacement, seems optimistic.

Apart from its possible effects on men's employment, women's labour became the subject of much concern at the turn of the century, centring particularly on the issue of 'sweating'. The term had originated in the 1840s to describe developments in the tailoring and shoemaking trades and was fully explained by Henry Mayhew in the 1850s, but from the 1880s it became a matter of official investigation and, ultimately, of public control. Sweating was characterized by unregulated hours and conditions of work, extremely low wages and tedious, monotonous processes, mainly hand-operated: the place of work was the home or small workshops, backrooms, cellars and attics where subdivided processes could be carried out without the need for powered machinery: organizationally, it was characterized by manufacturers putting out work to middlemen who hired workers on piece-rates for specific parts of the end product. Such workers, with a high proportion of women and youths, were unorganized and ununionized and unable to put up any real resistance to exploitation in an over-stocked labour market containing many casual and part-time workers. It is estimated that in the 1880s women's wages in homework occupations averaged 8s. to 9s. a week, while Charles Booth found that tailoresses' wages ranged from 5s. to 13s. 6d. and skilled dressmakers and milliners from 13s. to 20s.:[107] these rates were for regular, full-time work, taking no account of frequent periods of unemployment and under-employment.

Women workers in dress numbered 755,964 in England and Wales in 1911, the largest occupational category after domestic service and slightly larger than those employed in textiles: 339,240 were dressmakers and 127,115 tailoresses.[108] Around a third of these were homeworkers, the rest factory hands. Both groups were subject to periodic unemployment, though factory work was the more regular and in the textile industries slackness of trade was usually met by short-time work-sharing rather than by dismissals. Nevertheless, Clementina Black found that in the Bradford woollen industry, which specialized in dress stuffs for women's clothes, the work was much more irregular than in Huddersfield where cloth for men's wear was made since this was less subject to seasonal fluctuations.[109]

In a survey undertaken by the Women's Industrial Council in 1908 into the employment of married women in many parts of the country it was concluded that most worked because there was no continuity of employment for their husbands: this applied whether the men were Yorkshire miners, Liverpool dockers, Sheffield cutlers, Reading bricklayers, or casual workers in any trade. In Yorkshire the interviewer was told that 'no [married] woman would go out to work if she could afford to stay at home', and concluded that, 'In short, poverty and low wages in nine cases out of ten are the causes that drive married women into the labour market'.[110]

The sweated outwork trades suffered especially from seasonal fluctuations as well as an overall glut of female labour trying to make good the loss of male earnings: this applied not only to milliners and dressmakers, but to other sweated trades such as box-makers, artificial flower-makers, hook-and-eye carders and paper-bag makers which all had their 'seasons'. In the East End 'slop' tailoring trade women worked approximately two-and-a-half days a week when averaged over the year, and it was noted that the use of the sewing-machine, by speeding up production, had actually shortened the 'season' for dressmakers and milliners: a contemporary observer, Sherwell, believed that such women were 'frequently driven upon the streets in the slack season, returning to their shops with the advent of the new season's trade. In other words, morals fluctuate with trade'.[111] In the coatmaking branch of bespoke tailoring the slack season covered half the year, and during this time 'slackness deepens into unemployment', while in boot and shoemaking it was said that 'permanency . . . means work for a few weeks at the most, never more':[112] in this trade by the end of the century outworkers were only fully employed when the factories could not meet orders, and women workers in Norwich averaged only 3s. a week over the year because of irregularity of demand. Similarly, in straw-plait work a factory inspector in 1912 reported that homeworkers had only twenty weeks a year of full employment, twenty-two weeks with some work and ten with none.[113] Even in trades where women's wages were highest, such as West End dressmaking where a 'first hand' could earn 20s. to 30s. a week in the best houses, the same problem of seasonality could reduce actual earnings to half this amount, as the Secretary for the Women's Trade Union Association reported:

> The majority of workers are simply season hands, and if they begin work at the end of March they will perhaps be kept busy until August. . . . They may get a few more weeks' work from October to December, but this is not to be relied upon. What they do until the season begins again, cannot be said.[114]

Direct evidence about the extent of unemployment was gathered by an enquiry into the London clothing trades in 1908:[115] a few typical reports by the investigators are as follows:

161. Waistcoat maker. 'This girl works in a small workshop. About 10 employed. . . . Their busy times are from March to July, then they are on ¾ time and ½ time. They are never sent quite away, although she had only a ½ day in one week.'

180. Widow with 3 daughters, homeworkers. Work entirely for one firm which specialises in high class work, including selling to the Royal Family. 'If there is any work in the shop this family gets it, as they are considered good, quick workers. In this way, they have not quite so much slack time as others. Still, there are several months when they make very little or nothing.'

248. High class shirt finisher. 'There is a great deal of slack time all through winter. Sometimes they only have a couple of days' work in a week.'

366. Children's dresses, medium quality. 3d. an hour when fully employed, 21 years old. 'The mother says this girl gives her 6s. 6d. weekly towards her support: some weeks she is so distressed because she has not got it to give. They won't allow the girls to come home even if there is no work . . .'

51. Cheap quality work – servants' print dresses. 'Piece wages averaging 8s. a week when work is plentiful (there is none to speak of in autumn or winter. Last winter they were 6 months without).' Gets 4s. a dozen for servants' dresses.[116]

SKILLED WORKERS

Unlike the unskilled and casually employed, the skilled worker normally expected security for life in a job for which he was specially trained. Having sacrificed the immediate gratification of a youth's wages for five or seven years of apprenticeship when, at least for the first year or two, he was paid little or nothing, he looked forward with deferred expectation to a safe, honourable job with relatively high earnings and membership of a craft union. Such hopes had often, though not always, been realized in the past, as previous chapters have shown, but in the period after 1870 unemployment among skilled workers reached new levels and was no longer accepted as an inevitable hazard of life by a better educated, organized and articulate workforce. The Reform Act of 1867 had brought the franchise to the town worker, the Trade Union Acts between 1871 and 1875 had given legal recognition and protection: by the 1880s the traditional alliance of the working man with Liberalism was beginning to yield to claims for separate political representation, culminating by the end of the century in the emergence of the Labour Party. Issues about unemployment, couched in campaigns such as the Right to Work and the Eight Hour Day, were uppermost in the new political agenda, led by radical members of the trade unions often supported by middle-class Social Democrats. In the autobiographies of this period political involvement becomes inescapable, both as a frequent cause of unemployment and as a reaction to it. It is no longer to be suffered in silence or relieved by charity: public remedies for a national problem are sought and unemployment for the first time takes the stage as an issue of social policy.

The large group of building craftsmen shared with their unskilled labourers the uncertainties of weather and of gaps in employment between jobs: although the comparatively few large firms could expect to offer regular employment to their first-class men, the much larger number of small, speculative builders had no regular flow of contracts and notoriously frequent bankruptcies. Skilled bricklayers, carpenters, painters and others therefore often had to move between employers within a town or even between towns. This was especially true of stonemasons, whose usual employment on large, geographically scattered buildings, necessitated a peripatetic existence. Thus, in the bad year 1879, 8 per cent of members of the Stonemasons' Union were 'on tramp', drawing travel and lodging allowances in their search for work.[117] Alfred Ireson's father and grandfather had both been masterbuilders and stonemasons, working wherever the jobs took them, often away from home: as a young man in the 1870s Alfred worked on castles, churches, London mansions, Holloway's Hospital at Egham in Surrey, Cambridge colleges and other public buildings, journeying south to Portsmouth and Southampton and north to Glasgow, eventually marrying and hoping to settle in Birmingham in 1876. 'One Saturday, quite unexpectedly, I with several others was dismissed from work. For the first time being out of work troubled me. The prospect of a long, cold winter brought anxious thoughts.'[118] After temporary work with a coalmerchant at 5s. a week, Ireson was converted to Christianity and, disillusioned with the life of a stonemason, became a London City Missionary for the next forty-five years.

> To thousands of workers the dreadful, bitter, haunting experience that eats the soul away, is the lack of security. This deliverance brought to me the same joy that comes to a slave when his chains and shackles are knocked off, and he is told to go a free man. My tool chest, with its contents, would be sent at once to my father. How thankful I was to see the last of a stone-mason's life.[119]

Fred Bower's father, another stonemason, first became unemployed in 1868 during a lockout in London, when 'blacklegs' were brought in from Scotland, France and Germany, and emigrated to America for six years:

his son, Fred, was born there in 1871, 'because my father refused to be an English blackleg and sell the principles of his trade organisation'. Following his father in the trade back in England, 'I shifted about, up and down the country, picking up experience all the while', and beginning to take an interest in union affairs.

> Most of the thankless work, such as spokesman for the men at interviewing bosses, etc., was undertaken by one or two individuals in each lodge or branch. And these men couldn't seem to hold a job down for long. These, I found, were the most fearless and independent-minded of my fellow-members. Yet they did not seem to suit the bosses. . . . I found that these men, who did the speaking up for the other men, who risked their jobs, with what that meant of poverty to themselves, their wives and children, were socialists.[120]

Like Ireson, Bower travelled the length and breadth of the country for work, using his union card for lodging at the club houses.

> Our Union gave us, when out of work, a cheque book good for 98 days, which cheques we cashed at towns as we came to them and at our club houses, the said cheques being good for one and three-pence per day, with an extra three pence for Sunday, but – only if you travelled.

> > Our Domain, our 'stamping ground'
> > Was Carlisle to the Chesil Beach,
> > From Newcastle down to Penrhyn Town,
> > Wherever the foot could reach.
> >
> > For it was fifteen pence for a working day,
> > Eighteen for the day between,
> > And a penny for three miles over twelve
> > When Victoria was Queen.
> >
> > And that was six for a bed, and two for a pint,
> > And four for a 'rough stuff' meal,
> > And three for an ounce of twist or shag
> > To smoke when our innards did squeal.

This was in the early 1890s, when the Operative Stone Masons were among the last unions to continue the tramping system. Unlike Ireson, Bower enjoyed his wandering life, working in America, Canada and Australia and never marrying: in the years before 1914 he became a trade union delegate and Socialist lecturer, active in local labour politics.

Tramping was never so common in the other building trades, where by this time 'static' unemployment pay was usual for carpenters, joiners, plumbers and other skilled workers. On the day of the unemployment survey in York (7 June 1910), 116 of the building craftsmen out of 1,240 (9.4 per cent) were unemployed: they included thirty-five bricklayers, thirty-four joiners, twenty-five painters, nine plumbers, seven plasterers and six stonemasons.[121] In a highly seasonal trade, these percentages were likely to worsen with the onset of winter – thus, at the end of November 1908 11.6 per cent of carpenters and joiners in the UK were out of work and 16.3 per cent at the end of January 1909.[122] For a skilled carpenter a harsh winter or a depression in trade could mean no more security than for an unskilled hand. In Dundee in 1895 Bob Stewart, a joiner, found that 'Unemployment in the city was high. The hard winter had closed the building sites and all outside work was at a standstill. Labour was plentiful, jobs were scarce. After much searching and standing at work gates, I started on the railway'.[123] Later he moved to carpentry work in a shipyard at Renfrew.

> I held this job for a few months. Then, after the ship was launched, there was a big pay-off. . . . For me it meant looking for another job immediately. I tramped the whole of the reaches of the Clyde, Greenock, Yoker, Partick and Govan, but at every yard the position was the same, no work. Trying to find a job was humiliating. At the yard gates hundreds of men would wait each morning. . . . The unemployed got 10s. a week from the union for thirteen weeks and then it was reduced. My position became desperate.[124]

All he could find to do was hawking tickets in a lottery: 'The whole thing revolted me, and I had the feeling of being degraded'. Back at shipyard work in 1903 and now married, he again lost his job when the order books became thin: he was by now a local Committee member of the Amalgamated Society of Carpenters and Joiners, and active in Dundee politics: 'When the pay-offs came, I was one of the first to go, as was usual for shop delegates'.[125]

Victimization, real or imagined, becomes a frequent theme of autobiographers in this period, often resulting in militant political activity. Other building craftsmen who, like Walter Hannington's bricklayer father, who suffered long periods of unemployment between 1901 and 1911 but refused to take jobs at lower than the agreed union rates, made sure that their sons did not follow them in such an uncertain trade. When Walter left school in 1910, 'Unemployment was still present in the building trade, so my father decided, as he had done previously with two of my older brothers, that I must seek employment elsewhere'.[126] Walter was apprenticed as an engineer.

In fact, if security was the object, this would have been an unwise choice, since engineering and its allied metal and shipbuilding trades had higher rates of unemployment than almost any other. As these trades produced the materials for manufacturing industry and transport, they were particularly affected by periods of depression, when potential purchasers at home or overseas were generally unwilling to extend their plans for a doubtful future. The group of engineering, shipbuilding and metal trade unions had particularly bad years in 1879 (15.3 per cent unemployment), 1884–7 (always over 10 per cent), 1893–4 (over 11 per cent) and 1908–9 (over 12 per cent):[127] in the single year 1908, from the middle of August until the end of the year it rose to over 16 per cent, while in shipbuilding alone it reached more than 25 per cent.[128] These figures refer to the percentage of workers who were unemployed at the same time, but as Beveridge pointed out considerably higher percentages were unemployed at some time within a year. Statistics compiled by the Amalgamated Society of Engineers gave 8.1 per cent as the average unemployment at the same time in 1887, but 39.5 per cent of members were unemployed at some time in that year for an average of sixty-two days: over a nine-year period, 1887–95, an average of 29.7 per cent of members were unemployed at some time for an average of 63.1 days a year – the highest 117.8 days in 1893.[129] The fact that between one- and two-fifths of all members could expect to be out of work for an average of ten weeks in the year throws a much gloomier light on what were already sombre statistics. Unemployment was also regionally differentiated, London and the south-east having consistently lower than average rates while its incidence progressively increased through the Midlands, Yorkshire and Humberside, Lancashire, Tyneside and Scotland.[130]

George Barnes described the early 1870s as 'the heyday of London engineering', though its fortunes were to decline after 'the black year', 1879.[131] After completing his apprenticeship in Dundee and a couple of years at Vickers' shipyard in Barrow-in-Furness, 'I was restless and wanted to see more of the world': he moved to London in that unfortunate year to find no work.

> I faced the winter as one of London's unemployed. And then began for me the hardest struggle of my life, a real struggle for existence. . . . I had to get work, and I laid myself out to get it. But it was a weary job. . . . From my lodgings in Sadlers Wells I have set out day after day with no better guidance than the advertisements in the *Clerkenwell News*, subsequently expanded into the *Daily Chronicle* – which was the best advertising medium of the London dailies. I acquired a knowledge of London which, like Sam Weller's, was extensive and peculiar, for I knew every engineering workshop from Thorneycroft's of Chiswick to Vicker's of Erith. . . . That was the condition of things in my unemployed days. The unemployed were ignored except when vociferous as well as numerous, and even then the general view was that they were a lot of wastrels.[132]

After ten weeks he found work for a fortnight but then was out again.

W. F. Watson, who described himself as an 'Itinerant Mechanic', was born in 1881 in London and had eight different jobs by the age of eighteen: his parents had not been able to afford a premium of £40 and he remained unapprenticed. Towards the end of the century 'The industry was torn with dissension over the manning of machines, piecework and overtime, and the widespread agitation for an eight-hour day was rapidly approaching a crisis'.[133] Watson was frequently unemployed because of labour disputes such as the eight-hour day strike of 1897, and experienced much hostility from the craftsmen when he worked on the new American capstan lathes 'producing more crank bolts in a day than two turners could make in a week'. Between 1896 and 1914 he had at least fifteen different jobs, some only for a week or a month, the longest for three-and-a-half years: jobs usually terminated when the firm dismissed men when short of orders, sometimes because of rows with foremen over working conditions or because he refused to accept less than union rates. Watson became a union militant and known agitator, which probably accounted for some of his dismissals. 'Loss of character' could seriously restrict chances of employment, and even in London the engineering world was small enough for a man's reputation to be widely known. At Howdens engineering works in Glasgow, where Harry McShane began his apprenticeship in 1907, he found a different sort of discrimination, as freemasonry was strong in the firm:

> The freemasons were often members of the union, the Amalgamated Society of Engineers. They escaped unemployment because they were in with the management, whereas the socialists were always the first to be paid off. In a place like Howdens there would be six or nine months' work followed by a slack period. The foreman used to go round quietly on a Friday night to the men he was going to pay off. We watched him; each man would keep his back turned, hoping he would pass by, but the men he stopped at were the ILP members and the other Socialists. They were good, skilled workers, and when trade was busy they would be taken on again, but at the next pay-off it would be they who went first again.[134]

In terms of wage levels and social status printers and compositors had always stood very near the top of the craft hierarchy. Strongly unionized, the London Society of Compositors had been able to resist damaging changes in the past, but from the 1870s printing firms were beginning to move out of the capital to employ cheaper provincial labour less resistant to new work practices: this became particularly pronounced in the 1890s with the introduction of the new composing machines, especially the linotype, which were causing displacement of hand compositors. Activists in the Unemployed Chapel successfully pressed for restrictions, including a reduction in the ratio of apprentices from one to three to one to six, and strongly supported the movement for a forty-eight hour week: after a strike in 1911 a fifty-hour week was gained.[135] But the technological difficulties only added to the existing problems of a trade which always fluctuated with the state of the economy and with seasonal, local factors such as the sittings of Parliament and the lawcourts. The year 1879 was a particularly bad year for printing, as for other trades; 1885 another bad one, when the London Society of Compositors reported to the Royal Commission on the Depression of Trade that one-fifth of its members were more or less unemployed during the year.[136] In 1899 there were 2,166 claimants for union relief out of the membership of 11,415, in 1908 1,509, but the proportion of unemployment fluctuated widely from around 2 per cent in a good year to 10 per cent in a bad one.[137] The Society provided a range of reliefs – static pay of 10s. a week for six weeks in each quarter, a travel grant rising to 55s. after five years' membership, an emigration grant of £15, and a tramping allowance, which continued in this union as late as 1913. The 'tramping comp' was almost a distinct group in the trade, partly composed of 'unfree' single men who, with less than a year's membership, did not qualify for static pay, partly of those who for a variety of personal reasons, preferred an unsettled life: numbers on the road probably peaked in 1879, when tramping printers were paid for 336,000 miles, equivalent to fourteen times round the world,[138] though they remained a common feature of the trade down to the outbreak of war. As with other unions, the percentage of printers out of work at the same time gives little indication of the number who experienced it at some time in the course of a year. For the ten-year period 1894–1903 the average unemployment rate in the London Society of Compositors was 4.3 per cent, but the proportion of members claiming benefit at some time in the course of a year was 20.9 per cent:[139] among those drawing benefit the average time unemployed was fifty-two days in 1898 and seventy-one days in 1902.[140]

Autobiographers of the period make frequent reference to tramping comps who had learned by experience where seasonal work was to be had on county directories, voters' lists and the like. As an apprentice in Colchester at the turn of the century Paul Evett found that 'During the summer months itinerant comps would call in on us, sometimes for a whip round to help them on their way from London to Bungay or Beccles, some selling books, setting rules, sticks, type-gauges, etc.' Having served his time, Evett was not offered full journeyman's rates, and decided to join the travellers. 'Now I had made up my mind that, as I was always likely to remain poor as a compositor, I would in very deed be a journeyman, and stay in one job no longer than about two years, and so see as much of England as I could in this way. I was very fond of cycling, and I loved the country.'[141] Between 1907 and 1912 he worked in Colchester, Clacton, Ware, Portsmouth, Warwick, Newport, Chatham and St Albans, sometimes moving from choice, sometimes from necessity when jobs came to an end: as a member of the Typographical Association (TA) he was sometimes refused work by non-union shops but at other times was found work by the local TA secretaries. In his youth, George Rowles 'worked in all sorts of offices in all sorts of places, and although I was not actually a tramp printer I met and worked with many who came into that class'.[142] Rowles believed that it was not only unemployment that put a printer on the road, but also 'wanderlust, loss of pride through drink, resentment of authority, unhappy marriage, inability to cope with life and trying to find the way out. It was difficult to get out of the groove once in'.[143] The saddest cases were the non-unionists, who had no relief except the poor law, because in addition to their other benefits, unemployed trade unionists could 'have the organ' – 'Most Chapels had mutual loan clubs, the official of which was an elected "Organ Master". Members paid a weekly subscription and could borrow money and pay a little interest weekly on it'.

The furnishing and woodworking trades also suffered from seasonality, and to a greater extent than almost any other. Averaged over the years 1897–1906, unemployment in December and January stood at 7.5 per cent compared with 2.4 per cent in April and May, a range of three-and-a-half times:[144] again, many more men were unemployed at some time during a year than at the same time, the former figure for millsawyers and woodcutting machinists rising to 26 per cent over the decade 1894–1903.[145] In Lancashire at the end of November 1908, 13 per cent of workers in the furnishing trades were unemployed and 10.9 per cent of coach-builders, while at the end of January 1909 the figures were 13.9 and 9 per cent respectively.[146] The experiences of autobiographers confirm the uncertainties of employment in these trades. As a young cabinet-maker in London in the 1890s, George Acorn heard that 'On the following Saturday I was told to "pack up" at the workshop as trade was too quiet for my employer to keep me employed. Of course, I was dejected, but went out on the following Monday morning full of the hope that something would turn up'. His main source of information was advertisements in ironmongers' shop-windows, who apparently posted vacancies in any trade: 'I tramped to the ends of London answering advertisements, but they were always "suited" if, indeed, they had ever wanted anybody. I firmly believe that many firms advertise for hands simply to pretend they are busy. . . . Day by day my nerves became more tense and strained'.[147]

Although apprentices were usually the last to be dismissed since they represented cheap labour, this was not always the case, as Bill Elliott found at the Wolverton Railway Works where he was serving his time as a coach-builder about 1900: 'There were a hundred apprentices sacked out of the Works one week, and another 250 some weeks afterwards. I was in the 250, that was when the Railway Companies were doing badly'.[148]

He was taken on again when work became busy. Herbert Hodge's parents in London at the turn of the century had 'a hard time of it'.

> Dad was an upholsterer, and a good one. When he was working he sometimes earned as much as two pounds a week. The trouble was, he so often wasn't. He had been unemployed all through my gestation. Mother had lived, so she told me, mainly on porridge, and filled in the hungry intervals with beautiful thoughts so that her baby might be beautiful. (She must have been disappointed in the result. I was rickety.)[149]

One of the few trades in which the usual seasonal pattern was reversed was piano-making, which had its busiest demand in winter followed by summer slackness. Frank Goss's father, a skilled piano-action and piano-case maker, had frequent spells of summer unemployment in London at the end of the century, but one day in the spring of 1902 he was sacked earlier than usual. He announced:

> It's never been quite like this before. Before, there has always seemed a chance of getting in somewhere. Getting out of work was only for a week or two, or at most a couple of months. But it's not like that now. I could name a dozen of my pals who were out all last winter: now I've joined them. We have always had work in the winter before. Once out now, you can't get in anywhere.
>
> This was the beginning of our second period of dire poverty. Poverty in itself is bad enough, but while you survive and have hope it is endurable; it is despair that destroys the fibre of a man. To see the bones and structure of life disintegrate, to feel the patterns and habits of living, in which the future has been envisaged as a procession of normalities, destroyed, and replaced by a living fear of greater and greater destitution and want, becomes an interminable progress into a greater hopelessness that surely breaks the spirit.[150]

In some industries fluctuations in demand, whether caused by seasonal or cyclical factors, were often met by short-time for all workers rather than dismissals for some. This was common in the cotton industry, which Chapman and Hallsworth in their study of unemployment in Lancashire believed 'is a form to be encouraged, since thereby the adversity associated with business depression is spread over the whole trade. Low wages for the many are certainly better than no wages for the few': they estimated that in the bad year 1908 a contraction of output of 13.3 per cent was met by 5 per cent dismissals and 8.7 per cent short time.[151] Coalmining experienced regular seasonal fluctuations – a heavy demand in winter and slackness in summer, usually met by varying the number of shifts worked per week: over the period 1897–1906 the average number of days worked per week was 5.46 in December and 4.93 in June,[152] though some collieries worked only three or four days at this time, with conse-quent reductions of pay. But in all trades employers always had the option to dismiss workers in times of real or alleged depression, and at this point a range of personal, 'character' factors came into play. Unpunctuality, insubordination, heavy drinking and advancing age were often given as the reasons for inefficiency, but in this period it becomes clear that trade union militancy was frequently the real reason for dismissing men who were troublesome and potentially disturbing to existing work practices and wage rates. Thomas Williams, a Yorkshire miner, was sacked in 1912 for complaining about having to wait for empty tubs, which thereby reduced his piece-work earnings: he declined the union's offer of victimiz-ation pay because his name would have been circulated as a trouble-maker to every pit in the county.[153] 'Bronterre' Emsley, a Yorkshire spinner, was frequently sacked for bad behaviour and disagreeing with the manage-ment, emigrating to Belgium and twice to Canada and America but eventually returning to open his own business as a photographer.[154] Many men of ability who could not accept the conditions and insecurity of waged labour, and wished to change them, moved into positions in trade unions or politics, as we have seen: others found escape in self-employ-ment or by immersing themselves in religion, Socialism or attempts at writing. Frederick Parkin, a skilled pottery worker, was constantly dis-missed for his activities at a time when many Staffordshire firms refused to employ trade unionists: the reason given was always 'shortage of work'. After repeated sackings when his union pay ran out, Parkin found himself 'on the slippery slope to semi-starvation'. He became a pedlar and part-time gardener, and did not return to the pottery trade until the outbreak of the Second World War.[155]

RESPONSES AND REMEDIES

What was new in this period was the development of forms of state provision for the unemployed outside the poor law – a recognition that unemployment was a national, industrial problem rather than an indi-vidual, moral one, and that it was no longer acceptable to condemn its victims to the workhouse and the principles of 'less eligibility'. But most unemployed people still looked to public provision last rather than first. The immediate responses to unemployment remained as they had in the past – to search for work and to try to raise enough money to survive a period of uncertain length. Any savings which such families had went first, and it seems that some workers in seasonal trades did their best to save against the slack season: an immigrant Polish tailor records that 'As it was a seasonal business, in fact only eight months in the year gave full employment, it was necessary to work exceedingly hard in order to save for the slack periods which were not paid for'.[156] Members of trade unions were, of course, more fortunate in being able to draw tramping allowances or, more usually now, 'static' pay or 'donation', the amount varying with length of membership, but typically around 8s. to 10s. a week at the end of the century. Also, in the engineering and some other trades, 'Trade union club-houses served as employment exchanges ... The landlord of the pub was the Branch Treasurer. He had charge of the vacant book, paid members their donation benefit on Friday ... when a working member knew of a vacancy, he put a note in the book, and members discussed who should go after it. Foremen and managers in need of mechanics inquired in the shop'.[157]

This was a somewhat idealized account. Club houses no doubt helped with frictional unemployment but were virtually powerless in times of general depression: the unemployment donation normally ceased after thirteen weeks, and even skilled workers were forced to look outside their trades for anything that would bring in a few shillings, however degrading. In some rare instances, wealthy individuals supported the union's funds at such times as a Staffordshire potter discovered:

> Unemployment caused a great drain on the Society's funds. The present generation of potters have probably never heard of a lady named Miss Bennet. She was a real benefactor, and many workers whose union benefits had become exhausted received from Mr. S. Clowes vouchers for groceries, etc. ... Miss Bennet defrayed the cost, placing cheques of £50 at his disposal from time to time.[158]

Non-unionists, the overwhelming majority of the working class throughout the period, had no such support. For them, the first recourse was always the family – the earnings of wives at washing, charring, sweated homework or seasonal factory work, and of children as errand-boys, milk-boys, lather-boys, step-girls and baby-minders before and after school or as young, full-time workers. It has been estimated that even in normal times as many as 48 per cent of all manual workers were dependent on women's earnings,[159] and at times of crisis these could become the principal or sole support: especially in the casual trades such as London dock-work it was normal for wives to tide over the uncertainties with work in the sweated industries. Relatives, friends and neighbours came next in the order of informal support networks. Whether the poor helped each other from natural generosity or as an insurance against their own future needs is uncertain, but it is clear that the local community was often the major support at times of need, and one of the reasons why the poor in inner cities remained so immobile. Few can have been more generous than Mrs Jacobs of Cambridge Heath who worked at home at boot-sewing. When Walter Southgate's father was unemployed and no more credit was available:

I remember the broker's men in our own front parlour, considered by every respectable working-class family as the holy of holies. My parents never looked upon poverty as a crime or as something to be ashamed of, neither did they adopt all sorts of subterfuge to make others think they were different to what they really were, poor, and the victims of a bad economic system. The presence of those bailiffs in our own front parlour was, in my youthful eyes however, a visit of men from the dark regions. They sat there in our parlour smoking their clay pipes and drinking beer from a tin can. . . . My mother would be busy going round to various neighbours, almost as poor as ourselves, for temporary small loans to save the bits and pieces of furniture that had been earmarked by the broker's men for removal at sundown.

It was Mrs. Jacobs, who lived in North Street, who came to the rescue, as she had done on other occasions. She had no money readily available, but such was her natural disposition to help, she had no hesitation in taking off her gold wedding ring, saying to mother, "'Ere you are Liz, pawn it and get it out Sat'day'.[160]

The extent of credit, whether from friends and neighbours, from the local 'community shop', the pawnshop or the landlord, was vast and mentioned by almost all autobiographers who experienced unemployment. Shop credit was usually short term, but, as Booth found, could be long term from winter to summer for known, reliable customers. The number of pawnbrokers in Britain rose steadily to an all-time peak of 5,087 in 1914: it is estimated that each London pawnbroker took an average of 60,000 pledges a year, provincial brokers 40,000, equivalent to at least one pledge a fortnight for every family in the country.[161] For those who regularly pawned the frequency was, of course, greater still, and for many the pawning of Sunday clothes was a regular Monday occurrence even in 'normal' times: in distress, other clothes, boots and shoes, bedding, ornaments and small articles of furniture all went the same way. The working-class economy at the lower end was always frail and precarious, the line between respectability and destitution easily broken by a spell of unemployment, an illness, a death or another birth. In 1911, when the first National Insurance Act was being debated, the average adult working-class assets per head were estimated at a mere £11 2s. 0d., and Lloyd George believed that 'not a tenth of the working-classes have made any provision at all' against unemployment.

In these circumstances pawning and short-term borrowing from the unlicensed 'dolly' shop at the exorbitant rate of 1d. a day for a shilling, afforded life-support systems which could be manipulated with financial wizardry by the cognoscenti. Rose Gamble describes how her mother, with no home and no money, set about raising the 6s. advance rent required for new lodgings. She first borrowed 1s. from the street money-lender: with this, she obtained a pair of sheets at 15s. from the credit draper, immediately pawning them for 7s. 6d.: the rent was then paid, the money-lender repaid, and 5d. was left over. There was, of course, then 1s. a week to be repaid for the sheets.[162] Local publicans were often involved in credit relations, running savings clubs of various kinds and organizing Benefit Nights of entertainment to raise money for unemployed or sick regulars. But the inevitable response to a lengthy period of unemployment was to run up credit to the maximum possible and to cut down on food, always the major item of expenditure, to the minimum consistent with survival. When Frank Goss's father, the piano-maker, was unemployed, furniture went to the pawnshop, food became 'scraps and scant purchases', the rent was unpaid, the milkman and grocer allowed some 'tick', friends rallied round, his mother took in washing, the children ran errands for the better-off houses and Mr Goss unsuccessfully tried selling sweets on the Lincolnshire beaches, having answered an advertisement which promised that 'For an outlay of 5s. you can earn 10s. a day: apply Bill's Boston Sweeteries, Boston, Lincs'.[163] In Lambeth around 1910, Mrs Pember Reeves discovered an unemployed family of husband, wife and five children surviving on a budget of 5s. 5d. a week, another, with only one child, on 2s. 6d. a week: in these cases, the children had free school meals in term-time, but at home the families were existing on 1¼d. or 1½d. a day per head for food.[164] In households like this bread was the staple, often the only food, made more palatable by whatever 'relishes' of jam, margarine or dripping could be afforded and washed down with cheap tea. In their study of the diets of eight unemployed families in York in 1910 Rowntree and Lasker found that the energy value varied from 1,086 calories per man per day in the worst fed to 2,374 in the best fed, when the amount required for 'physical efficiency' was 3,500: protein ranged from 39 to 74 gms. a day, compared with the required 125 gms. In short, some families were existing on only a third of the food required for efficiency, and none on more than two-thirds: the authors pointed to the 'physical deterioration following on unemployment', especially when long-continued.[165]

Temporary unemployment might occasionally act as a spur to activity and ambition, a determination to overcome difficulties by a change in the direction of one's life. James Turner, an unemployed Yorkshire carter in the early 1880s, tried to emigrate but could not raise the £10 passage for his family of three: believing fervently in self-education, he joined the YMCA, tried to learn shorthand and French, persuaded a friend to teach him tapestry weaving and eventually got factory work at £1 10s. 0d. a week.[166] But extended unemployment and the trauma of constant rejection, coupled with a debilitating diet, gradually produced psychological as well as physical effects. A Charity Organisation Committee was told by an employer in 1886 that, 'if he [an artisan] happens to be out of work for three months, he is never the same man again. He becomes demoralised',[167] and the same point is made by Joseph Stamper: 'Constant failure to get decent employment crushed my spirits. . . . I became as my associates, listless, apathetic. . . . Ambition ceased to exist'.[168] Poverty and unemployment were so closely linked that it is virtually impossible to separate the particular effects of each. As previously noted, Booth had calculated that 51 per cent of the poverty of Classes A and B was caused by casual and irregular earnings, and 43 per cent of that in Classes C and D, estimates endorsed in a survey by Squire and Steel-Maitland in 1907 which found the major cause of pauperism to be 'casual and irregular employment'.[169] But extended unemployment could have effects in some ways distinct from those of poverty in general; it could deprive a man of what Victorian values regarded as responsibility to work, could ultimately destroy his will to labour and so render him unemployable. Most commentators in the period still found it difficult to accept this, and while admitting that unemployment might be a primarily industrial problem – even an industrial 'disease' as Beveridge put it – continued to believe that many of its victims were the result of 'character' deficiencies or physical or mental disability.

This assumption that many, if not most, of the unemployed were at best the 'inefficients' of society or, at worst, idlers, loafers, charity-seekers and semi-criminals, powerfully influenced the forms of public relief devised during this period. Those of this persuasion seemed to have their views confirmed by the fact that such men no longer hid themselves away but paraded their poverty and their demands in public processions, often led by agitators and Socialists. The organization of the unemployed to demand relief and the Right to Work was a new phenomenon, the first, perhaps, the Trafalgar Square demonstration in 1870 at which leaders of the Land and Labour League argued for nationalization of the land and the establishment of home colonies.[170] From the 1880s onwards such demonstrations became frequent and widespread in practically every town, large or small. In Portsmouth the unemployed marchers were 'more threatening to the public than diphtheria or scarlet fever';[171] in Walworth they chanted 'Eight hours work. Eight hours play. Eight hours sleep and Eight bob a day' and were condemned by local residents as 'greedy agitators';[172] in some towns the unemployed paraded to Church, as the Chartists had done half a century earlier, to demonstrate their distress,[173] and in Tottenham the marchers sang, 'We have got no work to do. We have got no work to do. We're all froze out, poor labouring men. We have got no work to do', but after collecting what money they could from passers-by, quenched their thirsts at the Bell and Hare or the Spotted Dog.[174] During his residence in Hastings, Robert Noonan (Tressell) observed well-organized marches of up to 400 men, accompanied by police escorts, but believed that 'the majority of the men belonged to what is called the unskilled labour class. The skilled artisan does not, as a rule, take part in such a procession'.[175] Nevertheless, the unemployed demonstrations generally had important effects both in raising the collective consciousness of the unemployed themselves and in contributing to force the issue on to the political agenda. In Glasgow in 1908 Harry McShane witnessed mass demonstrations in George Square every week until the magistrates banned them, but 'A large number of socialists became involved in the fight for the unemployed. . . . The agitation transformed the labour movement in Glasgow. A number of new people joined the different socialist organisations. Many ILP and SDF members had not been unemployed, but they had been affected by the agitation'.[176]

Whether through fear or compassion, from a wish to contain unrest and maintain social stability or to respond to what was now an enfranchised working class beginning to flex its political muscle, the public responses to unemployment took on a new scale and direction in this period.[177] Social policy is always a compound of philanthropic and instrumental motives having political, social or economic foundations, and the precise ratio of these elements is not discoverable. It is certain, however, that the recognition of widespread unemployment at this time aroused much public sympathy, which initially responded in the traditional form of charity. Especially in London, considerable sums were raised by special public appeals, beginning with the Lord Mayor's Mansion House Fund of 1886 which raised £78,629: these were repeated in 1892–5, 1903–4, 1904–5, (£51,904) and 1905–6 (£63,455). The first produced what Beveridge described as 'an orgie of relief'. Although the intention was not to relieve chronic poverty but to direct assistance to acute cases suffering from the winter's unemployment, administration of the fund largely broke down into handouts of small doles to almost all applicants. The 1903–4 scheme was quite different, establishing two farm 'colonies' outside London at which applicants were required to work as a 'test' of their genuineness: their families were maintained at home, the men being allowed to visit once a fortnight or once a month. This 'device of rustication' ended in 1904, by which time it was found that only 26 per cent of the colonists had recovered 'more or less regular employment'. Under the scheme of 1904–5, initiated by the Local Government Board, some 3,500 men were employed on relief works in parks and gardens or on farm colonies, one of which was run by the Salvation Army at Hadleigh, only a tiny proportion of the 46,000 who had applied for relief.[178]

In provincial towns charitable responses followed a similar pattern, though at a lower level of resource and usually with even less well-planned remedies. Thus in Sheffield, relief funds were opened in 1878–9, 1884–5 and 1893–5 and Distress Committees were presided over by the Lord Mayor in 1902 and 1903. Under pressure from the Trades Council, on which the trade unions were strongly represented, the city's Works Construction Department in 1904 found temporary employment for 1,200 men, mainly on roadworks, and between 1908 and 1910 the Council spent £80,000 on relief works. Large as this was, it had little impact on what was mass unemployment in the city at this time: of 14,000 unemployed, only 7,000 were on the Register, and only half of these were provided with short spells of work.[179] On many occasions, voluntary soup-kitchens were opened, with free distribution of bread and soup to children. In a very different town, Hastings, relief followed a similar pattern in the depressed years 1902–10. Here there were as many as six soup-kitchens, a Mayor's Appeal in 1904 and a Distress Committee which provided three days' work a fortnight for the unemployed: additionally, the local Charity Organisation Society received almost 2,000 applications for assistance each year, relieving 1,284 in 1906, mainly with bread, grocery and coal orders to a maximum of 5s. weekly.[180] The COS strongly condemned the indiscriminate almsgiving of the early Mansion House Appeals, and attempted to discriminate between the 'helpable', deserving applicants and the 'undeserving' who were refused relief, usually on the grounds of moral failings. The Salvation Army, on the other hand, never refused relief, but developed its own policies aimed at regenerating the physical and moral fitness of the unemployed. This was to be achieved by progressing him through a series of 'elevators', beginning at Food and Shelter Depots and moving through City Colonies where workshops and labour yards were provided to farm colonies which would be self-supporting, co-operative communities. Some would settle permanently here, but the majority would pass, when fully trained, to overseas colonies arranged by the Emigration Bureau.[181] The Army's 'social salvation' schemes made a not insignificant contribution to the relief of unemployment, mainly through its Labour Bureaux: in the decade 1903–12 it found permanent or temporary work for not less than 12,000 applicants a year, rising to as many as 42,493 in the depression of 1908.[182]

The expansion of philanthropy in the late nineteenth century was in part a response by the propertied classes to fears of social and political unrest, but also a recognition that the main instrument of public relief, the poor law, was both inadequate and inappropriate for dealing with the scale and complexity of the unemployment problem. The Amendment Act of 1834 had intended that outdoor relief should be forbidden to the able-bodied, who would only be offered workhouse relief under conditions of 'less eligibility', but this had been abandoned as early as the severe depression of 1842 and thereafter the able-bodied never formed as much as 20 per cent of workhouse inmates: between 1886 and 1912 they only once exceeded a figure of 12,000,[183] due partly to even more rigorous conditions introduced by the Local Government Board after 1871. Up to 1914, therefore, the poor law made very limited provision for the unemployed. The offer of the workhouse was rarely accepted by respectable working men, involving as it usually did the break-up of the family and home. An alternative developed in this period was relief of the family outside the workhouse on condition that the head of the family entered the institution – the 'modified test workhouse'. This plan was initiated by the Charity Organisation Society at the Whitechapel Union and adopted by one or two others: it had some advantage in keeping the home together, but prevented the man from seeking other employment. Thirdly, most unions, especially in the cities, offered out-door relief subject to the performance of a 'labour test', usually stone-breaking or the unravelling of so much oakum per day. This form of relief had been allowed by the Outdoor Relief Regulation Order of 1852 provided that at least half the aid was given in food or fuel rather than cash and it continued to be used by Guardians at times of particular distress, when stoneyards would be opened. This kind of relief was, how-ever, much criticized. It was found that no specified task could be enforced: stoneyards attracted those other than the genuinely unem-ployed and the nature of the work tended to further demoralize those who applied. The stoneyards utterly failed to solve the problem common to all relief works of how to enforce work of a deterrent nature in return for an allowance at anything like the economic cost – in Southwark in the winter of 1895, for example, an average of 900 men were paid 3s. 6d. a day to break stones at a cost of £7 a ton, the market price of which was 12s.[184] A final remedy, used sparingly, was to grant outdoor relief without a labour test. This discretionary power of the Guardians, which flew directly in the face of the principles of 1834, was specifically permit-ted by the Order of 1852 in cases of 'sudden and urgent necessity', a phrase which led to much controversy and uneven application. The extreme instance of its use, or abuse, was the case of the Poplar Guardians who, under the leadership of the Socialist George Lansbury, granted outdoor relief to virtually all applicants without investigation and without any labour test in the winter of 1904–5. This episode, which achieved notoriety in poor law history, partly explains the maximum figure of 7,872 able-bodied persons relieved outside the workhouse in 1905 on account of unemployment: normally before 1914 the figure ranged from 1,000 to 4,000, a quite insignificant contribution to the problem.[185]

The poor law had, of course, never been designed or intended to deal with industrial unemployment on a large scale. What was new in this period was the development by the state and local municipalities of new forms of relief which would not attach the stigma of pauperism to the genuine unemployed. One deceptively obvious approach seemed to be to provide useful public works in return for a wage which would support a family but not be too high to attract idlers or deter a man from seeking better-paid employment. Following the exceptional distress of the winter of 1885–6, Joseph Chamberlain at the Local Government Board issued a circular urging Boards of Guardians to co-operate with local authorities to provide relief works 'on which unskilled labour may be immediately employed'. Government loans on favourable terms were offered as an inducement to authorities.[186] The circular went on to detail the kinds of work considered appropriate which would not compete with that of other labourers in employment – spade husbandry on sewage farms, laying out new cemeteries, recreation grounds, paving new streets and cleansing those not normally cleaned by the authorities. The circular was issued five times between 1886 and 1893, and in the words of Jose Harris was 'an almost complete failure'.[187] Local authorities usually had their own staff for such work, much of which was not suitable for winter employment anyway: the schemes failed to attract the artisans and respectable unemployed for whom they were intended, while most applicants were general labourers and the chronically underemployed: subsequent Conservative Presidents of the Local Government Board were unsympathetic and failed to make public funds available quickly enough. A few councils such as West Ham applied the provisions almost every winter, but even in the exceptional trade depression of 1892–3 only seventy-three authorities out of 673 provided relief works, giving employment to a mere 26,875 persons.[188]

Much the same criticisms applied to the more ambitious Unemployed Workmen Act of 1905, passed against a background of demonstrations and a mounting labour campaign for government action led by Keir Hardie and Will Crooks. The Act provided for the establishment of Distress Committees in all local authorities with populations greater than 50,000, the Committees to consist of Councillors, Poor Law Guardians and persons experienced in philanthropic work. After enquiring into their circumstances and the establishment of genuine need, unemployed applicants could be put to temporary relief work, could be assisted to emigrate or remove to another area, and local authorities could levy a rate of a halfpenny in the pound towards the costs of administration. The Act was primarily intended to co-ordinate and extend the relief activities of local authorities, the poor law and charities rather than to initiate radical schemes, though it did bring central government for the first time into the arena of unemployment policy. By 1906, eighty-nine provincial Distress Committees and twenty-nine Metropolitan Committees had been established, covering a population of 16,340,000 in England and Wales: by 31 March 1908, a total of £540,000 had been expended, approximately two-fifths from the rates, two-fifths from the Exchequer and the remainder from voluntary contributions. The Act remained in force until 1914: in the early years the number of applications for assistance varied between 90,000 and 110,000 a year, rising to a maximum of 197,000 in the depression of 1908–9 and then falling steadily to only

24,000 by 1913–14.[189] More than half the applicants were general or casual labourers and a further fifth building workers, so that the kind of relief work provided – almost always rough labouring on projects similar to those of the 1886 Circular – was reasonably appropriate for the majority though unsuitable for the relatively small numbers of skilled men: a few authorities leased land for cultivation, including the London Central Body which set up a farm colony at Hollesley Bay in Suffolk. In general, there was great difficulty in finding useful work, and the inefficiency of much of the labour meant that costs were often three times as much as normal labour: work was supplied for a maximum of sixteen weeks and very few men succeeded in finding permanent employment thereafter, mainly because the majority had never had permanent work for years previously. As an experiment to deal with exceptional distress caused by trade depressions outside the poor law – the original intention of the Act – it was a total failure: as a means of temporary relief to irregularly employed men who always lived on the edge of destitution, it was a modest palliative, though at a high cost and without providing any permanent cure.[190]

Two further measures complete the legislative provision for unemployment in the years before 1914. In 1909 the Labour Exchanges Act was passed, the creation of Winston Churchill at the Board of Trade and William Beveridge, the responsible civil servant. It reflected the latter's belief that organization of the labour market was the first step in the treatment of unemployment, that public Exchanges would reduce the wasteful 'hawking' of labour, the time and effort spent by workers seeking employment and employers seeking workers, and would bring greater mobility and efficiency into the labour market. The Act was put into operation with speed and efficiency, 414 Labour Exchanges being opened and staffed by the end of 1912. The vacancies filled by Exchanges rose from 1,400 a day in 1910 to 3,100 a day in the first half of 1914, while in the last full year of peace, 1913, 922,000 vacancies were filled out of 2,966,000 registrations.[191] The Act did not go so far as the Webbs wished by making registration of the unemployed compulsory, and it did not create a single extra job – the sarcastic comment of Arthur Henderson during the House of Commons' debate on unemployment in May 1909 that it was 'the right to work bill in penny numbers'[192] missed the point that it was merely a voluntary means by which workers and employers could be put in touch with each other on a nationwide scale. The large numbers using the Exchanges just before 1914, at a time when the general unemployment rate was low, indicates how successful the Act was in its main intention. In one respect, however, Beveridge had to admit its failure. The Minority Report of the Royal Commission on the Poor Laws in 1909 urged that Labour Exchanges should be used as a means of decasualizing labour and preventing chronic underemployment, especially in dockwork, but there was strong resistance to this in the docks from both employers and employees: here, the old methods of casual employment had certain advantages for both, and were to continue for many more years.

The other important measure sponsored by Churchill as 'the untrodden field' but again detailed by Beveridge and Llewellyn Smith, was unemployment insurance, introduced in 1911 as Part 2 of Lloyd George's 'ambulance wagon'. Workers in certain trades particularly subject to fluctuations – building, construction, shipbuilding, mechanical engineering, ironfounding, vehicle construction and sawmilling – were to be compulsorily insured against unemployment: they would pay 2½d. a week, their employer the same, and the state 1⅔d., which would provide benefits of 7s. a week for a maximum of fifteen weeks. It was a modest first step, initially covering only 2¼ million workers, but one on which a major structure was later to be built. It well illustrated Beveridge's firm belief in the insurance principle, based on a three-cornered contractual relationship which guaranteed benefits as of right, free from any taint of charity or the poor law, because they had been paid for. The newly established Labour Exchanges were responsible for registration of the insured workers and for payment of benefits. In one sense, of course, it was casual workers who most needed protection, but the actuarial basis for insuring them would have imposed impossible burdens: in fact, two-thirds of those insured by the Act were skilled workers not previously covered by trade union schemes. Given its limited extent, the 1911 Act was an immediate success, for even in the relatively prosperous year ended July 1914, 23 per cent of insured men claimed benefit[193] – an indication of how irregular employment was even for skilled workers in good times.

These measures went some way towards meeting the increasing pressure from trade union and Labour leaders for more positive policies towards what they regarded as the most pressing industrial problem of the age. Their proposals generally distinguished between 'palliatives' and more radical, longer-term remedies. Under the former, a revival of agriculture was often urged by Labour MPs such as G. N. Barnes, with improved wages, housing and availability of small-holdings to attract men back to the land:[194] afforestation schemes and land and foreshore reclamation were particularly advocated as adding to national resources. Labour 'colonies' were generally not approved, though Labour leaders were keen to distinguish the 'genuine' unemployed from 'loafers' and to accept that for the latter some degree of deterrent discipline was appropriate. Many continued to believe that properly organized relief works by local councils could absorb much unskilled labour (John Burns estimated as much as 200,000) if authorities would employ only minimum permanent staffs, restrict overtime and phase their work to give more winter employment,[195] but T. Good believed that the 'real' unemployed did not want pauperizing relief work, and that relief committees only came into contact with 'professional charity-hunters and expert whiners and wastrels'.[196] Other trade union proposals included shortening working hours to eight a day, work-sharing on the lines already practised in the cotton industry and coalmining and the restriction of boy labour by raising the school leaving age to fifteen followed by further specialized trade instruction.[197] The Eight Hour Day campaign had begun in the early eighties, initiated by the Social Democratic Federation and later supported by Keir Hardie, whose Parliamentary Bill of 1895 failed to pass.

More radical than these was the Right to Work campaign, first endorsed by the Independent Labour Party in 1895, but gaining strength after the end of the South African War in 1902 when depression returned. From this time marches and demonstrations were frequent occurrences in many towns, organized either by the National Committee on Unemployment, an ILP initiative, or the more militant SDF, and pressure for a Right to Work Bill mounted further after the General Election of 1906 and the return of twenty-nine Labour Party members. Introduced in 1907 it passed its first Reading with 116 votes, including a good many Liberal MPs, but in the deep depression of 1908 the campaign became more violent, with riots in Glasgow, Manchester, Sheffield and Nottingham and Hunger Marches in twenty Divisions of the Metropolitan Police. With this escalation of violence, the Labour Party abandoned its alliance with the SDF and the Right to Work campaign, turning its attention to the unemployment insurance proposals and the long-awaited report of the Poor Law Commission. The demand for a state guarantee of work at standard wages or maintenance at subsistence level which had dominated labour politics between 1904 and 1908, collapsed with its second Reading defeat by 267 votes to 118.[198]

The campaign was defused, or at least side-tracked, by the publication of the two (Majority and Minority) reports of the Royal Commission on the Poor Laws in February 1909. Even the Majority Report went further than many had expected in recommending the abolition of the Poor Law Unions and Boards of Guardians and the transfer of their functions to County Councils, the national adoption of Labour Exchanges, the extension of unemployment insurance to the unskilled and the establishment of local Public Assistance Committees to administer temporary relief to the 'necessitous unemployed' either by home assistance or by daily work in a Colony or Institution: for those who refused to work there should be Detention Colonies graded into three or four types of severity. It also advocated the spreading of work by employers in industries where demand was intermittent, raising the school leaving age to fifteen, and increased technical education for youths. The Minority Report, signed by four of the Commissioners including Beatrice Webb and largely written by her, went considerably further, receiving a warm welcome from the

Labour Party and almost all labour organizations except the SDF. Its broad proposal was for the break-up of the poor law and the replacement of 'The Framework of Repression' by 'The Framework of Prevention'. In respect of unemployment, it urged the creation of a Ministry of Labour to organize the national labour market, a reduction of working hours to thirty a week for those under eighteen, the withdrawal from industrial wage-earning of mothers of young children and the payment of 'termination dues' by employers of intermittent labour. It further recommended that the government should plan its public works over a ten-year period with the object of off-setting fluctuations and concentrating orders in 'lean years', and the systematic dovetailing of employment in seasonal trades: afforestation and foreshore reclamation schemes were specifically approved. Many of these suggestions had been common currency in the labour movement for up to twenty years previously, but what neither report endorsed was the right to work at standard wages: this was condemned as 'absolutely subversive of self-respect, self-exertion and independence, and ... detrimental to the industrial efficiency of the community'.[199] By this time, official labour opinion had dropped the issue anyway, and was happily digesting many good things in both reports. Only on unemployment insurance was there much disagreement. The Minority Report, under the influence of the Webbs, was opposed to a compulsory scheme: many in the labour movement were against a state-organized scheme of any kind, preferring the idea of government subsidies to the trade unions to extend their existing cover – a device known as the Ghent Scheme in use in some Continental countries. What transpired in 1911 was, as we have seen, the beginnings of a compulsory state scheme, which was to become the basis of national policy after the Great War. In the last year or two before that event economic recovery took some of the sting out of the unemployment issue, while further Liberal government measures, including Old Age Pensions, a Trade Boards Act regulating some of the sweated trades and a statutory eight-hour day and minimum wage for miners seemed to many to suggest that there were legislative solutions to social problems – given time, even to unemployment.

6

'THE WORST OF TIMES?' UNEMPLOYMENT BETWEEN THE WARS

THE CAUSES OF UNEMPLOYMENT

In *Unemployment: A Problem of Industry*, published in 1909, William Beveridge had written confidently about his diagnosis of the causes of unemployment and the remedies, if not the complete cure, for it. Twenty-one years later in 1930, and on the eve of the abyss which he only faintly sensed, he gloomily admitted that

> Unemployment in Britain since the war transcends in scale anything experienced in earlier years. Before the war the annual percentage of trade union members unemployed ranged from just under one to just over ten: the mean . . . from 1860 to 1914 is 4.5. . . . For the nine years from 1921 to 1929 the annual percentage unemployed in the insured population has ranged from a minimum of 9.7 in 1927 to a maximum of 16.9 in 1921, and has averaged 12.[1]

Much worse was to come, when after the Great Crash unemployment mounted to just under three million in 1932, a quarter of the insured workforce: over the whole period from 1921 to 1939 it averaged 14.7 per cent. The causes which Beveridge had identified before the war were still present: casual employment in the docks, the building trades and elsewhere had not diminished, seasonal unemployment was still widespread, public works were of limited value and the Labour Exchanges which he had largely created had failed to create jobs and had not had their expected effect of organizing the labour market. Cyclical and structural unemployment, the principal causes of the inter-war problem, received scant attention from Beveridge, and the newer, Keynesian theories were quickly dismissed: 'Organisation, not spending, [is needed]'.

From a longer perspective, the Great Depression, sudden and cataclysmic as it seemed at the time, can be traced back to flaws in the British economy which had already developed in the late Victorian and Edwardian periods. On the surface, Britain in 1914 was still a highly prosperous industrial society, a great exporter of capital and consumer goods, the

199

major centre of international finance and the heart of the greatest empire the world had ever known. The shipyards of the north-east coast alone produced one-third of the world's output: Britain was the second largest coal producer in the world, and the British merchant fleet amounted to half the world's tonnage.[2] But Britain was no longer the world leader she had been in 1870 when she had a one-third share of total world trade: by 1913 this had fallen to one-seventh, and more recently industrialized countries, especially Germany and the United States, had overtaken her in a number of fields. The British economy was narrowly based on the staple industries which had given her predominance in the earlier nineteenth century – textiles, coal, iron and steel and shipbuilding – but she had been slow to adopt later, more efficient processes in these, and slow to diversify into new industries such as electrical engineering and chemicals which other countries were developing apace. Technical retardation, inadequate domestic investment and a low rate of economic growth were all characteristics of the Edwardian economy, though masked by Britain's creditor position and substantial receipts on invisible exports. With labour plentiful and cheap, it did not seem necessary to invest in labour-saving automatic looms or mechanical coal-cutters, or to develop technical education and training beyond the traditional method of craft apprenticeship. If many of Britain's industrial leaders had grown complacent, some had perhaps acquired a distaste, even contempt, for the grittier aspects of entrepreneurship.[3]

The outbreak of war in August 1914 produced an almost immediate demand for extra labour of all kinds, so much so that after the first ten weeks involuntary unemployment was 'practically banished from the land for the duration of the War'[4]: by 1916 unemployment among trade union members was less than 0.5 per cent, the lowest on record.[5] A great stimulus was given to all industries which bore, directly or indirectly, on the war effort – munitions, engineering, chemicals, iron and steel, shipbuilding, textiles, vehicles, aircraft and agriculture: wartime demands produced what Beveridge described as an 'anomalous growth' so that some industries became 'bloated beyond any possible peacetime needs'.[6] At the same time, however, the war dislocated international trade and export markets on which the British economy had been so dependent, and increased the National Debt tenfold, reversing Britain's position to that of a debtor nation. In volume terms, British exports in 1918 were 63 per cent less than in 1913: there were particularly heavy losses to the Far East, Canada, America and Australia where the United States and Japan had been able to move in to former British markets.

For a brief period after the Armistice in November 1918 it seemed that economic conditions might return not only to pre-war 'normalcy' but to an even better Golden Age long past. A speculative boom lasted for about fifteen months, aided by a pent-up demand for consumer goods, rising prices and heavy investment in the cotton industry, shipbuilding and engineering. The collapse, beginning in the spring of 1920, was rapid and unexpected, caused by over-speculation and a loss of business confidence, a rise in bank rate and cuts in government expenditure: industrial production, which had grown 10.2 per cent in 1918–19 and 11.1 per cent in 1919–20, now fell by 18.6 per cent in 1920–1[7] while a decline in exports reflected disturbed conditions in many foreign markets. By 1921 unemployment suddenly leapt to 1,840,000, 17 per cent of insured workers: when those not covered by insurance (workers aged fourteen to sixteen, agricultural workers, indoor domestic servants and non-manual workers earning more than £250 per annum) are added, it is estimated that the true figure of unemployed was 2,212,000.[8] In 1922 cotton exports were less than half those of 1913 and coal exports only one-third: 'the long weekend' of mass unemployment had begun, and despite some ups and downs in the economy, was never interrupted by a wholesale return to work: in 1927, the best of the inter-war years, unemployment was still twice as high as the pre-war average.

The general course of the depression which followed is well known, though its causes have been the subject of debate ever since. After the slump of 1921 the economy revived somewhat in the mid-twenties, though at the peak of this recovery in 1929 exports were only 80 per cent of the 1913 volume: then, Britain shared in the world depression of 1929–32 when European and American markets collapsed after the Wall Street Crash, and primary producing countries reduced their demands because of lack of purchasing power. In 1932 British exports fell to 50 per cent of 1913, and unemployment rose to 22 per cent, 2,828,000 insured persons or an estimated 3,400,000 of the total workforce. Thereafter, some recovery based on the home market occurred, peaking in 1937, but was followed by another downturn in 1938 which was only halted by the outbreak of war in September 1939.[9]

The paradox of these two decades is that against the background of appalling levels of unemployment, declining world markets and derelict areas of industrial Britain, some parts of the economy prospered and those people fortunate enough to stay in work experienced a substantial rise in real wages and improvement in living standards. Since the fundamental problem was a structural decline in Britain's basic industries, and those industries were mainly localized in certain 'special' areas (south Wales, the north-east coast, west Cumberland and Clydeside), it was always possible to think of the depression as exceptional, untypical of the general state of the country. For those in work these were unusually good years – more disposable income, shorter working hours, increased leisure provision, more and better houses – and it was easy, especially for those living south of the line from Bristol to the Wash, to ignore the problem of unemployment or, at least, to believe with Philip Snowden, the Labour

Chancellor of the Exchequer in 1924, that 'there is nothing we can do about it'.

Outside the depressed staple industries, optimists could point to substantial growth in the economy, especially in the newer industries of the Midlands and Greater London, based on electrical power and a prosperous home demand. Motor vehicles and cycles, chemicals and drugs, artificial fibres, tobacco and food trades, radio and electrical industries, not to mention entertainment industries and an unprecedented boom in house building in the 1930s, were evidence of the considerable success of the economy to adapt to new consumer demands, sufficient for some recent economic historians to view the inter-war period as one of overall growth. 'Certainly, there were black spots in the economy', but the 1920s can be seen as 'a period of real economic progress', while Britain's recovery from the world depression of 1929–32 'not only started earlier but was more persistent' than in other countries. The index of production (1925–9 average 100) fell from 111 in 1929 to ninety-two in 1931, but then rose to 147 by 1937, the number of people in employment increased from 10.2 million in 1932 to 11.5 million in 1937, while profits rose by 10 per cent and wages by 7 per cent over the same period.[10] Gross Domestic Product rose 1.8 per cent per annum between 1924 and 1937, more than twice as fast as between 1900 and 1914 and faster even than between 1855 and 1900.[11] Clearly, one's view of the inter-war period depended on where one stood geographically, occupationally and socially. For the eight or nine million people who depended on an ungenerous dole in the early thirties, these were unquestionably the worst of times: for the burgeoning lower middle classes buying their new semi-detached house on mortgage, running a Ford or baby Austin car and enjoying the radio, the cinema and paid holidays, they were probably the best to date.

In trying to account for the unprecedented levels of unemployment it was evident to contemporary observers that the automatic 'match' between the supply of and demand for labour which classical economists had assumed, had broken down. In the early months of peace it was easy to believe that the labour market was temporarily dislocated by the demobilization of five million men and the closure of many wartime industries, and that a natural adjustment to peacetime production would inevitably follow. Any such optimism was shaken by the slump of 1921 and the continued fall in exports. By the mid-twenties explanations tended to concentrate on Britain's lack of competitiveness and high prices, especially after the return to the Gold Standard in 1925 at the pre-war conversion rate of $4.86, which Keynes and others believed over-valued the pound by 10 per cent. Beveridge considered that the war and brief post-war boom had led to the excessive development of some industries such as shipbuilding, coal and cotton, and a permanent surplus capacity in these in relation to a shrinking world demand and intense foreign competition, quoting with approval the report of the Industrial Transference Board in 1928 that 'The idea of a cyclical or transient depression must now be recognised quite unflinchingly as no longer tenable'.[12] The leading economist, Pigou, argued that a main problem was too high a level of wages, which had not declined in line with the deflation of the 1920s because of the greater power of labour organizations since the war: as there had not been an equivalent increase in productivity, the unit cost of labour was now one-sixth greater than pre-war, and Britain was bound to lose many of her former markets in the face of cheap-labour Japanese cotton, subsidized Polish coal and high tariff barriers in many other countries.

Most economists of the day therefore stressed the centrality of long-term structural factors as against the traditional cyclical, seasonal, frictional and personal explanations of unemployment. Beyond this, however, there was a wide gulf between the classical school which favoured cost-reduction and tight budgetary control and the few Keynesians who argued for an increase in aggregate demand to reflate the economy by government investment. In this debate, the effects of unemployment relief on wage levels became and have continued to be a highly contentious issue. Many contemporaries, including Beveridge, believed that the adoption of unlimited (in time) unemployment relief after 1921 strengthened the bargaining power of trade unions by, in effect, stopping undercutting and preventing a downward drag of wages which would have been normal in a period of falling prices. Criticisms reminiscent of those levelled at the Speenhamland System were again current a hundred years later – that allowances to the unemployed introduced rigidities and lack of mobility into the labour market and that the insurance rules helped to 'crystallize' casual labour by allowing men who worked only one day a week to draw benefit continuously.[13]

Recent writers of the 'new classical' school of economics have tended to return to this explanation of mass unemployment, and Benjamin and Kochin have gone so far as to see the unemployed as 'willing volunteers' attracted by generous benefits.

> The late 'twenties and 'thirties were characterised by high and rising real income, and the high unemployment at those times was the consequence almost solely of the dole. The army of the unemployed . . . was largely a volunteer army.[14]

The substantially lower rates of unemployment among women and juveniles, who were not insured workers, is cited as evidence for this assertion, but despite a good deal of hearsay accusation of 'malingering', numerous official investigations into the effects of unemployment relief constantly refuted this and concluded that the great majority of men genuinely desired work and actively sought it. A Ministry of Labour report in 1928 indignantly rejected such allegations:

> Every impartial body that has examined this [unemployment insurance] scheme ... has found that the allegations of general abuse are without foundation. The body of unemployed is not a standing army of vagrants and loafers, but a number of genuine industrial workers whose composition is constantly changing.[15]

In any case, the benefit levels were not sufficiently generous to attract any but a small minority, the allowance for a family of four in 1936 amounting to only two-thirds of Rowntree's Human Needs of Labour scale.[16]

The alternative, Keynesian, view was to stress the deficiency of aggregate demand rather than the over-supply of labour. Demand could be stimulated by investment policies which would create jobs, increase purchasing power and result in a multiplier effect which would reflate the economy as a whole: the economy had become locked in a position of chronic underemployment which could only be released by government policies of major investment in new industries and public projects. But this would involve government borrowing on a massive scale, so unbalancing the budget, a remedy which neither Conservative nor Labour governments, equally subject to Treasury control, could contemplate, and proposals of this kind, whether from a Mosley or a Macmillan, met with an equally flat rejection.

The fact was that there was no single cause or single remedy. Inter-war unemployment was a combination of structural, cyclical, seasonal and frictional factors, the last three of which had long plagued the economy but were now overlaid by the new phenomenon of a secular decline in basic industries. Probably the best analysis of the relative contribution of these different factors has been offered by Glynn and Oxborrow. They suggest a hard core of structural unemployment amounting to some 6 per cent of the insured workforce throughout the period: seasonal and frictional unemployment added another 3 or 4 per cent, which would explain the minimum level of around 10 per cent below which unemployment never fell. But on top of this was periodic cyclical unemployment which in particular periods of slump such as 1921 and 1930–3 could almost double the minimum level.[17] To closer details of the extent and incidence of unemployment we now turn.

THE EXTENT AND INCIDENCE OF UNEMPLOYMENT

We can be a good deal more confident about the extent of unemployment in the inter-war years than in the nineteenth century, though total accuracy is impossible. From 1920 onwards the extension of unemployment insurance covered the majority of manual workers over the age of sixteen and non-manual workers earning less than £250 a year, and these statistics of unemployment among the insured population are the ones most usually cited. Important groups were not included in the insurance scheme however – workers in agriculture, forestry and horticulture, domestic servants, teachers, nurses, civil servants, the police, armed services and the railways: in 1931 insurance covered only twelve-and-a-half million of nineteen-and-a-half million within the insurance age limits sixteen to sixty-four.[18] Statistics based on the insured working population therefore considerably under-represent the total number of unemployed people, but because the rate of unemployment among the excluded groups (which tended to be more stable occupations) was lower than among the insured, statistics relating to the latter over-represent the rate of unemployment in the total employed population. In Table 4 below, Professor Feinstein calculated the numbers and rates of unemployment among both the insured workforce and the total workforce.

Table 4 Employment and unemployment, 1921–38[19]

Employees at work		Unemployment		Percentage unemployed	
		Insured persons aged 16–64	*Total workers[a]*	*Insured unemployed as a proportion of insured employees*	*Total unemployed as a proportion of total employees*
	'000s	*'000s*	*'000s*	%	%
1921	15,879	1,840	2,212	17.0	12.2
1922	15,847	1,588	1,909	14.3	10.8
1923	16,068	1,304	1,567	11.7	8.9
1924	16,332	1,168	1,404	10.3	7.9
1925	16,531	1,297	1,559	11.3	8.6
1926	16,529	1,463	1,759	12.5	9.6
1927	17,060	1,142	1,373	9.7	7.4
1928	17,123	1,278	1,536	10.8	8.2
1929	17,392	1,250	1,503	10.4	8.0
1930	17,016	1,979	2,379	16.1	12.3
1931	16,554	2,705	3,252	21.3	16.4
1932	16,644	2,828	3,400	22.1	17.0
1933	17,018	2,567	3,087	19.9	15.4
1934	17,550	2,170	2,609	16.7	12.9
1935	17,890	2,027	2,437	15.5	12.0
1936	18,513	1,749	2,100	13.1	10.2
1937	19,196	1,482	1,776	10.8	8.5
1938	19,243	1,800	2,164	12.9	10.1

Note: [a]Insured persons plus those under 16 and over 64 and agricultural workers, private indoor domestic servants, and non-manual workers earning more than £250 per year.

Source: Adapted from C. H. Feinstein, *Statistical Tables of National Income, Expenditure and Output of the U.K., 1855–1965* (Cambridge, 1972), Table 58.

It illustrates the cyclical pattern of inter-war unemployment, with peaks in 1921–2 and 1930–3 with some recovery between; the figure for insured workers only fell marginally below 10 per cent in 1927, and over the whole period averaged 14.7 per cent. When the uninsured workers are added, the estimated total of unemployed people in the UK mounted to 3,400,000 in 1932, though this represented only 17 per cent of total employees compared to 22.1 per cent of the insured.

The aggregate figures tell something about the extent and pattern of unemployment, but not who the unemployed were. The fact that over the period between one in ten and two in every ten insured people were out of work disguises the fact that the likelihood of being among the casualties depended crucially on a number of variables – sex, age, region, occupation and personal characteristics – which determined who joined the queues at the Labour Exchanges and who held their jobs and bene-fited from a substantial rise in real wages. Male unemployment was much higher than female, mainly because with the exception of the cotton industry, women tended to be employed in more stable occupations. In April 1926, a fairly typical year, men constituted 77 per cent of all unem-ployed people while women and girls made up 19 per cent.[20] But such global statistics have to be seen against the fact that women were a much smaller proportion of the total labour force than men, and therefore a realistic measure is their rate of unemployment among their own sex. Much depended on the local employment opportunities for women, so that in a city such as York, where female labour was in strong demand for the chocolate and other factories, women's unemployment was low,[21] while in Bolton, a cotton-spinning town undergoing depression, 1,820 women and girls were out of work in July 1924 out of the town's 6,200 unemployed.[22] In 1931 14.7 per cent of male workers were unemployed nationally compared to 9.4 per cent of female workers, suggesting that women and girls had some advantages to employers as cheap labour, especially in semi-skilled occupations. But it is likely that the official statistics under-represent the real extent of female unemployment, especially among married women who after legislation in 1931 ceased to qualify for unemployment benefit unless they could show a 'reasonable expectation' of obtaining insurable work, and that their chances were not impaired by the fact of marriage. Thus if in a Lancashire town the only local mill closed down, married women workers lost entitlement to benefit, and between 1931 and 1933 nearly a quarter of a million claims were disallowed under this regulation.[23] Under such a disincentive it is probable that many married women declined to register as unemployed, and were therefore not counted.

Age was a factor which operated unexpectedly in that the chances of becoming unemployed did not increase regularly with advancing years. A boy or girl leaving elementary school at fourteen was likely to find work of some sort fairly easily, usually in unskilled or semi-skilled work in a factory, warehouse, coalmine or in a shop as assistant or delivery-boy: at this age they presented the great advantage to an employer of willingness and extremely low wages. Even so, a good many did not walk immediately into a job. In a survey of juvenile employment in Sheffield it was found that of those leaving school in October of the 'good' year, 1927, 12 per cent of boys and 22.5 per cent of girls spent between three months and a year before obtaining their first work: a further 3.8 per cent of boys and 11.7 per cent of girls spent more than a year before working.[24] The high figures for girls probably reflect the fact that some did not immediately seek work, staying at home to help with the domestic chores, though this would not apply to the boys on whom there would be a strong parental pressure to be earning as soon as possible. The majority entered 'dead-end' jobs providing little or no opportunity for developing skills or technical training: 18 per cent of the boys and 22 per cent of the girls changed jobs three times or more in the first three years either from choice or as a result of dismissal.

It is not possible to know the full extent of unemployment among juveniles because boys and girls under sixteen were outside the scope of unemployment insurance and were not, therefore, required to register at Exchanges: the statistics relate only to the sixteen- to eighteen-year-olds, and of this group in Sheffield in February 1933, 10 per cent of the boys and 9 per cent of the girls available for work were on the 'live register' of unemployed. The survey concluded that 'there is no doubt that complete figures would show a very much higher proportion', though this was a depressed town at a particularly bad time: national rates for unemployed juveniles generally averaged about 4 per cent.[25] A particular concern of the period was the waste of ability owing to the lack of training facilities by employers and the loss which this ultimately entailed for the economy. In a national enquiry into juvenile labour in 1926 it was found that only one in six of school-leavers had a chance of starting their industrial careers in a job that offered prospects of training or perma-nence.[26] The danger point consequently arose at age eighteen or nine-teen, when young men and women with no particular skills competed for jobs at adult wages, many being dismissed or replaced by new gener-ations of school-leavers: at twenty-one their numbers were swollen by discharged apprentices who had been taken on by unscrupulous employers as cheap labour with little or no chance of permanency. Unem-ployment therefore suddenly leapt for the age group eighteen to twenty-four at a time when many wished to marry and set up home, and remained high for the age groups up to forty-four: in May 1937 men aged twenty-one to forty-four were 55 per cent of all unemployed males while women of this age were 65.5 per cent of the unemployed of their sex.[27] After the mid-forties the risk of losing a job did not increase

207

with age, probably because experience now became an asset in those occupations which did not depend on the strength of youth, but once out of work after this age the chances of regaining it diminished rapidly. In 1931 unemployment for the twenty-five to forty-four age group was 13 per cent but for those aged fifty-five to sixty-four it rose to 22.6 per cent[28] and was far more likely to be long-term.

More important than age as a determinant of employment, however, was the nature of occupation. In this respect, some former patterns still applied in the 1920s and 1930s, in that employment opportunities in numbers of trades were still influenced by seasonal factors or the essentially casual nature of the work. Winter unemployment was always higher than in summer, as it had been for centuries past. The unemployment rate of all insured workers in the bad year 1922 varied from 12.7 per cent in September to 17.7 per cent in January, while in the good year of 1927 it ranged from 8.7 per cent in May to 12 per cent in January.[29] The incidence was, of course, much higher than this in outdoor work which depended even more on climatic conditions, especially the building trades which always suffered in winter; thus in January 1926, 30 per cent of painters were out of work and 16 per cent of building trade labourers[30] compared with the overall unemployment average of 11 per cent. Seasonal unemployment went wider than this however. English seaside resorts were booming in summer in response to increasing real wages and paid holidays for those in work, but shed much labour for at least six months in the year, while motorcar manufacturers in Oxford, Luton and Coventry experienced the strongest demand for new cars in spring and summer but went into short time in winter. These were skilled men, but casual workers were especially vulnerable, as they had always been. Before the war casualism had been a principal cause of unemployment and had attracted much of the attention of reformers like Beveridge. Twenty years on in 1930, he had to admit that it had not diminished, and that the two classic casual trades – dock-work and building – had remained as disorganized as ever despite the establishment of Labour Exchanges. Neither industry had a problem of reconstruction and scaling down after the war like the munitions industries, and building had faced a large unsatisfied demand for houses and had been favoured by government subsidies: nevertheless, between 1924 and 1929 unemployment in dock-work ranged between 24 per cent and 31 per cent, building averaged 11.3 per cent and public works contracting 19.3 per cent.[31] Officially there were only around 250,000 men identified as casual workers, but there was a much larger number of unskilled labourers whose work was always temporary, and at times of high unemployment their numbers were swollen by skilled men competing for low-grade work at almost any price.

The new, alarming feature of this period, however, was structural unemployment, caused by the decay of Britain's staple industries which had formerly accounted for a major part of exports, and the consequent economic collapse of those regions of the country where the industries were based. Coal, iron and steel, shipbuilding, heavy engineering and cotton accounted for more than 40 per cent of total unemployment, and in the areas where they were concentrated, for far higher proportions. At the worst time in 1932 a third of coalminers were out of work, half the workers in iron and steel and nearly two-thirds of shipbuilders: these high rates contrasted strongly with those in the new industries like chemicals (17.3 per cent), electrical engineering (16.8 per cent) and gas, water and electricity (10.9 per cent), bad as these would have been at any other time. The combination of a world collapse in trade and intense competition from cheaper producing countries reduced Britain's exports in 1932 to half the volume of 1913 and her share of world industrial production to one-tenth. This was therefore a problem different both in scale and kind from a cyclical downturn from which the economy would sooner or later bounce back: this was a permanent, seemingly irreversible decay of industries for which the world was over-supplied, leaving Britain, as their pioneer, with an unwanted, surplus capacity. The consequence was that even in 1936, a year of some recovery, 30 per cent of shipbuilders and iron- and steel-workers and 25 per cent of coalminers were unemployed.[32]

An inevitable result was the emergence of 'depressed', 'distressed', or 'special' areas of Britain where these industries were narrowly concentrated and which offered few alternative opportunities of employment – south Wales and Monmouthshire, Durham and Tyneside, Cumberland and the industrialized parts of lowland Scotland. These were the officially designated 'Depressed Areas', identified in a government report of 1934,[33] though abnormally high levels of unemployment extended well beyond them to other 'single-industry' towns, whether Redruth (Cornish tin-mining), Sheffield (metals and engineering) or Lancashire cotton towns. But although there could be pockets of extreme depression in almost any part of the country, the broad contrast was between the depressed regions north of a line from the Severn to the Wash and those south of it, especially the Midlands and the Greater London region where most of the new industries were developing and economic activity was generally booming except in the worst cyclical downturns. The fact that the seat of government was located in one of the least affected areas perhaps helps to explain the lack of concern which some politicians displayed towards a problem which could be regarded as remote and exceptional. In 1934 unemployment in St Albans stood at 3.9 per cent and in Oxford and Coventry at 5.1 per cent, different worlds from Maryport (57 per cent), Merthyr (61.9 per cent) or Jarrow (67.8 per cent). In this last, 'The Town that was Murdered', the closure of the principal employers,

Palmer's Shipyard, spelled disaster to a whole community, resulting in over 80 per cent unemployment in 1932 and 72.9 per cent in September 1935, at which point the Ministry of Labour amalgamated the Labour Exchange with that of the relatively prosperous Hebburn, so reducing the recorded percentage of unemployment by almost half.[34]

Jarrow was only an extreme instance of the blight which affected almost the whole of Tyneside and Teesside: the much larger town of Middlesbrough had 50 per cent of male unemployment in 1926 and more than 50 per cent from 1930 to 1933, while the closure of shipyards and Blair's Engineering Company in Stockton-on-Tees resulted in 67 per cent of male unemployment in 1932: the registered female and juvenile unemployment was also over 50 per cent at this time.[35] The government investigator for the Depressed Areas Report of 1934 noted that in Durham and Tyneside there were 147,940 people unemployed, only 10,499 of whom were females: 63,000 had been out of work for more than two years, 40,700 for more than three, 18,500 for more than four years and 9,250 for more than five. At Butterknowle 32 per cent had been out of work for five years, while at Witton Park practically all those available for work were unemployed.[36] In the iron-ore mining areas of west Cumberland, 10,500 of the insured 33,800 workers were idle, and the Rt. Hon. J. C. Davidson could see little prospect of any outlet locally for the surplus labour or of new industries being attracted to the region. Here there were 'villages where men have no work whatsoever. The local mine has closed, never to re-open', and many areas which were 'distressed and practically derelict', Maryport, Haltwhistle and Cleator Moor, had unemployment rates over 50 per cent, Cockermouth and Alston over 40 per cent.[37] In south Wales Sir Wyndham Portal believed that there was a 'permanent surplus' of 39,000 men and 5,000 boys even assuming a revival in trade. Places like Blaina, Brynmawr and Merthyr averaged 70 per cent unemployment, and were largely derelict: the coalmines had been worked out and abandoned and the great Dowlais Steelworks closed: over the whole area 45.3 per cent of coalminers were out of work and 40 per cent of iron- and steel-workers. A total of 28,500 men, or 35.3 per cent of all unemployed, had been continuously out of work for more than three years.[38] Finally, in the areas of Scotland investigated by Sir Arthur Rose, principally the heavy industrial regions of Lanarkshire, Renfrewshire and parts of Ayrshire, there was a permanent surplus of 60,000 men and juveniles: in the hardest hit areas unemployment ran at 60 per cent and in Glasgow over the previous three years had averaged 30 per cent.[39]

These investigations in 1934 revealed not only the escalation of the scale of unemployment after 1929, but also a virtually new phenomenon of long-term unemployment, defined as more than a year without three days of uninterrupted work. Through the 1920s this had been a rare and localized abnormality: in September 1929, less than 5 per cent of all the unemployed, mainly composed of 38,000 coalminers (of the national total of 53,000 long-term unemployed) many of whom had had no work since the great lockout of 1926.[40] But after the slump of 1930–2 the proportion of long-term rose dramatically to 480,000 by July 1933, 25 per cent of all unemployed people and, even more alarmingly, continued to rise in the next few years despite a substantial recovery in the economy: in the autumn of 1935, 26 per cent of unemployment was long-term and in August 1937, 27 per cent.[41] In the words of the Pilgrim Trust Report of 1938, 'a social problem of the first order' had arisen and through the 1930s a large hard core of long-term unemployment continued despite the economic revival. Much public interest now centred on analysing its causes. It was quickly apparent that long-term unemployment was concentrated in the old staples – coalmining, shipbuilding, cotton and iron and steel and, therefore, geographically localized in the depressed areas. In 1936 the Pilgrim Trust surveyed six towns taken to be reasonably representative of prosperous and depressed parts of the country: it was found that long-term unemployment ranged from only 6 per cent of the unemployed in the London Borough of Deptford and 11 per cent in the prosperous Midland city of Leicester to 56 per cent in Crook, County Durham and 63 per cent in Rhondda: Liverpool and Blackburn stood midway between the extremes, at 23 per cent and 38 per cent respectively.[42] Age was a critical determining factor, long-term unemployment increasing regularly with advancing years though with two marked jumps at twenty-one and fifty-five: after fifty the chances of re-employment declined sharply, and a man of sixty-two had only half the chances of one of fifty. Although long-term unemployment could affect all grades of labour within particular industries, its incidence was three times higher among unskilled than among semi-skilled and skilled workers.[43] To be out of work for a year was bad enough, but a good deal of the unemployment of the thirties was for considerably longer periods. The Pilgrim Trust survey drew attention to the phenomenon of 'very long-term unemployment' of five years or more, and showed that this had increased dramatically from 8 per cent of long-term unemployed men in the summer of 1935 to 16 per cent a year later: by then, as many men had been out of work for 5 years or more as had been unemployed for only one year in 1929.[44]

This meant that in some of the hardest-hit, virtually derelict, communities large numbers of men had been workless for years, with very little prospect of ever regaining it at their advancing age. The extreme case was Crook, in County Durham, where in November 1936, 71 per cent of the unemployed had been out for five years or more, but in Rhondda urban district the figure was 45 per cent and in Liverpool 23 per cent: in small communities the effects of this on local shops, pubs and social life generally could be devastating, and the social problems of such places began to receive some public attention in the later thirties. But the individual, personal problem of long-term unemployment was much the same in the Rhondda as in a generally prosperous town like York where, although the overall rate of unemployment in 1935 was not high, 21.9 per cent of the unemployed heads of families had been out of work for two to four years, 23.6 per cent for four to six years and 17.9 per cent for more than six.[45]

The Pilgrim Trust believed that some 30 per cent of long-term unemployment was 'residual' that is, due to personal, individual reasons rather than economic, and therefore existed in prosperous towns as well as depressed. Age and skill, or the lack of it, were major determining factors, and in Jarrow in 1939 unemployment was twice as high among the unskilled shipyard workers as among the skilled.[46] Physical or mental disability, actual or alleged, had always been a reason for shedding unwanted workers, and in the inter-war years this was more pronounced than usual since some two-and-a-half million men had been disabled as a result of the war: depending on the severity of injury, they received government pensions, but many were so small that most had to seek employment and tended to form a marginal group despite strong pressure on employers to retain them. Employers not unnaturally preferred to take young, healthy men who had not been long out of work, who did not yet look shabby and dispirited as did many of the long-term unemployed. And in this period of unprecedented labour militancy members of the recently-formed Communist Party, the National Unemployed Workers Movement or even trade union activists became natural targets for dismissal and victimization, however capable or willing workers they might be: 'troublesome' men who objected to deskilling, new work practices or reduced wage rates were equally likely to become casualties at a time of intense industrial competition. But whatever criticisms were levelled at the unemployed – whether work-shy 'malingerers' who preferred to live on the dole rather than earn an honest living, or revolutionaries who aimed at manipulating present difficulties to overthrow the capitalist system – the vast majority of the unemployed were neither of these, but ordinary men and women who wanted nothing better than an honest job and a decent wage. In a detailed survey of York's unemployed in 1935 Seebohm Rowntree found that 76 per cent were fit and capable and eagerly looking for work, 12 per cent were capable of work of some kind, but not making strenuous efforts to find it, and the remaining 12 per cent were unlikely to work again through old age or disability.[47] How the varying experiences of unemployment are represented in the words of autobiographers will now be discussed.

THE EXPERIENCE OF UNEMPLOYMENT

Becoming unemployed

In 1931 an American sociologist, E. Wight Bakke, conducted a detailed survey of the unemployed in the London borough of Greenwich, living among them in lodgings, befriending them in pubs and clubs, persuading them to talk openly and to keep diaries of their daily routines. His main aim was 'to try to discover by first-hand observation, in a limited working-class area, what view unemployed workmen themselves take of their own situation'.[48] Discussing with them the reasons for their unemployment at this critical period in the depression, he apparently revealed an extraordinary degree of ignorance, prejudice and lack of understanding of the nature of the economic crisis. Machinery was blamed first as the reason for dismissal:

> Machinery is the most prominent feature of his world. It is most quickly blamed for the uncertainties of employment. It is almost a personal, diabolical force to him. . . . The battle between labour and labour-saving machinery is a constant interest-centre in his conversation.[49]

Next cited was the dismissal of youths at eighteen, when the employer's insurance contributions increased, and of apprentices at twenty-one having served their time and qualified for skilled men's wages: the complaint was that these young workers were flooding the market and were prepared to undercut men in order to get work. The same objection was levelled at women in industry. Unemployed men believed that more women were being taken on, especially in semi-skilled jobs, again at impossibly low rates of pay for family men to live on. It was also believed that labour was moving into Greenwich from outside as a result of the depression, further increasing competition. But, beyond these factors, there was a widespread belief in impersonal forces which controlled a man's destiny: it was common to blame an unspecified 'them' for a man's bad luck, though sometimes 'they' were identified as the government, bankers, or the 'boss class'. Luck was usually on the side of the bosses, not the workers: a man who had work was lucky, an unemployed man unlucky. Overall, Bakke concluded that there was a strong sense of control from outside:

> It causes the worker to feel a minimum of responsibility for his own fate, for responsibility goes with control. No one who has not shared the life of the worker can realise the number of points at which the ultimate decision as to his way of life rests with others.[50]

Bakke chose Greenwich for his investigation because the extent of unemployment was average for the country as a whole, and was mainly intermittent not long term. London, with its large variety of industries and occupations, was not a 'depressed area', and the attitudes of the unemployed were not likely to be representative of those regions of the country where a complete closure of a major industry which had employed large numbers of workers was the obvious and well-understood cause of their dismissal. The writings of the many working-class autobiographers who lived through the 1920s and 1930s make clear the variety of reasons, personal and impersonal, for their unemployment.[51] For some women as well as men unemployment began as early as 1919 with the closure of munitions factories and other wartime demands. Lottie Barker of Beeston in Nottingham had filled shells for good wages but in 1919 'we were given our cards and cried all the way to the office':[52] Eva Shilton's father lost his job in 1918 – 'no more tanks needed' – and was unemployed for the next two-and-a-half years,[53] and Amy Gomm was sacked 'when the men returned from the War'.[54] The absence from the labour market of so many men during the war had created favourable employment opportunities for youths as well as women, but many lost their places with the return of the 'heroes' to claim their former jobs. Born in 1900, Joseph Stacey had been an estate clerk during the war, unusually young for so much responsibility, but was dismissed by a new squire shortly after the Armistice.

> I tried all the offices I could find [in nearby Liverpool]. I must have walked scores of miles up flights of steps alone, but always I had to descend without employment. The clerks who had gone to the war had returned; during the hostilities young ones had been taken on, now many of these had lost their jobs and were in a similar plight to my own. . . . The tremendous influx back from the Armed Services had done the same at the docks. The work force was now completely full . . . I joined queues of old men waiting at the gates for the chance of a day's work.[55]

In such cases there was an understandable preference of employers to give work to ex-servicemen, a patriotic duty encouraged by government and public alike. It was easier to blame remote, economic forces when a major industry collapsed, destroying the jobs of hundreds, thousands, or even a whole community. The results of structural decline in the textiles, coal, steel and shipbuilding industries had far-reaching and unexpected effects on individuals – the chauffeur whose employer in the cotton trade had to dismiss him in the slump of the 1920s with no unemployment insurance since 'in those days domestic servants didn't pay in'[56] or Henrietta Burkin's cousin who was 'suddenly made redundant after having worked in the office of an export woollen firm in the docks since he left school' – 'He used to come practically every week begging Dad [a foreman electrician in charge of cable-laying in London] to give him work, but he said, how could he offer a clerk work digging up roads, he hadn't the strength'.[57] Although the closure of a coalmine, shipyard or cotton mill affected many people, there was in these communities a shared loss and mutual support which was lacking in the individual cases, and commentators were struck by the remarkable degree of resilience which characterized depressed areas like south Wales or Tyneside. The resentment at the sudden closure of pits or steelworks was nevertheless intense, especially in south Wales after the collapse of the long strike in 1926 when pits were bought up cheaply by the Powell Duffryn Company and many 'rationalized' out of existence.

> The village of Aber Cridwr was one of two villages in the Aber Valley. The valley is only five miles long. But what went on there was going on all over South Wales. The other village in the valley is called Senghenydd. Two villages – two collieries. In 1927 P. D. bought Senghenydd colliery and shut it down, putting two thousand men out of work. Some of them got work at the other pit, the rest were left to rot.[58]

Two years later, in 1929, the giant steelworks at Dowlais, near Merthyr Tydfil, were shut down:

> There were at least half a dozen pits belonging to G. K. Nettlefolds supplying coal to the steelworks. They all went under. Twelve thousand men out, miners and steelworkers, all in one day. There was utter despair. Family businesses also disappeared overnight. The main shopping streets of Merthyr were boarded up overnight.[59]

Many pits never reopened after the General Strike and stoppage of 1926, either because they were flooded or unworkable through neglect or because the owners deemed them unprofitable in a period of falling prices: miners found it difficult to accept unexplained 'economic reasons'. 'Hire and fire, boom and slump, call it what you will, but in the 1930s we just did not know what it was all about.'[60]

There was, of course, nothing new about the closure of individual firms, but the impact of the loss of a major employer cut much deeper and wider into a local community. When the Leeds Steel Works closed for good in the depression of 1921, J. H. Armitage's father lost his job along with 2,000 others, and in consequence two of the three shifts at the nearby Middleton colliery were stopped, putting another 800 men out of work.[61] But probably the best-publicized destruction of the prosperity of a whole town virtually dependent on one industry was the case of shipbuilding in Jarrow, immortalized by the Jarrow March (1936) and Ellen Wilkinson's book, *The Town that was Murdered* (1939):

Jarrow in that year, 1932–3, was utterly stagnant. There was no work. No one had a job except for a few railwaymen, officials, the workers in co-operative stores and the few clerks and craftsmen who went out of the town to their jobs each day. The unemployment rate was over 80 per cent.[62]

The closure and dereliction of Palmer's great shipyard was the best-known of Jarrow's casualties but only one of several which shared the same fate; one autobiographer must stand for the many whose skill became redundant. Arthur Barton had left Jarrow Grammar School at sixteen in 1927 and, following the ambition of most local youths, had been apprenticed as a draughtsman at Chalmers Shipbuilding and Iron Co. The third year of his apprenticeship, 1929, was spent in the drawing office. 'At work, there was less and less to do' when the last of the thousand ships built since the firm began a century ago was launched. The Co-Operative Hall was commandeered as a Labour Exchange: one by one the draughtsmen left until on the day after his twenty-first birthday and the completion of his five-year training Barton received the now expected letter: 'Owing to the unprecedented slump in shipbuilding . . .' The company was now in the hands of receivers and work had stopped.[63]

In one respect the unemployed men of Greenwich who complained to Bakke of the increased competition of youths were right. Many school-leavers had always taken dead-end jobs for which there was no further use beyond the age of sixteen or seventeen: traditionally they had then gone into semi-skilled or unskilled jobs which were now experiencing the highest rates of unemployment. It seems clear that juvenile employment became even more insecure in the inter-war years, partly because apprenticeship was declining but mainly because employers took every opportunity of reducing wage bills by using the youngest and cheapest workers: an additional cost was the unemployment insurance stamp which employers had to pay at sixteen. Autobiographers constantly refer to the insecurity of their early jobs and the lack of training opportunities.

When I left school I went butchering. . . . The idea in my dad's mind was that I was going to learn a trade. . . . He give me five shillings a week. Then I got seven and sixpence. When I got about eighteen I come to ten shillings a week and he couldn't pay me any more. He said, 'I'll give you a reference, and that's about all I can do. I just hope you can get a job.' So that's when I had my first sample of the dole.[64]

All the gaffers want is cheap labour – kids from school. When they have to pay you a bit more money, they don't want you.[65]

I had a job until I was eighteen, and then I was too old, which is the old story again. I was working in the laundry then, doing stoking and helping in the wash house. . . . When I was eighteen I got slung out. I went on the dole.[66]

I became unemployed a fortnight before my twentieth birthday in 1933. I was a machine attendant at a small local factory, and it was the custom of my employer to discharge employees when they became older and more expensive to him and employ younger lads in their place. There was plenty of labour available. Young lads were hanging around the factory gates every day looking for work.[67]

Early sacking was felt especially keenly by apprentices, who had suffered low wages for five years in the expectation of good earnings and honourable status as skilled men. Employers had never guaranteed jobs to men out of their time, but in the inter-war years it seems that more employers abused the system by using apprentices as cheap labour, providing little or no training and dismissing them as soon as they qualified for skilled wages. Not a few autobiographers also write of 'broken' apprenticeships when sacked before the completion of their term: they then had the difficulty of trying to negotiate a transfer of indentures to another employer or, more often, trying to find work in an over-stocked semi-skilled market.

A lot of apprentices were used as cheap labour on the buildings. They'd be signed on as apprentices and work for about four years on the site, and all they'd be doing was wheeling a barrow and stacking bricks. . . . And then, when the building was completed, the apprentices would be out before they'd even started laying bricks.[68]

Harry Fletcher had started as an apprentice in Earle's shipbuilding yard in Hull in 1916, where a labour force of 3,000 to 4,000 had been kept very busy on war work: 'By 1921 the situation in the shipyards was very bad. . . . In May, when my apprenticeship finished, the yard was on short time, four days a week, and after working for a fortnight as a journeyman I was sacked. . . . Apprentices were generally sacked when they finished their time'.[69] Now married, Fletcher tried to get shipyard work for the next fourteen months, during which time he only had two-and-a-half days of labouring. Ernie Benson completed his apprenticeship as a fitter in Leeds in 1927 to be told, 'I believe you're twenty-one now, aren't you? We don't keep apprentices after they are twenty-one'.[70]

In fact, age operated as a limiting employment factor throughout the span of a man's life. If some were too old at eighteen to twenty-one for work which could be done by boys of sixteen to eighteen, men over forty-five faced special difficulty in keeping or obtaining jobs where physical strength was regarded as more important than skill and experience: in mining, steelmaking, dock-work and labouring generally older men were at a serious disadvantage, despite often pathetic attempts to disguise their age by darkening their hair, abandoning the use of spectacles and so on. But even at their most employable age in their twenties or thirties men and women might be told that their years were against them, particularly for semi-skilled factory work where cheap juvenile labour was preferred and readily available. John Evans had been a mechanic in the RAF before discharge in 1923, and thereafter had only four years' work in the next eleven at factory work as a fitter, brush salesman, traveller and pedlar, often losing jobs for younger men: 'I'm only 33, but I've been told time after time that I'm too old, and some of my friends who are over 40 know for a fact that they'll never get another job whilst we live under this present system'.[71] And Olive Gold, who tried to be the family bread-winner when her husband was sacked in 1928 was told that she was 'too old at 31 years of age' for factory work.[72] Age also operated against skilled workers whose trades had been made redundant by mechanization. Much of the transformation of woodworking, tailoring and boot and shoemaking had already occurred before 1914, but some lingering craftsmen continued to be ousted in the years of depression. A skilled woodcarver who had worked for thirty years on high-quality furniture, shop fronts, ship's fittings and railway coaches found that 'Machine-turned furniture and machine-carved wood have driven us out of business. I have now been without work for four months. I am 44, and have a wife and one daughter. . . . My unemployment allowance is 23s. a week'.[73] And Arthur Newton's father who worked in the domestic shoe industry in Hackney became unemployed in 1928 when the factory system began there. 'For eighteen months he didn't do a stroke of remunerative work.'[74] Arthur followed his father in the same trade, but into the factory, where he experienced much short time. From 1929 to 1939 he was frequently out of work, 'sometimes for short periods and sometimes for as long as six months. I seldom was able to have a full week: we were really at this time casual workers'.

Age was a major determinant of work opportunities, but in a period of intense labour competition, only one of a range of personal factors which influenced employment chances. Many of the two million more or less seriously disabled men who returned from the war found employment difficulties despite public sympathy and official encouragement of employers to make special arrangements. Like many others, Mick Burke was badly wounded in the head and arm and found that:

> Those of us who came back from the war ended up at the Labour Exchange. I got 29s. a week for three months, then £1, and after six months it was dropped to 17s. It's a good job I wasn't married then. There were two million unemployed, and big fellows with all their limbs in the queue.[75]

But the frequency with which autobiographers cite victimization as the reason for their dismissal suggests that this was one of the commonest personal reasons for unemployment in the inter-war years. It was usually concerned with taking a leading part in trade union activities, in a strike or in militant politics, especially the Communist Party, which was founded in 1920. The dismissal of 'trouble-makers' was especially common in coalmining after the strikes or lockouts of 1921 and 1926, when men regarded as agitators were blacklisted, sometimes for years to come. Even the protection afforded by his union's appointment as checkweighman did not prevent the sacking of Will Paynter, a Communist in the Rhondda, for allegedly interfering in the management of the colliery.[76] Another Communist, Arthur Horner, wrote: 'I had joined in strikes and helped to organise them in every pit I worked in. I had been put on the blacklist throughout the Welsh coalfield, and deprived of the right to work by the coal owners, whom I hated as bitterly as they hated me'.[77] Edward Cain, who took a leading part in the miners' strike at Seaham, County Durham, in 1926, was afterwards told by the manager: 'If you give up your ideas of Socialism you can start'; he refused and was evicted from his miner's cottage.[78] And George Bestford, also of County Durham, corroborates that

> It was a hard job for a 'politician' to get a job in the 'thirties. If he was a 'politician' he had to keep it under his cap, because if it once got out that he was a bit of an agitator and fighting for better conditions, there was no chance of a job for him. . . . There were a lot of good workers who never worked after the 1926 strike.[79]

In many other industries militants who declared themselves suffered the same fate. As a young man in Glasgow in 1920 Harry McShane took the chair at public meetings addressed by the Communist John Maclean. 'The third time, my foreman was in the audience, and I got the sack from A. and W. Smith's.'[80] George Hodgkinson had been a Shop Steward in Coventry during the war and later went to Ruskin College, Oxford, on a trade union bursary: he had been promised that his job with the Daimler Co. would be kept open for him, but 'the Company did not honour [it]. . . . The bar was down, and I was on the blacklist of the employers, I, a marked man who had to pay the price of pioneering and strike leading in the war years'.[81] After the General Strike, when Jack Braddock had been a member of the Merseyside Council of Action, his name was also on a blacklist and 'I couldn't get work. Anywhere'.[82] The blacklist also extended to women workers, as Mary Brooksbank discovered in Dundee in 1920. She had helped to organize an unemployed demonstration which was stopped by the police, and she was sentenced to forty days' imprisonment for breach of the peace. After her release 'I found that because of my activities I could not get a job, and if I did I could not keep it long'.[83]

Searching for work

'Hunting a job is the "job" of the unemployed worker. It is the most important part of his self-maintenance efforts.'[84] So concluded Bakke in his study of unemployment in Greenwich. From the daily diaries kept by unemployed men he calculated that an average of 4.2 hours a day for five-and-a-half days a week were spent looking for work, or twenty-three hours a week: some spent as much as forty-four hours a week, a few only four hours, and while skilled men averaged seventeen hours a week in job hunting, unskilled men averaged twenty-seven hours. This somewhat surprising statistic was explained by the fact that skilled men made more use of writing letters and of their trade union facilities, seldom starting off on a wandering tour but visiting known firms.[85] They also made more use of trams, trains and buses to take them further afield, whereas the unskilled tended to wander more aimlessly in restricted areas. Bakke was told that searching often began as early as 5.00 or 6.00 a.m., and that 'It's no use to look for a job after nine o'clock. All hands are taken on by then'. The main sources of information used for job-hunting were coffee-houses, described as 'casual workers' Free Masonry', informal trade union clubs meeting in public houses, and former workmates who would act as a 'stand-in' to speak to a foreman on your behalf. Newspaper advertisements were considered a poor source for industrial jobs, being mainly used for commercial, professional and domestic workers. When a shopkeeper advertised in a Birmingham paper for two men with cycles at a wage of £2 a week it was reported that a thousand had tried to get near the place and that the police had been called out to control the traffic.[86] The rows of unemployed men scanning the newspapers in public libraries may have included those seeking a warm place to sit or read the sports results rather than with any real hope of finding a vacancy.

Despite what some of the national press liked to refer to as 'scroungers' and 'loafers', there is no doubt that the overwhelming majority of the unemployed genuinely looked for work, often finding the dispiriting process more tiring than work itself. The joke which unemployed ex-servicemen told against themselves – 'Why should a working man work when he's got the health and strength to lie in bed?'[87] – was an ironic reaction to years of danger and over-activity and in no way implied a rejection of the work ethic. Bakke's researches concluded that the availability of unemployment insurance and subsequent transitional benefit had little or no effect on the willingness of workers to support themselves and their families, and showed that almost all men made strenuous efforts to find work, even when odds were heavily stacked against success. Nor was it the case that a large proportion of the unemployed were 'unemployable' through age or some physical or mental infirmity. On three occasions in 1924, 1927 and 1931 the Ministry of Labour conducted sample surveys of the degrees of employability of claimants for unemployment benefit: in 1927 69 per cent of claimants in Britain were classified 'A' (i.e. of full industrial capacity and in steady employment in normal times), while in 1931 77 per cent of London claimants were so rated, reflecting the worsened economic conditions between those years.[88] But the public sources of information about jobs were woefully inadequate, and the Labour Exchanges managed to fill only one adult vacancy in five nationally in 1930.[89] A skilled plumber told Greenwood that 'All the ones they have sent me on weren't much good. I can find better jobs myself' and an unskilled labourer commented

> I don't blame any fellow for dodging some of the jobs they send you on here. Rotten isn't the word for them. I've just finished one job – one they told me would last a long time – two days, that's all it lasted. It was on a building job that their own men wouldn't tackle. I was up to my knees in mud digging out a foundation ... I ruined a good pair of boots and trousers. . . . And you're not in a position to say 'no' to the vacancies manager. If you refuse a job when it's offered you, you're knocked off the dole for six weeks.[90]

This man believed that employers did not use the Exchanges except as a last hope for worthless jobs, and that they would only function as intended if employers were compelled to notify all vacancies. Unemployed juveniles were at a particular disadvantage in the Exchange, which only admitted them after sixteen when they qualified for unemployment insurance, and even then tended to reserve what worthwhile jobs they had for adults. Unexpectedly, in an enquiry carried out in 1932, it was found that secondary school-leavers were considerably less successful in obtaining jobs than those from elementary schools, and this was especially true for secondary school girls. The authors of the report commented:

> The depression has produced the paradox that the children who have had the longest training seem least able to obtain employment. . . . It runs counter to anything that is logical, that at a time when trained, flexible and imaginative minds are more than ever required, industry can find so little use for those who have had the privilege of extended education.[91]

It was easier for a fourteen-year-old to get a 'blind-alley' job as an errand-boy, newspaper-boy or shop assistant than for a sixteen-year-old with Matriculation to find a start in professional or clerical work, and even higher qualifications could be a serious disqualification for the jobs available. Peter Donnelly had trained for seven years for the priesthood at Ushaw College, Durham, and was proficient in Latin and Greek, but discovered that 'there is this to be said against such accomplishments,

221

that you cannot sell them'.[92] When Kay Garrett, a qualified shorthand-typist, returned from South Africa in 1929,

> I was under the happy impression that I would get a job the day after I landed. But the depression had set in. Wherever I went in answer to an advertisement, there were queues of shorthand-typists stretching out into the street. They all had up-to-date London references. What could I hope for straight from a frontier town (I don't suppose anyone had ever heard of Bulawayo in those days) in darkest Africa?[93]

Arthur Barton qualified as a teacher in Chester in 1937 to find the job market overstocked: 'I wrote dozens of letters of application and went to many education offices and even to the headquarters of the National Union of Teachers up in London, but there was nothing anyone could or would do for me.... There were absolutely no vacancies'.[94] So, too, Kathleen Betterton, a working-class girl who had fought her way to Oxford, graduating in 1933, to find that 'a degree counted for nothing in finding a job.... There was a glut of educated people in search of jobs: many became socialists'.[95]

Searching for work was an increasingly dispiriting occupation as days, weeks and even months passed without result, whether for skilled workers who anxiously waited for the postman to bring a reply to a letter or for the unskilled who retraced well-trodden routes in widening circles from home. From initial optimism there was almost always a gradual descent into frustration and despair, often accompanied by anger. When Alice Pidgeon's husband was out of work for two-and-a-half years in the thirties, 'he wrote hundreds of letters for jobs ... and not even a reply. It was heart-breaking'.[96] For Jack Jones, a Pontypool miner, unemployment in 1921 meant 'Going deeper and deeper into debt, until at last I was as bitter as gall, and ready for anything', and again in 1926:

> There is nothing interesting that one can say about looking for work in and about a little city which has twenty thousand unemployed. One just goes round and round, and when in need of a rest about midday one takes a threepenny bowl of soup at Woolworth's, a look through the paper in the Reading Room of the hospitable Central Library, then off we go again. On towards evening one goes home to the wife and children. 'Here's Dad. Any luck?'[97]

In areas dependent on a single industry which had collapsed it quickly became almost meaningless to look for work, mining communities being particularly vulnerable to this. In 1933 both Joseph Halliday and his father became unemployed when their pit at Wingate, County Durham, closed: his father, 'signing on' for the first time in his life at fifty-two, 'took it much to heart'. 'To look for work was absolutely hopeless.... To say "genuinely seeking work" was farcical in its way. There was none.'[98] The chances of alternative work depended on the area and the variety of local occupations, so that in a city like Hull the skilled shipbuilder, Harry Fletcher, had forty-six different jobs for brief periods between 1922 and 1938: casual dock-work, labouring on building sites, concreting and at gasworks, sometimes for only half a day.

> Some tried to make the best of a bad job, but it needed a very strong will to ward off the general feeling of helplessness.... It has made me very bitter. During the war we could not do enough for the country, but when it was over we were thrown on the scrapheap, where a good many of us stayed until the next war.[99]

Two further records suggest the gradual erosion of hope which many long-term unemployed experienced. Joe Loftus, a young labourer of Leigh, Lancashire, fell out of work in 1931.

> I trudged for miles to firms I knew of, sometimes alone, sometimes with mates in the same fix, asking for work of any kind and getting refusal after refusal, walking for what seemed to add up to little more than killing time, using up shoe-leather and good clog-irons, steadily becoming convinced there was 'nothing doing' before I even got there. Sometimes arriving and walking past the factory gates without asking, to avoid one more refusal. Many days I would turn out strangely hopeful, with a spring in my step, still hopeful after refusals, getting stiff and weary after pounding the stones, feeling my shoulders beginning to ache and droop, and so back home.... What was it I had to offer anyway?[100]

The same year a young cabinet-maker, Max Cohen, searched for work in London.

> I found it a harassing and nerve-racking ordeal to accommodate myself to the reduced rate of benefit... I lived in dread of those empty, boring, monotonous days of walking about searching for a job that was never there, and returning to a lodging bereft of warmth and stimulating food. The emptiness of the belly, and the accompanying tension and worry, produced an emptiness of the brain and of the spirit. I walked about looking for work as much to distract myself as to find work.[101]

Having exhausted local job prospects, some men took to the road to tramp further afield, as their fathers and grandfathers had done before the Great War. There were, however, differences from the former pattern. Trade unions no longer supported men on tramp with travelling allowances and registered 'houses of call'; there were no longer information services or established routes; on the other hand, tramping on foot was now supplemented for some by the use of trains, trams and buses, and for others by lifts from sympathetic motorists and lorry-drivers. These gave a new mobility to some tramps in the twenties and thirties, enabling them to cover longer distances at greater speed than their forefathers who had trudged their weary twenty miles a day. Walking remained the chief means of travel, however, as Hannington saw on the Bath Road leading from south Wales, 'hundreds of men, footsore and weary... trudging towards London, having left their families at the mercy of the Boards of Guardians'.[102] Nightly lodging was usually in the casual wards ('spikes') of workhouses, where a dormitory bed and unappetizing food were provided in return for a couple of hours' work, sometimes perfunctory, sometimes energetic wood-chopping or stone-breaking. Men who had 4 or 6d. to spare usually preferred a private lodging-house or the better-run hostels administered by philanthropic bodies.

It is not possible to estimate how many tramps were on the road at a given time, even less what proportion of them were genuinely unemployed men looking for work as distinct from 'professional' vagrants who might do an odd day's work if offered. Nevertheless, there seems to be a clear connection between the use of tramp wards and the state of the economy. The numbers using casual wards increased sharply from 3,188 at the end of May 1920 to 10,217 in December 1929 and reached 16,911 on the night of 21 May 1932, at the depths of the depression.[103] Additionally the LCC area alone contained 16,875 registered lodging-house beds in 1931, though it is not known how many were occupied at a given time. Autobiographers used both types of accommodation depending on their resources and location: some 'spikes' had a reputation for clean beds and better food while others were to be avoided except in extreme need. Inter-war tramps in search of work were almost always young, single men, not necessarily impelled solely by lack of work: tramping was also an adventure, sometimes pleasurable, sometimes not, but always a challenge and a change from the frustration of aimlessly seeking work. By the age of seventeen Joe Armitage had been bored by a succession of brief, dead-end jobs in a warehouse, a brickfield and a building site interrupted by spells of unemployment, and took to the road, spending the next six years tramping through England and Scotland, picking up casual work, sometimes for a few weeks, sometimes for half a day: he was generally able to sleep in Model Lodging-Houses at 1s. a night, and enjoyed his long tramp before settling down to regular work in Leeds at twenty-three.[104] Charlie Potter had been out of work since 1926 when he was sacked at twenty-one: in 1931, after the introduction of the Household Means Test, his dole was cut from 25s. to 17s. a week, and he and a mate went on tramp from home in Beeston, Nottingham, on the rumour of work at a new ironworks at Beverley in Yorkshire. They slept in haystacks or used 'spikes' (at Southwell it was skilly for breakfast – thin oatmeal porridge without milk or sugar), but though they found no work at Beverley, 'it was an experience we would not have missed'.

> To many of our mates, some of our friends and a few in our families, it had all been a waste of time. But not to Joe and me. It had been a mild adventure after weeks and months roaming the streets with hundreds of others looking more bedraggled and hopeless day by day. Meeting friends who asked the same question – 'Have you found anything yet? Never mind, something will turn up. Have you tried so-and-so? I hear they are setting on.' . . . I lost nothing and learned a lot. I was better in health, and felt fit enough to face the future, knowing that things had to get better economically – or that's what I thought.[105]

John Brown's tramp in 1927 became virtually a tour of England, undertaken when he lost his dock-work job after the General Strike at the age of nineteen. From home in South Shields he looked for work in Newcastle, York, Reading (having got a lift), Guildford, Winchester, Southampton, Dover, Canterbury, Reading, Bath, Gloucester, Chester, Manchester, Penrith, Carlisle, Dumfries, Newcastle, Leeds, London (where he had work for a spell) and back to South Shields, casual dock-work, and more unemployment. Now he looked on the queues at the Labour Exchange with fresh eyes:

> In the newspapers I had read a great deal of the men who drew the dole although they had large sums of money in the bank, and of others who lay in bed all day reading novels from the Public Libraries, going out only to sign on. But I soon found out that such statements were gross slanders on the unemployed. Many of the men in my queue went without cigarettes so that they could buy stamps to put on letters applying for jobs. . . . But as the weeks went on, they grew weary, and some of them adopted a defiant 'don't care' attitude. They resumed their cigarettes, and ceased tramping and 'made the best of a bad job.' This does not mean that they gave up their search for work . . . but they lost the first, vigorous urge which drove them on in the first month of unemployment.[106]

Tramping was a constructive alternative to the boredom of worklessness in local, familiar surroundings. So, also, was to seek alternative employments far removed from one's usual work – usually at a much lower level of skill or status, but occasionally using the opportunity of enforced leisure to change the direction of one's life and develop a new, more interesting career. Of the former response there are many examples, since mobility downwards was much easier than upwards during the depression. Kay Garrett, a qualified shorthand-typist with a child to support, took work as a 'daily' at £1 a week while her unemployed father peddled razor-blades and bootlaces from a suitcase.[107] Joseph Halliday, with a secondary school education, worked as a farmhand at 10s. a week, and, later, as a brush salesman, often earning less on commission than when receiving transitional benefit,[108] while Max Cohen similarly tried a short spell as commission agent for scouring powder[109] and George Hodgkinson, after ten months of failure to get engineering work, became a commission agent for a book publisher and, later, for a wireless company.[110] After his long tramp, John Brown also survived for a year as a commercial traveller selling celluloid labels.[111] A good many unemployed men joined the army if they could pass the strict, peacetime medical examination, and at 2s. a day with 'all found' it was a not unattractive alternative to the dole, with the added glamour of a uniform and the chance of overseas service. 'After the General Strike I went in the army', said a former miner: 'It was the only way to escape from unemployment'.[112] A few – it seems, very few – dropped out of normal life completely. Unemployed in 1921, Joseph Stacey decided that he would become a 'real' tramp and 'work at the trade': he did so, to his satisfaction, until conscripted into the army in 1940 (where, at forty-one, he was drafted into the Pay Corps). In the thirties 'If I had been offered permanent work I would have rejected it, for tramping was now my life. . . . After several years living in the nomadic way I was in love with the freedom'.[113]

Upward mobility was obviously much more difficult, usually constrained by lack of capital and experience, yet a number of autobiographers record successful adaptations to new occupations which provided more satisfaction than their previous work. Keeping a small shop was the ambition of many working men, and could be realized with small outlay in trades such as greengrocery, as Mick Burke demonstrated. Partly disabled in the war, he had worked for a market trader until becoming unemployed: his response was to set up his own business, obtaining £40 from the King's Fund by commuting part of his pension: this bought a pony, cart and stock of fruit and vegetables and he developed a successful round. Later he recalled, 'I've no regrets. I've had a good life. . . . If I'd had two arms I'd have been out of work and have nothing'.[114] A woodcarver driven out by machinery developed a new profession as a masseur,[115] while others became gardeners, clerks, organists, newsagents, bookmakers and fish and chip shop proprietors. Some men had always nursed literary ambitions and used their enforced leisure to develop writing skills which sometimes took them into professional authorship; besides the considerable number who wrote and published their own autobiographies, an ex-miner, Jack Jones published novels and plays, Walter Greenwood, unemployed three times as a clerk and council canvasser, became an acclaimed novelist, Peter Donnelly, a casual labourer, became a poet while others achieved success as journalists. Another group of men of strong political convictions and experience in the labour movement found salaried positions in trade unions or political parties of the left; George Hodgkinson became Agent for the Coventry Labour Party, Ernie Benson a branch Secretary of the Communist Party and, later, sales organizer for the *Daily Worker.* Harry McShane, Arthur Horner, Willie Gallacher and Walter Hannington were all early members of the Communist Party and took leading parts in the revolutionary politics and unemployed struggles of the inter-war years: all had experienced unemployment, usually as a result of victimization. McShane worked as a propagandist for the 'Tramp Trust Unltd.', touring Scotland with demands for a six-hour day, wages of £1 a day, rationing of work and full wages for the unemployed, later becoming Glasgow Organiser of the National Unemployed Workers Movement.[116] Hannington, sacked as a toolmaker in 1920, was a founder-member of the NUWM and quickly became its National Organiser,[117] Gallacher was elected the first Communist Party MP (for West Fife in 1935) after leading many strikes and unemployed demonstrations,[118] while Arthur Horner was successively elected as a colliery checkweighman, President of the South Wales Miners' Federation and, in 1946, General Secretary of the National Union of Mineworkers.[119] For such men the campaign against unemployment and for better rights for the unemployed was part of the greater struggle for a revolutionary change in the economic and social order by which the capitalist system and the exploitation of labour would cease to exist.

Psychological effects

Both autobiographers and social commentators on the effects of unemployment believed that lack of work had important and, over time, seriously detrimental effects on mental health. With the onset of world depression after 1929 the subject was explored by psychologists in several European countries and in America[120] and there emerged what became a widely accepted theory or 'stage model' which argued that the attitudes of the unemployed passed through a series of changes towards ultimate apathy and despair. The most influential of these studies was one carried out by a team of Austrian social scientists, Marie Jahoda, Paul Lazarsfeld and Hans Zeisel in 1931–2 in the small town of Marienthal, about twenty miles from Vienna.[121] Marienthal, a company town with a population of around 1,500 inhabitants, was solely dependent on its textile factory, which closed for good in 1930: the buildings and plant were demolished, and the workers' houses now overlooked the ruins of their former workplace. Three-quarters of all the families were dependent on meagre unemployment relief payments, which for some amounted to a mere quarter of their former wages: it was said that it was scarcely possible to live on these payments, and that 'When a cat or dog disappears, the owner no longer bothers to report the loss: he knows that someone must have eaten the animal, and he does not want to find out who'.[122] The factory had been the centre of social life of the town, with a range of clubs and cultural activities which had now disappeared or greatly declined: library loans had dropped by 49 per cent between 1929 and 1931, despite the abolition of loan charges, newspaper circulation had dropped drastically as had membership of political clubs. 'Now the whole place is dead', residents reported: there was a 'blunting monotony' about life, in which people 'have become accustomed to owning less, doing less and expecting less' than formerly. Although housewives were as busy or busier than ever, with the added burden of trying to stretch limited resources, the men had lost the structure of time which work had given to their lives and were now unable to fill their days usefully or interestingly: 'they drift gradually out of an ordered existence, standing around in the streets for hours or leaning against walls'. They have 'gone back to a more primitive, less differentiated, experience of time' in which the changing seasons of the year are important, but not the days of the week.[123] The researchers concluded that the unemployed passed through a series of psychological stages, forming a pattern or model. The first effect of loss of work was shock or panic, a lack of understanding of its cause and of how life could be managed: this was followed by an eager search for work (one man wrote 130 letters of application for jobs in the early months), but when this produced no results men became gradually resigned to a lower level of existence until, for some, a final stage of apathy and despair was reached: at this point there was a total lack of initiative, self-confidence and hope – a condition which the researchers described as 'broken'. Taking all the Marienthal families, they concluded that 23 per cent were 'unbroken' or relatively unchanged psychologically, 70 per cent were 'resigned' and 7 per cent 'broken' i.e. 'collapsed under the pressure of unemployment'.[124]

The British experience of unemployment was by no means an exact parallel with Marienthal. There the unemployment was virtually total and long-continued and there was virtually no possibility of alternative work: public relief was at a much lower level than in Britain, and the unfortunate inhabitants lived among the visible ruins of their former prosperity: half-demolished walls, dented boilers and old transmission wheels. Nevertheless, the Austrian study became extremely influential in both Britain and the United States, almost to the point of becoming received wisdom. The theory rested on the assumption of the importance of work in human life – that work gave identity and status, a structure of time and a sense of achievement and satisfaction, so that without it people became demoralized and purposeless. It was not difficult to find individual instances in the English studies of the descent from eager activity to apathy and hopelessness, though the full progression of the Marienthal model to the 'broken' stage required a considerable lapse of time, and as we have seen, long-term unemployment, though serious in Britain in the thirties, was never the experience of most. For the majority, who were in and out of work, hope could be constantly reborn, and the ultimate stage of total collapse was only rarely reached.

In Greenwich, studied by Bakke in 1931–2, unemployed men spoke of feeling 'lost' without work, and that they felt 'more important' when working. You feel that 'something is wrong with you' when unemployed, and several men told Bakke that they would 'jump at the chance' of a job even if the wage was no more than unemployment insurance benefit. 'Everybody does some work in this world. . . . That's one thing that makes us human; we don't wait for things to happen to us, we work for them. And if you can't find any work to do, you have the feeling that you're not human. You're out of place.'[125] Bakke cited a case which apparently closely parallelled the Marienthal model (of which he was at the time presumably unaware). Case 'A' was a mechanic and lorry-driver aged twenty-eight with ten year's experience. At first on losing his job he was confident: 'There's plenty of jobs for a man with my experience. I've never been out more than a week or so before. I'll soon be back'. After three weeks: 'I'm beginning to wonder how plentiful jobs are. It's a funny thing. It's never been like this before. . . . You feel like you're no good, if you get what I mean'. After eight weeks: 'I'm beginning to wonder what is wrong with me. I've tried every way. . . . They say, "How long you been out?" And you don't like to, but you lie . . . I know if I tell them two months, they'll say "What's wrong?" ' After eleven weeks: Confidence now gone, but still a dogged determination to find some kind of work: 'There's one of two things, either I'm no good, or there's something wrong with business around here . . . I feel when I walk down the streets here that all my old mates are looking at me and saying, "Wonder what's wrong with 'A'? He never used to keep away from work so long." Even my family is beginning to think I'm not trying'. After seventeen weeks, sullen, but not completely discouraged, and still searching for work: 'It isn't the hard work of tramping about so much, although that is bad enough. It's the hopelessness of every step you take when you go in search of a job you know isn't there'.[126] This case was, however, untypical of Greenwich, where most unemployment was short-term, and even here 'A' was still actively seeking work and not completely 'broken'. We are not told his later history.

Bakke believed that it was the more ambitious men, and those who got most satisfaction from work, who lost heart most quickly, and also that what was often mistaken for the 'laziness' of the unemployed was more a result of physical and mental exhaustion. The Pilgrim Trust survey of unemployment in 1938 also found that the former status of the worker played a large part in his attitude and ability to adjust to worklessness; it was more difficult for the skilled man, who had had pride in his work and, often, in his firm, than for the unskilled who had little interest in the job and no regular time routine.[127] By this time there was considerable medical interest in psychoneurosis and psychosomatic illnesses, which appeared to increase with the length of unemployment. In a survey of 1,000 sick insured persons carried out in Glasgow by Dr J. L. Halliday he calculated that psychoneurosis was the cause of ill-health among 27 per cent of those unemployed for up to three months, rising to 42 per cent among those out of work for between six and twelve months.[128] A number of cases were cited of long-term unemployed men suffering from disabling fears, anxieties and functional disorders for which there were no organic explanations, while it was also claimed that the mental effects on the wives of unemployed men were greater still. Given the state of psychiatric knowledge and practice at this time and the vagueness with which such terms as 'neurasthenia', 'neurosis' and 'strain' were used, the evidence of a direct link is persuasive rather than conclusive: nor is it possible to distinguish clearly between the effects of a reduced diet in causing, for example, anaemia among women, from the increased anxiety of maintaining the family on a reduced budget.

That the majority of unemployed people suffered, in varying degrees, anxiety, frustration and depression is beyond dispute and fully attested by autobiographers, but, as Hilda Jennings discovered in her study of unemployment in Brynmawr, south Wales, no two families had exactly the same reactions. There were certain common habits of thought imposed by the necessity of registering twice a week at the Labour Exchange and attending pay day on Fridays:

> If he has been out of work for some time, each Friday he will have a short period of sickening anxiety lest the clerk should single him out and tell him that he is to be sent to the Court of Referees: then will follow a few days' consequent dread lest his benefit should be stopped and he be cast onto the Poor Law.[129]

Beyond this, however, there was little similarity in attitudes: one man approaches the Exchange with impatience and bitterness at his dependence; one finds causes of complaint and irritation with the officials; another is apathetic, with no conscious feelings unless his pay is threatened; while another has an inflamed political conscience and argues the need for a fundamental change in the economic and social system. All these varieties of reaction, and more, are represented in the autobiographies, defying any universal pattern. Many writers describe a sense of impotence and powerlessness to control their situation, typically expressed by a former clerk in an advertising department for sixteen years, earning good wages and buying his house on mortgage: 'It seems like a devilish game of snakes and ladders – as if I had been picked up while well on in the game and put right back to the beginning'.[130] Or, in Terence Monaghan's words, 'You were nulled. . . . It means that you were afraid. You were humbled, cowed'.[131]

The monotony of searching for work and of life on a poor diet, without luxuries or diversions, is a theme commonly expressed: 'Life became a round of hateful sameness. . . . The long, monotonous days with nothing to do were maddening. . . . It was useless to look for work, it was useless to do anything at all'.[132] To relieve the boredom men were sometimes tempted into extravagance – some critics regarded visits by the unemployed to the cinema as this – and Max Cohen recalled that after days of hunger he would spend a good portion of his benefit money on a sumptuous meal in a restaurant.

> True, all this would mean that in one reckless hour I would be squandering money which I ought to be spreading carefully over a whole week. But what of that? I would at least have had one glorious and shining hour in the drab gloom of the week. Better one ecstatic repletion of the stomach than a succession of grey, unfilling palliatives, merely teasing, not satisfying.[133]

In the event, he could not eat more than half the meal placed before him.

As their unemployment lengthened, several autobiographers write of a sense of failure in their own abilities or personality. 'There is nothing quite so hard to bear as being a failure for the first time, when your spirit has not been accustomed to the recurrence of this experience.'[134] But recurrence of the experience could lead to a further sense of rejection by society, a feeling described by Syd Metcalfe as being 'useless, unwanted'[135] and by John Brown as an 'outcast':

> Perhaps the most remarkable feature of a long period 'on the dole' was the way in which a man felt himself to be fighting against the whole forces of the State. Treated as a mere cog in the bureaucratic machine, a man ceased to regard himself any longer as being a member of society, with the same rights as those possessed by a man with a job, and began to think of himself as an outlaw, granted a pittance with begrudging fingers so that his misery should not obtrude itself too much.[136]

For some, the result of this was increasing resentment, bitterness and anger, often levelled against the clerks at the Labour Exchange – the most tangible representatives of the bureaucracy – or against their more fortunate mates still at work, against particular employers, the government or, more rarely, the capitalist system generally. A skilled engineer, supporting two adults and five children on 33s. 3d. a week, wrote: 'Some of you think that an unemployed man gets apathetic. He doesn't. The chief mental effect to most, I am sure, is bitterness. . . . You feel you could break something'.[137] Resentment was usually personalized, levelled against individuals who could be held to blame rather than against the economic system or even a particular political party; a common view was that all parties were equally reprehensible, callous and unconcerned, and that nothing could be expected from them. Relatively few men, as we shall see, turned to active revolutionary politics. 'Men who had been unemployed for long periods were very unhappy and dejected and began to lose hope. . . . A few gave way to anger, which did not help either, but it did cause many men to become Communist in their thinking.'[138] Measured by the few who joined the party, this is a dubious assertion. Most unemployed men who had any strong political opinions supported the Labour Party, and the more typical view is expressed by John Edmonds: 'Hope, in varying degrees, was ever present . . . and, with it, a silent resentment at not knowing what or who was really to blame. . . . My father read the *Daily Herald*, stoutly supported the Labour Party, and blamed Mr. Baldwin for every and any thing'.[139]

Few autobiographers illustrate the full version of the stage model developed at Marienthal, though a natural progression from initial optimism towards an apathetic pessimism is often described.

> At first there was a period of brief euphoria for me, a tasty illusion of freedom. Soon enough I was jolted into realising that I needed a job, any job that would pay better than the measly dole. I was keen enough, hardworking enough, conscientious enough. . . . Then I'd be bouncing back, and fluctuating between youthful hope and adult apathy. . . . After all, though the newspapers talked about 20% unemployment, to me that meant that 80% were employed, and surely there must be a place in there somewhere for me?

But, after failure to find work,

> Becoming self-conscious about going out without purpose, having exhausted all the possible places to apply for work, I was almost in danger of becoming a loner, schizoid with loneliness, depressed with guilt – yes, guilt – too much alone with my thoughts. Being unable to keep up with my old friends, with no pocket money to spare. Losing touch, and knowing it.[140]

The transition from optimism to pessimism was natural and common enough, but from pessimism to fatalism and total despair much less so. One autobiographer who perhaps came nearest to the 'broken' stage was a forty-seven-year-old skilled engineer, unemployed when his firm closed for lack of orders. At first optimistic, after a year he was willing to take any work even if outside his trade, and had ceased to be active in his trade union. Hating to be dependent on his wife's and son's earnings, he left home after selling all his books and personal possessions, and now lived in lodgings on a dole of 15s. 3d. a week.

> I have thrown myself into revolutionary movements from time to time, but it all seems so futile. The one important thing is to get hold of money. I'd steal if I could get away with it. I'm disgusted with my former political and trade union associates. . . . It seems incredible that all this could have happened to me in four years. . . . The outlook as far as I am concerned is hopeless. I've given up dreaming of any return to my former life and work, and just hang on, hoping that something big will happen before I die. I don't believe things can go on like this much longer, and because of this I am willing to suffer this hellish existence for a few more months.[141]

Even here, it seems, were some remains of hope, if not for himself, for some change in society which would remove the evil of unemployment. Max Cohen suffered extreme misery, semi-starvation and 'the multifarious sources of worry that can afflict an out-of-work', but after two months,

> Nevertheless, man has to adjust himself to his environment if he is to survive. My attitude towards being out of work changed – in my surface consciousness at any rate. Slowly but surely the first keen edge of the urge to get work became blunted. I began to become accustomed to being without a job, and unemployment became the normal, not the abnormal, way of life.[142]

After several months Cohen became afraid of finding a job, feeling that he was no longer physically or mentally capable of holding down regular work. Nevertheless he still had sufficient courage to set up his own cabinet-making business on credit, which enabled him to survive until he found regular work in a new furniture factory.

Cohen believed that his experiences left long-lasting effects – a loss of vigour, lack of self-confidence, not knowing how to spend his money or how to enjoy a good meal. After five years on the dole Joseph Halliday commented: 'What a shocking start to a young life. . . . The marks it left upon me I shall carry as long as my life endures. They were soul-destroying experiences'.[143] An ex-Army officer stated that he would now do anything for money, short of murder, and that 'Sometimes I no longer desire to live at all',[144] while a Derbyshire miner who became unemployed at sixty said that 'We would both rather be dead than go on like this'.[145] But although there was considerable discussion in the thirties about unemployment as a cause of suicide, the evidence is sketchy given the difficulty of isolating one factor as the prime mover. Most of the cases reported in the press involved serious illness or marital breakdown as well as unemployment, making it impossible to know the proximate reason for the act. Max Cohen believed that he became 'mildly insane' at one point due to lack of food, but never contemplated ending his existence. On his greengrocery round in Lancashire Mick Burke encountered some of the tragedies of the depression: 'I served two brothers who had lost their jobs . . . one of them was sitting in the chair with his head down – at first I thought he was asleep, then I saw the large pool of blood on the floor. The poor devil had cut his throat'.[146] Ernie Benson stated that 'hardly a week passed by without deaths of this character being recorded in local and national newspapers', though the only one he detailed was the suicide of a young unemployed man who suffered from epilepsy.[147] In Sunderland, Jeremy Seabrook recorded the memoirs of a miner's son: 'After the General Strike he [my father] never worked again. He cut his throat one afternoon in July 1931. I can remember it like yesterday. I came home from school and found him'.[148] By chance, we have statistics for suicides in the nearby town of Darlington: between 1920 and 1939 they averaged nine a year, varying between two and twenty-one. The latter occurred in 1927 – the best of the inter-war years for unemployment, while 1931 and 1932, the worst years of the depression, had below average deaths from this cause.[149] On this admittedly small sample there was no general correlation between suicide and the extent of unemployment, but this does not preclude the possibility of unemployment depression as one factor in multiple causation.

A similarly negative conclusion applies to the statistics of crime, a notoriously difficult area to interpret since they depended on changes in the law, detection rates and variations in sentencing. Unemployed men might feel themselves to be 'outlaws' of society, might say that 'If I'm not allowed to earn bread I shall take it'[150] or 'I shall just become a thief if I can find a pal to come in with me',[151] but only one of the 200 autobiographers consulted actually admitted to a life of crime; this, a former electrician aged thirty-one now worked with a gang specializing in warehouse thefts and smash-and-grab raids, and gave his opinion that 50 per cent of burglars had drifted into crime 'through bad economic conditions': 'I am not writing this in any spirit of boastfulness – there is nothing to boast about. Nor do I regard myself as criminal by nature. I still have scruples, and have never done violence to any person. When I look back over the last five years I feel I am in some way justified in hitting back at society.'[152]

But a popular view that 'idleness' led directly to crime cannot be confirmed by the evidence. Although crime rates nationally rose over the inter-war years, the rise did not correspond with unemployment rates – for example, crime was particularly high in the prosperity of 1919–20 but lower in the depression of 1921, and it continued to rise in the later 1930s when unemployment was falling: similarly, at the local level, prosperous Norwich had higher crime rates than depressed Gateshead between 1934 and 1936[153] and in Middlesbrough in 1932, when 45 per cent of the workforce was unemployed, 801 indictable offences were reported compared with 1,099 in 1938 when 22 per cent were out of work.[154] It may, however, be of some significance that while offences against the person in Middlesbrough actually declined over the twenty years, offences against property without violence doubled[155] and juvenile crime showed a large increase of between two and three times. Increases in larceny and shopbreaking by juveniles were particularly common, and seemed to suggest that such offences were a by-product of a breakdown in work discipline on which social observers frequently commented.

In general, however, depressed areas were remarkably law abiding and did not exhibit any major changes in moral standards, religious observance, family or marital relationships peculiar to these regions. Despite all their difficulties, there was an extraordinary degree of resilience in these communities, akin to that displayed in heavily-bombed cities during the Second World War. Autobiographers write of 'the warm hospitality and the neighbourliness during adversity . . . the sense of a communal misfortune in which our little villages and towns seemed to share and feel stronger for the sharing'[156] and of the persistence of hope even in the most depressed areas. 'We felt, not only that work would pick up again in the yards and the pits, but that time was on our side.'[157] In Jarrow, of all places, Arthur Barton felt an 'eternal optimism . . . in a town where nearly 80 per cent were out of work',[158] and the wife of an unemployed riveter who once earned £8 to £10 a week and now supported a family of five children on 33s. commented: 'You must keep going for the children. . . . The only hope we have got is the hope to come. I've lived for hope, or as my husband would say, for faith, for thirteen years. Perhaps, after all, its worst for the men. The women have their work and their home'.[159] And a child could see unemployment through very different eyes: 'Home was happiest when Dad had no job and times were hard. . . . When times were bad, Mum and Dad couldn't go out to the pub'.[160]

Time to spare?

It was often claimed, particularly in the right-wing press, that the unemployed did not know how to use the time with which they suddenly found themselves, that once their work patterns had been disturbed men had no substitutes with which to fill five-and-a-half days a week and that this was a main reason why many degenerated into listlessness and apathy which unfitted them to take advantage of what work opportunities might exist, now or later. Such views often materialized in the shape of a stereotype – a bedraggled man, dressed in worn-out clothes which hung loosely on an undernourished frame, his cap pulled well down to conceal as much as possible of a careworn face, standing aimlessly at a street corner, propping up a lamp-post or a gable-end wall. Such men, it was believed, had given up hope, ambition and the search for work to become 'loungers' and 'loafers', content to live a low-level existence on public relief, now unfitted and unwilling to return to the normal life of work. Fears were often expressed that the long-term unemployed were becoming physically and mentally degenerate, and that young men who had never had regular work since leaving school would become a permanent liability to national fitness and the economy. Even some of those who were most sympathetic to the plight of the unemployed tended to take a low and condescending view of their ability to occupy themselves in rational ways: thus, the well-known author and broadcaster S. P. B. Mais:

> One thing is quite certain. Left to themselves the unemployed can do nothing whatever to occupy their spare time profitably. As *The Times*' correspondent pointed out with regard to derelict Durham, 'success depends entirely on the active presence of some individual on whom the unemployed people are ready to repose confidence'. The interminable worry of trying to budget on an inadequate benefit leaves them neither the spirit nor the initiative to think out any method of securing amenities without money.[161]

This was not the experience of any but a very small minority of the unemployed. The only sociological study of 'loafing' was that carried out by Bakke in Greenwich. He found that on an average day 210 men were standing in the streets apparently aimlessly and a further fifty-eight sitting in the public libraries – they represented less than 8 per cent of the unemployed men of Greenwich. Bakke further estimated that 45 per cent of these 'loafers' were young men under twenty-one, and that of the remainder about half were pensioners: the number of adults of working age who spent a significant amount of time aimlessly on the streets was, therefore, extremely small.[162] As we have seen, looking for work was the main work of the unemployed, and Bakke had observed that the unemployed spent an average of 4.2 hours a day at this. There was also the requirement of personal attendance at the Labour Exchange to register that one was available for work and 'genuinely seeking' it, and to draw one's benefit, usually on Fridays: in theory attendance was supposed to be every day, but in areas of high unemployment this was usually reduced to two or three times a week and, moreover, established something approaching a regular pattern or routine of its own. For many men further time was involved in appearing before committees and tribunals to plead or defend their entitlement to benefit – so much so that one autobiographer ironically observed that 'the staple diet of the unemployed is committees'.[163]

Much of the rest of an unemployed man's time was spent at home or at home-based activities, and there is little evidence that he was encouraged to spend much time in bed during the day. Domestic life and routines had to continue as before, and the home and family were the principal social and psychological support systems of a man whose former social contacts arising from work were now reduced. The importance of the home was now, if anything, enhanced. In the depressed Welsh town of Brynmawr, Hilda Jennings noted 'The common preoccupation with home and family, the warmth and colour in human relationships, the intense attachment to the place, proved by the constant return of emigrants from it . . . Brynmawr, apparently so disintegrated, has an underlying common life.'[164] In such places the local community was the family writ large, where friends, neighbours and relatives provided companionship, group associations and an extended network of support. According to the Pilgrim Trust's investigation, the unemployed man finds his life 'switched down to a lower economic plane . . . and no doubt at first he finds it hard [but] he ultimately settles down to a new routine of existence. And one thing above all makes this comparatively easy for him, if he finds himself a member of an unemployed community'.[165] 'Life in Darwen is still very cheerful', wrote Cecil Northcott after a study of a Lancashire town where only twenty-eight of the sixty cotton-mills were still working,[166] while in the Rhondda, 'Kindly country ways of neighbourliness and mutual help survive . . . to a degree of which suburban dwellers can have little conception'.[167]

From the diaries kept by unemployed men in Greenwich, Bakke calculated that they spent, on average, five hours a day at home exclusive of sleep: together with the time spent looking for work, this made up something very close to the hours of a normal working day.

> My impression from reading the diaries of the unemployed is that they are not idling their time away. Their time is fully occupied, for the most part at useful tasks. The extra time which is on their hands after time spent looking for work is deducted, is spent by most of the men at home, not in the 'pubs' or on the streets.[168]

Contrary to the stereotypical division of functions between husbands and wives in working-class households, it seems that a good many unemployed men were prepared to help in at least some domestic tasks, even going across traditional role boundaries. In Lancashire mill-towns Cecil Northcott found that most unemployed men helped domestically, and believed that this 'accounts for the extraordinary air of neatness and well-being in most unemployed homes'.

> One man showed me his backyard, which he had transformed with a cheap pot of paint and re-paved with old pieces of flagging. 'Helping the missus' in many cases is a permanent occupation. The

brass round the kitchen range and anything which shines come within the duties of the man.[169]

Some went much further than mere polishing: 'Although I was unemployed, I was never unoccupied. I did a lot of paper-hanging and painting, and any odd jobs my relations and friends wanted doing'. This man also made rag rugs, normally done by women: 'By working very hard I could finish one measuring 2 × 1 yards in sixteen hours, and I was allowed to earn the 10s. a week without losing the unemployment pay'.[170]

John Edmonds' unemployed father was 'always occupied in repairing and redecorating the house, and making and mending clocks and other items of household equipment for ourselves and for neighbours'. Like many others, he also cultivated an allotment, which he had reclaimed from a refuse dumping-ground: 'The vegetables grown on this patch helped balance the household's precarious budget, and provided father with a healthy, sunburnt appearance that caused adverse comment among unkindly neighbours'.[171] Mr Pallas spring-cleaned and decorated his house, patched old kettles with cocoa tins, cut his children's hair and repaired their shoes. He too had an allotment, and when a photographer gave him thousands of old glass negatives, he built himself a greenhouse.[172] John Evans re-equipped his house with furniture he made at the Occupational Centre;[173] Joe Loftus built himself a small workshop in the backyard, made a kitchen cabinet and built an extension to the scullery,[174] while many unemployed fathers helped to look after and amuse the children. A labourer reported by the Pilgrim Trust had eight children at home and was drawing 54s. unemployment assistance.

> His chief interest was evidently his family, and he had not much use for any amusements and interests which he could not share with them. He found that looking after them was practically a whole time job for two people, himself and his wife. 'You can't complain. It's a lot of money to get for nothing. I wouldn't get much more in work than out of work.'[175]

In Greenwich those unemployed men who kept diaries spent an average of 10.7 hours a week in reading, half the time on newspapers and half on books, mainly fiction borrowed from the public libraries.[176] It is not possible to measure this against the time spent when in work, but those who mentioned reading were unanimous in saying that it had increased. Donald Kear, a young factory worker, noted that 'It was during my dole days that I became a compulsive reader. I read anything and everything that came my way',[177] and Will Paynter, a miner, became an 'avid reader' while unemployed: 'Some can boast of being educated at Eton and Cambridge: for me, it was the elementary school and Cymnor Library'.[178]

And for Will Oxley, as for many others, the public library, or 'the Tomb' as it was known locally, was both occupation and warm retreat:

> I had no private library, no money to buy books, and I wanted to read. I went to the reading room in the public library. Here there were proletarian students swotting away from ten in the morning till late at night. It was a refuge for them from the cold, wet streets, and gave them comfort and a sense of doing something for themselves. ... I got to know many such students. We began to compare ideas and notes, and to visit meetings together. We mutually organised ourselves.[179]

When details of the types of reading are supplied they seem remarkably varied – 'revolutionary novels', 'electrical engineering', 'astronomy, physics, economics, history, photography, psychology, psychic phenomena', and from another, 'Fiction – Priestley, Dell, Orczy, Tolstoy, etc. (Russian writers are my favourites). Educational and interest subjects – philosophy, psychology, travel, Socialism, economics etc.'[180] Jack Jones, the Welsh miner, went so far as to argue that unemployment was creating a new reading public, and had three articles on the subject published in *Time and Tide* in 1931:

> People were reading for dear life now that they had no work to go to. I tried to show how the depressed mining communities were trying to read themselves through the depression, and how this was sending the borrowing figures in libraries such as Pontypridd, where there were six and a half thousand unemployed, up and up by scores of thousands.[181]

Recreational pursuits which had to be paid for necessarily declined somewhat under the pressure of financial constraints, though people rarely abandoned them altogether. A decline in drinking by the unemployed was noted in Brynmawr and Greenwich – 'You can't afford it, mate', 'You've got to eat first'[182] – though it appears that gambling, generally for very small amounts, remained as popular as before, offering the hope of a sudden big win on the Derby or the Irish Sweep: 'Why, of course its a good investment. It's your only chance to get out of a 26s. rut. It don't happen often, that's true, but think of when it does!'[183]

The cinema provided another kind of excitement and release, either in the form of drama or comedy, and was probably the main family entertainment through the thirties. In Brynmawr the two cinemas remained busy while the amount of drinking was heavily down, and the Greenwich unemployed who kept diaries calculated that they spent an average of 2.6 hours a week at the cinema. This represents a reduced attendance, however, given the long cinema programmes of the day, Bakke believing that those who had formerly gone to the pictures every week now went only once a fortnight, generally in the afternoon when cheaper matinée seats were offered.[184] Attendance at professional football matches was similarly affected, though some clubs gave special rates to the unemployed, admitting them at low cost at half-time and free ten minutes before the final whistle. Participant sport was a major interest of many younger unemployed men, for whom 'time to spare' gave added opportunities for cricket and football matches, for swimming or gymnastic training where local clubs had been formed. Most single men spent as much time as possible out of the house and, when not searching for work, would often be involved in some group activity based on sports or hobbies. One curious phenomenon was the formation of 'gazoot' (or 'kazoo') jazz bands by the unemployed, sometimes known as 'Tommy Talker' bands:[185] these dressed in homemade uniforms, marched, paraded and competed, sharing any prize or collected money among the members. Hiking, either independently or with the recently formed Youth Hostels Association, was also popular, but others preferred solitary rambling, mention of walking in the woods occurring not infrequently. Poaching, always a favourite sport for some, increased among the unemployed, providing the chance of a rabbit dinner with the element of excitement and danger to break monotony. George Tomlinson, a Nottinghamshire miner unemployed for four years, found his escape and solace in nearby Sherwood Forest 'when things are at their worst, when the future looks hopeless and one's inside is tormented with that awful, boiling feeling that makes one want to rush out of the house and curse everything to relieve the torment...'[186] In the woods he studied nature, read Shakespeare, Byron and Shelley and made up fairy stories about the Forest to tell to his little daughter, gradually reaching a new kind of contentment:

> I have read many novels in which the chief characters have been unemployed, but I cannot say that I have been impressed. They always seem to make their characters either totally miserable or totally unconcerned about their unemployment. Whilst it is true that there is much more misery than joy, it is also true that one finds happiness in things which one had never noticed before. One hoards pleasant little incidents in the mind, incidents which would never be noticed if one was at work. Often in the summer I have been starting off for a long walk through the woods just as the men have been going to the pits, and I frankly admit that I have been glad that I was free to go where I wished... I have actually found it in me to pity those who were sweating in the darkness beneath me.... Even after four years of unemployment I get a thrill out of ignoring the pit buzzer.[187]

Other men greatly missed the associational experience which work had provided. Unemployment contributed to the large decline in trade union membership after the General Strike, further limiting the social contacts which had arisen from work. In some unions membership lasted as long as a man was on benefit, and in a few cases, such as the Leicester boot and shoe industry, unemployment insurance was paid through the union. But when benefit ended trade union membership ceased unless the man continued to pay his dues – unlikely, both because of the cost and the disenchantment which many felt over the inability of trade unions to help them. This was less so in some mining communities where the unemployed were encouraged to stay in union membership on special low rates in order to use the social and recreational facilities of miners' clubs. Church and chapel membership does not appear to have been greatly affected by unemployment, and a number of autobiographers valued the support which these institutions provided. Thus, a Primitive Methodist: 'Church activities, in which I was happy to engage, filled a gap and were a great help relieving deadly monotony'.[188] A man who had formerly been active in his trade union and local Labour Party as well as being a football coach, a lay preacher and Sunday school superintendent, gave up all activities except his chapel work: 'I maintain my connection with the chapel and the Sunday School because I believe in the chapel as a necessary institution in the lives of our people'.[189]

The consolations of religion as well as the social contact and possible material benefits which went with it were clearly important, and in areas where Church or chapel membership had always been high there was little sign of falling away. In Brynmawr, for instance, there were reckoned to be 2,310 adult Church members in 1931 out of a total population of 7,247, while the proportion of the inhabitants on Church rolls or known as 'attenders' reached 70.9 per cent.[190] And in Jarrow in 1926 Arthur Barton observed that 'There seemed to be a great deal of evangelism about in those days. As employment decreased more and more ... one evangelist after another came to our town and played to packed houses. The vacuum left by the departure of a way of life was filled temporarily at any rate, by religious emotion'.[191]

In addition to such pre-existing institutions, there was a remarkable growth of new clubs and societies of many kinds – social, recreational, athletic and educational – aimed at occupying the time of the unemployed interestingly and usefully. They were usually the products of local initiative, sometimes aided by voluntary social service agencies, miners' lodges, the Workers' Educational Association (WEA) or the National Unemployed Workers' Movement: some were quite informal, like the 'cellar clubs' in Liverpool, others were highly organized settlements or occupational centres, providing a wide range of activities for men of all ages and, often, women, during the day and evening. These were especially effective in close communities like those of south Wales and Durham, less so in large cities like Leicester where the smaller numbers

241

of unemployed were scattered over a wide area. Thus in Crook, Durham, it was estimated that 49 per cent of the unemployed were members of such clubs, which as well as social activities included WEA classes, four occupational centres receiving grants from the National Council of Social Service, drama, craft and hobbies clubs and a library. In the Rhondda there were between thirty and forty unemployed clubs which ranged from choral and operatic societies to clubs for mining outcrop coal: they were described by the Pilgrim Trust as 'the most successful response to the unemployment problem which the community has yet found'.[192]

Autobiographies confirm this optimism. An unemployed seaman wrote, 'I don't really know what we should do without them. They are a wonderful help in our lives':[193] Mrs Keen, an unemployed Lancashire cotton worker, believed that 'the Club helps me to keep sane'[194] while William O'Neill, an out-of-work turner in Lincoln, thought that 'This Club of ours has been a tremendous stimulus to us. I don't know what I would have been like if I had no other interests'.[195] This was the People's Service Club, started by the unemployed themselves, which as well as organizing a range of classes, included a repair shop for household equipment, a nursery school, communal garden and allotments, and a cobbler's shop which had repaired 15,000 pairs of children's shoes. Clubs organized by the National Unemployed Workers Movement sometimes had more explicit objectives, like the one in Dundee in 1922 which ran classes in history, economics and organizational tactics.[196] One of the most successful was that run by Harry Goldthorpe, who was Secretary of the Bradford Unemployed Association and its Club in Quebec Street: he had previously organized open air demonstrations, had had a fight with a clerk at the Labour Exchange and a spell in the workhouse when his benefit was stopped for not 'genuinely seeking work'. With a membership of 3,000, the club had a canteen, dance-hall, billiards table, printing press and a transport system 'all obtained by our own efforts'; it provided free meals for the children, and took a thousand of them for a week's holiday in Morecambe; numbers of men whose benefit had run out were employed by the club and their insurance cards stamped in order to put them back in benefit: 'a wangle . . . but also a humane act of kindness among suffering workers and their families'.[197] As one member, Clarence Muff, remembered, the club became sufficiently well-known to be visited by the Prince of Wales on one of his tours of depressed areas:

> I remember well the day that the late Prince of Wales came to the Unemployed Club in Quebec Street. No plush red carpet down. The Prince sat down on an ordinary plain chair; with him was a very elegant lady, and they had tea and cakes just the same as the rest of us. He was a fine young man, and spoke well of Mr. Goldthorpe doing such a good job for everyone concerned. Later on,

242

the Prince and the lady went up the wooden stairs to the dance floor and had a dance. It was no Tiffanys, but still, all was scrupulously clean. After staying about an hour, the Prince left, accompanied by detectives and a police escort.[198]

Not many years before this, Goldthorpe had been visited by a CID officer who had advised him, 'Take my advice and give this up. If you don't, you'll never be out of trouble as long as you live'.[199]

Poverty

Not all the poor in inter-war Britain were unemployed, nor were all the unemployed necessarily very poor, but the likelihood of a connection between poverty and those dependent on unemployment relief was a subject which aroused much concern and debate among social investigators, propagandists and politicians of all parties. The twenties and thirties were remarkable for the large number of social surveys carried out in many towns of differing economic fortunes, several of which repeated similar investigations made before the Great War in order to determine whether poverty had increased or diminished. The investigators were in no doubt that overall poverty had substantially declined, and that, however defined, fewer people now fell below a poverty line. When A. L. Bowley and Margaret Hogg had surveyed five English towns (Northampton, Warrington, Bolton, Reading and Stanley) in 1912–14, they had estimated that 11 per cent of all working-class families were in poverty: repeating the exercise in 1924 they found the figure to be 6.5 per cent.[200] Later surveys showed increases on this figure, reflecting the worsened economic conditions as the depression deepened, but still well below the pre-war level. When in 1929 Hubert Llewellyn Smith updated Charles Booth's survey of London life and labour forty years earlier, he found 11 per cent of families in poverty in the eastern area compared with 30.7 per cent previously,[201] while in his second survey of poverty in York in 1936, Seebohm Rowntree calculated that only 6.8 per cent of the working-class population was living in 'primary poverty' compared with 15.46 per cent in 1899, although on a more generous 'human needs' scale than that adopted earlier, he believed that 31.1 per cent of the working-class population were in poverty through inadequate income in 1936.[202] In Merseyside Caradog Jones placed 16 per cent of working-class families in poverty, but 30 per cent on a 'human needs' scale, closely similar to Rowntree, while in Bristol in 1937, a year of prosperity, 11 per cent of the working class were estimated to be in poverty, but another 21 per cent with insufficient income 'who are hard put to it to make a decent home'.[203] These definitions of poverty, and, therefore, the conclusions, are not strictly comparable, and it is significant that no comparable studies were carried out in the most depressed areas of Britain. However, some things seem clear despite the differences: that absolute poverty was substantially lower than formerly, perhaps only about half that at the beginning of the century, but that taking a definition somewhat above the mere subsistence level and more in line with the improved standards of living of the working classes generally, there was still around one-third of the class whose income was insufficient for human needs.

What was also clear, and more disturbing, was that the causes of poverty had changed substantially. Before the war the principal reasons had been low, irregular and casual earnings, the death or disability of a chief breadwinner, large families of dependent children and old age: now, although some of these factors were still important, family size was smaller, old age was partly protected by state pensions and, above all, those who had work could usually exist on their earnings, admittedly at a fairly low level in the case of unskilled workers. But unemployment had now emerged as a principal cause of poverty. In York it was the cause of poverty in 28.6 per cent of cases, second only to low wages at 32.8 per cent:[204] in the five towns they surveyed, Bowley and Hogg found that the proportion of poverty due to unemployment had increased more than three times since before the war, while in London in 1929 unemployment and short time were the causes in 38 per cent of the families of the poor, and 55 per cent of the families of the unemployed were living below the poverty line.[205]

These were important findings, but, so far as the unemployed themselves were concerned, statistical abstractions. What mattered to them was the extent to which their incomes were reduced by unemployment, and how far they could be made to stretch to support their families. Both are difficult questions to generalize, depending on a variety of individual circumstances – the kind of occupation and wage previously received, the size and ages of the family, the region of the country and, therefore, the variations in rent and cost of food, and, not least, the skill and ingenuity of the individual or, more usually, his wife, in managing a limited budget. Added to these were the frequent changes in the levels of unemployment insurance benefit and public assistance payable after insurance had expired. Table 5 below gives the scales of benefit under the various Unemployment Insurance Acts from 1919 to 1939.

For the majority of the unemployed, these levels represented a gap between their normal income and what they now received, greater or lesser depending mainly on the number of children. Industrial wages in the thirties lay between £2 and £3 a week, less for agricultural workers and rather more for the most skilled, but it will be seen that insurance benefit did not even reach the lower level for a family of husband, wife and two children, even at its best in the late thirties. The same is true of the scales paid by the Unemployment Assistance Board after 1934. The

Table 5 Scales of benefit under Unemployment Insurance Acts, 1919–39
(in shillings)[206]

	Single men	Single women	Wife	Child	Family of four
December 1919	11	11	0	0	11
December 1920	15	12	0	0	15
March 1921	20	16	0	0	16
June 1921	15	12	0	0	15
November 1921	15	12	5	1	22
August 1924	18	15	5	2	27
April 1928	17	15	7	2	28
March 1930	17	17	9	2	30
October 1931	15	13	8	2	27
April 1934	17	17	9	2	30
May 1934	17	17	9	3	32

Out of work donation

Man	29
Woman	25
First child	6
Other children	3

Source: 1921 and 1931 Census

Pilgrim Trust estimated by how much these scales fell short of wages for men of different age, allowing for the fact that most men in their twenties and thirties would be receiving allowances for a wife and children.

Table 6 Income in and out of employment under Unemployment Assistance Board (men only)[207]

Ages	(1) Average wage	(2) Average UAB allowance	(3) (2) as % of (1)
	s. d.	s. d.	
18–24	33 7	22 4	66
25–34	45 0	29 3	65
35–44	50 1	32 5	65
45–54	51 0	26 8	52
55–64	49 9	22 6	45

On this estimate, unemployment relief was at best 66 per cent of wages, but fell progressively with age to less than half for men over fifty-five who no longer had dependent children: relief came closest to wages for those aged twenty-five to thirty-four who were supporting a young family. This was due, of course, to the fact that wages took no account of dependents (a man's wage was usually the same whether he was single or married with eight children) while unemployment relief included allowances for them, though at a low level. This meant that a low-paid unskilled worker with several young children could be almost as well off or badly off when unemployed as when in work. In a survey of semi-skilled workers in Wales, the difference was negligible for families with three or four dependent children, and with six or more there could be a positive advantage in not working. Nationally, the Pilgrim Trust concluded that around one-fifth of all those receiving unemployment assistance were as well off, or better off, than they would be working.[208] It should be emphasized, however, that this does not mean that they were not in poverty, as were many low-paid workers with large families. And the largest gap between unemployment assistance and wages was for the married man with only two children, a family pattern which was becoming increasingly normal in the thirties.

A question hotly debated in the thirties was whether the allowances were sufficient to maintain the unemployed and their families at a civilized level of existence. No one suggested that they should be maintained in comfort, but beyond this opinions tended to diverge on political or ideological lines between those who thought that benefits were inadequate for basic human needs and those who believed that they were an over-generous encouragement to the 'work-shy': although not accepting the latter view at its face value, governments and administrators were also concerned that benefits should not act as a disincentive to work. The debate largely centred on the cost of an adequate diet, since food was by far the largest item in working-class budgets, normally taking half or more of income, whereas the second largest item, rent, was usually not negotiable. With the development of nutrition science since the war, and the recognition of the importance of vitamins and minerals in the diet as well as calories and proteins, it was now theoretically possible to construct and cost a minimum diet which would satisfy bodily needs. These specimen diets produced by the experts usually ranged around 5s. to 6s. a week for a moderately active man, with smaller amounts for women and children: they allowed little meat and no luxury foods, and assumed that the housewife would buy in the cheapest markets and cook the most economical dishes. George Orwell cited with incredulity a budget carried in the *News of the World* which claimed that a man could be adequately fed on 3s. 11½d. a week: this was a vegetarian diet, based on three wholemeal loaves, 1lb. of cheese, 2lbs. of dates and ten oranges per week together with one tin of evaporated milk and half a pound of margarine.[209]

A more realistic estimate which was widely used in assessments of poverty was drawn up by a committee of distinguished nutritionists and doctors of the British Medical Association in 1933. Its brief was 'to determine the minimum weekly expenditure on foodstuffs which must be incurred by families of varying size if health and working capacity are to be maintained, and to construct specimen diets': these were carefully

Table 7 Average weekly costs of a diet to maintain nutritional health, BMA, 1933[210]

	s.	d.		s.	d.
Adult male	5	11	Child 8 and under 10	4	2
Boy over 14	5	11	Child 6 and under 8	3	7
Adult female	4	11	Child 3 and under 6	3	5
Girl over 14	4	11	Child 2 and under 3	3	1
Child 12 and under 14	5	4	Child 1 and under 2	2	8
Child 10 and under 12	4	9			

drawn up to provide cheap but palatable meals which would satisfy nutritional requirements. Their average weekly costs worked out as in Table 7. For a family of man, wife and two children aged eleven and nine this would cost 19s. 9d. a week in 1933 out of unemployment benefit of £1 7s. 0d., though Dr McGonigle, the Medical Officer of Health for Stockton-on-Tees, estimated the food cost at only 16s. 9d. in this particularly low-price area. The unemployment allowance of only 2s. per child up to fourteen meant that larger families were particularly under-resourced compared with the BMA scales: thus a family of two adults and four children aged eleven, nine, seven and five would receive £1 13s. 0d. a week compared with £1 6s. 9d. on the BMA scale for food alone. Beyond this was rent, heat, light, clothing, repairs and replacement of household equipment, club payments (commonly for clothing or shoes) and occasional 'luxuries' such as travel costs, a newspaper or packet of cigarettes, even assuming that the whole of the allowance was handed over intact for housekeeping expenses. In Stockton-on-Tees the rents for old, slum cottages averaged 4s. 8d. a week and for new council houses to which some former slum-dwellers had been transferred, 9s. 0d.,[211] while in York in 1936 the average rent for three rooms was 7s. 5d. and for four rooms 8s. 11d.;[212] and in London (eastern area) for three rooms 12s. 6d.[213] It follows that very many unemployed families would not be able to afford the BMA minimum diet if they paid their rent and allowed anything for other necessary expenditure.

This is confirmed by many of the individual budgets collected in this period. In Brynmawr an unemployed family with three children was spending 17s. 9d. a week on food, when the BMA scale would allow around 23s.[214] while in Rochdale an unemployed man with a wife and two-year-old child spent only 9s. 3d. on food instead of 13s. 11d.[215] The Pilgrim Trust's investigation showed that 44 per cent of the families of the unemployed were existing on or below the BMA standard, and that many mothers were literally starving themselves in order to feed their husbands and children. Larger-than-average families were particularly at risk: even in the prosperous city of Bristol in 1937 a quarter of all families with three children were below the poverty line and slightly more than half of those with four or more. Child poverty became a major social issue in the thirties, publicized by organizations such as the Children's Minimum Campaign and the Family Endowment Society urging the adoption of state-funded child allowances[216] and, in more polemical terms, by Fenner Brockway in the 'Hungry England' debate. The alternative view, often expressed in the right-wing press, was that unemployment benefit was adequate for a nutritious diet if wisely spent by housewives who were prepared to take the time in careful budgeting and preparation of cheap but nourishing dishes: the problem was not so much one of poverty as of ignorance. It was true that there were wide differences of food consumption in individual families, that some wives were incompetent managers and some husbands spent so much on drink or gambling that what remained for housekeeping was totally inadequate on any standard. A carefully controlled study of the diets of sixty-nine representative working-class families in Newcastle-on-Tyne showed huge variations in the consumption of nutrients. The intake of calories per man-value ranged from only 1,846 to as much as 5,261 a day compared to the 3,000 to 3,400 calories which nutritionists thought necessary; protein ranged from 51 to 161gms. a day. The unemployed families in the sample were generally towards the lower end of these values, and it was noticeable that unemployed families on a new council estate were worse fed than those remaining in the slums who paid lower rents. But the amounts of energy and protein obtained per penny were 23 per cent higher among the unemployed families than in the employed, suggesting that the unemployed generally got good value from their expenditure on food.[217]

This does not mean that they were well or even adequately fed. Most unemployed families had a monotonous diet, heavily dependent on bread and potatoes, the cheapest filling food, which provided a third or more of energy: margarine usually replaced butter, meat was restricted to a small quantity of cheap cuts, milk was often tinned, condensed rather than fresh – only two-thirds of the unemployed Newcastle families bought any fresh milk, and then only one-and-a-half pints a week. Vegetables, especially for those who had an allotment, were valuable additions to diet, but fruit consumption among the poor generally was very small.[218] Many families went hungry, especially towards the end of the week before benefit was drawn on Fridays, but Brockway's assertion that 'frequently, the allowances provided under the Means Test involve semi-starvation'[219] is not capable of a precise assessment. George Orwell's claim that 'twenty million people are underfed',[220] a figure which would include a high proportion of the unemployed, would have had support from the eminent nutritionist, Sir John Boyd Orr, though Orwell's belief that 'the less money you have, the less inclined you feel to spend it on wholesome food' is not borne out by actual expenditure patterns. 'Semi-starvation' could best be claimed for the diets of some wives of unemployed husbands, who Margery Spring Rice saw as the chief victims due to their self-sacrifices for their families: some of their diets yielded as little as 1,305 calories and 36gms. of protein a day, around half of requirements. Small families generally managed better than large, and Spring Rice believed that wives from Scotland and Wales were better managers than those from the south of England, citing the homemade bread, porridge, puddings, soups and stews as more characteristic north of the Trent. One budget, described as 'magical' was provided by a Birmingham wife for a family of four on 15s. a week: before marriage she had been a cook: 'She says she has grapefruit, bacon and egg, bread and butter and marmalade for breakfast: meat, green vegetables and a boiled suet pudding for dinner and boiled cod twice a week. She says she never uses tinned food, "not even milk." She has good health'.[221]

Budgeting and food are frequently mentioned by autobiographers, and it is clear that experiences varied greatly. In 1937 George Tomlinson, an unemployed Nottinghamshire miner, was receiving 30s. 6d. for two adults and one child, paying 12s. 6d. rent, 1s. for electricity, 2s. 6d. for coal, 1s. 6d. on a bill for boots and shoes and 10d. for insurance: food took the remaining 12s.

> We can't be miserable on Friday, Saturday and Sunday because we are feeding fairly well. On Saturday afternoon we mostly have a few chips, but we don't bother much about supper because we still have a bit of bacon left for Sunday morning. Sunday dinner is a thumping big meal of potatoes, bread, a small portion of roast beef and more potatoes and bread. That's the real secret of living on the dole – potatoes and bread.
>
> Monday and Tuesday are not too bad. There is usually a bit of meat left from the 'Sunday joint,' and with a few potatoes and greens it is possible to make a decent meal or two. It is on Wednesday and Thursday that the real pinch comes.[222]

Mrs Pallas in Sunderland had only 16s. a week for food for her family of seven: 2s. 0d. went for milk, 3s. 0d. or 3s. 6d. for meat and 10s. for groceries:

> Every week regular I get two pounds each of margarine and butter, four pounds of sugar, two tins skimmed milk, two stone of flour and a quarter of yeast for the bread. I have tried to work it out. I find I get half a pound of tea every week for three weeks, then I can make do the fourth week with a quarter of a pound... I manage to get a 2lb. jar of jam once a month, and make it last the four weeks. Some weeks I can get a quarter of a pound of bacon

for threepence or threepence-halfpenny. Now that eggs are cheap I use quite a lot. We very, very rarely get cheese. We all like it, but it is a bit of a luxury. When there are birthdays we have it.[223]

Mr Pallas had an allotment, for which he paid rent, but this provided potatoes and other vegetables. But John Evans, on transitional benefit of 27s. 3d. to support his wife and two children, could spare only 8s. a week for food after other fixed commitments, which included 11s. for rent and 1s. 1d. a week for membership of the Friends Occupational Centre. Of the 8s., 3s. went on bread, with 1½lbs. of margarine, 1lb. of jam, 2lbs. of oats, ½lb. of cheese and ½lb. of lard: 'Bread, bread, bread! I hate the very word! The sight of bread makes me feel sick. . . . If you want to vary it you change from marg. to lard, and when you're tired of that you go back to jam, if there's any left'.[224]

Mrs Keen in Lancashire supported two adults and six children on transitional benefit of 35s. 3d. and her husband's war pension of 8s.: 'We get one proper meal a day, and we're frightened, eating, wondering where the next is coming from'. Here there was no Sunday dinner, only 4d. of stewing-meat on Friday when the money came in.[225]

Perhaps budgeting was even more difficult for a single man living in lodgings, like Max Cohen who had 6s. a week for food left out of his 15s. 3d. For the better part of each week he was intensely hungry, sometimes 'mildly insane on the question of food',[226] yet on Tyneside two adults were existing on a food bill of 5s. 7½d. a week[227] and two adults and a sixteen-year-old daughter were 'living well' on 10s. 6d. a week.

My wife bakes the bread, and we eat wholemeal bread because it is more sustaining than white bread. We have a cake occasionally, the vegetables out of the garden, tea, cocoa and home-made stout. We spend 1s. 6d. a week on frozen meat. We live well on our allowance because my wife is a first-class cook and manageress.[228]

Such cases illustrate the varying experience of unemployed families dependent on benefit. Some managed by the exercise of strict economy and the good housekeeping of wives and mothers: others could not balance their budgets, usually because of the size of their family or an unorganized household, and had to fall back on some kind of survival system. Debts to landlords for rent, to shopkeepers for groceries, to tally-men for shoes and clothing and to relatives, friends and neighbours were the commonest resort, followed by pledges, often not redeemed, to the pawnbroker. A Sunday suit, children's best clothes, shoes, sheets, small pieces of furniture were all regularly pawned from Monday until Friday or Saturday, realizing the few shillings which could feed hungry children or prevent eviction by an impatient landlord. Street money-lenders also performed a useful if lucrative function at 1d. in the shilling interest per week. Many poor families survived through their resilience and ingenuity – the key role being that of the mother in organizing the finances and manipulating credit. Not untypical was John Edwards' mother, who 'managed the household on strictly businesslike lines', always put aside a tiny amount of money into an emergency reserve, shopped late on Saturday night when perishable foods were going cheap and clothed her children from jumble sales and gifts from neighbours.

> Mother was not above the practice of petty fraud in her attempts to repair the deficiency, and would consider it a lucky day if a purchased egg proved to be bad. This provided an opportunity to halve the smelly contents into two teacups, add another half shell to each, and send the children with them to two different shops, thereby gaining two replacements for the price of one.[229]

The neighbourhood and the extended family provided a major survival network based on co-operation rather than charity; the poor helped each other when they could because they never knew when they might be recipients instead of donors. Jerry White has described this as 'a collective response to mutual problems', citing one poor family in Islington in the thirties which had forty relatives living in and around the same street.[230]

Self-sufficiency and 'making do and mending' were important aids to survival in many homes. Mending, repairing and remaking clothes, especially for the children, mending boots and shoes with rubber from old tyres, repairing furniture and household utensils were all useful ways of saving money as well as spending time. Fuel was a costly item at 2s. or more a week, and in suitable parts of the country could be economized by collecting wood or 'scratting' for coal on slag-heaps. Clifford Steele and his friends in Barnsley sawed up a whole wood for logs,[231] while Will Paynter, his father and brother in the Rhondda spent one day every week on the outcrops and slag heaps to fill one bag each: 'To get three bags could involve turning over twenty to thirty tons of slag, which was hard work in any language'.[232] 'Scratting' was at best a quasi-legal activity and in some areas look-outs had to be posted to warn of the police, but it seems to have been universal in the coalfields, sometimes carried on on an organized basis by the unemployed. Poaching, even in its commonest form, rabbiting, was clearly illegal, but very widespread, combining excitement with the prospect of a meat dinner. Even in apparently unlikely places, such as around Hastings, unemployed men made nets for the poachers and were paid for them in rabbits.[233] In such activities there was some echo of the Marienthal return to a more primitive way of life, to survival by growing or catching food, gathering fuel and making clothes. But few unemployed were totally cowed and apathetic; most were remarkably stoical, resourceful and resilient in the face of exceptional difficulties.

251

Health

One of the many public concerns about mass unemployment was its likely effects on health. On the face of things, it seemed obvious that long-term unemployment, accompanied as it often was by poor standards of diet, would almost inevitably lead to physical deterioration of adults and under-nourishment of children. Several autobiographers noted the mental and physical depression, the low state of health and vitality, which they ascribed to their unemployment: 'Jack Linton, a pal of mine, had reached a very low ebb with nervous debility, and he would weep apparently at nothing. He was convinced that he was a victim pursued by relentless enemies with no tangible form, and compared his industrial death with his own physical death'. He had been unemployed for ten years. His panel doctor sent him to hospital where, after three months of proper nourishment, he made a good recovery.[234] Max Cohen experienced periods of extreme hunger when he lay on his bed in the daytime 'in a state fluctuating from torpid indifference to intolerable craving for food and tobacco'[235] when he even wondered whether the top of a table might be edible. One cold January night Major Blackburn had no lodging and had not eaten for two days.

> Perhaps it was my army training that helped me. Of course, hunger makes one feel sick, and there's nothing to be sick on. After a while, one's mind gets a curious sense of detachment, the physical suffering hardly seems to belong to one. It becomes impersonal. It is at this stage that one gets one's worst fears.[236]

Although there are many illustrations in the literature of severe hunger, mental and physical debility, harder evidence of the direct effects of unemployment on health is difficult and controversial, partly because it is often not possible to separate unemployment from poverty, insanitary and overcrowded housing and other environmental contributors to ill-health, partly because the statistics of mortality and morbidity are capable of differing interpretations. Official opinion represented by the Ministry of Health remained staunchly optimistic that unemployment, even in the depressed areas, was not having discernible effects on what were, overall, improving health standards. In 1928 a Ministry investigation into conditions in the coalfields of south Wales and Monmouthshire concluded

> Our observations did not disclose any widespread manifestation of impaired health which could be attributed to insufficiency of nourishment. In this view we are confirmed by the opinions of the medical practitioners who have the best opportunities of watching the physical condition of families.[237]

Similarly, in 1932 Sir George Newman, Chief Medical Officer at the

Ministry, wrote in his Annual Report that 'There has been no general excess of sickness, ill-health or physical incapacity attributable to unemployment'.[238] Politicians and administrators could take comfort in such apparently authoritative statements, and in the published vital statistics which indicated that the population generally was enjoying substantially better health and greater longevity than before the war. The crude death rate in England and Wales improved from 14.0 deaths per thousand in 1919 to 11.6 in 1938 (1900 18.2) and infant mortality, often regarded as the more sensitive indicator of health standards, from eighty-nine to fifty-three per thousand over the same period (1900, 154).[239] Even in a depressed town like Middlesbrough the death rate fell from 18.39 in 1919 to 13.30 in 1939, and the infant death rate from 139 to seventy-three per thousand, reflecting an even greater improvement in an area which had always had high infant mortality, while in nearby Stockton-on-Tees, with an even higher unemployment rate, the improvement in infant mortality was equally impressive, from 105 per thousand to sixty-eight.

On the other hand, it is certain that these improvements were very unevenly spread between different regions, different towns and different social classes, indicating that economic status was still a major determinant of health. Although Sir George Newman could justly claim in 1932 that no county in England and Wales now had an infant death rate over 100, it still reached as much as 170 in some parts of depressed industrial towns. Furthermore, there did seem to be evidence that infant death rates might be directly related to unemployment, since they rose significantly between 1930 and 1931 as the depression deepened and unemployment rose.[240] One of the few direct comparisons between the mortality rates of employed and unemployed families was made by Dr M'Gonigle, the Medical Officer of Health for Stockton-on-Tees. In 1931 the crude death rate of unemployed was 31.79 per thousand compared to 18.80 for the employed; in 1934, 22.49 compared to 18.07. When the death rate was standardized to allow for age differences within the groups, families with incomes from 25s. to 35s. a week had a death rate of 25.96, those with incomes over 75s., 11.52.[241] In other areas of high unemployment the standardized death rate was well above the average for England and Wales: in the Rhondda 1.44 times the average; in Jarrow 1.3 times.

Other concerns were about maternal mortality and child health. Charles Webster has argued that governments, faced with mass unemployment, wished to present its effects in the most favourable light, even to the point of playing down embarrassing statistics: he points out that the deaths of mothers in childbirth actually increased by 22 per cent between 1923 and 1933 and did not show a sustained fall until after 1935.[242] In an experiment in the Rhondda, Lady Williams showed that the maternal death rate could be dramatically improved by extra feeding of expectant mothers though ante-natal programmes had had little effect. There was also anxiety in the thirties about a possible increase of malnutrition among children since surveys had shown that more than a quarter of all children in the country lived in the lowest income households, which included many unemployed. In fact, the doctors and nurses who conducted the school medical inspections had no fixed standards for malnutrition, and produced widely different results from which no satisfactory conclusion can be drawn. Again, the official view was optimistic – a reduction in malnutrition from 15 to 20 per cent of the school population before 1914 to 5 per cent in 1925 and a mere 1 per cent by 1925–32.[243] The diversity of medical assessment is shown by the fact that in Aberdare and Ebbw Vale not a single child was reported as having 'bad nutrition', while in Stockton in 1934, probably under the influence of the energetic Medical Officer of Health Dr M'Gonigle, 53.8 per cent of children were diagnosed in this category and a further 22.8 per cent as suffering from subnormal nutrition.[244]

A fair judgement on the statistical evidence would be that the unemployed, in common with the poor generally, shared unequally in the improvements in health standards which the British people experienced between the wars. The judgements of social investigators, though generally not medically qualified, clearly indicate poor physical status, especially of the long-term unemployed, the Pilgrim Trust categorizing 19 per cent of unemployed men in the Rhondda as 'out of condition', 17 per cent as 'unfit' and 8 per cent as having 'obvious physical defects', a total of 44 per cent here and 38 per cent in Liverpool.[245] It was noticed that unemployed men who attended Government Instructional Centres ('Training Camps') in the countryside for three months usually put on an average of 7lbs. in weight, and in one recorded instance, 18lbs.[246] In depressed Brynmawr Hilda Jennings recorded that

> Nurses, doctors, Public Assistance Officers and other competent observers agree that the general vitality of men who have been unemployed for a long period is lower, and it is remarked that when such men return to work they find difficulty in standing the strain of heavy manual labour.[247]

But all investigators concurred in the belief that it was the health of wives and mothers of unemployed families which suffered most, that they denied themselves in order that their children should be fed and clothed as well as possible and their husbands kept ready for work should it become available. In a study of unemployed families in Liverpool, one third of wives were reported as unhealthy, anaemia and nervous debility being the main symptoms:[248] in Brynmawr 'mothers generally now suffer more from debility, and have less recuperative powers than formerly',[249] while Margery Spring Rice found many mothers going without proper food, suffering from anaemia, faintness and chronic indigestion: 'It is abundantly clear that in an undernourished family, she is certainly the worst sufferer'.[250]

Politics

A commonly held view was that, far from revolting or even protesting collectively over their conditions, the unemployed generally were remarkably quiescent and apolitical: unemployment bred apathy, not revolution. This was the conclusion of the Marienthal study, where the chief characteristic of the unemployed was found to be a resigned acceptance of their lot, and where membership of political parties and clubs fell by up to 60 per cent. British investigations reached similar conclusions, finding little evidence of class consciousness or common hatred of 'the system' among the unemployed. In Greenwich talk of revolution was 'conspicuous by its absence', and Bakke believed that unemployment insurance had brought 'a sufficient degree of security' to prevent it. He acknowledged that there were occasional disturbances in many cities, but they did not start as disturbances, only as peaceful demonstrations for more liberal relief, and 'the publicity which these demonstrations get is out of proportion to their importance as indications of unrest'. Demonstrations and marches appeared to offer hope to those who had failed to adjust to their circumstances, but 'in the field of political activity there was little evidence of any difference between the employed and the unemployed workers'.[251] Other commentators stressed that the anger which unemployed men often displayed was directed against individuals who they believed were responsible, but very rarely against the capitalist system, and that the few areas where there were signs of militant solidarity, such as Clydeside, Poplar and Mardy in Wales, were quite unrepresentative of the generally peaceful and law-abiding conduct of the unemployed.

Such comforting views seemed to be confirmed by the extremely small membership of political parties and organizations which might have been expected to have strong appeal to the unemployed. Membership of the Communist Party did not rise above 11,000 until the anti-Fascist campaigns of the late thirties increased it to a maximum of 18,000, partly by the recruitment of middle-class intellectuals. The British Union of Fascists, with a maximum membership of 40,000, drew its main support from the lower middle class and did not make significant inroads among the unemployed, being no more successful in depressed areas than elsewhere.[252] The one organization which explicitly set out to recruit and further the interests of the unemployed was the National Unemployed Workers' Committee Movement (the 'Committee' was dropped after two or three years), formed in 1921 out of a London group led by three Communists, Wal Hannington, Percy Haye and Jack Holt. The NUWM linked up some seventy or eighty local organizations, many of which had been founded to protect the interests of ex-servicemen: at the first National Conference the oath of membership was agreed – 'never to cease from active strife until capitalism is abolished', and Hannington was appointed as national organizer, the effective leader of the movement throughout the inter-war years. Its membership fluctuated wildly in response to levels of unemployment and the publicity which demonstrations and hunger marches received. After the big 1922–3 March it claimed 100,000 members organized into 300 local committees in almost every town in the United Kingdom, but by 1926 its effective membership had shrunk to no more than 10,000. The early thirties saw a recovery with the campaign against the means test and the Anomalies Regulations which excluded many women from benefit: membership rose to 35,000 in 1931, and 100,000 were claimed in 1933 at the high point of the movement following the hunger march of 1932. Thereafter it declined again in the recovery years and was virtually moribund by 1937 when the last National Conference was held. Hannington later claimed that a million people had passed through its ranks during its lifetime, but the recent historian of the movement has observed that

> The average member of the NUWM had only a fleeting association with the movement, paying only a few penny subscriptions before he or she fell out of touch, found work ... or moved. These people tended to be young, unskilled, and not afraid either of the Communist image of the movement, nor of the prospect of violence on demonstrations.[253]

Organizing the unemployed effectively was a formidable, perhaps impossible, task. The NUWM was cold-shouldered by the TUC and the Labour Party, it lacked adequate financial support, it suffered from its dependence on the Communist Party of Great Britain and from government harassment, even to the extent of penetration of its National Council by a police spy. Its achievements were to publicize the plight of the unemployed by demonstrations and hunger marches, to bring pressure to bear on the bureaucratic procedures of relief which helped to humanize them somewhat by the late thirties, and to represent the unemployed in tribunals and Courts of Referees in order to obtain their legal rights under the highly complicated benefit systems. Although its influence on raising benefit levels is debatable, it did have some success in fighting off cuts in the thirties, while its hundreds of local branches provided social and recreational facilities giving mental and often material support to the unemployed and their families. National hunger marches to London from many parts of the country took place in 1922–3, 1932, 1934 and 1936, as well as a south Wales miners' march to London in 1927 and many local marches in Liverpool, Belfast, Birkenhead and elsewhere. The 1932 march against the means test and the 10 per cent cut in benefits had

2,000 marchers in eighteen contingents: it had very close police scrutiny and was marred by violence and baton charges when the marchers reached Hyde Park. The national government after 1931 consistently refused to meet deputations of the marchers on the ground that extra-Parliamentary pressure should not be encouraged, and this also applied to the Labour Party-organized Jarrow March of 1936, a small affair of 200 men led by the MP Ellen Wilkinson, petitioning for the opening of a steelworks to replace the closed Palmer's shipyard: ironically, this received more public sympathy than the much larger NUWM march at the same time.

A number of Communist Party leaders left records of the unemployed struggles, the demonstrations and marches, and their own frequent periods of imprisonment for incitement and riot.[254] The memoirs of more representative unemployed men suggest that though they were not members of the CP or the NUWM many were in favour of a radical change in society and were certainly not more politically apathetic than the working-class generally. Disillusionment with the Labour Party and the trade union movement, neither of which seemed to offer much to the unemployed, was often mistaken for apathy – a former Labour Party member wrote that after two years of unemployment 'my interest in politics has completely vanished. I am embittered against all politicians of all parties', but went on to say, 'I am still a Socialist'.[255] An engineer who had held office in his trade union branch gave up his membership because: 'I had found my position in the trade union movement considerably weakened. . . . In spite of the existence of thousands of unemployed skilled engineers, to be workless is somehow related in the minds of the employed with inefficiency'.[256] Men who felt excluded from their former associations did not necessarily change their fundamental beliefs: on the other hand, more were drawn towards radical politics by their experiences. A thirty-three-year-old mechanic wrote, 'The whole system's wrong . . . I'm not a revolutionary in the sense of violence, but we do want a revolutionary change in our conditions'.[257] For Ernie Benson the years of unemployment were 'years in which the seeds of discontent were sown and from which a new spirit rose. Rebellious men were looking for leadership'.[258] John Edmonds in the Surrey Docks wrote, 'Religion has been called the opiate of the masses, but the majority of the poor in the neighbourhood preferred the tonic of political thought',[259] while Dick Beavis, an unemployed collier in the thirties who went poaching for food, wrote, 'That's how I learned my politics – who owned the land?'[260]

The evidence from autobiographies is that unemployment increased political awareness but not political participation: if it produced an apathetic resignation in some, it burnt into the souls of the many who found no acceptable remedy for their discontent until 1945. More typical than

those who 'loafed' at street corners or lay in bed in daytime was Will
Oxley, who wrote

> Though industrially dead, legally destitute, physically half starved
> and deteriorating, I was mentally and spiritually restless and vital. I
> was living the proletarian day-to-day struggle for existence, and in
> the bitterness of that struggle, I set up my own philosophical
> tactics.[261]

Few of the unemployed found their philosophy in Communism which
they thought utopian, alien and un-British: patriotism, respectability and
even deference remained strong in the working class, and the NUWM
suffered both from its association with Communism and from the scenes
of violence which often accompanied its demonstrations, and which its
leaders were believed to initiate in the hope of encouraging class hatred.
No doubt there was sometimes a hooligan element which looked for
trouble, and Will Paynter admitted that 'A strong feeling of adventure
enlivened our activities during the early 1930s. This was as true of Liverpool or Glasgow as it was of the Rhondda. There was excitement and a
certain element of danger in our struggles'.[262] But meetings, demonstrations and marches were the legitimate, democratic means by which
protest could be made public: they were usually licensed by the local
authorities and began peacefully, though sometimes abused by the militants and by the police who over-reacted to provocation and hit out
indiscriminately at men and women who had committed no offence.[263]

Public relief

Between the wars governments concentrated on relieving the main symptoms of unemployment by providing financial support, but did not
seriously attempt to create employment by regulating the economy in
ways which John Maynard Keynes and minority parties like the Liberals
advocated. Full accounts of unemployment policies and proposals are
readily available:[264] all that is needed here is the briefest sketch of the
complex, largely unplanned responses to an unprecedented problem.

Remedial measures began in November 1918 with an Exchequer-
funded Out of Work Donation for ex-servicemen and civilians unable to
find work in what were thought to be the temporary, emergency conditions following the Armistice. This expensive scheme was replaced in
1920 by the Unemployment Insurance Act which extended the 1911 Act
to cover manual workers and non-manual workers earning up to £250
per annum with the exception of agricultural workers, domestic servants,
teachers and civil servants: it provided 15s. a week for men (12s. a week
for insured women) for a maximum of fifteen weeks in any one year.
Like the pre-war insurance scheme, it was intended to be self-financing

from contributions, but as unemployment increased and lengthened in 1921, this quickly proved unworkable: a new Act in 1921 introduced 'extended benefits', not covered by contributions, for up to forty-seven weeks in a year, and also added dependents' allowances of 5s. for a wife and 1s. for a child. The rates of relief were increased in 1924, 1928 and 1930, and given also the effects of falling prices, were by then worth approximately double the value of 1920. However, from 1922 onwards certain restrictions were applied to extended benefit. It was only available to those 'genuinely seeking whole-time employment', an attempt to exclude 'loafers', but which in fact disallowed many women who were not prepared to accept the domestic service work which Labour Exchanges offered: also introduced was a means test for extended benefit which applied to single persons living with relatives and to married persons whose spouse was in work. This was bitterly resented by the unemployed and condemned by the Labour Party: it involved inquisitorial procedures reminiscent of the poor law and in effect, disqualified those with incomes over 13s. a week. In the brief economic recovery in 1927 a new Unemployment Insurance Act replaced 'extended benefit' by 'transitional benefit' which it was optimistically assumed could be phased out altogether within eighteen months.

The Labour government in 1929 introduced some modifications to the 'genuinely seeking work' condition, but in the crisis of 1931 the national government cut benefit rates by 10 per cent and reduced transitional benefit to a maximum of twenty-six weeks: it also introduced a household means test under which all the earnings and capital assets of a family could be assessed in determining the extent of relief. Through the 1920s claimants who had been 'disallowed' for one reason or another could appeal to Courts of Referees: if unsuccessful their only recourse was to the poor law and the local Boards of Guardians, who generally now gave out-relief in cash and food tickets, often on the condition of 'test work' such as road-building, land drainage or sewerage work. The Local Government Act of 1929 abolished the Guardians, replacing them by Public Assistance Committees which continued to cater for those who had run out of transitional benefit. Locally appointed and financed by the rates, their policies were very uneven, some Labour-controlled councils providing relatively generous levels of relief, others continuing on strict 'less eligibility' principles inherited from the poor law. A new Act in 1934 superseded the local PACs by a national Unemployment Assistance Board which was intended to provide uniform levels of relief for the uninsured. The Household Means Test continued to apply, but the proposal to lower some more generous local scales to the national level met such a storm of protest that the government was forced to relent with a 'standstill' arrangement by which the old rates continued if higher than the national scales.

By the mid-thirties, then, something like a national scheme of relief for the unemployed had emerged out of a series of *ad hoc* responses. There were very few attempts to create jobs, though many proposals from minority parties and individuals which did not receive government support. They ranged from suggestions that the unemployed could be settled on the land – 'A Cottage and an Acre'[265] to Ernest Bevin's 'Plan for 2,000,000 Workless'[266] and Lloyd George's Liberal Party plan, 'How to Tackle Unemployment':[267] both Oswald Mosley in the Labour Cabinet and Harold Macmillan, a Conservative MP, proposed the planned reconstruction of the economy with government funding and loans on the Keynesian principle of reviving activity by stimulating demand. Governments, whether Conservative or Labour, remained faithful to the belief in the importance of a balanced budget, and were equally in thrall to the Treasury and the Bank of England, which could not contemplate massive increases in debt. The few positive measures, such as the Special Areas Acts of 1934 and 1937, which offered tax incentives to industry to locate factories in the depressed areas, provided some semi-skilled assembly work for women but had little effect on male unemployment. Somewhat more significant was the encouragement of labour transference from depressed areas to the more prosperous Midlands and south-east: over the ten years 1929–38 government-assisted migration averaged 32,000 per annum, peaking at over 40,000 in 1929 and 1936.[268] Wales and Tyneside lost considerable numbers of their young men under these schemes with some effects on the social composition of their former communities, though it is not known how many subsequently returned home. There were also some limited government attempts at training, especially for the young unemployed, and for juveniles attendance at an Instructional Centre (or Domestic Training Centre for girls) could be made a condition of receiving relief. These were quite marginal interventions in the labour market, and more jobs were created by government rearmament orders from 1934 onwards than by any specific unemployment policies: there were still a million-and-a-half unemployed when war was declared in September 1939.

Autobiographers were predominantly hostile, sometimes violently so, to the procedures of unemployment benefit. There were, however, a few exceptions to this.

> I have no objection to the visits of the Public Assistance Officer. I believe in the principles of the Means Test, for I think it is a necessary safeguard. . . . The official investigation is less objectionable than the former method of questioning the applicant for relief at the Labour Exchange before a crowd.[269]

A Nottinghamshire coal miner wrote,

During four years of unemployment I can honestly say that I have met with almost unfailing courtesy and much practical sympathy. The clerks show an interest in the men. . . . When the 'means test' visitor calls, there is little of the hostility between him and the family that is so often depicted in novels.[270]

These were exceptional opinions. The typical experience began with 'signing on' at the Labour Exchange, humiliating in itself for someone who prided himself on independence.

What a place that turned out to be in 1931. Dreary, dismal, gloomy, dirty and hopeless, painted a typically standard olive drab, with clerical staff to match. Staff with little or no knowledge of life or work outside the dole office. . . . Their main concern, it seemed, was to cut you down and pay out as little as possible, not even your entitlement, to keep you at arms length by humiliation, by assuming you guilty of wilful idleness before you even opened your mouth.[271]

Max Cohen found the inside of the Exchange 'dirty and repellent. There appeared to be a large number of notices forbidding one to do this and warning one of the penalties incurred by doing that'. Pay day on Thursday or Friday could take all the morning and even into the afternoon, and one might have to wait three weeks before receiving a full week's benefit because of an unpaid 'waiting period'.[272] Others wrote that the clerks 'treated us like dirt', while several mention physical attacks on clerks by infuriated men whose benefit was cut or disallowed: police were normally on duty inside the Exchange and outside to regulate the queues and to observe the public meetings which the NUWM often called on pay days.

The strongest complaints were against the Labour Exchange investigators, the Courts of Referees and the means test officials. Men who were considered not 'genuinely seeking work' or had turned down offers made by the Exchange would be directed to explain themselves to a committee which had the power to stop or reduce benefit. In the opinion of the unemployed these interviews merely 'put a premium on dishonesty'[273] because in many depressed areas there was simply no work, however hard it was sought, but 'if you were honest, you lost your benefit'.[274] Claimants were expected to remember which employers they had visited on which days over a period of two or three weeks, and believed that the committee would often try to trick and confuse them by going over the days in a different sequence. Some would therefore bring in diary notes concealed in their caps (which they would take off in the interview), and Arthur Horner, who led a hunger march of Rhondda miners to London in 1927, remembers that: 'At Mardy we used to draw up a list of places where we knew there was no work, but where men were supposed to call to ask for a job. We handed out the lists. The man memorised them and repeated them to the officials. In that way he was able to prove he was looking for work'.[275] The bitterest objections were generally reserved for the means test, however: 'Of all the curses put on the unemployed worker the Means Test tops the list. There are hundreds of homes broken up here in Glasgow'.[276] This referred to the fact that the total income of the family was assessed, so that if a son or daughter was earning, an unemployed father's benefit was reduced: the result was that children often left the family home for lodgings so that a parent could qualify. Again, subterfuges were sometimes adopted – a son would temporarily be accommodated in an outhouse or allotment shed if a visit was expected. The system also worked the other way, of course, and an unemployed son could have his benefit stopped if his employed father was adjudged to have sufficient income to support him. Also much resented was the rule that occasional earnings must be declared, and neighbours were encouraged to report on those who earned a few shillings 'on the side'. 'Mostly they didn't, but there was always the few that would.'[277]

The invasion of privacy seems to have been resented almost more than the principle of means testing. Alf Hodd in Hastings remembers that a means test officer walked into his grandmother's house where they were all living:

> My father went in and said 'Who invited you in?,' and he couldn't say because he hadn't been invited in – he just thought he was 'It,' and he walked in and sat down. So he was thrown out. . . . And he was saying 'You've got this you could sell' and 'You've got that you could sell'.[278]

Unemployment relief beyond the insured period was discretionary, not a right: in effect, it involved a test of 'character' of the claimant, who became a supplicant forced to accept the conditions laid down. Transitional benefit involved completing a complicated form of income and expenditure each month: up to 1929 Boards of Guardians could require 'test work' in return for assistance, which for Harry Fletcher meant twenty-six hours' work a week for 26s., digging out a boating lake in a Hull Corporation park – he was a skilled shipbuilder.[279] Conditions of this kind were designed to meet the charge that over-generous local authorities were giving 'something for nothing', partly also to try to keep up the physical and mental fitness of the unemployed. This was also the aim of Training and Instructional Centres, designed principally to restore the vitality and employability of young, single men. The opinions of the unemployed varied greatly about these. Sometimes described as 'concentration camps', Anthony Divers of Liverpool thoroughly enjoyed his time at the Fermyn Woods Instructional Centre where he had good food, mild discipline and a variety of work in afforestation, gardening and carpentry: he put on one-and-a-half stones in weight while there: 'The staff are really kind and helpful. They go to endless trouble on our behalf. . . . There's no punishment – but a fellow can be sent home. That's the worst thing that can happen to him'.[280] Joseph Halliday, a miner of County Durham, volunteered to go to a Training Centre at Bourne, Lincolnshire, where he worked at roadmaking and quarrying: he enjoyed his ten weeks there so much that he applied to go again.[281] On the other hand, Donald Kear had quite different feelings about his six-month stay at a Government Training Centre. Each trainee received 22s. a week, 17s. of which was deducted for his board and lodging with local families. Kear was trained as a fitter:

> The atmosphere of the Centre was the exact opposite of what it should have been. Instead of giving the impression that here was the chance of a new life with a trade in your hands, you felt this was a place of punishment for a collection of idle layabouts on the criminal fringe. From the Chief Instructor down to the timekeeper at the gates, the main job of them all appeared to be to bully, to frighten, to squeeze the trainees to an even lower sense of degradation.[282]

And at a Labour Camp in County Durham, Len Edmondson's brother organized a strike about the poor quantity and quality of food supplied: he was subsequently transferred to a camp at Carshalton, Surrey, where he collapsed with pneumonia.[283]

Reactions to the forms of relief depended on individual circumstances and personality as well as on differences in local administration. Some officials were petty tyrants determined to enforce the letter of the law, while others used their discretionary powers to humanize procedures as much as possible: similarly, while most unemployed people accepted the system, if grudgingly, some constantly tested its limits, often at much cost to themselves. Ernie Benson had completed his apprenticeship as a fitter in 1927, married, joined the Communist Party and was sacked on reaching twenty-one. In the Labour Exchange he abused and tried to attack the clerk: he then formed a local Leeds branch of the NUWM and acquired a reputation for defending workers at the Court of Referees. Still unemployed in 1930 he had to attend a committee meeting as the result of an anonymous letter which accused him of earning money by boot-repairing: here he caused a disturbance, insulted the members and was thrown out: his relief money stopped for five weeks. Subsequently directed to attend 'test work' navvying organized by Leeds City Council, he was determined 'to smash this scab-making and soul-destroying scheme': he organized the men to disrupt the work and the physical training classes which were intended to prevent 'muscle atrophy'. ('It's stomach atrophy we are likely to suffer from because of lack of good food.') Jobs offered him by the Labour Exchange were snow-shifting in winter and selling ice-cream in summer, but by now he was a paid local organizer for the Communist Party and rejected these affronts to his dignity and skill. He was also involved in numerous unemployed demonstrations and sentenced to fines or imprisonment.

Only a few men were prepared to take on the authorities in this way (Benson did so at the cost of his personal life and the break-up of his marriage). Levels of relief and administrative procedures were often felt to be niggardly and bureaucratic, but, whether by luck or careful judgement, they were so pitched as to prevent revolution or even widespread disturbance. This does not mean that the unemployed were 'broken' or cowed into apathetic acceptance of whatever was handed out to them. Communities remained strong – perhaps even strengthened; families generally remained united and supportive; men accepted their insurance benefit and also their transitional benefit as rights, not as charity for which they had to be deferentially grateful. Resilient, resourceful and always hopeful, the unemployed endured what was for most an unprecedented change in the pattern of their lives and reduction in their standard of living. Their experiences, however, followed no universal or simple pattern: on the contrary, autobiographies demonstrate a wide variety of reactions – of success and failure to adapt, acceptance and anger, frustration and creative activity – which defy any single model.

7

BACK TO UNEMPLOYMENT, 1970–90

The return of mass unemployment since the early 1970s inevitably invites comparisons with the 1930s, and this chapter does so at numerous points. Autobiographical writing comparable with the earlier period has not yet been produced, but there has been extensive social research by official bodies and private investigators which provides direct evidence of the experience of unemployment: as in earlier chapters, this is set against brief accounts of the extent and characteristics of contemporary unemployment.

THE EXTENT OF UNEMPLOYMENT

The inheritance of over a million unemployed continued into the early months of the Second World War, but by 1940 the heavy demands for manpower had reduced it to a negligible 100,000: by September, 1944 there were no applicants for unemployment relief in Reading or Rugby, only six in Leicester and eight in Birmingham.[1] As in so many areas of social policy, the war engendered an impetus for change and, most notably, a determination not to return to the mass unemployment of the 1930s, though precisely what the emerging commitment to 'full employment' meant has never been clear. In his Report on Social Insurance and Allied Services in 1942, which became the foundation-stone of the post-war Welfare State, William Beveridge based his proposals on 'the avoidance of mass unemployment', but assumed that 'Over the whole body of insured employees unemployment will average about 8.5 per cent. It is right to hope that unemployment can be reduced to below that level ... but it would not be prudent to assume any lower rate of unemployment in preparing the Security Budget'. The Report went on to say that his scheme did not require the abolition of all unemployment, 'but the abolition of mass unemployment and of unemployment prolonged year after year for the same individual'.[2]

In the growing euphoria towards the end of the war these reservations seem to have been either forgotten or ignored, and expectations arose that a commitment to 'full employment' would mean work for everyone who was fit, able and willing to do it. No official target figure was ever pronounced by government. The coalition government's White Paper on Employment Policy, published in June 1944 was discreetly unquantitative: 'The Government accept as one of their prime aims and responsibilities the maintenance of a high and stable level of employment after the war'. The same year Beveridge himself defined full employment as a situation where 'those who lose jobs must be able to find new jobs at fair wages, within their capacity, without delay': he believed that some degree of frictional unemployment was necessary for the efficient working of the economy, but that this should not average more than 550,000 or around 3 per cent of the labour force.[3]

In fact, Beveridge's belief that there was an 'irreducible minimum' of 3 per cent unemployment to allow for job changes proved unduly pessimistic for the next twenty years or more. Between 1948 and 1966 unemployment averaged a mere 1.7 per cent: labour shortages after the war invited public condemnation of 'drones' and 'spivs' who profited on the margins of a strictly-regulated economy without legitimate occupation, while in the 1950s immigrants and married women were encouraged to add to the workforce. A study of men registering as unemployed between 1961 and 1965 showed that of an average of 57,000 new registrations each week, 54,000 could expect to leave within one month,[4] though Professor Paish believed that there existed a small, hard core of 'noneffectives' who were unlikely to be employed even in areas of high demand and which he placed at 180,000 (c. 0.8 per cent of the employed population) in 1964.[5] It was widely assumed that Keynesian policies of demand management and fine tuning of the economy, pursued by both political parties during the 'Butskell' consensus, were mainly responsible for this good result, though with low fuel prices, stable Commonwealth markets for exports and comparatively low US interest rates at this time major manipulations of the economy to preserve high levels of employment were scarcely required.

The first warnings of a change were noticed in 1967 – the previous year the total registered unemployment stood at 192,000 men and 63,000 women,[6] but from 1967 onwards the figure was never less than half a million. Questions of efficiency and overmanning in industry began to be discussed from the mid–1960s, productivity agreements with trade unions were encouraged and, significantly, in 1965 the government introduced the Redundancy Payments Act making compensation a statutory requirement. Nevertheless, it was not until the winter of 1971–2 that the official unemployment total touched a million during the recession, widely regarded as a sufficiently symbolic figure for the Conservative government to generate an expansionary boom which reduced the figure by half. In retrospect the Middle East oil crisis in the autumn of 1973 and the sudden surge in fuel prices marks a turning-point in the fortunes of the British economy and the future of employment. In the previous March growth rates had reached over 8 per cent and *The Economist* believed that Britain was 'right in the middle . . . of an economic miracle':[7] by the end of the year a ban on overtime by the miners' union had resulted in the three-day week, to be followed by a deflationary budget, a total coal strike in February 1974 and the electoral defeat of Edward Heath's government.

From 1975 unemployment rose steadily from 3.9 to 5.6 per cent in 1978, then, after a slight fall, steeply after 1980 (1980 6.8 per cent, 1981 10.5 per cent, 1982 12.4 per cent): in November 1980 the registered figure topped two million for the first time at 2,162,874, though W. W. Daniel, the Adviser to a House of Lords Select Committee on Unemployment put the real figure, allowing for non-registrations, even higher – his calculations would give a total of 2.9 million at the end of 1980.[8] By this time Margaret Thatcher's administration was committed to monetarist policies, seeing wage pressure and inflation, which had risen to 25 per cent in 1975, as the greatest evils and impediments to economic recovery. Sir Keith Joseph's statement in 1978 that 'Full employment is not in the gift of governments. It should not be promised and it cannot be provided', became the received wisdom, at least of the powerful right wing of the party, and, significantly, unemployment, standing at one-and-a-quarter million at the time of the General Election next year, did not dominate the campaigns or prevent a Conservative victory.

From 1980 the number of unemployed continued to rise to a peak in July 1986 – a longer period of increase than that of 1930–4. In 1981 the monthly adjusted stock figure for December stood at 2,940,000 and in 1986 at 3,120,000, a rate of 11.2 per cent and a total almost three times greater than in June 1979: from this high point unemployment fell each year to 1990, by which time it had almost halved to 1,670,000 or 6.3 per cent.[9] Although 1990 is the end of the period under review, it is worth recording that hopes of a continued decline were dashed in 1991 when the figure climbed to 2,385,000 and in 1992 to 2,732,000:[10] at the time of writing it has again passed three million.

The statistics quoted are derived from those registered as unemployed and available for work at local employment offices, but the total figure of those looking for work is unknown and unknowable. For a variety of reasons people who are actively seeking work may not register: in 1979, for example, the General Household Survey found that an additional 25 per cent of people declared themselves to be unemployed but had not registered: about half of these were married women, the other half men and single women.[11] A further complication occurred in November 1982, when the count was changed from those registered as seeking work to those entitled to unemployment benefit, a change which is estimated to have reduced the total by around 6 per cent.[12] There have been many subsequent changes in the administrative counting procedures since then – according to the unofficial Unemployment Unit as many as thirty – which significantly reduce the real number of unemployed: the Unit estimates that the true figure for June 1990 was 2,494,000, not 1,617,100.[13] Similarly, Jon Shields has estimated that a more comprehensive count may well have shown a peak of over four million in the mid-1980s.[14] Those who argue for the higher figures do so mainly by including the 600,000 or so people employed on government-financed special employment programmes, including the Youth Training Scheme, and the large numbers of those who are not eligible for benefit, such as many married women. On the other hand, in 1984 there were 740,000 people receiving benefit – and therefore counted – who were not economically active, mainly because they had given up seeking work which did not exist, because they were sick, disabled or retired or, in the case of women, because they had domestic duties. The fairest judgement on the dispute over numbers is probably that of Hawkins: 'On balance, therefore, it seems likely that the stock figures based on the monthly count marginally understate the real level of unemployment'.[15]

THE CAUSES OF JOB LOSS

As earlier chapters have shown, the causes of unemployment may be frictional, structural or cyclical, each of which has operated in different degrees since 1945. Technological change has also often been claimed as a major cause of labour displacement, most recently associated with semi-conductors, microprocessors and information technology: in the view of some, this has been a principal and irreversible reason for 'the collapse of work', and the full employment of the two decades after the war an 'aberration' dependent on post-war rebuilding, external finance and the Cold War.[16] On the other hand, Professor Layard contends that it is a myth that technology replaces people, and that this is not what history shows: there is labour displacement, but also the creation of new jobs, and in periods of high productivity such as the 1950s and 1960s unemployment was very low despite technological innovations and new sources of energy. More important as causes of unemployment in his view was lack of competitiveness and inflation of costs which contributed to an 'astounding' collapse of manufacturing employment after 1979 and the loss of nearly two million jobs by 1985 – a much greater proportion than in any other major country.[17]

Until the oil crisis of 1973–4 cyclical unemployment was not a serious problem despite some minor falls in output in 1957–8 and 1967–9. When W. W. Daniel conducted the first National Survey of the unemployed immediately before this, the total standing at 502,000 (2.3 per cent), he found that 47 per cent had left jobs of their own accord, 20 per cent had been dismissed (for reasons of ill-health, disability, disputes with employers or workmates), 5 per cent had retired and 28 per cent had been made redundant, for which the main reason was the ending of a contract, season or fixed term of employment: nearly half of these had known that the job would so terminate when they took it.[18] Unemployment at this time was still largely short term and frictional, consisting of people moving between jobs from their own choice. Some 85 per cent of the registered unemployed were male, concentrated in the under-twenty-five and over-fifty-five age groups, two-thirds of whose last jobs had been semi-skilled or unskilled: 19 per cent had some physical disability and a further 12 per cent suffered chronic ill-health; a third of those over fifty-five had volunteered for redundancy.

The euphemism 'redundancy' was already well established in the vocabulary of unemployment. Structural changes in some of the older industries like coal and textiles resulted in substantial job losses, and even in the late 1950s some employers were making *ex gratia* payments to encourage 'shedding' before the statutory scheme of 1965 made compensation compulsory after two years' employment. The first official guess of the scale of redundancies was 200,000 a year from 1958–61; in 1962 it was estimated at 470,000 to 590,000 and in 1968 at 764,000 to 1,014,000 or 3.4 to 4.5 per cent of all employees.[19] Some Lancashire cotton-mills were being closed as early as 1952: faced by a 'crisis of over-production' and the competition of oil, pit closures began in 1959 in south Wales, Durham and Scotland and accelerated between 1965 and 1970 when the coalmining labour force halved from 659,000 to 305,000.[20] Cushioned by relatively generous levels of compensation in a nationalized industry, some of this 'de-manning' could be regarded as voluntary, but it is clear that the overall pattern of reasons for job loss changed markedly during the 1970s. In a later study Daniel found that in 1980–1 only 37 per cent of unemployed had left their last job of their own accord and 14.5 per cent had been dismissed, but the proportion made redundant had risen to 36 per cent.[21] The years 1973 and 1974 were beginning to seem like 'another world', but by 1987 the trends were even clearer – only 18 per cent of unemployed men had given up their jobs voluntarily, only 1 per cent gave health reasons as the cause of leaving and 41 per cent of the unemployed men were skilled workers or had worked on their own account, now substantially more than the 33 per cent of semi-skilled and unskilled.[22] There were also important differences in the reasons for job loss between men and women, who by the mid-1980s constituted 42 per cent of the labour force, though many of these were part-time workers. A survey of unemployed women in 1984 found that 39 per cent were 'domestic returners', in three-quarters of cases because of pregnancy: of the remaining 61 per cent who had suffered job loss the reasons were

269

(in order) redundancy, job dissatisfaction, health reasons, childcare prob-lems and moving house, and 18 per cent classified themselves as 'off-market' (i.e. not interested or not available for work). Fewer than half of those who had lost their jobs had registered as unemployed, mainly single women, a typical comment of the married women being 'I don't class myself as unemployed. I just class myself as looking for a job . . . I'm a housewife looking for a job'.[23] The author of the survey concluded that 'The male model of unemployment usually does not hold good for women'.

Through the 1970s and 1980s structural changes in the economy became increasingly the major reason for job loss as British manufactur-ing industry declined in the face of foreign competition and changes in consumer demand. British levels of unemployment increasingly became a function of the international economy: on the one hand, Britain suf-fered from high oil prices, high unit labour costs, inflation and over-manning which discouraged exports, and on the other, from cheap imports from newly industrialized countries such as Taiwan, Korea and Hong Kong. Fundamental structural changes in the world economy affected all the formerly advanced industrial countries, but perhaps most particularly Britain with her long inheritance of traditional industries, rigidities of labour and management and generally conservative attitudes. Between 1975 and 1983 the penetration of imports of manufactured goods increased from 22.2 to 30.8 per cent, while between 1974 and 1980 alone the penetration of motor vehicle imports rose from 23 to 39 per cent.[24] Overall, British manufacturing production fell by 15.75 per cent between 1979 and 1983 despite the effects of North Sea oil and gas, and by then Britain stood fourteenth in the table of international industrial competitiveness among OECD countries.[25] The 'fall-out' affected virtually all sectors and levels of industry, from small businesses to giant 'household name' companies such as GKN which shed 35 per cent of its labour force between 1973 and 1981 and British Leyland which lost 40 per cent in the same period.[26]

Overall, the changes in employment patterns between 1966 and 1982 were dramatic as Table 8 illustrates.

The growth in the service industries and public sector had by no means compensated for the huge falls in employment in manufacturing, widely spread across the range of industries. This was in sharp contrast to the 1930s, when the decline was concentrated in particular sectors – coalmin-ing, textiles, metal manufactures and shipbuilding – and in particular regions of the country: then, other industries such as vehicles, electrical goods, food, drink and tobacco, building materials, paper and printing were expanding, so that total employment in all manufacturing industries fell by only 3.3 per cent between 1920 and 1938.[27] In the 1980s there was no compensating growth in any industrial sector and again, unlike the thirties, a major decline in building and construction. Despite some recov-

Table 8 Employment in Great Britain, 1966–82 (in thousands)[28]

	1966	1982	% change
Agriculture, forestry, fishing	464	346	–25
Mining and quarrying	574	325	–43
Food, drink, tobacco	832	605	–27
Metal manufacture	623	294	–53
Shipbuilding and marine engineering	200	140	–30
Vehicles	845	547	–35
Textiles	757	298	–60
Clothing and footwear	528	260	–51
Other manufacturing industry	345	236	–32
Construction	1,637	1,011	–38
Insurance, banking, finance and business services	639	1,305	+104
Professional and scientific services	2,512	3,650	+45
Miscellaneous services	2,196	2,484	+13
Total manufacturing industries	8,976	5,644	–37
Total service industries	11,226	12,960	+15

ery of the economy after 1986, the employment trends established in 1982 continued to the end of the decade. By 1989 manufacturing accounted for only 5,234,000 people in the UK, or 23 per cent of the employed population, compared with 31 per cent ten years earlier. The only significant growth was in parts of the service sector – banking, finance, insurance and business services – which grew from 7 to 12 per cent of total employment over the same period.[29] (At the time of writing manufacturing industry has further declined to four-and-a-half million.)

Unemployment in the early 1980s stood at a total remarkably close to that of the 1930s, but it struck more widely across occupations, regions and levels of skill. Contemporary unemployment is less a respector of persons than in the past, though there exists a range of factors which make particular groups and individuals more vulnerable than others, and which are examined in the next section. There are now no 'typical' unemployed, but the experiences of one family, the Smiths of Peterlee, County Durham, encapsulate many aspects of the present situation and can stand as not unrepresentative of the 'new' unemployed.[30] Peterlee was designed as an early new town, mainly to replace some of the old pit villages of Durham, but pit closures in the 1960s resulted in many redundancies which were not absorbed by the Development Corporation's efforts to attract new industries in clothing, food and engineering. In 1987 the official unemployment rate stood at 17.6 per cent, but if those on government training schemes and those ineligible for benefit are included, nearer 30 per cent: three-quarters of school-leavers went on to Youth Training Schemes, though only 40 per cent of these found future employment.

John Smith, aged forty, with a wife and two sons, had been unemployed for nine months, the third time in three years. A skilled technician in non-destructive testing, he was employed for seventeen years until the collapse of the shipbuilding and steel industries: he believes that there are now practically no jobs in his expertise in the UK – 5,000 men recently applied for twelve short-term contract jobs – and he has started a Manpower Services Course in ultrasonics. His wife, Carol, works four afternoons a week in a general store: before her husband began the MSC course her wage was deducted from his benefit so that she worked for £4 a week. John Smith Jnr aged nineteen has six 'O' Levels and went to a local college for a year: he has been unemployed for two years, has made 300 applications for jobs but only worked for three weeks in a Yorkshire hotel and had been offered one other job selling loft insulation on commission. 'Firms prefer to take school-leavers who they can pay on the 16-year-old rate. I've got no chance at 19.' His pessimism seems to be confirmed by the experience of his younger brother Paul, who left school at sixteen and got taken on at a tailoring factory in the cutting-room: 'If you are offered a full-time proper job at 17 you are very lucky. . . . You call yourself a training scheme lad until you are 18 now'. Paul considers it ironic that he is the only man in his family with a job when he has the fewest qualifications of all: his wages pay for the family's food (the Smiths began buying their house in better days and now pay £48 a week mortgage) and he sometimes takes his father to Newcastle football matches.[31]

WHO ARE THE UNEMPLOYED?

Unemployment strikes unequally but not randomly. In the modern period age is the principal determinant, the young and the 'old' being especially vulnerable. Between 1951 and 1981 unemployment rates for young people under eighteen increased from 1 to 25 per cent, and a researcher in 1988 estimated that without YTS and other Special Employment measures the real rate might then be nearer 50 per cent:[32] the same effect continues, though somewhat less markedly, for the next age group, so that in 1985 unemployment for all under twenty-five stood at 21.5 per cent, 600,000 of whom had been out of work for more than six months. (In March 1993 one million people under twenty-five were unemployed, one-third of the total.) This represents a major change since 1973, when only 5 per cent of those between the ages of eighteen and twenty-four were without work,[33] and even more since the 1930s when it was relatively easy for school-leavers to obtain work, though they might well lose it on approaching twenty-one. Explanations of high youth unemployment include their enhanced wages since adult rates now often begin at eighteen rather than twenty-one, and their lack of skills, qualifications or training for the type of jobs available. In the past it was consoling to believe that young workers were 'trying out' different jobs and only suffered relatively brief spells of unemployment, but by July 1985 28 per cent of registrants under twenty-five had been unemployed for more than a year compared with only 7.5 per cent in 1977.[34]

Older workers have long been at a disadvantage in the labour market, and their disadvantage has increased in a period of rapid technical changes: 'Technology, which has lengthened the time for which our lives could be useful, shortens the span for which society finds use for us'.[35] In 1973 the largest group of unemployed men (27 per cent) were in the fifty-five to sixty-four age group, though the pattern for women was quite different: here the largest group of the unemployed was the eighteen to twenty-four age group (41 per cent).[36] Marriage and family formation were the crucial influences, effectively removing younger women from the labour force despite the desire of many to work if suitable employment were available which fitted in with domestic duties. Most men selected for redundancy tend to be in the older age groups, and the availability of lump-sum payments related to length of service has often made early retirement attractive, whether or not encouraged. A study in 1980 of redundancy at the Firestone Tyre Co. showed that more than half were over fifty, 68 per cent of whom had been in unskilled or semi-skilled jobs.[37] Once unemployed, the older worker has greater difficulty in finding re-employment and many therefore join the ranks of the long-term unemployed. At around fifty it has been argued that the unemployed man enters an 'age trap' – too old for employment, but too young for state benefits until sixty-five – 'It's an in-between status', according to one interviewee.[38] Even fifty may now be putting the readily employable age too late. Daniel believed that a man was now firmly in the 'older' category by the time he was in his forties, while Jeremy Seabrook interviewed a long-distance lorry-driver who could not get work at thirty-eight: 'They told me I was too old. At 38! You're too young to be employed in your teens and twenties and too old at 38. When will they employ you – for a fortnight around your 30th birthday?'[39]

Despite the major expansion of women's employment since the last war, they are considerably less likely to be casualties than men. In 1973, 85 per cent of the registered unemployed were male, and of all unemployed (based on the General Household Survey in 1971, which included the unregistered) 66 per cent.[40] In the eighties unemployment of women under nineteen was high, and closely similar to that of men of the same age, but after that it declined sharply: in 1983 the registered unemployment rate for women was 8.6 per cent compared with the male rate of 15 per cent, though these official statistics conceal the 'invisible' unemployment of women, especially of married women who may not be eligible for benefit because not available for full-time work.[41] This is a more important factor than formerly, since over 60 per cent of married women wish to work, a high proportion of these only part-time; otherwise the pattern of women's unemployment is quite similar to that of the 1930s when in 1932, 9.5 per cent were out of work compared with 21.8 per cent of men. The reasons for the disparity are also quite similar: in the 1930s women workers were partly protected by opportunities in the 'new' semi-skilled assembly and light industries (the cotton industry was the only major industry in which women's employment contracted drastically), while in the 1970s and early 1980s they were cushioned by work in the service sectors where employment held up better than in manufacturing: most recently, however, they have been vulnerable to the microprocessor revolution, so that opportunities for young women are now little better than for young men. In some occupations age appeared to limit job prospects very seriously: 'I couldn't believe it when they said, "Well, we were looking for a younger girl." They wanted eighteen, nine-teen-year olds, I suppose' (aged twenty-five). 'When you're over 50 they don't wish to know – it's either 30, 35 is all right. . . . Over 40 they don't seem to want to know' (aged fifty).

But research into unemployed women suggests that only in a third of cases – mainly single mothers and those with low-paid or unemployed husbands – was there an acute financial need to work, and many in all age groups subscribed to very traditional views about the roles of the sexes:

> Men are supposed to be the bread-winners. . . . At least when a woman's unemployed she can do housework. She can generally busy herself.

> Working mothers should be banned in favour of men and school-leavers . . . I think a man is more entitled to work than a woman. . . . Just the pure fact that he is a man, and it's a man's place.[42]

In a multi-racial society colour has now become an important determinant of employment. A survey of 1973 found that half the young unemployed black people had not registered at Careers Offices or Employment Exchanges because they did not see registration as a means of getting a job: the unemployment rate of sixteen- to twenty-year-olds born in the West Indies was 16.9 per cent compared with 7.6 per cent for Great Britain as a whole, and for all ages 8.4 per cent compared with 5.4 per cent. The survey concluded that lack of educational attainment was the main factor affecting employability: in the sample 71 per cent of young black people did not have any 'CSE' passes, only 8 per cent one 'O' Level and 2 per cent one 'A' Level, but the authors also accepted that 'discrimination in employment, despite the Race Relations Act 1968, remains extensive'.[43] With the general growth in unemployment in the

1980s, black and Asian school-leavers became increasingly disadvantaged, a study of Bradford Asians in 1982 finding that of those who had left school a year before only 28 per cent were in real paid jobs: of the rest, 41 per cent were unemployed and 31 per cent on YOP schemes.[44] The disparity has not lessened in the most recent period, 1986–8, when in the sixteen to twenty-four age group 31 per cent of Pakistanis and Bangladeshis were unemployed, 28 per cent of Caribbeans and 22 per cent of Indians compared with 15 per cent of young white people: for all age groups 17 per cent of males from ethnic minorities were without work compared with 10 per cent of whites.[45]

Unemployment is closely related to occupation. Historically, unskilled and semi-skilled workers earning low wages were the most vulnerable, non-manual professional and managerial employees the least so, and as late as 1980 unemployment was six times greater among unskilled manual workers than among non-manual. In turn, the type of occupation linked closely with educational qualifications and skills training: in Newcastle in 1973, 91 per cent of the unemployed had no educational qualification (only 4 per cent possessed any 'O' Levels) and in Coventry 80 per cent: here, 15 per cent of a sample of the unemployed said that they could not read or write very well and 5 per cent said that they could not read or write English at all.[46]

The collapse of much manufacturing industry during the early 1980s has tended to accentuate the vulnerability of manual workers, who in 1983 constituted 84 per cent of unemployed men: the unemployment rates for different occupations were then non-manual 5 per cent, skilled manual 12 per cent, semi- and unskilled 23 per cent.[47] No groups are now wholly immune, and the phenomenon of unemployed managers and professionals has also received much recent publicity: in 1989 of all unemployed 9.7 per cent were in this category, almost as high as craft-workers at 10.8 per cent.[48] Recent unemployment has therefore been more widely distributed across occupations, levels of skill, education and social class than it was in the 1930s, and it follows that it has also been more widely spread geographically. As we saw in the previous chapter, inter-war unemployment struck particularly in the depressed areas of south Wales, Lancashire, the north-east and Clydeside where the old staple industries were concentrated, while the Midlands and south of England largely escaped serious depression and mass unemployment. This continued to be broadly the pattern in the period of overall low levels of unemployment up to the early 1970s, with Scotland, Wales, Northern Ireland and the north of England having rates twice or three times higher than the Midlands or south of England. But in the depression of the first half of the 1980s the gap closed noticeably as the West Midlands, East Anglia and the south-east experienced major shake-outs. Table 9 indicates that by 1986 unemployment in the West

275

Midlands was not far below that of the north or Scotland, and even the south-east, with a rate of 8.3 per cent, had moved much closer to the UK average of 11.2 per cent.

Table 9 Unemployment rates in 1966, 1976, 1986 and 1989, by region[49]

| | Unemployment rate | | | |
| | *1966* | *1976* | *1986* | *1989* |
	%	%	%	%
North	2.4	5.3	15.4	10.0
Yorkshire & Humberside	1.1	3.9	12.6	7.7
North-west	1.4	5.1	13.8	8.4
East Midlands	1.0	3.5	9.9	6.2
West Midlands	0.8	4.3	12.6	6.7
East Anglia	1.4	3.5	8.1	4.4
South-east	0.9	3.1	8.3	3.9
South-west	1.7	4.7	9.5	4.5
England	–	3.9	11.3	6.2
Wales	2.7	5.3	13.9	7.8
Scotland	2.7	5.1	13.4	9.3
Northern Ireland	–	7.1	17.4	15.1
United Kingdom	–	4.2	11.2	6.3
Britain	1.4			

Source: Regional Trends, Table 10.19, HMSO, 1990 edition, and *Employment Gazette*, Department of Employment, June 1973

Comparisons of the 1980s with the 1930s therefore yield some similarities and some major differences. The total number out of work is much the same, though it is a smaller proportion of the enlarged labour force. Unemployment has struck much more widely across occupations and regions; it has hit the young of both sexes much more than in the past; it has seriously disadvantaged ethnic minorities, those with low educational attainments and lack of relevant skills. One of the most disturbing aspects has been the increase in the average duration of unemployment and the consequent growth of long-term unemployment. Even at its worst in 1936–7 this affected a quarter of the unemployed, and was largely confined to older workers in decayed industrial regions: in 1985, 38 per cent of all unemployed had been out of work for over a year, including many young people, some of whom had never worked since leaving school.[50] In the thirties, in spite of the size of the problem, unemployment could be regarded as exceptional, untypical, socially and geographically remote: the recent experience has been more pervasive and, following a long period of full employment, rising living standards and expectations, has entered more into the heart and consciousness of the nation.

for a single householder, but the 'typical' unemployed person does not have any dependent children, let alone four.

For almost all, therefore, unemployment means a substantial fall in disposable income, often up to half. Are these in poverty? The difficulty of defining poverty in contemporary Britain has already been noted, but if one accepts the level of Supplementary Benefit as the operational test (since this is what the state regards as the level of need) in 1987, 10,200,000 people (19 per cent of the population) were living on or below this level compared with 6 per cent in 1979: in 1987, 2,890,000 (5 per cent) were living *below* the Supplementary Benefit level. On a different measure, of relative deprivation, in 1987 10,500,000 people were living below 50 per cent of average income, yielding a closely similar result.[69] Unemployment is not, of course, the only reason for this relative inequality, albeit a major one. Of the ten-and-a-half million with less than half the average income, 28 per cent were in unemployed households (2,910,000), compared with 26 per cent in full-time but low-paid work and 22 per cent were pensioners: smaller groups of single parents, disabled people, widows and others made up the remainder.[70]

The experience of living on a budget suddenly reduced by up to a half varied greatly, as it did in the 1930s, with a range of individual factors, material and psychological; it also depended importantly on the length of unemployment, because the immediate effects may be cushioned by redundancy payments and real hardship may not commence until after a few months: 'The living standards of the long-term unemployed are lower than those in short-term unemployment, and . . . the living standards of both are below those of the poorest families in work'.[71] Asked what they considered the main hardship of becoming unemployed, 72 per cent of a national sample said lack of money, three times as many as those who said boredom, inactivity or depression.[72] Typical comments include 'I don't think about anything except the money, and how to stretch it'; 'Life is limited. It all revolves around what benefits you get'.[73]

A study of the unemployed on Tyneside found that they spent only half as much on food as the average, cutting down on fresh meat and fruit and luxuries such as cakes and biscuits, very similar to comments in the 1930s except that beefburgers, fish fingers and frozen chips have entered into the budgets of the poor. A report on food and drink manufacturing noted that a decline in the overall volume of consumption between 1981 and 1983 was related to an erosion of net disposable income, and that consumption of beer and whisky had slumped especially in areas of high unemployment.[74] 'We can manage now. . . . We're not rock bottom, but I think if it goes on much longer we could be going that way . . . it's getting harder to manage each week.'[75] Especially for families with children, lengthening unemployment almost necessarily meant the accumulation of debts, often associated with housing and heating costs but also with arrears on hire-purchase payments. A study of the living standards of those on Supplementary Benefit in Tyne and Wear found that nearly all families were in debt, the average amount £441, including weekly repayments of 11 per cent of their income.[76] Comments by Newcastle unemployed include: 'We're not living, we're just existing'; 'We can't even think about buying clothes'; 'I never go out now'; 'It's alright for the first month'.[77]

Other commentators stressed the anxiety and frustration which financial constraints brought:

> The worst thing, the thing that really gets you down, is the uncertainty, that you've got no future. The future is the next electricity bill, and whether you can pay that.

> If you want to put up some shelves, even if you've got the wood left over from something else, you find you can't afford to go out and buy the brackets. I could have repainted the whole damn house, but I can't afford to go out and buy paint.

Frequently mentioned by parents is the anxiety, almost shame, they feel in being unable to meet their children's requests for things that others enjoy.

> The children can't understand why they never have a holiday. They can't understand why they don't get new clothes like their friends do. We try to tell them, but they don't understand. It's a strain when they cry. . . . At Christmas they won't go out of the house because the others are bragging about what they've got.[78]

In this connection, many of those interviewed in surveys mention the support given by grandparents to buy clothes and presents for the children.

In some respects budgeting in the 1970s and 1980s was more complicated and difficult than in the 1930s because the scale of commitments and expectations was so much greater than in the simple lifestyles of the past. The Smiths' budget for example, meticulously noted each week by Mrs Smith, included home and property insurance (they were buying their house), telephone, television licence and car tax and insurance (though John Smith could now rarely afford the petrol and was considering selling it). Their weekly outgoings totalled £89, leaving just 94p from their benefits: the family's food was bought from their younger son's wage, carefully costed at 90p per head per day. Mrs Smith buys the cheapest, filling foods – bread, potatoes, margarine, cornflakes, tins of beans – 'Potatoes are a large part of our diet now: they go a long way and they fill you up'. They no longer have a Sunday joint: their meat is sausages, mincemeat, sometimes liver, and fresh vegetables are bought only 'when the price is right': formerly they had two pints of milk a day and a dozen eggs a week, now one pint and half-a-dozen. Despite their not uncomfortable home, the television and the telephone, the privation they feel when measured against their former standard of living is perhaps more acute than it was for families in the thirties, many of whom had always existed on the margins of poverty. And in one respect there was a remarkable parallel with the past. Although they spend £12 a week on coke for their central heating boiler, this is never enough, so every week John and his wife go foraging in the woods for timber: like their prede-cessors on the slag-heaps, 'Logging is a necessity, it's not through choice'.[79]

The availability to some of sizeable redundancy payments has admit-tedly softened the immediate impact of unemployment compared with the 1930s when compensation for manual workers was unheard of, but lump-sums may be mixed blessings in creating a false sense of security. In any case, both the extent and amounts of redundancy payments are much exaggerated, and the numbers receiving some tens of thousands of pounds are extremely small: a survey in 1971 found that only 7 per cent of the unemployed received payments under the Redundancy Act of 1965 and 11 per cent refunds of a lump-sum from pensions, but the largest proportion (39 per cent) received only quite trivial holiday pay and 43 per cent none at all: the numbers receiving any forms of payment rose steadily with occupational level up to the professional/managerial class. More than three-quarters of all surveyed received less than £100 or nothing, and even in the top grades only a quarter received more than £2,000 compared with 1 per cent in the unskilled grade. Most unem-ployed people used their lump sums to contribute towards living expenses and home improvements or, partly, on holidays.[80] Mr Weston, who received £500 redundancy pay, reported: 'I had three weeks' holiday, the best holiday I've ever had'. And in the early days, his wife said: 'We've not cut down on anything. In fact, the children have had more . . . they've had clothes and that. We've not had to cut down on food'.[81]

How long such a happy state of affairs lasts obviously depends on the size of the lump sum and how carefully it is husbanded. In a recent study of the unemployed the proportion receiving redundancy pay had risen to 21 per cent in 1987 but even so, 57 per cent of unemployed men and their partners had no savings and only 16 per cent had £1,000 or more.[82] Once any severance payments are exhausted – and for the long-term unemployed this is likely to be the case – standards of living become eroded to subsistence level. A recent commentator has observed, 'Loss of job does not mean starvation, but almost inevitably it will lead to a growing loss of mobility and reduced access to social interaction'.[83] A survey by the Department of Health and Social Security found that one-third of men had given up going out for a drink or a meal, a third no longer took the family on outings and a quarter had given up attending football matches or other sports.[84] Financial constraints limit participation and enjoyment in what society accepts as a normal lifestyle, resulting in anxiety and frustration when 'dole day is the decentest meal we get'[85] or when after collecting his benefit on a Friday afternoon a husband would buy pasties, bacon and eggs 'to cheer us up'.[86] The desire occasionally to relieve the monotony is very reminiscent of comments in the thirties, as also are the battles which some claimants have with the authorities, especially over extra discretionary grants for exceptional needs.

> We were pretty lucky to get a grant for shoes . . . but, another certain person that we know, they came into the house and he sat and she told him all her troubles, and he said 'Well, I don't think you need anything myself. You've got a beautiful home. If you're that hard up, sell the sideboard, and when the money goes for that, sell that'.[87]

In general, however, the harshness of means-testing in the past does not seem to be replicated recently, and the more common complaints are about the wages-stop and bureaucratic delays in receiving benefits rather than the tyrannical treatment by petty officials which was so often alleged in the thirties. Given the long history of a welfare state since the last war, benefits are now more widely regarded as 'rights' derived from citizenship and former contributions to the body politic, not as charitable handouts for which the recipient has to be grateful. And because unemployment has been much more widely experienced across regions and social classes, the sense of personal blame and shame which was often expressed in the previous 'Great Depression' has, at least to some degree, declined. 'There's no stigma attached to it because it's so common in Peterlee and in the North-East generally.'[88]

SOCIAL AND PSYCHOLOGICAL EFFECTS

The return of mass unemployment inevitably invites the question whether those affected have suffered similar emotional experiences to the unemployed of the 1930s which were illustrated in the previous chapter. In the former period they frequently included apathy and a sense of purposelessness, a loss of status and identity which had been defined by the nature of employment, a lack of time structure to the day, an absence of social contacts and a sense of being isolated from the rest of society – of being 'on the scrap-heap'. It might be assumed that because the material standards of the unemployed have not been reduced to the levels of absolute poverty of fifty years ago, that because health and nutritional standards are higher, education, housing and social services all much improved, the unemployed of today have been better able to cope with the loss of work without suffering the kind or degree of traumas of the past.

It was the observation by social scientists of the behavioural character-istics of the unemployed in several European countries and the USA in the thirties which led them to propose models of a series of stages through which individuals passed as a result of job loss. The first of these, developed in 1932–3 by Jahoda and others from their observations in Marienthal, Austria, was described in Chapter 6: it argued that as the income of the unemployed declined month by month down to around half that at the beginning of unemployment it was paralleled by a pro-gressive emotional deterioration from the initial 'unbroken' stage to resig-nation, despair and, ultimately, apathy. By 1935 Zawadski and Lazarsfeld had elaborated the model with two additional stages:

1 Initial reaction of fear, injury, sometimes hatred and desire for revenge;
2 Numbness and apathy;
3 Calming down, adaptation, a belief that things will improve;
4 Hope fades when no job arises;
5 Fear and hopelessness as resources diminish;
6 Acquiescence or apathy, with alternating hope and hopelessness 'according to momentary changes in the material situation'.[89]

More recent studies in the 1970s have tended to reduce and simplify the transitions: thus Harrison (1976) suggested a sequence of shock – opti-mism – pessimism – fatalism, while Hill (1977, 1978) has only three stages:

1 Initial trauma *or* optimism;
2 A process of accepting a new identity, involving boredom, stagnation;
3 Adaptation to unemployment – hope resigned, but anxiety may be partly relieved.[90]

These models clearly have much in common and have come to have almost the authority of received wisdom, but they should not be accepted without several qualifications. They suggest an almost inevitable pro-gression, whereas, depending on the length of unemployment, an indi-vidual may never reach the final stage: moreover, his experience is probably not the linear one which the models suggest, but he may well swing backwards and forwards, with periods of optimism recaptured even in the later stages of the transition:[91] indeed, as many autobiographies suggest, hope is often never completely abandoned, even in the most unpromising circumstances. Also, the models are based mainly on the experiences of men in middle life suffering long-term unemployment, whereas women, school-leavers and men nearing retirement age may well feel the effects of unemployment differently. Finally, any model which ignores individual differences of personality and temperament is likely to

285

be too simplistic, and we should be very cautious about any generalization such as the suggestion that the 'settling down to unemployment' stage begins at around nine months to a year[92] – some may never settle down, others may do so much earlier. The reactions of a forty-year-old unskilled labourer who has previously experienced several short spells of unemployment are likely to be very different from those of a fifty-year-old manager who for the first time in his successful career has been declared redundant because of company restructuring. For many, the idea of a fixed pattern of reactions and stages is not appropriate.

Further, how traumatic the effects of job loss will be must depend partly on the individual's feelings about his former job: at one extreme, he may feel devastated by the loss of power, status and respect; at the other, a sense of relief at giving up excessively unpleasant or uncongenial work. In that sense, the losses of unemployment can only be understood by reference to the benefits of employment. Professor Marie Jahoda points out that in modern industrial society employment is the main source of certain 'categories of experience' which are relevant to psychological well-being. Employment has the 'manifest' function of providing financial rewards, but also involves important 'latent' functions:

1 Enforced activity;
2 Brings the individual into social contacts outside the family and household;
3 Involves him in collective purposes which go beyond personal, immediate goals;
4 Provides a time structure for the execution of activities;
5 A social status linked to the prestige of the occupation.[93]

In short, these functions support Freud's thesis that work constitutes man's strongest tie to reality, and that without it he is likely to be psychologically damaged. Jahoda argues that nothing prevents the unemployed person from fulfilling the five latent functions for himself, 'but the psychological input required to do so on a regular basis, under one's own steam entirely, is colossal'.

It is certainly not difficult to find illustrations of stages among unemployed men interviewed in recent surveys. The first stage of 'shock' is often mentioned as a feeling of disbelief or numbness: 'It was a shattering experience, absolutely shattering. You see, insecurity has always been a sort of bogey with me. . . . Desperate when that went: been desperate ever since, really. I'm not used to it yet'. (A former manager in his early fifties with a good salary, buying a bungalow, unemployed for four years.)[94] One man described his sensation at being dismissed as 'like being cut by a knife', another as 'like a ship going down'; for others, the realization sank in only when they first visited the Job Centre: 'When the man behind the desk saw my age, 59, he said, "You don't stand an earthly of getting a job", I could have burst into tears'.[95] But a warning against stereotyping even the initial reaction to unemployment is given by others:

> At first it feels marvellous. It's as though you've left the rat race . . . and you can look at it and wonder why people bother. You look at them setting off in the morning at 7.30 and coming back at night at half-past five, and you think 'Why bother?' The first few days you sit at home and relax, and it's like a holiday.[96]

A man who collected £1,900 redundancy pay felt 'like a millionaire. At first, great, you don't have to get up in the morning. That goes on for a few weeks. Then you have a twinge of anxiety. You think, "Next week I'll look for a job" '.[97] And another: 'It's alright for the first month'.[98]

How quickly these reactions are replaced by anxiety and pessimism depends partly on the size of resources in relation to expenses, partly on a wide range of personal factors; but for many it seems that hopes are first dashed by the initial visit to the Job Centre and the realization of how few vacancies exist. In the recent jobs crisis this seems to contrast with the situation for many in the 1930s or the early 1970s when the average length of unemployment was shorter, there was more short-term frictional unemployment, and the period of optimism about finding work would be sustained longer. Furthermore, in the thirties the job search occupied more time and energy, and visits to the Labour Exchange twice or three times a week gave more structure to time than the now usual fortnightly call. In the recent accounts, the period of optimism about finding work is generally briefer and sometimes non-existent.

Evidence about the feelings of people during unemployment has been gathered in several surveys. Asked what things about unemployment caused concern, 72 per cent in 1973 said lack of money: 'having to cut down'; 'not being able to afford things'. Boredom or inactivity was given by 28 per cent, depression/apathy by 14 per cent, feeling a failure/ useless by 11 per cent and social isolation/rejection by 5 per cent. (Several respondents listed more than one factor.) But although financial concerns came out most strongly, 58 per cent mentioned at least one item of psychological or social concern, and when asked what was the 'worst thing' about being out of work, lack of money fell to 45 per cent, while boredom/inactivity rose to 36 per cent: a total of 64 per cent mentioned some social/psychological factor, and only 4 per cent found 'nothing wrong' with being unemployed.[99] Similarly, in a study of the long-term unemployed in 1980 lack of money and boredom were the concerns most strongly represented: to the question 'Can the unemployed get as much out of life as those in work?', three-quarters of respondents replied 'No': 37 per cent of men and 28 per cent of women had given up one or more leisure activities because they could no longer afford it, the activity most frequently stated being 'going out socially'.[100]

In all the recent enquiries the problem of spending time, and the consequential boredom, is the most frequently mentioned social effect of unemployment.

> The best thing you can look forward to is running a Hoover around the living-room and washing-up.... You go mad.... The kids are running round, screaming their heads off, you tend to get ratty, the more often you lose your temper it has an effect on you ... I think it does have an effect on your health both physically and psychologically. It depresses you.[101]

A Middlesbrough boilermaker, a single man:

> You can so easily feel it as a personal failing, even when you know it's a fault in the system.... [After visiting his ageing mother each day] Then I come down here in the middle of the day, have a pint, make it last. I wake up at five in the morning: by the time I've been to see Mam and the Bramble opens, half my day's over. I sit here till three, have a bite to eat, get my head down in the afternoon, wake up at six, have a wash, look at the paper, come back here at half-past seven (to the Bramble), make another pint last till ten. Then I go to bed at eleven, only I'm not tired, so I'm awake again at five.[102]

The habit of waking at the same time as when employed is often mentioned, but in the above case the unemployed man had found a new routine which imposed a time structure on his day, however unsatisfying, and his visits to The Bramble may well have supplied him with social contacts. A range of other comments illustrate a deterioration in morale which parallel the stage models, though drawn from several witnesses, not merely one:

> I miss the people at work.

> By the end of the first month you're bored stiff.

> I'd rather be working now, and have no time (for other things).

> I keep waking up. I usually watch the telly till about one o'clock.... When I was at work I was always in bed about eleven o'clock...

> Oh, he'd love to get a job.... You look at him, and he looks really tired and ill, and he hasn't eaten a thing for four days. I'll make a meal and put it on his plate, and he'll take a couple of spoonfuls and say he doesn't feel hungry. (A wife.)

> I just find I can live on one meal ... and a couple of pints.

Then after a couple of months you started getting lazy, like you
cannot be bothered to doe nowt, just feel like stopping in bed all
day.

I think I'm at a peak now. I sit here dead worried, and I think, 'I've
got to get a job'. But in a month or two I'll be saying, 'I can't get
a job'.

We haven't much sense of time . . . I have developed the capacity to
do nothing, absolutely nothing. But it worries me a bit . . . I was
writing a letter, and I began this letter and I got broken off, and
when I went to finish this letter I looked at the date and it was four
days between starting and finishing. Christ, man, four days! Where's
it gone?

I stopped even looking for a job. In these two years I lost all bloody
interest. I thought, 'What's the bloody point of it all, anyway? What's
the reason for it all?' Then you start to become, well, deranged . . .
I can't pronounce the word when you're thinking about things, I
can't get it out . . . psychologically. You start thinking about it, 'What
the bloody hell's the point? Why are yer here?'[103]

You felt you were playing a part in the community (when working):
it was right for someone to go to work from nine till six and bring
a certain amount home. . . . You weren't shoved on the scrap-heap,
rendered useless. . . . Well, you might as well be dead.

So you draw the curtains, put the television on, and that's the only
thing really you've got left.

One of the problems is that the working-class has never experienced
having leisure time: we just don't know what to do with our leisure
time . . . This is the main thing about being out of work, absolute
boredom.[104]

There is clear evidence here and in the comments of other respondents
that some men reach a final stage of becoming institutionalized in unemployment, with a sense of helplessness, futility and lack of control over
their destiny. Losing friends, workmates and social contacts, they are
thrown in upon themselves and their own diminishing material and
emotional resources: 'I've lost interest. I'm disillusioned with society'; 'I
became something of a hermit'; 'I don't know where I'm going any
more'; 'If I had my way they could have their £10,000 (redundancy
payment) back and I would go back to my job'.[105]
Such responses apply particularly to men in their middle years with
family responsibilities who feel their role as the breadwinner diminished
and their status in the household and society 'demeaned' – a word often

used. The effects for other groups are usually less acute – for men nearing retirement age, especially if they have received substantial redundancy payments, or for school-leavers who have never experienced the routine of employment. These have, however, moved from a structured school environment, and if the summer holiday extends into long unemployment it seems that many experience great difficulty in filling their time: a study of young unemployed in Birmingham in 1981 found that over a period of twenty-four weeks there was a progression from initial pessimism to resignation and apathy, closely similar to the stage model.[106] The danger for school-leavers is that without the stimulus of loss of former income and family responsibilities they may adjust more quickly than the adult to acceptance and resignation.

> **Carol** I have been on the dole ever since I left school about a year and a half ago . . . I get £22 a fortnight, but by the time I give my Mum some money and have bought something for myself it does not leave me much . . . I go to the Job Centre every week, but they do not have anything for me. . . . It's most boring just sitting at home doing nothing all day long, only going to the shops with my Mum and carrying whatever she gets.

> **Roger** The last year at school we started clowning about, having fun and a laugh like. . . . Now I wish I could have stayed on or done better when I was there. I suppose I didn't appreciate what exams would mean to me, but I never got interested while I was still at school. . . . It's boring with nothing to do being unemployed. I get depressed. Everyone gets in your way and starts arguing with you.

> **Andrew** I don't know what the dole will do to you, but I used to be a really good-tempered and friendly chap, but while on the dole someone just says something I don't like and I'll have a good go to give them a fat lip. I'm still quite friendly but I've got a really wild side. . . . When my parents and I had rows all the time they just used to get on my wick. They used to be shouting at me that I had to get a job or go and live elsewhere. . . . So I used to just walk out, slam the door, and be ready to set on the first person who spoke to me.[107]

Such symptoms of rejection and alienation from family and society seem to be shared quite widely by the young jobless, especially by those without qualifications living in areas of high unemployment. A study of young people from ethnic minorities, whose unemployment rates were twice or three times the average, showed especially strong feelings of inferiority and alienation from white standards and a turning inwards on their own cultures: there was a high level of distrust and suspicion of the police in areas such as Brent, where 35 per cent of young unemployed blacks reported being taken to a police station for questioning.[108]

The psychological effects of unemployment on women depend very much on whether they were sole earners, contributing earners or house-wives not normally engaged in paid work, but in all groups studies show that women feel the lack of social contacts more acutely than men. Beyond this generalization, however, the effects are difficult to categorize, since a majority of formerly employed women worked only part-time and generally had a less strong attachment to work than men, and also because, as Cragg and Dawson observe, 'marriage complicates official (and personal) perceptions of unemployment among women'.[109] Their study of 1984 found, for example, that the mothers of families did not regard themselves as 'unemployed' though they might be looking for paid work, and that for many married women the primary motive for employment was not so much financial as independence and desire to escape the confines of domesticity. But for a third of their sample – mainly single mothers and those with low-paid or unemployed husbands – the loss of work caused major problems, both financially and psycho-logically.

> We're on the dole. We've got no savings. We're on the breadline. And now there's gas and electric due before Christmas and the television licence. Well, how do you pay. . . . Where am I going to get that?

> £38 (Supplementary Benefit) for all of us (mother and three children) plus the family allowance. £10 rent, £10 electricity, £2 club money, and that's it. It's all right until one of the children needs a pair of shoes . . . I was earning £60–70 a week before, so it's a big drop. . . . Mostly, I suffer.[110]

> You walk into a room, and don't have any way into the conversation. If you've got a job, even if it's disgusting, you can make people laugh by telling them how horrible it is. But if someone asks you what you do, and you have to say, 'I'm unemployed', that's it. End of conversation. They just say, 'I'm sorry.'[111]

In such cases the stress of unemployment, unshared with a partner and with the knowledge that childcaring responsibilities greatly limit the chances of paid work, must be much worse than for the single man. This is a neglected area of research, and most of the recent studies have been on the effects on family relationships where a husband is unemployed. Here the consensus is that unemployment increases tensions between husbands and wives, leading to frequent arguments, sometimes violence and even divorce.[112] 'You feel you have nothing to say to each other. . . . What have I done in a day that interests her? . . . I don't want people coming in here, seeing how shabby it is.'[113] Yet, exceptionally, and where a marriage was very firmly based, unemployment and shared suffering may bring the partners closer together.

> The only good thing that's come out of unemployment is that the families are more together: men take more care of the kids, they know a bit more what it's like for a woman. But the first time I took the pram out, I felt awful. But then I looked round and saw that no end of men were doing it. I just hadn't noticed.[114]

But other evidence suggests that male unemployment does not generally result in any major reversal of traditional sexual roles: the man still sees himself as the provider, having a public profile in his search for work, attending job interviews, engaging in informal work outside the home, and this role was still accepted by wives, even when reduced income leads to an enlargement of their own domestic role.[115]

Unemployment may be experienced collectively as well as individually. In the 1930s the common suffering in depressed areas seems to have helped to sustain morale and the hope that things would eventually improve. A former shipyard worker who had experienced unemployment before the war, told Seabrook in 1980:

> What really appalls me now is that they don't have hope, and we did. We felt not only that work would pick up again in the yards and the pits, but that time was on our side. We saw a future possibility for socialism. . . . The young have no such hope now. Their only hopes are centred on individual salvation – the dream of the pools, the big win, the stroke of good fortune. We hoped for the whole of the working class, not just for ourselves.[116]

Most of the old working-class communities he spoke of – perhaps with an enthusiasm heightened by nostalgia – no longer exist, dispersed by migration and redevelopment. Pit villages are almost the only survivors of such close communities, though few of these now remain, and the sense of collective mourning when a pit closes (even to the extent of carrying a coffin in procession) suggests the deep emotional feelings which bereaved communities share on the loss of a local industry. Writing in 1967 about the pit closures then beginning, Will Paynter said:

> I wonder sometimes if those who decide policies to precipitate the contraction of the coal industry have any idea as to what a pit closure means to the community built around it. It is the death of a creation that gave the community life. . . . Closure represents a disaster as poignant and harrowing as a death in the family.[117]

Comments by miners during the coal strike of 1984–5 affirm these emotions: 'If they close the pit, they're closing down my life'; 'The pit's your own community. . . . It's the family pit'; 'You work with all your mates, so it's good'; 'It was a happy pit. It was a place full of laughter'.[118]

It is, perhaps, too easy to romanticize both about the emotional rewards of such work and about the social and psychological support of the communities in which it was carried on, but in the more privatized lives of the late twentieth century there clearly seems to be less mutual consolation in adversity from extended families and neighbourhoods, and fewer spontaneous collective activities designed to help fill the gap left by the loss of work.

HEALTH

There is abundant evidence that unemployment frequently leads to psychological stress, but it is more difficult to establish whether it can be a direct cause of ill-health. In interviews with unemployed people, depression is very frequently mentioned, together with problems of sleeping, loss of appetite, headaches and indigestion, and it may well be that psychological stress is a preliminary to a decline in physical well-being. John Smith lost a stone in weight while unemployed, suffered from frequent headaches, felt lethargic and lacking in energy[119] partly, perhaps, because he could no longer afford his former sports at the leisure centre: 'Being out of work, and not getting enough grub, I was getting so I wouldn't eat. I mean, when you're out of work you worry, and you don't feel like eating'. His wife remarked 'He's complaining with his stomach all the time, and he's edgy, like, he's on edge all the time'.[120] Unstructured comments can, of course, be unrepresentative, and it is possible that a pre-existing illness or disability may be a cause of unemployment rather than a consequence: a study of male unemployeds in 1981 found that 29 per cent had some physical disability, though only 9 per cent were registered as disabled.[121] Comparing the results of a standardized General Health Questionnaire administered to a sample of employed and unemployed people allows a more scientific measure of respondents' own feelings about their 'state of well-being', and on this measure those in work had a substantially higher level than the unemployed.[122]

Most research on unemployment and health has stressed that hard evidence of a causal relationship is sparse. But it is known that poverty can be a major factor in the production of ill-health, and that 'the onset of disease is related to the degree of life change an individual has to cope with'.[123] Studies have found increased blood pressure and higher cholesterol levels among long-term unemployed men as well as fatigue, weight loss, stomach ulcers and increased drinking of alcohol,[124] while an official report in 1983 found death rates among unemployed men considerably higher than among comparable groups of the employed, particularly in respect of accidents and violent deaths.[125] A number of deeply depressed men have told interviewers about feelings of suicide – 'You feel like killing yourself. Perhaps somebody'd notice you then'.[126] A limited investigation of men admitted to an Edinburgh hospital between 1968 and 1983 showed 'a marked association' between unemployment rates and parasuicide (attempted suicide) rates: in the last year, the attempted suicide rate among unemployed males was 1,149 per 100,000 compared with 110 per 100,000 among the employed – a rate more than ten times higher. But the author of this study cautiously concluded that although 'the findings are entirely consistent with the hypothesis that unemployment is *a* cause of parasuicide (my italics)', it is only one cause, and that 'parasuicide almost certainly results from the complex interaction of many factors'.[127]

Despite the easy assumptions of the media, a similar verdict probably applies to the relationship between unemployment and crime. Overall crime rates did not rise during the depressed 1930s, when the view of researchers was that the unemployed were remarkably law abiding, and they rose during the affluent 1950s and 1960s as well as in the depressed early 1980s. Again, it is not difficult to quote statements by the unemployed which appear to point to a connection:

> I was out one Tuesday night and was very bored, because I didn't have a job. I decided to go joy-riding. This is taking and driving a car without the owner knowing. The first car I took was a Jaguar, and I meant to take parts from it, to sell to get some money . . . I then walked down to Temple Meads and took a Morris Oxford . . . I stripped the car of radio/cassette player, speakers and battery.[128]

> I gang into town every day now. I go shoplifting. Me Mam says, 'Get a job.' I say 'I've got one'. She says, 'What is it?' I say, 'Signing on.' I've been caught lifting things. I've been away for it. . . . What I really want is to be rich. Buy a house, have adventures. Get other people to do what you want them to.

> If you want things, you have to go roguing. . . . It gets you all excited while you're doing it, then afterwards you feel relaxed, it feels good. You feel you've achieved something.[129]

There is more here than the mere desire for gain – the filling of time, the sense of achievement, the excitement of the job and the evasion of discovery which compares closely with the accounts of poaching in the thirties. On a wider scale, the inner-city disturbances of 1981–5 have also been associated with unemployment and anomie, as well as with deprivation, racial tensions, family breakdown and a range of environmental factors: it may be that in the less cohesive communities of today, the effect of mass unemployment is further to undermine and destabilize authority, though this was not the case in the stronger communities of the past. As with health, the problem is to isolate the effects of one predisposing factor from others, and to assess which is first or predominant. Since Mannheim first studied the relationship between crime and unemployment in 1940 there have been at least thirty investigations: their conclusions are widely varying – a few found no link, a few a very powerful one, while in between the majority believe that unemployment contributes to crime, but only as one of many factors.[130] The relationship appears to be closest in the middle age range rather than in young offenders, yet the peak age for criminal convictions is the mid-teens, perhaps suggesting that economic motives for crime may not be the paramount ones for this group. However, a study of sixteen- to eighteen-year-old offenders in Northern Ireland has found them twice as likely to commit crimes when not in work, education or training,[131] apparently confirming the adage that idle hands find mischief to do. It also seems important to distinguish between different sorts of crime, a United Nations study concluding that periods of recession are particularly associated with property offences and petty 'social crimes' such as vagrancy and drunkenness. From the welter of sometimes conflicting evidence, a fair judgement would be that unemployment is an important determinant of the social conditions in which crime becomes more prevalent.

ADAPTATIONS TO UNEMPLOYMENT

Employment brings certain social as well as financial rewards: even if levels of benefit are sufficient to satisfy economic requirements adequately, including participation in social activities, can the other, psychological rewards of employment be met in a life of enforced leisure? The weight of evidence suggests that for the majority they cannot. In their study of the unemployed, *Workless* (1973), Marsden and Duff concluded:

> We had wondered whether unemployment might be a sort of release and opportunity for some men whose work we would consider to be harsh and unrewarding either in itself or financially. We found that so strong are the pressures and informal sanctions supporting work in our society that some of the workless cling to the desire to work to a much greater degree than our society has a right to expect. . . . Indeed, in our small study we found no really convincing evidence of the emergence of any viable alternatives to work.[132]

Jock Keenan, a fifty-year-old unemployed miner, well described the ambivalent attitudes of many people towards work and leisure:

> Frankly, I hate work. Of course, I could also say with equal truth that I love work. . . . Nor have I ever met anyone who liked work, or to be precise, liked what blokes such as myself understand by

the term. . . . It would seem clear that it isn't really work that we are talking about, not the thing in itself, but its associations.[133]

In theory, these 'associations' of work could be met outside of waged labour, the actual processes of which men like Keenan often found dreary, monotonous and unfulfilling. It is important here to distinguish between work, in the sense of activity which is natural and necessary, and employment for wages, which in a longer historical perspective is not 'natural'. Unemployed people may be able to find the satisfactions of 'work' in active leisure, in self-provisioning, in voluntary social or political activities, by engaging in the informal ('black') economy or by making a career change into self-employment, though each of these involves difficulties of adjustment, material and psychological resources which the individual may lack. The evidence suggests that in recent times leisure activities have been generally curtailed rather than enlarged by unemployment, that, as previously noted, boredom is one of the chief characteristics of worklessness, and that men in particular often find much difficulty in filling time.

> We just don't know what to do with our leisure time. I'm quite fortunate with having a garden, but that can't last for long – you can only spend so much time in a garden. One really gets bored stiff. This is the main thing about being out of work, absolute boredom. This comes before the financial position, I think.[134]

> What happens is, after they've been on the dole for a long time they lose their spirit, they've got no fight in them, they crawl into their bloody holes, they sit round the fire, they get used to doing nothing, they stand at the bloody window watching the world pass them by. . . . When I'm working I can go on my holidays, I can go away to the coast several weekends in the year, I have a car which I used to replace every three years – that's gone. There's a tremendous loss straightaway. I'm used to going out to clubs . . . that's gone. I'm used to buying clothes and getting dressed up and going out, and so is the wife – that's gone. . . . The attitude now to a man on the dole is that his place is in the house: 'If you're not working, then you sit up home, boy, and be thankful that we're feeding you'.[135]

The last remark, whether true or merely felt to be so, is significant. There is often a sharp divide between the employed and the unemployed in which the latter are increasingly squeezed out of the public realm and reduced to increasingly lonely, privatized lives. Yet those living on benefit are subject to public scrutiny, both by the authorities and by neighbours who may share a common prejudice against 'scroungers', a prejudice which seems to have increased since the 1930s partly because tax thresholds have been lowered to include many of the working class. The involvement of the unemployed in public social activities has become more difficult both because of ostracism and because the costs of many forms of entertainment are prohibitive for them. In his survey in 1973, Daniel found that more than half of the unemployed who had previously been used to going out with friends for a drink or a meal, taking the family for outings, attending a football or cricket match, or going to the theatre or cinema, had in each case given up the activity: between a third and a half who had previously entertained at home, had gambled, or engaged in hobbies such as photography, had given these up.[136] Other studies have clearly shown that the unemployed are less satisfied with their leisure time than the employed, and that such activities as are available to them are largely home-based. These may be satisfying up to a point, though one of the commonest complaints is of being 'shut away' or 'cooped up' at home, where watching television has become a major time-killer and palliative. It is not known how much time is spent in viewing by the unemployed: in 1989 the average time in all households was twenty-four-and-a-half hours a week or twenty-six hours for the thirty-five to sixty-four age group,[137] and almost certainly the figure would be higher for the unemployed. This is another contrast with the 1930s, when television was not available and the radio far from universal in poorer homes. Then, as noted in the previous chapter, a weekly or fortnightly visit to the cinema was common, but the difference, as Kelvin and Jarrett have observed, is that going to the cinema took one out of the house and among other people – a positive action akin to a tonic rather than the drug of passive viewing in an all-too-familiar environment.[138]

Of course, there are exceptions: those who have not been diminished by unemployment but have grown through it. Mr Keach was a skilled joiner with large building firms before becoming unemployed after twenty years:

> I should have tried to break away earlier, but when you've a family you can't think of the luxury of getting yourself educated or whatever. . . . You do feel that earning a living has got nothing to do with you as a person. That's why I can bear unemployment. My relationship with the family has always been my greatest support. . . . With my wife being ill, some days she can't do anything, it's given me a purpose. I can take some of the burden from her, and I don't feel useless. We've always got on well together. We share everything.[139]

Colin, an energetic thirty-year-old, told Seabrook that 'There's too much work to be done to take paid employment': he was a voluntary worker in a neighbourhood centre, a health food co-operative and a campaigner against racism. Voluntary work of this kind can clearly be deeply satisfying, though unemployed people are not best equipped to engage in it by experience, education or tradition. While men's voluntary activities have been concerned mainly with political and labour organizations, some unemployed women have found outlets for their energy and compassion in caring activities: one such was described who

> rushes around all the time, organises hundreds of different things, working in an adventure playground and doing shifts at a women's centre. Last week she was at my house when a man asked her what her job was. She just mumbled, 'I don't do anything really, I'm unemployed.' Because she isn't paid for the things she does, she won't count them as a proper job.[140]

Mr Davis, an unemployed boilermaker, developed a passionate interest in collecting butterflies: 'Unemployment definitely gave me a fascination and an interest that saved me'. His wife added, 'I think the satisfaction comes from looking at something of beauty, and also learning about them, their habitat and their lifecycle. I'm not a professional, only a passionate amateur'.[141]

Home improvements, decorating and other 'do-it-yourself' activities have long been a satisfying, creative activity for some men to which the growth of home-ownership and pride in possession has given an added importance. This can merely be at the level of 'pottering about, trying to fill your time up. You try to keep up a routine, doing little jobs here and there', though for a minority more ambitious projects can develop into small, money-making enterprises. Mr Coxon turned his woodworking skills to making and wiring electric lamp-holders – 'I made about three or four hundred of them' – and Mr Vickers spent regular hours in his garden shed until five o'clock every day: 'I think I wouldn't work if I didn't have to. I think I'd like to set up my own little workshop, with a bandsaw in it and a lathe, and turn out bits of furniture, even if it was only to give my wife'. Another man made kites for sale; another pictures: 'Work has gone right to the back of my mind, because I feel so free doing these pictures, that if I can make a living wage without the dole, I just won't be interested in going back to work'.[142]

But these are exceptions. Many men say that they cannot now afford to do so much handywork about the house as formerly because of the cost of materials, though whether it is this or the apathy which often accompanies unemployment is not possible to know. Similarly, self-provisioning by the unemployed has been found to be less than among the employed, and appears to be considerably less than in the thirties when coal-gathering from tips, tending allotments, rabbiting and poaching were frequently mentioned. Opportunities for such activities may well be less in a highly urbanized society, but Professor Pahl's study indicates that all forms of work, whether formal or informal, tend to be concentrated in the better-off households, and that a polarization occurs in modern society in which the poor can do little more for themselves than scavenging. Opportunities to engage in informal work tend to arise out of formal work and the contacts which go with it rather than out of unemployment and its relative isolation. In his study of Sheppey, Pahl also found that unemployment tends to reinforce traditional sexual roles within the household, and that far from increasing the sharing of domestic tasks, the great majority (89 per cent) of families in which the husband was unemployed fell into the most conventional category in which the female partner did most of the tasks.[143] The conclusion is paradoxical – that households with work and money are productive and busy, those without money are idle and unproductive.[144]

Both today and in the thirties, public policy has sought to prevent informal work from developing into the 'black economy' where payments for work are not disclosed to social security or revenue authorities. How widespread are forms of minor 'fiddling' among the unemployed is, by definition, unknowable, though it is likely that it is limited by lack of equipment and that where it does exist the amount of money involved is generally small. A typical example is probably that reported by Marsden:

> I've got a little bit of a fiddle, window-cleaning. Champion. . . . Now I make me own baccy money and me own couple of pints. . . . On a fine week I'd say I make about five or six quid, like. You won't have to mention that, or else me dole's stopped.[145]

That was in the early 1970s. More recently, the opportunities for casual work 'on the side' have diminished with increasing competition.

> When things are easy, it isn't such a tragedy to be out of work. There are all kinds of fiddles, little jobs you can do; but as the level of unemployment rises these avenues close down, you can't get the little jobs window-cleaning, car-repairing. On my estate, in the little road where I live, there were eight out of fourteen households that had cars; there's one now.[146]

In areas less open to public scrutiny some degree of domestic provisioning undoubtedly continues, as in Sheppey where an unemployed man kept himself very busy gardening, decorating, fishing and rabbiting with a gun, bringing meat and ducks into the house, while his wife was involved in (undisclosed) outwork industry and home selling,[147] but such cases now look like rare survivals from a more primitive stage of economy. Doing occasional work for friends, neighbours and relatives obviously continues, and for a few may develop into virtually full-time voluntary activity, as we have seen, though even here the enlargement and professionalization of welfare agencies may have reduced the scope for the amateur volunteer compared with the 1930s. Similarly, the extent of mutual aid systems among the unemployed, which was strongly in evidence then, has almost certainly been eroded by the destruction of some old industrial and mining communities, by urban renewal, new town development and, not least, by the growth of materialism and consumerism which have tended to encourage individual rather than collective values. A national survey by the Economist Intelligence Unit in 1982 found that 23 per cent of the unemployed had done some work for other people, but only 4 per cent of these had received payment in cash, and were mainly people who had received some further education.[148] A not dissimilar conclusion was reached by a government report in 1981 that around 8 per cent of the unemployed had undisclosed work, mainly part-time.[149] Most of the 'black economy' consists of second jobs by those already employed.

Previous chapters have shown that in earlier periods significant numbers of people escaped from unemployment by moving into new occupations, sometimes making successful career changes, though more usually, moving from one semi-skilled or unskilled job to another. At a time when general labouring work was in demand from a wide variety of industries, this was often not a difficult transition – an agricultural worker could move to navvying, a building labourer to other forms of construction, a factory worker to another factory. Such possibilities now seem less, partly because of the widespread collapse in almost all manufacturing and construction sectors, partly because the jobs that do exist usually require levels of skill, experience and qualifications which the unemployed lack. Occupational mobility is inevitably reduced by the increased division and specialization of processes and the expertise required by modern technology, while at the same time geographical mobility has been limited by the recent growth of home-ownership to more than half the population, including the unemployed. Some unemployed people still speak of their desire for a small-holding, a corner shop or small business where they can be their own master, but successful moves into entrepreneurship require resources and abilities not usually available to the majority of the unemployed – it is easier for a former senior manager to take over the running of a children's home, and to find fulfilment in so doing[150] than for unqualified manual workers to become teachers, technical college lecturers or youth leaders, however strong their feelings of vocation.[151] One of the largest growths in the British economy in recent years has been a 50 per cent increase in the numbers of self-employed between 1971 and 1989, to reach 3.2 million at the latter date, two million of these in service occupations,[152] but the casualty rate of small businesses is notoriously high, and start-up government grants to those without experience hard to obtain. An unemployed man with the dream of starting a gardening business summed up the problems:

> If I had a pair of grass cutters you could make a bomb like, as I say, and you had transport. Then you'd need money for a van, tax

and insurance, then your machines are about £40 apiece ... you'd want two working. You could do it, but you know, you've got to get up and go.... I'm bad in saving up, you know. I canna save.... But if I had the capital, I think I could start me own business.[153]

One of the sharpest contrasts with the 1930s is the negligible amount of political activity and involvement of the unemployed in organizations intended to further their interests. In the recent depression there has been no equivalent of the National Unemployed Workers Movement, no swing towards either extreme left or right in politics, no large-scale hunger marches: on the contrary, there has been a general decline in radicalism, a seeming apathy and submissiveness among what is a very large, disadvantaged group. In the many recent interviews with unemployed people only a small minority report an increased interest in the political dimensions of their problems: one of the few, John Smith, commented that 'I've become much more politically aware since I've become unemployed',[154] but much more typical is the comment that 'I used to be interested in politics at one time, but I don't bother much now ... I don't know. It all seemed to be the same old scene, you know'.[155]

The reasons for this change have puzzled commentators. The labour militant, Will Paynter, who lived through both periods, believed that the long period of prosperity after the war had denuded the radical movement of leaders:

The men who led the great fight against unemployment and for the right to work were themselves now in work. My old friends Len Jefferies, Phil Abrahams, Jack Jones and a host of other unemployed leaders were in employment, active in the trade unions, trades councils and local government.[156]

That was in 1973, but full employment and the affluence which accompanied it seems to have left a legacy of division and isolation within the ranks of the workless. Others have written that in the 1930s the unemployed still had hopes of a fundamental change in the economic and social order, a hope which grew during the war years and the post-war Labour government with expectations of a new world of welfare, publicly owned industries and work for all: against that background of rising, and partially realized, expectations, the economic and political changes since the seventies have been acutely disillusioning and numbing. It is also argued by some that relatively more generous levels of benefit have taken much of the sting out of unemployment and that the growth of the informal 'black economy' provides some with work as well as additional resources. Both these assumptions have already been questioned. With more justice, sociologists have pointed out that the unemployed are a 'negative reference group': being unemployed defines what one is not, not what one is and as such it is not a status with which others naturally wish to identify, especially if it is one which carries public distrust rather than sympathy. Far from creating the conditions for solidarity and a common bond, the unemployed are a group to which its members do not wish to belong.

This does not mean that there has been a total absence of concerted action by unemployed organizations in recent times. There have been some attempts by 'work-ins' to continue employment in plants threatened with closure, a few workers' co-operatives have been formed with varying success, and a demonstration in 1975 claiming 20,000 supporters out of which a Right to Work campaign was launched. This was not supported by the TUC or Labour Party, and appears to have had only a brief existence: significantly, one of the eighty members who took part in a march from Manchester to London described it as 'an anger march, not a hunger march'.[157] There have been other, small-scale marches from London to Brighton in 1976 to petition the TUC and a sizeable demonstration in Merseyside in 1980, but nothing comparable in scale of sustained protest of the inter-war years. An Unemployed Workers Union was established in Tyneside in 1979 and managed to set up a few branches elsewhere for a time. Probably the most successful concerted action has been the formation of Claimants Unions (or Centres) whose main function is to give advice on welfare rights and to represent clients in dispute with the authorities: the best-known of these was the Barnsley Claimants and Unemployed Workers Union organized by the veteran Joe Kenyon, who had been a branch secretary of the NUWM in the thirties. Several Claimants Unions were formed in Scottish towns in the seventies and a few in England, though Kenyon complained of the lack of militant leadership in many places.[158] From 1980 the TUC has sponsored Centres for the Unemployed, providing advice and also some recreational and educational facilities, similar to the unemployed clubs of the thirties: some have obtained support from the Manpower Services Community Programme for full-time staff while others have obtained concessions from local authorities, cinemas and sports clubs. Again, however, the scale of these activities and the membership seem very limited by comparison with the pre-war clubs. In 1987, 190 Centres were in operation, half of which had 100 plus users per week: the total membership was estimated at under 20,000, only a tiny proportion of the unemployed.[159]

Adaptations of the unemployed to satisfying or ameliorating activities appear to be considerably less than in the 1930s. The unemployed are more isolated and inward-looking, more locked into narrow, privatized lives than their predecessors: they are less radical, less active politically, less organized either to promote change in the system or to engage with others in constructive activities. This is partly because many of the old industrial areas which were strongholds of communal support have been dispersed by urban redevelopment, partly because demographic changes have greatly reduced household size and broken up extended family networks. But the collective apathy which seems to characterize today's unemployed still presents a puzzle: have the relative improvements in levels of benefit, social services and material standards of living produced more contentment, less anger and frustration than in the past, or have the unemployed, faced with two deep recessions within a decade and the widely publicized collapse of Britain's industrial base, resigned any hopes for the future and sunk into silent despair – have 'drawn the curtains and turned on the TV'?

CONCLUSION

History is about continuity as well as change, and this study of unemployment illustrates some remarkable consistencies over time in public attitudes and personal responses despite the major economic and social transformations which have occurred during the last two centuries. The causes of unemployment changed greatly as Britain passed from a rural, agrarian society to an urban, industrial one. In the early nineteenth century the principal occupation of the people – agriculture – which had always suffered from seasonal unemployment, was unable to absorb a rapidly increasing population, and consequently experienced a surplus of labour until many farmworkers took their own remedy by deserting the land. Autobiographies clearly indicate the economic insecurity of labourers throughout the century, and the inappropriateness of using crude wage rates as a measure of their standard of living when work was so irregular. Their problem should not be lightly dismissed as 'underemployment' when their hold on subsistence was already precarious, and a few days or weeks without wages could plunge families from poverty into destitution. While accepting that labourers who wrote their life histories were not 'typical' of their kind, their accounts suggest a considerably greater extent of geographical and occupational mobility than has been supposed of a group 'imprisoned' by poverty and ignorance. The recruitment of agricultural labourers into construction, navvying, factory work and a range of other industrial employments, not to mention domestic service, the army and police forces, suggests much more fluidity between rural and urban labour, between country and town, both before and after the railway age, than previous studies have allowed.

The case of the handloom weavers also illustrates the interdependence of many workers on a combination of agriculture and industry, either on a seasonal basis or within a familial division of labour, typical of a pre-industrial system but persisting in some areas well into the middle of the nineteenth century. The brief prosperity of the trade, however, had already begun to attract a surplus of full-time weavers before the adoption of power-looms: as well as a secular decline, the trade suffered serious cyclical fluctuations resulting in much short-time and periods of total unemployment. Many autobiographers who began life as weavers took the official advice to 'flee the trade', some making successful adaptations to new and diverse occupations, but many older weavers had a deep attachment to their calling and persisted in it long after it was economically doomed: mobility into factory weaving came largely from younger generations. The skilled trades of the mid- and later nineteenth century experienced different employment problems. The traditional handicrafts suffered a gradual erosion of skill and increasing insecurity as their numbers were swollen by 'invasions' of unskilled men, women and children working for undercutting 'slop' masters: some trades, such as wooden shipbuilding, rope and sailmaking, woodworking, bespoke tailoring and shoemaking, also faced technological unemployment as new machines or materials successfully competed with traditional methods. On the other hand, those skilled workers who, in good times, were the beneficiaries of the machine, such as engineers and iron shipwrights, had different problems as their industries were heavily dependent on foreign demand and passed through cycles of boom and slump, causing periodic high unemployment.

Seasonal and cyclical unemployment tended to be relatively short-term, though in combination spells of worklessness could be frequent. In industries such as textiles and coalmining employers often tried to meet fluctuations in demand by work-sharing, putting their workers on half-time or on two or three shifts a week. But autobiographies indicate that many workers did not experience their unemployment only from a single cause: seasonal factors were added to cyclical downturns, the overall, long-term decline of an industry or the failure of a particular employer. Again, the end of apprenticeship often resulted in unemployment, while a range of personal factors – ill-health, disability, intemperance or insubordination, real or alleged – could often be the occasion for dismissal. The reason for an individual's lack of work was often multi-causal, an important fact which tends to be obscured by an economic categorization of the types of unemployment.

Despite its periodic ups and downs, the generally expanding British economy before 1914, aided by increasing mobility, was able to absorb and redeploy much of the surplus labour from declining occupations into new, and often better-paid, employments. That there continued to exist both a 'residuum', which included many unemployables, and a much larger group of casual workers who had no regular employment, became a major concern of late Victorian and Edwardian social reformers, while the growing influence of the labour movement contributed to the 'discovery' and politicization of unemployment at this time. In fact, as earlier chapters have shown, there was nothing new about unemployment except its elevation to the political agenda and its increasing articulation by the unemployed themselves. Only with the onset of depression after 1921 did an apparently new type of unemployment emerge – that of structural decline in basic industries – and even here it is possible to trace its origins back to the earlier Great Depression of the 1880s. What was different in kind between the wars was the extent and length of unemployment in former staple occupations, where old skills could now be permanently redundant and worklessness could last for years. Not surprisingly, this period was particularly rich in autobiographical accounts, and authors were able to provide more detailed descriptions than previously of their loss of work, their searches for it and their emotional reactions to unemployment. These illustrate desperate efforts to find work by almost all and much mobility out of depressed areas, especially by younger workers: there was extremely scant evidence of the will to work being eroded by state benefits.

Outside the old staple industries other sectors of the economy were considerably expanding, allowing substantial labour transference. Despite their often great privations, very few autobiographers resigned all hope, but continued to believe in a better future for themselves and their fellow men, often through political change. For a quarter-century of virtually full employment and substantially rising living standards after 1945 such hopes seemed to be fulfilled, but the return of high levels of unemployment from the late 1970s now makes that brief period when all who wanted work could find it seem exceptional and historically untypical. Recent unemployment is more widespread geographically and occupationally than between the wars: it includes high proportions of young people and of long-term unemployed, and the drastic reduction of jobs in manufacturing industry has not been compensated by comparable increases in other sectors. The problems of a post-industrial economy seem of a different order from the past, when a large manufacturing base survived through periods of depression, available to re-employ labour during the next cyclical upturn.

If the causes and circumstances of unemployment have changed, public reactions to it show remarkable similarities over the past 200 years. Attitudes towards those without work have always been a combination of humanity and distrust, the balance between them changing in line with the ideological values of the time. As Chapter 1 describes, employers giving evidence to an official report on agriculture in 1816 were already complaining about improvident labourers who regarded support by the parish as their 'right': when in work they were careless and difficult to control. In 1824 it was said that 'There are but two motives by which men are induced to work; the one, the hope of improving themselves and their families, the other the fear of punishment'. Yet, before 1834 some parishes adopted humane and remarkably 'modern' policies towards their unemployed, providing make-work schemes and training in crafts, aiding migration and supplying tools by which men could become self-supporting. In others, deep suspicion of the unemployed as work-shy scroungers was predominant, not only among poor law administrators but among jealous neighbours, as Joseph Mayett discovered when one reported him for 'feigning' illness. As the costs of poor relief mounted after 1815 the official view gained ground that unemployment was largely artificial, created by over-generous and indiscriminate benefits, a view which culminated in the deterrent principle of 'less eligibility' introduced in 1834.

Deterrence, of course, did not create jobs, and forms of relief for the unemployed outside the detested workhouse were quickly resumed, usually under a 'labour test' which required work of the recipient. The 'ticket system' in mid-century, by which an unemployed labourer had to carry round a card to potential employers which they signed if they could not offer work, has close parallels with the later requirement of 'genu- inely' or 'actively' seeking work. Despite variations in local practice, official attitudes in the half-century after 1834 generally hardened, and voluminous public enquiries into the plight of the handloom weavers offered no more consolation than that they should abandon the dying trade and 'beware of setting their children to it'. In the context of expanding industrialization that made good economic sense, however painful the required adaptations might be. But by the later nineteenth century a poor law which had been designed principally to combat rural pauperism began to look increasingly irrelevant as a remedy for industrial unemployment, especially as social investigators were now demonstrating that its causes were not generally due to faults of character, but to impersonal forces. After the disturbances of 1886, local authorities were allowed to establish make-work schemes for the unemployed outside the stigmatizing poor law: these, and their successors organized by Distress Committees after 1905, proved costly and inefficient, and of little interest to the genuinely unemployed. Social reformers at this time concentrated more on the casual worker and the 'residuum', believing that these distorted the labour market and prevented other groups from obtaining regular work: some advocated removing the residuum altogether into home colonies or, as the Salvation Army proposed, reforming them physi- cally and morally through a series of 'elevators' until they were fit to enter the labour force. For the casual worker much could be done by an efficient system of Labour Exchanges, which would bring demand and supply together and prevent much aimless, demoralizing searching for work. But even William Beveridge, the architect of the scheme in 1909, did not believe that unemployment could ever be totally abolished, and that 'There may be worse things in a community than unemployment. The practical reply is to be found in reducing the pain of unemployment to relative insignificance. In this, there seems to be no impossibility'. 'Reducing the pain' came to be the principle of unemployment insurance, introduced partially in 1911 and generally for manual workers in 1920. Left-wing labour leaders before 1914 campaigned for more radical policies to create jobs or spread the available work more evenly – an eight-hour day, compulsory reduction of overtime, longer schooling and better job training. But unemployment, as Beveridge knew, was divisive. The powerful voices in the Labour Party and the TUC mainly represented those who had regular employment and were anxious to draw a sharp line between themselves and the 'ineffectives': work-sharing of any kind would almost certainly mean less for them.

The extension of unemployment insurance in 1920 was a political response to a new, mass electorate and a social response to fears of instability and a perceived Socialist threat in the wake of the Great War. Insurance gave the claimant the right to relief for a limited period on the basis of his contribution to the scheme: beyond that period, his resort was still to the poor law until 1930, thereafter to public assistance which, under various names and procedures, has continued to the present day. The continuity with the past was, and still is, evident. To qualify for public assistance the claimant must be 'actively seeking work' to demonstrate his or her willingness to re-enter the labour market: relief is subject to means-testing so that it is granted only to those in need, and levels of relief are pitched substantially below average wages in order to act as an incentive to work: assistance may be refused to unemployed married women whose husbands are in work, and to young applicants except on condition of training. In these and other ways the principle of 'less eligibility' which has underlain social policy since 1834, is still alive, and the campaigns to root out welfare 'scroungers' in the 1930s and the 1970s closely parallel the Victorian anxiety to distinguish between the 'deserving' and the 'undeserving' and refuse help to the latter. Similarly, current concerns about a 'dependency culture' which allegedly saps morale and initiative, are almost identical to the strictures levelled at the allowance system of the early nineteenth-century poor law.

Insurance was at best a palliative, and was never designed to meet long-term unemployment. Government attempts to create work, both in the 1930s and recently, have been modest in scale, too often artificial, and have had little impact on the size of the problem, while efforts to preserve jobs in ailing industries by public funding would now have no more likelihood of success than the attempts of the handloom weavers to gain financial support for their dying trade in the 1840s. The statement in 1978 by Sir Keith Joseph, the former Conservative minister, that 'Full employment is not in the gift of government. It should not be promised, and it cannot be provided', echoes the despairing comment of the Labour Chancellor of the Exchequer, Philip Snowden, in 1924:

'Unemployment... there is nothing we can do about it'. Almost a hundred years before that, Nassau Senior, a leading economist and one of the chief framers of the new poor law in 1834, wrote:

> We know that to attempt to provide by legislative interference that in all the vicissitudes of commerce and the seasons all the labouring classes, whatever be the value of their services, shall enjoy a comfortable subsistence, is an attempt which would in time ruin the industry of the most diligent and the wealth of the most opulent community.

These are still the policy dilemmas – not to make unemployment so attractive that it deters those who would work, not to make benefits so generous as to alienate the tax-payer and ruin the economy but not so niggardly as to encourage social unrest in a democracy which clings to values of fairness and humanity. And above such local constraints, the world economy is now so interdependent that what an individual nation can do – especially one which is no longer 'the most opulent community' – is subject to powerful forces over which it has little control.

From the evidence of autobiographies, the reactions and responses of individuals to their unemployment indicate both major continuities and some changes. The psychological effect of loss of work in causing anger, frustration and hostility is consistent over the whole period discussed, and it is remarkable that descriptive terms such as 'apathy' and 'broken' were used in the 1840s, almost a century before they entered the psychological vocabulary. Beyond this, however, there are some important differences in attitudes over time determined by the changes in the nature of employment and the context in which it occurred. For much of the nineteenth century unemployment was relatively short term. It was within the normal experience of an agricultural labourer to be underemployed in winter, of a building worker to lose time in bad weather, of a tailor, shoemaker or painter to be out of work in the slack season: a stonemason expected to have to live a semi-peripatetic life, and a casual dock labourer was well used to trudging up and down the waterside to get half a week's work. A few occupations were geographically more immobile, notably the textiles and mining, though both of these were very subject to short time. But however likely and frequent spells without work might be, their effects on budgets which were often little above subsistence could be catastrophic. The frequency with which autobiographers mention debt and pawning, the reduction of their diets to the point of hunger, the effects on their clothing, shoes and bedding and their reliance on help from relatives and neighbours clearly demonstrates that unemployment was a major cause of primary poverty, long before social investigators provided the statistical proof. Much nineteenth-century working-class life was lived in and out of work and in and out of poverty and debt. In the good times of full employment families replenished their clothes and household goods, indulged their tastes for food or drink, treated their children and helped their neighbours in distress: in the bad, their possessions became their source of credit, and together with some help from others, their survival strategy. The writings suggest strong reciprocity in working-class communities. People helped each other when they could, probably not from any deep humanitarian motives, but because they did not know whose turn it would be next to need assistance.

What seems different in this period is that the sense of shock on losing work which twentieth-century writers often describe is rarely mentioned, and that the anger and frustration which is expressed is usually directed against an individual employer rather than the economic system as a whole. The master is to blame for wrongful dismissal, for greed in stinting wages or work when it suits him, for favouritism, drunkenness, dishonesty or mere business incompetence. Exceptionally in the earlier part of the century, there were some radicals and Socialists who condemned the existing order and looked for fundamental economic and political change as the only salvation of the working class, but their numbers were at least equally matched by those of deep religious conviction whose hopes for happiness centred on the next world rather than this. The prevailing reaction of most writers to unemployment at this time was closely similar to their feelings about poverty or the all-too-common death of a loved one – a mixture of pain, sorrow and resignation, a fatalistic belief in bad luck but also an almost unquenchable hope in a change of fortune. Those who had always had few expectations and little ambition for material things could, perhaps, adjust more easily to the familiar experience of loss. Yet some autobiographers of this early period stand out from the crowd by their possession of unusual abilities and intelligence, often developed through self-education, and for them unemployment acted as a spur to more satisfying occupations, to self-employment, shopkeeping, even to authorship, political or religious leadership.

Between the 1880s and the First World War autobiographical writing about unemployment becomes more articulate and, frequently, more strident. As John Burns wrote in 1893:

> The unemployed laborer today is not a replica of the out-of-work of a few years back. His predecessor was a patient, long-suffering animal . . . looking upon his enforced idleness as inevitable, and with blind submission enduring his lot. . . . The unemployed worker of today is of different stuff. He has a grievance, and thinks he has a remedy.[1]

Following the extensions of franchise to the majority of adult males in 1867 and 1884 there was a growing political awareness, aided by the universal provision of elementary education and increased literacy among the lower working class: at the same time, the formation of trade unions among some semi-skilled workers began to break the monopoly of the craftsmen who enjoyed some protection against unemployment through their trade benefits. 'New Unionism' was more militant and less accommodating to the employers: the right to work – or, in the absence of it, the right to maintenance at normal wages – now became the subject of organized campaigning and demonstrations, while labour relations before 1914 were characterized by frequent strikes and lockouts, demands for minimum wages and shorter working hours. Autobiographers engaged in these movements, either as militants or merely as active trade unionists, often complain of victimization, of the circulation of blacklists among employers which denied agitators work. That some men who had not previously been politically conscious became converts to Socialism as a result of their unemployed experiences is clearly demonstrated, while even among those who did not there was markedly more antagonism towards a system which still offered little to the workless beyond the humiliating poor law. Some writers at this time began to articulate their frustration in terms which would become familiar during the next hundred years: 'It is despair that destroys the fibre of a man', and 'Ambition ceased to exist'.

The 1914–18 war had major effects on attitudes towards unemployment. Virtually full employment and higher wages had raised the living standards of many of the working class: politicians had promised a better future to compensate for the sacrifices, while the brief post-war boom had raised expectations still further. The experience of unprecedented levels of unemployment during the next twenty years was, therefore, even sharper than previously, and produced an unparalleled quantity of autobiographical writing as well as social investigation. Some memoirs clearly illustrate the 'stage model' identified by psychologists as their authors passed from initial shock to optimism, pessimism, despair and apathy, but this was typical mainly of older, long-term unemployeds as the depression deepened and lengthened in the 1930s. The majority describe stages which are not linear, but which alternate between pessimism and hope, constantly reborn even in the most unpromising circumstances: few of these reached the permanently 'broken' stage in which all hope was resigned. This may be explained in a number of ways. Unemployment between the wars was mainly recurrent rather than permanent. The period included some years of improved economic prospects as well as a substantial growth of new industries which afforded work opportunities and career changes for some. There was also much collective activity by the unemployed – the National Unemployed Workers' Movement, hunger marches and demonstrations, which helped to sustain hopes of government action as well as providing some emotional outlet, while in the depressed areas there was a remarkable growth of clubs for the unemployed with a wide range of practical, cultural, sporting and educational activities. Above all, there was still much communal support for the unemployed in these areas from extended family and neighbourhood networks, and a good deal of public sympathy, especially for war veterans. In these circumstances, the hopes of the unemployed frequently faded, but rarely died completely.

The recent return of high unemployment suggests some unfavourable comparisons with the past. In material terms the unemployed are marginally better off than formerly, the degrees of poverty which still exist are not so harsh, actual hunger and malnutrition are now rare and even the photographic images of the unemployed do not present the stark contrasts with the rest of society which were evident in the 1930s. But in important ways, the emotional impact of loss of work now seems greater, following a generation of full employment and rising living standards unique in modern history. The marked fall in average household size, the break-up of old communities in industrial and mining areas and the increased privatization of domestic life and leisure appear to have internalized concerns and inhibited collective responses. There has recently been no comparable emergence of organizations for the unemployed, either political or social, and little expectation that the trade unions or the Labour Party would develop viable strategies for a return to work: there now seems less sense either of the 'shared predicament' or of public sympathy which formerly provided some encouragement and support.

It is significant that recent unemployment has not given rise to the wealth of autobiographical writing which it did in the past and that most of the evidence about its psychological effects is drawn from social investigations. These suggest that less time and effort is now absorbed by the job search, that geographical mobility has declined (probably due partly to the spread of home-ownership and housing difficulties), that self-provisioning is less than formerly and that alternative forms of work, whether legitimate or in the 'black economy', occupy a very small amount of time. Unemployment also appears to have strengthened, rather than loosened, traditional sexual roles, and there is little evidence that unemployed males take a larger share in household tasks than those in work. To all these generalizations there are exceptions, as noted in Chapter 7, but the overwhelming impression is that less activity and more inertia now characterizes the unemployed than in previous periods. This apparent quiescence does not, of course, necessarily imply greater contentment of the unemployed with their condition: it may well suggest that more have passed through the course of the stages to resignation and apathy. The recent surveys indicate deep and widely held emotions of sorrow and loss, contracted ambitions and lifestyles, above all, feelings of powerlessness and exclusion from the mainstreams of society. As yet, evidence about the longer-term effects of recent unemployment, either from autobiographies or longitudinal surveys, is not available; this would clearly be an important area for future research.

The persistence of unemployment throughout the whole period of Britain's economic growth and its escalation in recent years inevitably poses questions about the future of work and employment. In the first place, it is important to distinguish between these two – between 'employment' in the sense of waged labour and 'work' in the wider sense of activity. Activity is natural to human beings and desired by the vast majority, and there seems little truth in the Haitian proverb that 'If work were a good thing the rich would have found a way of keeping it all to themselves':[2] wealth enabled the leisured class to choose their activity, but most were active in something, whether in politics and government, sport, the arts, philanthropy or merely social interaction. But regular employment in waged labour is historically recent, mainly the result of the development of an industrial economy in the last 200 years or so: before that, a high proportion of people were at least partly self-employed, engaged in a variety of activities not dependent on a single industry or employer. Well into the nineteenth century, the opposition of handloom weavers to factory employment, the survival of 'Saint Monday' (and even Tuesday) as days of leisure in a number of industries and the strategies employed by engineers and others to 'dodge' work[3] are evidence of strong hostility to the routinization of labour which employers required. The new machine age imposed a strict division between work and leisure, unusual in pre-industrial society: as one of its leading advocates, Henry Ford, put it:

> When we are at work, we ought to be at work. When we are at play, we ought to be at play. There is no use trying to mix the two. The sole object ought to be to get the work done and to get paid for it. When the work is done, then the play can come, but not before.[4]

Furthermore, disciples of the new philosophy sought to elevate work not only as an end in itself but as a Christian virtue which brought rewards in this world and the next. From the seventeenth century onwards the Work Ethic was preached from the pulpit and inculcated by the schools and the poor law, giving moral authority to long hours of disciplined labour and condemning many forms of traditional recreation. The evidence from a previous study of autobiographies is that many of the working classes in the nineteenth century rejected the 'gospel of work' as an alien creed, that with some exceptions, mainly among craftsmen, work was not seen as an end in itself but only as a means to an end.

> Work, it seems, was not a central life-interest of the working-classes. For most it was taken as given, like life itself, to be endured rather

313

than enjoyed. . . . Such happiness and satisfactions as life has to offer are to be found in social contacts within groups – the family, the work-group, the chapel or the public house: here, meaningful relationships can be made, experiences exchanged, joys and sorrows shared.[5]

But in describing their largely negative attitude towards 'work', writers were referring to 'employment' since the two had become largely synonymous in circumstances where working hours were so long and exhausting that other kinds of activity were almost excluded. The campaigns by employees for shorter hours from the 1830s onwards are clear evidence of a conviction that life should not be only about 'work'. From a different perspective, sociologists have argued widespread alienation from work in modern industrial society, especially from assembly-line and other repetitive processes. Some have gone as far as Marx in believing that

> The worker feels himself at home only outside his work, and feels absent from himself in his work. . . . His work is not freely consented to, but is a constrained, forced labour. Work is thus not a satisfaction of a need, but only a means to satisfy needs outside work.[6]

A good deal of autobiographical evidence, both past and present, indicates strongly ambivalent attitudes towards work – 'I hate work. Of course, I could also say with equal truth that I love work' (an unemployed miner); 'It has no value as work. It is drudgery done in congenial surroundings' (a clerk).[7] The present study has shown that a small minority of people welcomed their liberation from employment and were able to engage successfully in autonomous, creative and satisfying activities: as an unemployed joiner explains, 'Earning a living has got nothing to do with you as a person. That's why I can bear unemployment'.[8] As we saw in Chapter 7, the problem is that few unemployed people seem able to fill their time satisfactorily, partly because opportunities and costs inhibit this and partly because they have been so conditioned to employment that leisure has become compartmentalized into an annual holiday and brief spells of commercialized recreation. The objection to the Marxist analysis is that work (i.e. employment) does, in fact, fulfil certain important needs apart from earning a wage – the 'latent functions' of providing a time structure to the day, social interaction with others, self-esteem, identity and a sense of order.[9] Can these functions be fulfilled outside waged employment? The evidence from studies so far is not encouraging. Marsden and Duff concluded in 1975 that 'We found no really convincing evidence of the emergence of any viable alternatives to work. For those we interviewed, talk about the "opportunity" or "leisure" afforded by unemployment seems decidedly premature'.[10] Even among people who had retired at the normal age and who, it might be expected, had looked forward to a release from work, only 35 per cent had found a satisfying form of life while 65 per cent, mainly former manual workers, were placed in the 'negative' category of those who had been unable to create a new time structure for themselves and were unhappy with life in the Third Age.[11]

It now seems likely that higher levels of unemployment than were imaginable in post-war Britain before the late 1970s will be a continuing feature of the economic and social structure; that while economic growth will undoubtedly create some more jobs, the dramatic decline in Britain's industrial base will scarcely be compensated by expansion in other sectors. Government policies can influence the level of unemployment by expanding training, by 'workfare' schemes and investment in housing, construction and public services, but no political party now promises a return to full employment. It may be, of course, that nothing very much need be done – that provided benefits can be maintained at a level which the unemployed find tolerable and the tax-payer acceptable, this is the price which a de-industrializing society has to pay for the continued well-being of the great majority of its members. But if that is politically or morally unacceptable in the longer term, the alternative appears to be that the existing quantity of employment should be shared so that all who want work can get some. Work-sharing has a long history in some industries, as previous chapters have shown, and could, theoretically, be greatly extended by a combination of strategies – progressively shorter hours and earlier retirement, longer education, a four-day week, the 'twinning' of jobs and so on: such changes would need to be accompanied by increased provision for leisure, recreation, adult education and voluntary service so that the released time could be structured purposefully. This may be an impossibly Utopian solution, the economic and social costs and consequences of which are far from clear: it would require major sacrifices from those in work and fundamental changes in public attitudes towards employment and unemployment, 'work' and 'leisure'. Early this century William Beveridge wrote of 'reducing the pain of unemployment to relative insignificance'. For the great majority of the unemployed this has not yet been achieved: although the financial hardship has been somewhat eased, the social and psychological losses from worklessness remain as great, or greater, than before. The continuing need is to find useful and satisfying activity for 'idle hands'.

REFERENCES

The place of publication of works other than autobiographies is London unless otherwise stated: autobiographies and memoirs are fully referenced in the accompanying Bibliography.

INTRODUCTION

1 John Burnett, David Vincent and David Mayall, eds, *The Autobiography of the Working Class. An Annotated, Critical Bibliography*, Harvester Press, Brighton, and New York University Press; Vol. I, 1984, Vol. II, 1987, Vol. III, 1989.
2 The principal guides are those by P. and G. Ford, *Select List of British Parliamentary Papers, 1833–1899*, Blackwell, Oxford, 1953, *A Breviate of Parliamentary Papers, 1900–1916*, Irish University Press, 1969, Shannon, and *A Breviate of Parliamentary Papers, 1917–1939*, Blackwell, 1951.
3 Peter Sinclair, *Unemployment: Economic Theory and Evidence*, Blackwell, Oxford, 1987, 1.
4 *Social Trends* 17, HMSO, 1987, 30.
5 W. H. Beveridge, *Unemployment. A Problem of Industry*, Longmans, Green and Co., 1909, 69–70.
6 ibid., 29–34.
7 Troughs of cyclical depressions and peaks of unemployment occurred in 1816, 1825, 1831, 1839–42, 1847–8, 1858, 1862, 1868, 1879, 1886, 1893, 1904, 1909.
8 Stephen Constantine, *Social Conditions in Britain, 1918–1939*, Methuen, 1983, 6–7.
9 Sinclair, op. cit., 18.
10 *Social Trends*, op. cit., 79–80.

1 UNEMPLOYMENT IN THE COUNTRYSIDE, 1790–1834

1 J. L. and Barbara Hammond, *The Village Labourer*, 1st edn (1911), Guild Books edn (1948), Vol. II, 44.
2 These extracts are taken from the *Autobiography of Joseph Mayett of Quainton, 1783–1839*, Ann Kussmaul, ed., Buckinghamshire Record Society, 23, 1986, 1–23. His untitled manuscript of 149 pages (*c.* 50,000 words) is in Buckingham Record Office: an abstract of his memoir is in *The Autobiography of the Working Class. An Annotated Critical Bibliography*, Vol. I, 1790–1900, John Burnett, David

Vincent and David Mayall, eds, Harvester Press, Brighton, and New York University Press, 1984, 223–4.

3 B. R. Mitchell and Phyllis Deane, eds, *Abstract of British Historical Statistics*, Cambridge University Press, 1962, Labour Force, Table 1, 60.

4 For the categories and wages of farm labour in the late eighteenth century, G. E. Mingay, 'The Transformation of Agriculture' in *The Long Debate on Poverty. Eight Essays on Industrialisation and 'The condition of England'*, Institute of Economic Affairs, 1972, 39–43.

5 Ann Kussmaul, *Servants in Husbandry in Early Modern England*, Cambridge University Press, 1981, 4 et seq.

6 ibid., 18.

7 ibid., 131.

8 Alan Armstrong, *Farmworkers. A Social and Economic History, 1770–1980*, Batsford, 1988, 25.

9 Table quoted in John Burnett, *A History of the Cost of Living*, Penguin Books, 1969, 137. This includes many labourers' budgets of the period, wage and price statistics.

10 David Davies, *The Case of Labourers in Husbandry, Stated and Considered*, G. G. and J. Robinson, 1795, 24.

11 ibid., 6.

12 Sir Frederic Morton Eden, *The State of the Poor*, 3 vols, J. Davis, 1797, Vol. III, Appendix: Expenses and Earnings of Agricultural Labourers, cccxlii et seq.

13 ibid., Vol. II, 29, 548, 383–4.

14 Davies, op. cit., 74–81.

15 Burnett, op. cit., 206. The table on pp. 206–7 cites the annual average gazette price of wheat, 1801–1914, from Sir Walter T. Layton and Geoffrey Crowther, *The Study of Prices*, Macmillan, 1938, 234.

16 This has long been an issue of dispute between 'optimistic' and 'pessimistic' historians. The debate is well reviewed in Armstrong, op. cit., 52–4.

17 K. D. M. Snell, *Annals of the Labouring Poor. Social Change and Agrarian England, 1660–1900*, Cambridge University Press, 1985, 147 et seq.

18 The classic history is still that of Sidney and Beatrice Webb, *English Poor Law History*, Parts I and II, Longmans, Green and Co., 1927–9. More recent studies include Derek Fraser, ed., *The New Poor Law in the Nineteenth Century*, Macmillan, 1976; M. E. Rose, *The English Poor Law, 1780–1930*, Macmillan, 1971; M. E. Rose, *The Relief of Poverty, 1834–1914*, Macmillan, 1972.

19 Elizabeth Melling, ed., *Kentish Sources*, Vol. IV, *The Poor*, Kent County Council, 1964, 147–69.

20 Maude F. Davies, *Life in an English Village. An Economic and Historical Survey of the Parish of Corsley in Wiltshire*, Fisher Unwin, 1909, 75–8.

21 A. W. Ashby, *One Hundred Years of Poor Law Administration in a Warwickshire Village. In Oxford Studies in Social and Legal History*, Paul Vinogradoff, ed., Clarendon Press, Oxford, 1912, Vol. III, 147–61.

22 M. K. Ashby, *Joseph Ashby of Tysoe*, Merlin Press, 1974, 278–80.

23 *Report of the Select Committee of the House of Lords on the Poor Laws*, 1818, V. Evidence of Revd Hugh Wade Gery of Eaton Socon, Bedfordshire.

24 *Report of the Select Committee on Labourers' Wages*, 1824 (392), VI. Evidence of Thomas Smart.

25 There are at least three editions of John Clare's autobiography, which covers the years 1793–1824. The extracts quoted here are from the most recent and authoritative edition by Eric Robinson, ed., *John Clare's Autobiographical Writings*, Oxford University Press, 1983. This edition includes both the *Sketches in*

The Life of John Clare, Written by Himself and Addressed to his Friend, John Taylor Esq. and *More Hints in the Life of John Clare.*

26 Armstrong, op. cit., 44–5. If the local militia (199,000) and volunteers (189,000) are added, the proportion is one in every six men.

27 Annual average gazette price of British wheat per quarter: 1813, 109s. 9d.; 1815, 65s. 7d.; 1817, 96s. 11d.; 1822, 44s. 7d.; 1830, 64s. 3d.; 1835, 39s. 4d. Layton and Crowther, op. cit., 234. A general price index indicates a fall of approximately half over this period: 1812–14, 211; 1815–20, 164; 1821–30, 126; 1831–5, 122.

28 *The Agricultural State of the Kingdom in February, March and April, 1816,* Board of Agriculture, 1816. Reprinted with Introduction by Gordon E. Mingay, Adams and Dart, Bath, 1970.

29 ibid., 7.

30 ibid., 25.

31 ibid., 357.

32 Mayett, op. cit., 66.

33 ibid., 72.

34 ibid., 84–5.

35 ibid., 92.

36 Alexander Somerville, *The Autobiography of a Working Man, by One Who Has Whistled at the Plough,* Robert Hardwicke, 1855, 82.

37 ibid., 115.

38 ibid., 134.

39 Russell M. Garnier, *Annals of the British Peasantry,* Swan Sonnenschein, 1895, 328.

40 James Dawson Burn, *The Autobiography of a Beggar Boy,* edited with an Introduction by David Vincent, Europa, 1978, 123. (The first edition was by William Tweedie, 1855.)

41 *Notes on the Life of Joseph Ricketts, Written by Himself, c.* 1858, *Wiltshire Archaeological and Natural History Magazine,* Vol. 60, 1965, 120.

42 ibid., 123.

43 *Autobiography of John Blow,* J. Parrott, 1870, 3, 6.

44 ibid., 23.

45 *The Autobiography of Robert Spurr. A Social Study of Nineteenth-Century Baptist Working Class Fortitude,* R. J. Owen, ed., *Baptist Quarterly,* Vol. 26, April 1976, 282.

46 ibid., 283.

47 ibid., 286.

48 E. L. Jones, 'The Agricultural Labour Market in England, 1793–1872', *Economic History Review,* Second Series, Vol. XVII, Nos 1, 2, 3, 1964–5, 326.

49 William Cobbett, *Rural Rides, 1821–32,* Everyman's Library, with Introduction by Professor Asa Briggs, 1967, Vol. II, 55.

50 James George Cornish, *Reminiscences of Country Life,* Vaughan Cornish ed., 1939, 33.

51 *Report of the Select Committee of the House of Lords on the Poor Laws,* 1818, V. Evidence of Revd Hugh Wade Gery.

52 *Report of the Select Committee on Emigration,* 1826, IV, 136 et seq.

53 *Report of the Select Committee on Labourers' Wages,* 1824 (392), VI, 12.

54 Armstrong, op. cit., 64.

55 E. J. Hobsbawm and George Rudé, *Captain Swing,* Peregrine Books, 1985, 51, citing J. Thirsk and J. Imray, eds, *Suffolk Farming in the Nineteenth Century,* Suffolk Record Society, 1958, Vol. 1, 134–5.

56 N. Gash, 'Rural Unemployment, 1815–1834', *Economic History Review*, First Series, Vol. VI, 1935, 90–3.

57 Somerville, op. cit., 31.

58 Burn, op. cit., 107.

59 Ricketts, op. cit., 121.

60 Select Committee on Criminal Commitments and Convictions, VI, 1826–7, 22, 31–7, 43–54. Cited in Snell, op. cit., 350.

61 Armstrong, op. cit., 71.

62 J. L. and B. Hammond, op. cit., Vol. I, 173–5.

63 Armstrong, op. cit., 73.

64 *Report from the Select Committee to whom the Several Petitions Complaining of the Depressed State of the Agriculture of the United Kingdom were Referred*, 1821 (668), IX, Report, 3.

65 ibid. Evidence of R. C. Harvey, farmer, of Aldburgh, Norfolk, 38.

66 Select Committee of the House of Lords, 1818, op. cit., 50–2.

67 Report on Labourers' Wages, 1824, op. cit., 3.

68 ibid., 4, 6.

69 *Report from the Select Committee on That Part of the Poor Laws Relating to the Employment or Relief of Able-Bodied Persons from the Poor Rate*, 1828 (494), IV, 4.

70 ibid., 10, 22.

71 Ashby, op. cit., 282–3.

72 Peter Ellacott, *The Poor of the Parish, and the Work of The Westbourne Select Vestries, 1819–1835*, Westbourne Local History Group, 1986, 6–11.

73 ibid., 13.

74 ibid., 22.

75 *Report from the Select Committee on Agriculture*, 1833, (612), V. Evidence of Robert Hughes, 55–6.

76 *Report of the Committee of the House of Lords on the Poor Laws*, 1817. Quoted in Gash, op. cit., 93.

77 J. H. Clapham, 'The Growth of an Agrarian Proletariat, 1688–1832: A Statistical Note', *Cambridge Historical Journal*, Vol. I, 1925, 93.

78 Snell, op. cit., 147–58.

79 'William Plastow's Story', 6–7. Transcript of an interview when Plastow was aged eighty-seven. TS in Modern Records Centre, University of Warwick.

80 Davies, op. cit., 79–80.

81 John Buckmaster, *A Village Politician. The Life Story of John Buckley.* With an Introduction by John Burnett, Caliban Books, 1982, 47–8 (1st edn 1897).

82 Hobsbawm and Rudé, op. cit., 51.

83 ibid. Appendix IV: The Problem of the Threshing Machine, 317–22.

84 A. J. Peacock, 'Village Radicalism in East Anglia, 1800–1850' in J. P. D. Dunbabin, *Rural Discontent in Nineteenth Century Britain*, Faber & Faber, 1974, 29–30.

85 Hobsbawm and Rudé, op. cit., 266–7.

86 *Cambridge Chronicle*, 8 January 1830, quoted in Peacock, op. cit., 60.

87 George Edwards, *From Crow-Scaring to Westminster. An Autobiography*, Labour Publishing Co., 1922, 16–17.

88 *Report from the Select Committee on Agriculture*, 1833 (612), V. Evidence of Mr Smith Woolley, Qs. 11, 947–12, 015.

89 *Report from His Majesty's Commissioners for Inquiring into the Administration and Practical Operation of the Poor Laws*, 1834, XXXIV. Supplement No. 1, 16–53.

90 ibid., 36–9.

91 ibid., 57.

92 ibid., 88, 94.

93 ibid., 228.
94 The Poor Law Amendment Act of 1834 has been extensively discussed by historians, and it is unnecessary to duplicate it here. See, for example, Sidney and Beatrice Webb, *English Poor Law History*, Part II 'The Last Hundred Years', Longmans, Green & Co., 1929; Fraser, ed., op. cit.; Rose, op. cit. (1972).

2   A DYING TRADE: THE CASE OF THE HANDLOOM WEAVERS, 1790–1850

1 R. M. Hartwell, Introduction to Duncan Bythell, *The Handloom Weavers. A Study in the English Cotton Industry During the Industrial Revolution*, Cambridge University Press, 1969, xi.
2 Royal Commission on the Handloom Weavers, *Reports of Assistant Commissioners*, Part III, West Riding, Ireland, 1840 (43-II), 590.
3 J. L. and Barbara Hammond, *The Skilled Labourer, 1760–1832*, Longmans, Green and Co., 1920.
4 E. J. Hobsbawm, *Industry and Empire*, Penguin Books, 1969, 59.
5 J. H. Clapham, *An Economic History of Modern Britain. The Early Railway Age, 1820–1850*, Cambridge University Press, 1939, 565.
6 F. H. Hayek, ed., *Capitalism and the Historians*, University of Chicago Press, 1954, 28.
7 Bythell, op. cit., 268.
8 ibid., 21.
9 These are located in John Burnett, David Vincent and David Mayall, eds., *The Autobiography of the Working Class. An Annotated, Critical Bibliography*, Harvester Press, Brighton, and New York University Press, Vol. I, 1984, Vol. II, 1987, Vol. III, 1989.
10 Robert Stewart, *Breaking the Fetters. The Memoirs of Bob Stewart*, Lawrence and Wishart, 1967, 7.
11 John Wood, *Autobiography of John Wood, written in the 75th Year of his Life*, Chronicle and Mail, Bradford, 1877, 5.
12 Ben Turner, *About Myself, 1863–1930*, Cayme Press, 1930, 5.
13 Joseph Livesey, Autobiography, in *The Life and Teaching of Joseph Livesey*, National Temperance League, 1885, 4.
14 E. P. Thompson, *The Making of the English Working Class*, Penguin Books, 1980, 298–9.
15 Bythell, op. cit., 29–30.
16 L. C. A. Knowles, *The Industrial and Commercial Revolutions in Great Britain during the Nineteenth Century*, Routledge and Kegan Paul, 1950, 55.
17 Clapham, op. cit., 69–70.
18 ibid., 554.
19 ibid., 179.
20 Bythell, op. cit., 54.
21 Norman Murray, *The Scottish Handloom Weavers, 1790–1850: A Social History*, John Donald, Edinburgh, 1978, 18–23.
22 B. R. Mitchell and Phyllis Deane, *Abstract of British Historical Statistics*, Cambridge University Press, 1962, 187.
23 T. Exell, *Brief History of the Weavers of Gloucestershire*, cited in H. P. R. Finberg, ed., *Gloucestershire Studies*, 1957, 247.
24 W. Radcliffe, *Origin of the New System of Manufacture*, James Lomax, Stockport, 1828, 65.

25 Peter Gaskell, *Artisans and Machinery. The Moral and Physical Condition of the Manufacturing Population*, John W. Parker, 1836, 24.

26 Radcliffe, op. cit., 12.

27 Neil J. Smelser, *Social Change in the Industrial Revolution. An Application of Theory to the British Cotton Industry*, University of Chicago Press, 1973, 137, citing G. H. Wood, *The History of Wages in the Cotton Trade in the Past Hundred Years*, Sherratt and Hughes, 1910, 125.

28 *Report of the Select Committee on Disputes between Masters and Workmen engaged in the Cotton Manufacture*, 1802–3, VIII, 44.

29 *Report from the Select Committee on Emigration from the United Kingdom*, 1827, (237). Evidence of Joseph Foster, Qs. 24–8.

30 *Report from the Select Committee on Handloom Weavers' Petitions, with the Minutes of Evidence*, 1835, (341) Report, XIII.

31 Wood, op. cit., 140.

32 William Thom, *Rhymes and Recollections of a Handloom Weaver*, ed. with a biographical sketch by W. Skinner, Alexander Gardner, 1880, 3.

33 William Marcroft, *The Marcroft Family, and the Inner Circle of Human Life*, E. Wrigley and Sons, Revised edn 1888, 5–6.

34 William Hanson, *The Life of William Hanson, written by himself (in his 80th year)*, Whitaker and Son, 1883, 3.

35 Cornelius Ashworth, *The Diary of Cornelius Ashworth*, in Frank Atkinson, ed., *Some Aspects of the Eighteenth Century Woollen and Worsted Trade in Halifax*, Halifax Museums, 1956. Ashworth was born in 1752 and died in 1821: these references are from Vol. I of his four diaries, covering October 1782 to November 1783.

36 Thom, op. cit., 4.

37 Smelser, op. cit., citing G. H. Wood, 140.

38 Murray, op. cit., 52.

39 John Burnett, *A History of the Cost of Living*, Pelican, 1969, 206, citing Sir Walter T. Layton and Geoffrey Crowther, *An Introduction to the Study of Prices*, Macmillan, 1938, 234.

40 Report of the Select Committee on Hand Loom Weaving, 1835, XIII, 355–6.

41 Clapham, op. cit., 209.

42 Bythell, op. cit., 148–55.

43 Ivy Pinchbeck, *Women Workers and the Industrial Revolution, 1750–1850*, Virago, 1985, 164.

44 Murray, op. cit., 185.

45 Bythell, op. cit., 74.

46 ibid., 191.

47 Frank Peel, *The Risings of the Luddites, Chartists and Plug-Drawers*, 1880, 4th edn, Frank Cass, 1968, 24.

48 Smelser, op. cit., 219.

49 For an account of Lancashire Luddism in 1812, see Thompson, op. cit., 618–22.

50 Dr Robert Taylor, *Letters on the Subject of the Lancashire Riots in the Year 1812*, 1813, 9.

51 Murray, op. cit., 186–90.

52 Bythell, op. cit., 57.

53 Murray, op. cit., 23. G. H. Wood estimated 240,000 by 1820.

54 G. H. Wood, op. cit., 112.

55 Bythell, op. cit., 99, 105.

56 Alexander Bain, *Autobiography*, Longmans, Green and Co., 1904, 3.

57 William Farish, *The Autobiography of William Farish. The Struggles of a Hand-Loom Weaver, with Some of his Writings*, printed for Private Circulation, 1889, 3–8.
58 Thom, op. cit., 4–6.
59 Livesey, op. cit., 5–15.
60 Bythell, op. cit., 123.
61 Murray, op. cit., 52–4.
62 Samuel Bamford, *Passages in the Life of a Radical*, 1st edn 1844, Macgibbon and Kee, 1967, 14–15.
63 Thompson, op. cit., 709.
64 Peel, op. cit., 307 et seq., where the incident is described as the Grange Moor Rising.
65 Murray, op. cit., 223–4.
66 William Varley, *Diary of William Varley of Higham. Memorandum Book for the Year of Our Lord 1820*, in W. Bennett, *The History of Burnley*, Burnley Corporation, Vol. III, 1948, 379–89.
67 Thom, op. cit., 11.
68 Farish, op. cit., 9.
69 Marcroft, op. cit., 29–30.
70 William Hanson, *The Life of William Hanson (in his 80th Year)*, Whitaker and Son, 1833, 8.
71 Estimates by Edward Baines, *History of the Cotton Manufacture in Great Britain*, H. Fisher and P. Jackson, 1835, 235–7.
72 Select Committee on Emigration from the United Kingdom. Second Report, 1827, (237), 4.
73 Murray, op. cit., 55.
74 Bythell, op. cit., 56.
75 ibid., 123.
76 Quoted in Brian Inglis, *Poverty and the Industrial Revolution*, Hodder & Stoughton, 1971, 218.
77 Edward Baines Jnr., *An Address to the Unemployed Workmen of Yorkshire and Lancashire on the Present Distress and on Machinery*, James Ridgway and Edward Baines, 1826, 7–8.
78 James Phillips Kay, MD, *The Moral and Physical Condition of the Working Classes Employed in the Cotton Manufacture in Manchester*, reprint of 2nd, enlarged edn of 1832 by E. J. Morton, Didsbury, 1969, 43–4.
79 Peter Gaskell, *Artisans and Machinery. The Moral and Physical Condition of the Manufacturing Population*, John W. Parker, 1836, 383.
80 Friedrich Engels, *The Condition of the Working Class in England in 1844*, 1st edition, 1845; trans. and ed. by W. O. Henderson and W. H. Chaloner, Stanford University Press, 1968, 50.
81 ibid., 97–8.
82 It was reported that in 1823 there had been a total of 568 emigrants: 182 men, 143 women, fifty-seven boys between fourteen and eighteen and 186 children. *Report from the Select Committee on Emigration from the United Kingdom*, 1826, (404), 6.
83 ibid., 3.
84 ibid., Second Report, 1827, (237), 3.
85 ibid., Second Report. Evidence of William Spencer Northouse, Qs. 659.
86 ibid., Second Report. Evidence of John Maxwell, Qs. 626.
87 ibid., Third Report, 1827, (550), II-VII.
88 'Handloom Weavers'. Speech by Dr Bowring MP in the House of Commons

on Tuesday, 28 July 1835, London, 1835, in *The Framework Knitters and Hand-loom Weavers: Their Attempts to Keep up Wages*. Eight pamphlets, 1820–45, Arno Press, New York, 1972, 8, 14.

89 Bythell, op. cit., 268.

90 Murray, op. cit., 125–8.

91 *Report of the Royal Commission for Inquiring into the Condition of the Unemployed Handloom Weavers in the United Kingdom*, 1841, (296), X.

92 W. Cooke Taylor, *Notes of a Tour in the Manufacturing Districts of Lancashire, 1842*, 3rd edn, with a new Introduction by W. H. Chaloner, Augustus M. Kelley, New York, 1968, 67–8.

93 Smelser, op. cit., 207, footnote 1.

94 B. R. Mitchell and Phyllis Deane, op. cit., 187, citing G. H. Wood's statistics.

95 Norman Murray, op. cit., 23.

96 Robert Stewart, *Breaking the Fetters. The Memoirs of Bob Stewart*, Lawrence and Wishart, 1967, 7. (Stewart was born in 1877.)

97 Ben Turner, *About Myself, 1863–1930*, Cayme Press, 1930, 34.

98 Edward Baines estimated that in 1833 a power-loom weaver aged fifteen to twenty, assisted by a twelve-year-old girl, and attending four looms could weave nine to ten times the quantity of an adult handloom weaver.

99 Smelser, op. cit., 148.

100 John Fielden, *The Curse of the Factory System*, 1st edn, 1836, 2nd edn Frank Cass and Co., 1969: Introduction by J. T. Ward, xvii. (In fact, Fielden gradually moved to the improved power-looms and built a factory for 800 in 1829, though still employing domestic handloom weavers for at least another twenty years.)

101 Cited in Bythell, op. cit., Tables 2 and 3, 279–80.

102 John Maxwell, *Manual Labour versus Machinery, exemplified in a Speech on Moving for a Committee of Parliamentary Enquiry into the Condition of Half a Million Hand-Loom Weavers*, Cochrane and M'Crone, 1834. Eight pamphlets, 1820–45, op. cit., 18 et seq.

103 ibid. 'Manufacture of Cotton, of Woollen and of Silk', Table opposite 31.

104 Clapham, op. cit., 552–4. (The wage statistics were collected in 1838–9.)

105 Maxwell, op. cit., 31.

106 Murray, op. cit., 56–7.

107 *Report from the Select Committee on Hand-Loom Weavers' Petitions, with Minutes of Evidence*, 1834, (556), X. Evidence of John Lennon, Qs. 6,256.

108 ibid. Evidence of William Longson, Qs 7,080.

109 ibid. Evidence of Richard Oastler, Qs 3,735–50.

110 ibid., 1835, (341), XIII. Report, XIII.

111 ibid., 1835. Analysis of Evidence, 6–7.

112 Joseph Gutteridge, *The Autobiography of Joseph Gutteridge*, in *Master and Artisan in Victorian England*, Valerie E. Chancellor, ed., Evelyn, Adams and MacKay, 1969, 99–121. Gutteridge's fortunes subsequently improved somewhat, though he again experienced unemployment in the 1840s and in the great Coventry strike and lockout of 1860–1 when he was out of work for a year. He died in 1899.

113 Thom, op. cit., 13–31. Thom was rescued from extreme poverty (and, possibly, insanity – there are close parallels with the life of John Clare) by having some of his poems published and becoming a protégé of Mr Gordon of Knockespock. His *Rhymes and Recollections of a Handloom Weaver* was published in 1844 and he was briefly lionized in London before returning to the

handloom in Aberdeen. His early death in 1848 at the age of forty-nine was hastened by heavy drinking.

114 John Castle, *The Diary of John Castle*, MSS. Essex County Record Office, written 1871; typewritten copy duplicated by Colchester Co-Operative Society in 1961 to mark their centenary, (38 pp). Castle later became foreman for a London firm employing weavers in the Colchester area, and a founder-member of the co-operative society there: he died in 1889.

115 E. J. Hobsbawm, 'The British Standard of Living, 1790–1850', *Economic History Review*, Second Series, Vol. X, 1957, 54.

116 Joseph Adshead, *Distress in Manchester. Evidence of the State of the Labouring Classes in 1840–42* (Henry Hooper, 1842), 55 pp.

117 Royal Commission on Hand-Loom Weavers: Assistant Commissioners Reports: Scotland by J. C. Symons (159), XLII, 1839, 8.

118 ibid., 23.

119 ibid., 25.

120 ibid., 55.

121 ibid., 232–3.

122 ibid., 291.

123 ibid., 305.

124 ibid., 429.

125 ibid., 436.

126 ibid., 531.

127 Ben Brierley, *Home Memories, and Recollections of a Life* (Abel Heywood & Son, 1886). Brierley was born at Failsworth near Rochdale in 1825 and died in 1891.

128 Thomas Wood, *Autobiography, 1822–1880*, offprint from serialized version in the *Keighley News*, 3 March–14 April 1956, 16. Wood was born at Bingley, Yorkshire, in 1822: in later years ill-health obliged him to give up engineering, and he became a school attendance officer.

129 William Heaton, *The Old Soldier, The Wandering Lover, etc., Together with a Sketch of the Author's Life*, Simpkin, Marshall and Co., 1857, xxii. The volume is principally a collection of his romantic poetry.

130 Joseph Greenwood, 'Reminiscences of Sixty Years Ago' (Articles in *Co-Partnership*, New Series, Vols XV–XVII, Nos 177–200, 1909–11).

131 Farish, op. cit.

132 William M'Gonagall, *The Authentic Autobiography of the Poet M'Gonagall. Written by Himself* (Luke, Mackie and Co., n.d.). M'Gonagall was born in Edinburgh in 1830: his first collection of poems and songs was published in 1878.

133 Charles F. Forshaw, ed., *The Poets of Keighley, Bingley, Haworth and District*, Thornton and Pearson, 1891. Includes the Autobiography of Abraham Holroyd, born at Clayton near Bradford in 1815, died in 1888 at Saltaire, where Titus Salt had been a patron.

134 Alexander Bain, *Autobiography*, Longmans, Green and Co., 1904.

135 Andrew Carnegie, *The Autobiography of Andrew Carnegie*, Constable and Co., 1920, 12–13.

136 Royal Commission, op. cit., Assistant Commissioners Reports, Part III, (43-II), 1840, 590.

137 Karel Williams, *From Pauperism to Poverty*, Routledge, 1981, 47–8.

138 David Ashforth, 'The Urban Poor Law', Ch. 6 in Derek Fraser, ed., *The New Poor Law in the Nineteenth Century*, Macmillan, 1976, 133.

139 Williams, op. cit., Table 4.9, 181.

140 Michael E. Rose, ed., *The Poor and the City. The English Poor Law in its*

Urban Context, Leicester University Press, 1985. Introduction, 8–9. (In 1846 'irremovability' was introduced after five years of continuous residence.)

141 Report of the Select Committee on the Poor Law Amendment Act, 1838, (681–I). Eighth Report by Assistant Commissioner Alfred Power, Qs. 2,848–57.

142 Report of Royal Commission on Hand-Loom Weavers (159), 1839. Report from J. C. Symons, 'General Mental and Moral Condition', 44–5.

143 Adshead, op. cit. Report by Dr H. Baron Howard, Princess St., Manchester, Jan. 1842, 52.

3 UNEMPLOYMENT AMONG SKILLED WORKERS, 1815–70

1 William Dodd, *The Laboring Classes of England, especially those concerned in Agriculture and Manufactures*, 2nd American edn, 1848; reprinted 1976 by Augustus M. Kelley, New Jersey, 9–10.

2 John Rule, 'The Property of Skill in the Period of Manufacture', in *The Historical Meanings of Work*, Patrick Joyce, ed., Cambridge University Press, 1987, 101.

3 See, for example, Thomas Wright, *Some Habits and Customs of the Working Classes*, by a Journeyman Engineer, 1867; reprinted 1967 by Augustus M. Kelley, New York: Part II, 'On the Inner Life of Workshops', 83–108.

4 R. Dudley Baxter, *National Income: The United Kingdom.* (Macmillan and Co., 1868), 51.

5 Quoted in Sally Alexander, *Women's Work in Nineteenth-Century London. A Study of the Years 1820–50*, Journeyman Press, 1983, 35.

6 K. Marx and F. Engels, *On Britain*, Foreign Languages Publishing House, Moscow, 1962, 179.

7 P. E. Razzell and R. W. Wainwright, eds, *The Victorian Working Class – Selections from Letters to the Morning Chronicle*, Frank Cass, 1973, 185.

8 J. H. Clapham, *An Economic History of Modern Britain*, Vol. I, 1820–50, Cambridge University Press, 1939, 558.

9 Alexander, op. cit., 36.

10 Clapham, op. cit., 551.

11 E. P. Thompson and Eileen Yeo, *The Unknown Mayhew. Selections from the Morning Chronicle, 1849–1850*, Penguin Books, 1973, 273–86.

12 ibid., 291.

13 ibid., 290.

14 E. P. Thompson, *The Making of the English Working Class*, Penguin Books, 1980, 282–3.

15 Thompson and Yeo, op. cit., 222–3.

16 Gareth Stedman Jones, *Outcast London. A Study in the Relationship between Classes in Victorian London*, Penguin Books, 1976, Table 11, 376.

17 Thompson and Yeo, op. cit., 263–4.

18 ibid., 231.

19 ibid., 527–8.

20 ibid., 525.

21 ibid., 405–21.

22 ibid., 430.

23 ibid., 435.

24 ibid., 449.

25 ibid., 460.

26 Razzell and Wainwright, op. cit., 192.

27 ibid., 196.
28 *The Great Unwashed*, by The Journeyman Engineer (Thomas Wright), 1868; repub. by Augustus M. Kelley, New York, 1970, 246–52.
29 Baxter, op. cit., 42–7.
30 Henry Mayhew, *London Labour and the London Poor*, Vol. IV, *Those That Will Not Work*, Griffin, Bohn and Co., 1862, 23.
31 ibid., Vol. II. *The Condition and Earnings of Those That Will Work, Cannot Work, and Will Not Work*, Charles Griffin and Co., 1861, 338.
32 ibid., 364–5.
33 For use of trade union returns as a measure see W. R. Garside, *The Measurement of Unemployment, 1850–1979*, Blackwell, Oxford, 1980, 9–16.
34 H. R. Southall, *The Tramping Artisan Revisits: Labour Mobility and Economic Distress in early Victorian England*, (*Economic History Review*, Vol. 44, May 1991), 727–96.
35 ibid., Table 1.
36 ibid., Table 2.
37 Humphrey R. Southall, *The Origins of the Depressed Areas: Unemployment, Growth and Regional Economic Structure in Britain before 1914*, Economic History Review, Second Series, Vol. XLI, No. 2, May 1988, Table 6, 251.
38 B. R. Mitchell and Phyllis Deane, *Abstract of British Historical Statistics*, Cambridge University Press, 1962, 'Table of Certain Trade Unions, 1851–1926', 64.
39 Thompson and Yeo, op. cit., 231.
40 Razzell and Wainwright, op. cit., 129.
41 Cited by Ellic Howe, *The London Compositor*, 1947, 228.
42 Charles Manby Smith, *The Working Man's Way in the World*, 1857; reprinted by the Printing Historical Society, 1967, 19–20.
43 Thompson and Yeo, op. cit., 272.
44 Report Relative to the *Grievances Complained of by Journeyman Bakers*, 3080 (1862). Appendix of Evidence, para. 80, 29.
45 ibid., Evidence of Mr Mackness, para. 383, 83.
46 Brian Lewis, *Life in a Cotton Town: Blackburn, 1818–48*. Carnegie Press, Preston, 1985, 31.
47 W. W. Rostow, 'Cycles in the British Economy, 1790–1914', Ch. 1 in *British Economic Fluctuations, 1790–1939*, Derek H. Aldcroft and Peter Fearon, eds, Macmillan, 1972, 77–87.
48 *Journal of the Statistical Society of London*, Vol. II, 1839. W. Felkin 'Statistics of the Labouring Classes and Paupers in Nottingham', Charles Knight and Co., 1839, 458.
49 *Journal of the Statistical Society*, ibid., Vol. V, 1842. H. Ashworth, 'Statistics of the Present Depression of Trade in Bolton', 74.
50 Cited by E. J. Hobsbawm, 'The British Standard of Living, 1790–1850', *Economic History Review*, Second Series, Vol. X, 1957, 53.
51 Sidney Pollard, *A History of Labour in Sheffield*, Liverpool University Press, 1959, 39.
52 J. Finch, *Statistics of the Vauxhall Ward, Liverpool, Shewing the Actual Condition of More than Five Thousand Families*, Joshua Walmsley, Liverpool and London, 1842, 28–30.
53 H. M. Boot, *Unemployment and Poor Law Relief, Social History*, Vol. 15, No. 2, May 1990, 219.
54 ibid., 222.
55 George Barnsby, 'The Standard of Living in the Black Country during the Nineteenth Century', *Economic History Review*, Second Series, XXIV, 1971, 234.

56 *The Autobiography of Robert Spurr. A Social Study of Nineteenth-Century Baptist Working Class Fortitude*, R. J. Owen, ed., (*Baptist Quarterly*, Vol. 26, April 1976), 283.

57 Smith, op. cit., 18.

58 *Autobiography of Thomas Wilkinson Wallis*, J. W. Goulding and Son, 1899, 25. Wallis set up business on his own account in 1844 and later became a distinguished prize-winning wood carver.

59 *Autobiography by Thomas Wood, 1822–1880*, offprint from serialized version in the *Keighley News*, 3 March–14 April 1956, 12.

60 ibid., 15.

61 J. H. Powell, *Life Incidents and Poetic Pictures*, Trubner and Co., 1865, 10–13.

62 W. E. Adams, *Memoirs of a Social Atom*, Hutchinson and Co., 2 vols, 1903, Vol. I, 288–93.

63 W. J. Francis, *Reminiscences*, Francis and Sons, 1926, 33.

64 John O'Neil, *The Journals of a Lancashire Weaver, 1856–60, 1860–64, 1872–75*, Mary Briggs, ed., The Record Society of Lancashire and Cheshire, Vol. CXXII, 1982, 113–44.

65 *The Life of Sir William Fairbairn, Bart., Partly Written by Himself*, Edited and Completed by William Pole, Longmans, Green and Co., 1877, 83.

66 James Dawson Burn, *The Autobiography of a Beggar Boy*, David Vincent, ed., Europa, 1978, 134–5. (The first edition was in 1855.)

67 John Francis Bray, *A Voyage from Utopia*, edited with an Introduction by M. F. Lloyd-Prichard, Lawrence and Wishart, 1957, Introduction, 9.

68 William Lovett, *The Life and Struggles of William Lovett in his Pursuit of Bread, Knowledge and Freedom*, Trubner and Co., 1876, 20–30.

69 *The Autobiography of Francis Place, 1771–1854*, edited with an Introduction and Notes by Mary Thale, Cambridge University Press, 1972, 79–94.

70 Burn, op. cit., 127.

71 John Bedford Leno, *The Aftermath: with Autobiography of the Author*, Reeves and Turner, 1892, 24.

72 Colin (pseud.), *The Wanderer Brought Home. The Life and Adventures of Colin. An Autobiography*, edited and with reflections by the Revd B. Richings, 2nd edn, W. Tweedie, 1864, 14.

73 William Dodd, *The Factory System Illustrated in a Series of Letters to the Right Hon. Lord Ashley, Together with a Narrative of the Experience and Sufferings of William Dodd, a Factory Cripple, Written by Himself.*, 1842, repub. Cass, 1968, 113.

74 ibid., 116.

75 ibid., 14–15.

76 Thompson and Yeo, op. cit., 415.

77 ibid., 395–402.

78 Iorwerth Prothero, *Artisans and Politics in Early Nineteenth Century London. John Gast and his Times*, Methuen, 1981, 215.

79 ibid., 221–2.

80 Keith McClelland and Alastair Reid, 'Wood, Iron and Steel: Technology, Labour and Trade Union Organisation in the Shipbuilding Industry, 1840–1914' in Royden Harrison and Jonathan Zeitlin, eds, *Divisions of Labour*, Harvester Press, Brighton, 1985, 161.

81 Mark Hirsch, 'Sailmakers', in *Divisions of Labour*, ibid., 95–8.

82 Lovett, op. cit., 20.

83 Place, op. cit., 80, 112.

84 Wood, op. cit., 8.

85 Clapham, op. cit., 165.

86 Gareth Stedman Jones, *Outcast London. A Study in the Relationship between Classes in Victorian Society*, Penguin Books, 1976, 41, note 47.

87 ibid., 34–6.

88 Ellic Howe, Preface to *The Working Man's Way in the World*, op. cit., VIII.

89 *Report upon the Condition of the Town of Leeds and of its Inhabitants*, by a Statistical Committee of the Town Council, October 1839, *Journal of the Statistical Society of London*, Vol. II, Charles Knight and Co., 1839, 422. (The survey was conducted over the previous eleven months.)

90 Fairbairn, op. cit., 85, 91.

91 *Henry Broadhurst, M.P., The Story of his Life from a Stonemason's Bench to the Treasury Bench, Told by Himself*, Introduction by Augustine Birrell, Hutchinson and Co., 1902, 16–17.

92 Alfred Ireson, *Reminiscences*, unpub. TS., written 1929–30, Brunel University Archive, 78.

93 Burn, op. cit., 137–8.

94 George Herbert (1814–1902), *Shoemaker's Window. Recollections of Banbury in Oxfordshire before the Railway Age*, Christiana S. Cheney, ed., Phillimore, for the Banbury Historical Society, 2nd edn, 1971, 21.

95 Thomas Carter, *Memoirs of a Working Man*, with an Introduction by Charles Knight, Charles Knight and Co., 1845, 136.

96 ibid., 151.

97 ibid., 163.

98 Smith, op. cit., 19.

99 ibid., 272.

100 Lucy Luck, 'A Little of My Life', J. C. Squire, ed., *London Mercury*, Vol. XIII, No. 76, 1925–6, 373.

101 Burn, op. cit., 129–30.

102 John James Bezer, *Autobiography of One of the Chartist Rebels of 1848*, in *Testaments of Radicalism: Memoirs of Working Class Politicians, 1790–1885*, David Vincent, ed., Europa, 1977, 181.

103 John Buckmaster, *A Village Politician. The Life Story of John Buckley*, Introduction by John Burnett, Caliban Books, Horsham, 1982, 105, 1st edn, 1897.

104 Place, op. cit., 115.

105 Leno, op. cit., 26–8.

106 Edward A. Rymer, *The Martyrdom of the Mine, or A 60 Years' Struggle for Life*, Introduction by Robert Neville, *History Workshop Journal*, Spring 1976, 2–13. (First published as a pamphlet, 1893.)

107 Powell, op. cit., 14.

108 ibid., 34.

109 George Haw, *From Workhouse to Westminster, The Life Story of Will Crooks, M.P.*, Cassell and Co., 1907, 44.

110 William Neild, 'Comparative Statement of the Income and Expenditure of Certain Families of the Working Classes in Manchester and Dukinfield in the Years 1836–1841', *Journal of the Statistical Society of London*, Vol. IV, 1841, Charles Knight and Co., 1841, 322.

111 C. B. Fripp, 'Report on the Condition of the Working Classes in Bristol', *Journal of the Statistical Society of London*, Vol. II, 1839, Charles Knight and Co., 1839, 372.

112 Paul Johnson, *Saving and Spending. The Working-Class Economy in Britain, 1870–1939*, Clarendon Press, Oxford, 1985, 74.

113 ibid., Table 6.2, 169.

114 John Finch, *Statistics of Vauxhall Ward, Liverpool, 1842*, op. cit., 12.

115 ibid., Report by James Parker, 53.
116 Ireson, op. cit., 47.
117 ibid., 76.
118 Wood, op. cit., 13.
119 Carter, op. cit., 133.
120 Smith, op. cit., 13.
121 R. A. Leeson, *Travelling Brothers. The Six Centuries' Road from Craft Fellowship to Trade Unionism*, Allen & Unwin, 1979, 112–3.
122 ibid., 149.
123 Wright, *The Great Unwashed*, op. cit., 159.
124 Burn, op. cit., 135.
125 Leno, op. cit., 35–6, 39.
126 Broadhurst, op. cit., 11.
127 ibid., 16–22.
128 ibid., 41.
129 Wright, op. cit., 102.
130 Pollard, op. cit., 72.
131 ibid., 150.
132 Place, op. cit., 113–4.
133 Lovett, op. cit., 40–41.
134 Fairbairn, op. cit., 91.
135 Brian Lewis, *Life in a Cotton Town: Blackburn*, op. cit., 31–2.
136 Pollard, op. cit., 110.
137 Felkin, 'Statistics of the Labouring Classes and Paupers in Nottingham' (1839), op. cit., 458.
138 H. M. Boot, 'Unemployment and Poor Relief in Manchester, 1845–50', op. cit., 222–3.
139 ibid., 224–5.
140 Charlotte Erikson, 'The Encouragement of Emigration by British Trade Unions, 1850–1900', *Population Studies*, Vol. III, No. 3, December 1949, 254–5.
141 Leeson, op. cit., 184.
142 Erikson, op. cit., 264. Table and footnote 4.
143 Leeson, op. cit., 185.
144 Dudley Baines, *Migration in a Mature Economy*, Cambridge University Press, 1985, 71.
145 Place, op. cit., 115–17.
146 ibid., 119.
147 Powell, op. cit., 13, 34.
148 Bezer, op. cit., 183.
149 Ireson, op. cit., 92.
150 Smith, op. cit., 20.
151 Bray, op. cit., 9.
152 Bezer, op. cit., 187.
153 Haw, op. cit., 47–8.
154 Wright, op. cit., 260.
155 Haw, op. cit., 52.

4 UNEMPLOYMENT ON THE LAND, 1834–1914

1 *Cambridge Chronicle*, 17 April 1835. Cited in A. J. Peacock, 'Village Radicalism in East Anglia, 1800–1850', in J. P. D. Dunbabin, *Rural Discontent in Nineteenth-Century Britain*, Faber & Faber, 1974, 49.

2 Nigel E. Agar, *The Bedfordshire Farm Worker in the Nineteenth Century*, Bedfordshire Historical Record Society, Vol. 60, 1981, 80.

3 *Cambridge Chronicle*, 27 August 1842. Cited in Peacock, op. cit., 59.

4 Select Committee of the House of Lords on the Poor Law Amendment Act, 1837–8 (719), XIX. Minutes of Evidence. Evidence of Daniel Goodson Adey, 23 March 1838.

5 Select Committee appointed to Inquire into the State of Agriculture and Agricultural Distress. First Report, 1836 (79), VIII. Evidence of John Brickwell, Qs. 312–459.

6 ibid. Second Report, 1836 (189), VIII. Evidence of John Ellman of West Firle, Sussex, Qs. 4,699–700.

7 ibid., Qs. 4,529.

8 ibid. Evidence of Thomas Bennet, Qs. 8,193–200.

9 Select Committee of the House of Lords on the State of Agriculture, 1837 (464), V. Evidence of John Lewin, Qs. 960, 1060.

10 See the account of this in E. P. Thompson, *The Making of the English Working Class*, Pelican, 1980, 880–1.

11 Alan Armstrong, *Farmworkers. A Social and Economic History, 1770–1980*, Batsford, 1988, 83–4.

12 J. T. Burgess, *The Life and Experiences of a Warwickshire Labourer . . . as Told by Himself*, Routledge, 1872, 5–11.

13 James Bowd, *The Life of a Farm Worker*, (MSS 1889). Extracts in *The Countryman*, Vol. 51, Part 2, Summer 1955, 293–300.

14 Mrs Burrows, *A Childhood in the Fens about 1850–60*, in Margaret Llewelyn Davies, ed., *Life As We Have Known It*, by Co-Operative Working Women, 1st edn 1931; Virago, edn 1977, 109–113.

15 George Edwards, *From Crow-Scaring to Westminster: An Autobiography*, Labour Publishing Co., 1922, 17–22.

16 *The Autobiography of Joseph Arch*, with a Preface by Frances, Countess of Warwick, John Gerard O'Leary, ed., Macgibbon and Kee, 1966, 22–5, 1st edn 1898.

17 *The Life History of Isaac Anderson, a Member of the Peculiar People*. Essex Record Office, 10 pp, n.d., after 1882. Anderson joined the sect of the Banyards, or Peculiar People, in 1851, later being ordained as an Elder. The Peculiar People had twelve chapels, mostly in Essex and London.

18 *The Autobiography of a Working Man*, Hon. Eleanor Eden, ed., Richard Bentley, 1862, 42.

19 George Bourne, *The Bettesworth Book. Talks with a Surrey Peasant*, Duckworth, 1920, vii–ix. The conversations with Bettesworth took place in the 1890s, when he was in his sixties and working as a gardener for George Sturt ('Bourne' was a pen-name) near Farnham, Surrey.

20 *The Hungry Forties, Life Under the Bread Tax*, Introduction by Mrs Cobden Unwin, T. Fisher Unwin, 1905, 12–13.

21 ibid., 28.

22 George Nicholls, 'On the Condition of the Agricultural Labourer, with Suggestions for its Improvement', *Journal of the Royal Agricultural Society of England*, Vol. 7, (1846), 7–8.

23 *Reports of Special Assistant Poor Law Commissioners on the Employment of Women and Children in Agriculture*, 1843, (510), XII, 219.

24 ibid., 249.

25 ibid., 225.

26 ibid. Evidence of Mr Vaughan, 132.

27 Select Committee of the House of Lords on the Poor Law Amendment Act, 1837–8, op. cit. Evidence of Dr Kay, 467 et seq.
28 W. Hasbach, *A History of the English Agricultural Labourer.* Trans. by Ruth Kenyon, P. S. King and Son, 1920, 234.
29 James Caird, *English Agriculture in 1850–51*, Longman, 1852, 85.
30 ibid., 148.
31 ibid., 514, quoting Parliamentary Return, no. 735 (1848).
32 ibid., 517.
33 Alexander Somerville, *The Whistler at the Plough, and Free Trade*, James Ainsworth, Manchester, 1852, 23.
34 ibid., 385.
35 M. E. Rose, *The English Poor Law, 1780–1930*, David & Charles, Newton Abbot, 1971, 129.
36 ibid., 140–8, quoting the Orders in full.
37 Anne Digby, 'The Rural Poor Law', Ch. 7 in Derek Fraser, ed., *The New Poor Law in the Nineteenth Century*, Macmillan, 1976, 156.
38 Anne Digby, *Pauper Palaces*, Routledge and Kegan Paul, 1978, Table 4d, 112.
39 Digby, op. cit., 166.
40 Full details of the notorious Andover case are in Ian Anstruther, *The Scandal of the Andover Workhouse*, Alan Sutton, Gloucester, 1984.
41 Arthur Redford, *Labour Migration in England, 1800–1850*, edited and revised by W. H. Chaloner, Manchester University Press, 1964, 70.
42 ibid., Table 1, 108.
43 ibid., 110.
44 John Dent Dent, 'The Present Condition of the English Agricultural Labourer, 1871', *Journal of the Royal Agricultural Society of England*, Vol. 32, 1871, 344.
45 ibid., 346.
46 Poor Law Returns, 1871. Quoted in Francis George Heath, *The English Peasantry*, Frederick Warne and Co., 1874, 9–24.
47 P. Anderson Graham, *The Rural Exodus. The Problem of the Village and the Town*, Methuen and Co., 1892, 12–13.
48 Dudley Baines, *Migration in a Mature Economy. Emigration and Internal Migration in England and Wales, 1861–1900*, Cambridge University Press, 1985, 216, quoting the Welton-Cairncross estimate.
49 Maude F. Davies, *Life in an English Village. An Economic and Historical Survey of the Parish of Corsley in Wiltshire*, T. Fisher Unwin, 1909, 80–8.
50 M. K. Ashby, *Joseph Ashby of Tysoe, 1859–1919. A Study of English Village Life*, Merlin Press, 1974, 85–9.
51 Heath, op. cit., 146.
52 Frederick Verinder, 'The Agricultural Labourer', in Frank W. Galton, ed., *Workers on their Industries*, S. Sonnenschein and Co., 1895, 156–7.
53 Heath, op. cit., 41–2.
54 ibid., 58.
55 Royal Commission on the Employment of Children, Young Persons and Women in Agriculture, 1867–8, (4068), XVII, First Report (1868), 24.
56 ibid., First Report, 72.
57 ibid., Second Report, 1868–9, (4202), XIII, ix.
58 Arthur R. Randell, *Sixty Years a Fenman*, Routledge and Kegan Paul, 1966, 8. Randell's father was born at Wisbech *c.* 1853, and began work as a crow-scarer at five.
59 *I Walked by Night, Being the Life and History of the King of the Norfolk Poachers, Written by Himself*, Lilias Rider Haggard, ed., Boydell Press, 1974, 4.

60 ibid., 89–90.
61 ibid., 178.
62 William J. Milne, *Reminiscences of an Old Boy, and Autobiographic Sketches of Scottish Rural Life from 1832 to 1856*, John MacDonal, 1901. He later published a further series of reminiscences, *Railway and Commercial Life*.
63 F. E. Green, *A History of the English Agricultural Labourer, 1870–1920*, P. S. King and Son, London, 1920: Reg Groves, *Sharpen the Sickle, The History of the Farm Workers' Union*, Porcupine Press, 1949: J. P. D. Dunbabin, *Rural Discontent in Nineteenth-Century Britain*, Faber & Faber, 1974, Chs 4 and 5.
64 Arch, op. cit., 32.
65 Green, op. cit., 36.
66 J. P. D. Dunbabin, 'The Incidence and Organization of Agricultural Trades Unionism in the 1870's', *Agricultural History Review*, Vol. XVI, 1968, 117.
67 Frederick Clifford, *The Agricultural Lock-Out of 1874*, William Blackwood and Sons, Edinburgh and London, 1875, 21. (Quoting *The Labourers' Union Chronicle*.)
68 Green, op. cit., 55.
69 Clifford, op. cit., 179.
70 Richard Jefferies, 'Travelling Labour', in *Chronicles of the Hedges, and Other Essays*, Samuel J. Looker, ed., Phoenix House, London, 1948. The essay on 'Travelling Labour' was first published in 1877.
71 *Memoir of John Kemp, First Pastor of 'Ebenezer' Strict Baptist Chapel, Bounds Cross, Biddenden, Kent*, C. J. Farncombe and Sons, 1933.
72 *The Autobiography of John Hockley*, in Mark Sorrell, *The Peculiar People*, Paternoster Press, Exeter, 1979.
73 Isaac Mead, *The Story of an Essex Lad, Written by Himself*, A. Driver and Sons, 1923.
74 C. Henry Warren, *Happy Countryman (The Reminiscences of Mark Thurston)*, Geoffrey Bles, 1939.
75 Edwards, op. cit., 50.
76 ibid., 75.
77 Report of the Royal Commission on the Depressed Condition of the Agricultural Interests (C 3309), XIV, Final Report, 1882, 22.
78 ibid., 23.
79 ibid., Minutes of Evidence, Qs. 58, 422, 60,354.
80 *The Land*, The Report of the Land Enquiry Commission, Vol. I, Rural, Hodder and Stoughton, 1913, 32.
81 ibid., 33.
82 Verinder, op. cit., 156.
83 William E. Bear, 'The Farm Labourers of England and Wales', *Journal of the Royal Agricultural Society of England*, Dec. 1893, 677–8.
84 P. H. Mann, 'Life in an Agricultural Village in England', *Sociological Papers*, Vol. 1, 1904, 176–8.
85 ibid., 192–3.
86 C. R. Buxton, 'Minimum Wages for Agricultural Labourers', *Contemporary Review*, August, 1912, 194–5.
87 B. S. Rowntree and May Kendall, *How the Labourer Lives. A Study of the Rural Labour Problem*, Thomas Nelson and Sons, 1913, 299 et seq.
88 Ann Kussmaul, *Servants in Husbandry in Early Modern England*, Cambridge University Press, 1981, 131.
89 Fred Kitchen, *Brother to the Ox. The Autobiography of a Farm Labourer*, J. M. Dent and Sons, 1940.

90 *The Land,* op. cit., 1.
91 ibid., 20–2.
92 Based on Mary MacKinnon, 'Poor Law Policy, Unemployment and Pauperism', *Explorations in Economic History,* Vol. 23, 1986, Table 1, 304.
93 Sidney and Beatrice Webb, *English Poor Law History, Part II: The Last Hundred Years,* Longmans, Green & Co., 1929, 403.
94 W. H. Barrett, *A Fenman's Story,* Routledge and Kegan Paul, 1965, 30.
95 Lord Snell, *Men, Movements and Myself,* J. M. Dent, 1936, 37–9.

5 THE 'DISCOVERY' OF UNEMPLOYMENT, 1870–1914

1 General Booth, *In Darkest England and the Way Out,* International Headquarters of the Salvation Army, 1890, 30.
2 Bennet Burleigh, 'The Unemployed', *Contemporary Review,* Vol. LII, December 1887, 773.
3 John Belchem, *Industrialization and the Working Class: the British Experience, 1750–1900,* Scolar Press, Aldershot, 1990, 183.
4 J. E. Cronin, *Strikes, 1870–1914,* in Chris Wrigley, ed., *A History of British Industrial Relations, 1815–1914,* Harvester Press, Brighton, 1982, 74 et seq.
5 The events of 1886 and 1887 are well described in Gareth Stedman Jones, *Outcast London. A Study in the Relationship between Classes in Victorian Society,* Penguin Books, 1976, 291–6.
6 John Burns, *The Unemployed,* Fabian Society Tract No. 47, Nov. 1893; reprinted March 1905, 4.
7 *The Times,* 7 April 1882 and 2 Feb. 1888, quoted Roger Davidson, *Whitehall and the Labour Problem in Late Victorian and Edwardian Britain,* Croom Helm, Beckenham, 1985, 55.
8 Samuel A. Barnett, 'A Scheme for the Unemployed', *Nineteenth Century,* Vol. XXIV, Nov. 1888, 754–5.
9 Sir John Gorst, Preface to Percy Alden, *The Unemployed: A National Question,* 2nd edn, P. S. King, 1905, iii.
10 Kenneth D. Brown, *Labour and Unemployment, 1900–1914,* David & Charles, Newton Abbot, 1971, 14.
11 Jones, op. cit., 300.
12 Arnold White, *The Problems of a Great City,* Remington and Co., 1886, 226.
13 J. P. Freeman-Williams, *The Effect of Town Life on the General Health,* W. H. Allen and Co., 1890, 5.
14 Sidney and Beatrice Webb, *English Poor Law History, Part II, The Last Hundred Years,* Longmans, Green and Co., 1929, Footnote to 632–3.
15 Sir John Clapham, *An Economic History of Modern Britain,* Vol. 3. *Machines and National Rivalries, 1887–1914,* Cambridge University Press, 1951, Footnote 4, 419.
16 Jose Harris, *Unemployment and Politics. A Study in English Social Policy,* Clarendon Press, Oxford, 1972, 4.
17 Davidson, op. cit., Table 2.1, 35.
18 Clapham, op. cit., 4, quoting the contemporary economist, Alfred Marshall.
19 See S. B. Saul, *The Myth of the Great Depression, 1873–1896,* Macmillan, Studies in Economic History: the Economic History Society, 1969, and the Select Bibliography therein.
20 Davidson, op. cit., 43, citing W. A. Lewis, *Growth and Fluctuations, 1870–1913,* 1978, 51 et seq.
21 Saul, op. cit., Table IV, 37.

REFERENCES

22 Rostow, *Cycles in the British Economy, 1790–1914*, in Derek H. Aldcroft and Peter Fearon, eds., *British Economic Fluctuations, 1790–1939*, Macmillan, 1972, 87.

23 ibid., 77.

24 W. H. Beveridge, *Unemployment. A Problem of Industry*, Longmans, Green and Co., 1909, 13.

25 G. H. Barnes, MP, *The Problem of the Unemployed*, Independent Labour Party pamphlet, 1907, 3.

26 W. R. Garside, *The Measurement of Unemployment, 1850–1979*, Blackwell, Oxford, 1980, 12–13, which contains a full discussion of the many problems of this subject.

27 The trade unions making unemployment returns in 1908 included building, woodworking and furnishing, coalmining, engineering, shipbuilding, other metal trades, printing and bookbinding, and textiles. (Beveridge, op. cit., 20.)

28 Clapham, op. cit., 29.

29 B. R. Mitchell and Phyllis Deane, *Abstract of British Historical Statistics*, Cambridge University Press, 1962, Table, Labour Force 3, 64–5.

30 Average unemployment rates quoted are from Mitchell and Deane and specific industries from Clapham, op. cit.

31 Davidson, op. cit., 186 et seq.

32 S. J. Chapman and H. M. Hallsworth, *Unemployment. The Results of an Investigation made in Lancashire*, Manchester University Press: Economic Series No. XII, 1909, 67.

33 Beveridge, op. cit., 154, citing the Association of Workhouse Masters.

34 Select Committee on Distress from Want of Employment, Third Report, 1895, (365), ix, iii.

35 ibid., First Report, 1895 (III), viii, iv.

36 ibid., First Report, Minutes of Evidence. Evidence of Keir Hardie, 69–71.

37 Beveridge, op. cit., new edition, Longmans, Green and Co., 1930, Table XXVI, 448.

38 Chapman and Hallsworth, op. cit., 67.

39 ibid., 71.

40 B. Seebohm Rowntree and Bruno Lasker, *Unemployment: A Social Study*, Macmillan and Co., 1911, 301. The size of the York wage-earning class, 17,457, is from Rowntree's *Poverty. A Study of Town Life*, Macmillan and Co., 1901, which would yield an unemployment rate of 7.3 per cent.

41 Beveridge, op. cit., 1909, 27.

42 Arnold White, 'The Nomad Poor of London', *Contemporary Review*, Vol. XLVII, May 1885, 715–17.

43 *Suggestions and Suggested Rules for Dealing with Exceptional Distress by Local Committees*, Charity Organisation Paper No. 11, 1886, 1.

44 *The Government Organisation of Unemployed Labour*, Report by a Committee of the Fabian Society, 1886, 3–4.

45 C. Booth, *Life and Labour of the People in London, Vol. I; East, Central and South London*, Macmillan and Co., 1892, 147, 149–50.

46 H. Llewellyn Smith, Evidence to Select Committee on Distress from Want of Employment, Third Report, 1895, (365), IX.

47 'The Problem of the Unemployed', Report of a Conference held by the Sociological Society, 4 April 1906, *Sociological Papers*, Vol. III, Macmillan and Co., 1907, 323–41.

48 Beveridge, op. cit. (1909), 4.

49 ibid., 70.

50 ibid., Conclusion, 235.

51 Chapman and Hallsworth, op. cit., 82.

52 Rowntree and Lasker, op. cit., Ch. 3, 'Casual Workers', 85 et seq.

53 C. Booth, op. cit., Vol. I, 147.

54 ibid., 37–8.

55 ibid., 42–3.

56 ibid., 44.

57 Jones, op. cit., 56.

58 Percy Alden and Edward E. Hayward, *The Unemployable and Unemployed*, Headley Bros., 2nd edn, 1909, 25.

59 Beveridge, op. cit. (1909), 101.

60 Sidney and Beatrice Webb, *English Poor Law History: The Last Hundred Years*, Longmans, Green and Co., 1929, 416.

61 *Report of Departmental Committee on Vagrancy*, Cd. 2,852, 1906, 22.

62 Webbs, op. cit., 403.

63 Alden and Hayward, op. cit., 32.

64 For a first-hand account of women tramps and their treatment, see Julia Varley, 'Life in the Casual Ward. Experiences of an ex-Bradford Guardian "On the Road" and in the Workhouses', (*Varley Papers*, Brynmor Jones Library, Hull University). Julia Varley, a trade union activist and member of Bradford Board of Guardians, posed as a tramp in Yorkshire and Lancashire and published her experiences in a local newspaper. No source or date is given, but probably *c.* 1910.

65 Will Thorne, *My Life's Battles*, George Newnes, 1925, 30–1. Thorne later worked at gasworks in Birmingham and London, joined the Social Democratic Federation, founded the Union of Gas Workers in 1889, was MP for West Ham, 1906–45, and was made a Privy Councillor in the latter year. When he married in 1879 neither he nor his wife could write.

66 Albert Pugh, 'I Helped to Build Railways', in Charles Madge, ed., *Pilot Papers: Social Essays and Documents*, Vol. I, No. 4, Nov. 1946, 87–91. Pugh was born in Wigan in 1867, the son of a foreman navvy: his later life is unknown.

67 Joseph Stamper, *Less than the Dust. The Memoirs of a Tramp*, Hutchinson and Co., 1931, 7, 31, 100. Stamper was born in Lancashire in 1886. In later life he was employed by a magazine publishing company and wrote several novels including *Violence* (1933) and *Slum* (1934).

68 Patrick MacGill, *Children of the Dead End. The Autobiography of a Navvy*, Introduction by John Burnett, Caliban Books, 1980: facsimile of 1st edn by Herbert Jenkins, 1914, 114, 117, 140. MacGill became a successful author, publishing at least twenty-six novels and collections of poems and emigrating with his novelist wife to California in 1924: his best works were based on navvying characters and experiences and on his life as a private in the First World War.

69 Harsh winters were a particular cause of distress in London in 1879, 1880, 1881, 1886, 1887, 1891 and 1895 (Jones, op. cit., 48).

70 Maud Pember Reeves, *Round About a Pound a Week*, Virago 1979, 196–200, 1st edn G. Bell and Sons, 1913.

71 General Booth, op. cit., 27–9.

72 Rowntree and Lasker, op. cit., 232–4.

73 On the decline of London as an industrial centre see G. Stedman Jones, *Outcast London*, op. cit., Ch. 1.

74 C. Booth, *Life and Labour*, op. cit., Vol. 3, 89.

75 C. Booth, 'Inaugural Address', *Journal of the Royal Statistical Society*, Vol. 55, Dec. 1892, 528–32. Cited Harris, op. cit., 20.

76 Beveridge, op. cit. (1909), 88.

77 ibid., 92.

78 Gordon Phillips and Noel Whiteside, *Casual Labour. The Unemployment Question in the Port Transport Industry, 1880–1970*, Clarendon Press, Oxford, 1985, 41.

79 ibid., 27, 30.

80 Ben Tillett, *Memories and Reflections*, John Long Ltd., London, 1931, 69, 75–6. Tillett later became Secretary of the Dock, Wharf, Riverside and General Labourers Union (1887), a leading trade unionist and Socialist and MP for North Salford (1917–24, 1929–31).

81 ibid., 87.

82 Beveridge, op. cit. (1909), 97.

83 Norman B. Dearle, *Problems of Unemployment in the London Building Trades*, (J. M. Dent, 1908), Appendix D, 205.

84 ibid., 101.

85 The Robert Tressell Papers, *Exploring 'The Ragged Trousered Philanthropists'*, Introduction by Fred Bell, Workers' Educational Association, Rochester, Kent, 1982, 49, 79.

86 Dearle, op. cit., 46.

87 ibid., 97.

88 Rowntree and Lasker, op. cit., 132.

89 Mrs Yearn. 'A Public Spirited Rebel', in *Life as We Have Known It*, by Co-operative Working Women, Margaret Llewellyn Davies, ed., Virago, 1977, 103, 1st edn Hogarth Press, 1931.

90 Louise Santer, in *Hastings Voices*, Hastings Modern History Workshop, University of Sussex Centre for Continuing Education, 1982, 15–17.

91 Jack Lanigan, *The Kingdom Did Come*, TS. Brunel University Archive, 10, 21. Lanigan later got work with the Council and became a qualified Sanitary Inspector in 1914 after passing examinations at Manchester College of Technology.

92 Robert Roberts, *The Classic Slum. Salford Life in the First Quarter of the Century*, Manchester University Press, 1971, 66.

93 Thorne, op. cit., 36.

94 Jones, op. cit., 44.

95 Wal Hannington, *Never On Our Knees*, Lawrence and Wishart, 1967, 25–6.

96 Aubrey S. Darby, *A View from the Alley*, Borough of Luton Museum and Art Gallery, 1974, 12. The author was born in Luton in 1905 and began part-time work for a butcher at the age of eight.

97 Walter Southgate, *That's the Way it Was. A Working-Class Autobiography, 1890–1950*, New Clarion Press in association with History Workshop, 1982, 55. Southgate left school in 1904.

98 Alexander Paterson, *Across the Bridges. Life by the South London River-Side*, Introduction by the Right Revd E. S. Talbot, Lord Bishop of Southwark, Edward Arnold, 1911, 126–7.

99 Rowntree and Lasker, op. cit., Ch. 1, 'Youths Under 19', 2 et seq.

100 Cyril Jackson, *Unemployment and Trade Unions*, Longmans, Green and Co., 1910, Ch. IV, 'Boy Labour', 60–4.

101 Chapman and Hallsworth, op. cit. An Examination of the Report of the Poor Law Commission on Unemployment, 2–13.

102 Quoted James H. Treble, *Urban Poverty in Britain, 1830–1914*, University Paperbacks, Methuen, 1982, 83.

103 James A. Schmiechen, *Sweated Industries and Sweated Labor. The London Clothing Trades, 1860–1914*, Croom Helm, Beckenham, 1984, 36.

104 Lloyd P. Gartner, *The Jewish Immigrant in England, 1870–1914*, Allen & Unwin, 1960, 30.

105 E. H. Hunt, *British Labour History, 1815–1914*, Weidenfeld & Nicolson, 1981, 182.

106 Schmiechen, op. cit., 35–6.

107 ibid., 63–4.

108 B. L. Hutchins, *Women in Modern Industry*, 1st edn 1915; repub. E. P. Publishing Ltd., Wakefield, 1978, 85.

109 Clementina Black (ed.), *Married Women's Work. Being the Report of an Enquiry Undertaken by the Women's Industrial Council*, 1st edn 1915; new edn by Virago, 1983, 132.

110 ibid., 138–9.

111 Quoted John Belchem, *Industrialization and the Working Class: the English Experience, 1750–1900*, Scolar Press, Aldershot, 1990, 200.

112 Quoted Schmiechem, op. cit., 59.

113 Duncan Bythell, *The Sweated Trades. Outwork in Nineteenth Century Britain*, Batsford, 1978, 117, 123.

114 Frances Hicks, in Frank W. Galton, ed., *Workers on their Industries*, Swan Sonnenschein, 1895, 17–18.

115 Mrs Carl Meyer and Clementina Black, *Makers of our Clothes. A Case for Trade Boards. Being the Results of a Year's Investigation into the Work of Women in London in Tailoring, Dressmaking and Underclothing Trades*, Duckworth and Co., 1909.

116 ibid., Appendix C, Tabulated Cases, 214 et seq.

117 R. A. Leeson, *Travelling Brothers. The Six Centuries' Road from Craft Fellowship to Trade Unionism*, Allen & Unwin, 1979, 249.

118 Alfred Ireson, *Reminiscences*, TS. Brunel University Archive, 77. Ireson was born in 1856 at Whittelsea, near Oundle.

119 ibid., 92.

120 Fred Bower, *Rolling Stonemason. An Autobiography*, Jonathan Cape, 1936, 19, 43.

121 Rowntree and Lasker, op. cit., 149.

122 Chapman and Hallsworth, op. cit., Table, 42.

123 Robert Stewart, *Breaking the Fetters. The Memoirs of Bob Stewart*, Lawrence and Wishart, 1967, 23.

124 ibid., 27–8.

125 ibid., 33. Stewart was elected to Dundee Town Council in 1908: in 1921 he became Scottish organizer for the British Communist Party and was an unsuccessful Parliamentary candidate.

126 Hannington, op. cit., 25.

127 Beveridge, op. cit. (1930), 39, 432.

128 Chapman and Hallsworth, op. cit., Graph, 36, and 38.

129 Beveridge, op. cit. (1909), Table XIII, 73. The statistics relate to the Manchester and Leeds Districts of the ASE.

130 Humphrey Southall, 'The Origins of the Depressed Areas. Unemployment, Growth and Regional Economic Structure in Britain before 1914', *Economic History Review*, Second Series, Vol. ixl, No. 2, May 1988, Table 6, 'Unemployment among skilled engineers, 1858–1909', 251.

131 George N. Barnes, *From Workshop to War Cabinet*, Herbert Jenkins, 1924, 8.

132 ibid., 24–6. Barnes became General Secretary of the Amalgamated Society of Engineers (1896–1908), MP for Blackfriars, Glasgow (1906–22), Chairman

of the Labour Party (1910) and Minister of Pensions in the War Cabinet (1916–18).

133 W. F. Watson, *Machines and Men. An Autobiography of an Itinerant Mechanic*, Allen & Unwin, 1935, 13.

134 Harry McShane, *No Mean Fighter, by Harry McShane and Joan Smith*, Pluto Press, 1978, 19–20.

135 Jonathan Zeitlin, 'Engineers and Compositors; a Comparison', Ch. 6 in *Divisions of Labour; Skilled Workers and Technological Change in Nineteenth Century England*, Royden Harrison and Jonathan Zeitlin, eds, Harvester Press, Brighton, 1985, 212–18.

136 Ellic Howe and Harold E. Waite, *The London Society of Compositors. A Centenary History*, Cassell and Co., 1948, 195.

137 ibid., 255.

138 Leeson, op. cit., 249.

139 Beveridge, op. cit. (1909), Table XII, 71.

140 ibid., 145.

141 Paul Evett, *My Life In and Out of Print*, TS. Brunel University Archive, 2–3. Evett eventually settled in Dartford and Gravesend, becoming a reader for the *Law Times* and *Financial Times*, 1928–1940.

142 George Rowles, *Chaps Among the Caps*, TS. Brunel University Archive, 37.

143 ibid., 66. Rowles became an editorial proof-reader, a freelance journalist and writer of short stories.

144 Beveridge, op. cit. (1909), 30–2.

145 ibid., 71.

146 Chapman and Hallsworth, op. cit., 42.

147 George Acorn (pseud.), *One of the Multitude*, Introduction by Arthur C. Benson, William Heinemann, 1911, 194–6. Acorn later tried to set up business on his own, 'buzzing' the furniture he made from one shop to another, but failed and returned to employment.

148 Bill Elliott, *Piano and Herrings, Autobiography of a Wolverton Railway Worker*, The People's Press, Milton Keynes, 1975, 10.

149 Herbert Hodge, *It's Draughty in Front. The Autobiography of a London Taxidriver*, Michael Joseph, 1938, 6–7.

150 Frank Goss, *My Boyhood at the Turn of the Century: An Autobiography*, TS., Brunel University Archive, 53.

151 Chapman and Hallsworth, op. cit., 38–9, 51.

152 Beveridge, op. cit. (1909), 30.

153 Lord Williams of Barnburgh (Thomas Williams), *Digging for Britain*, Hutchinson, 1965, 22. Williams became Labour MP for Don Valley, 1922–59, was Parliamentary Private Secretary to the Minister of Labour, 1929–31, Privy Councillor in 1941 and Minister of Agriculture in 1945.

154 J. W. Emsley, *Social Questions and National Problems, their Evils and Remedies, with Autobiographical Introduction*, 2nd edn, Matthews and Brooke, 1902, 9–28.

155 Frederick Parkin, *Autobiography of a Pottery Trade Unionist. Reminiscences of 45 Years*, MS. Horace Barks Reference Library, Hanley, Stoke-on-Trent, 29. Parkin was born *c.* 1884 and became Secretary of the local branch of the ILP and was on the management committee of the Burslem Co-operative Society.

156 Samuel Goldstein, *Resumé of the Life, Business and Social Activities, etc.*, TS. Brunel University Archive, 2. Goldstein arrived in London in 1905, aged sixteen; he ultimately established the highly successful clothing empire of Ellis and Goldstein Ltd.

157 Watson, op. cit., 29.

158 Frederick Parkin, op. cit., XIII–XIV.

159 Jenny Morris, *Women Workers and the Sweated Trades. The Origins of Minimum Wage Legislation*, Gower Pubs, Aldershot, 1986, 100.

160 Walter Southgate, *That's the Way it Was. A Working-Class Autobiography, 1890–1950*, New Clarion Press, 1982, 23.

161 Paul Johnson, *Saving and Spending, The Working-Class Economy in Britain, 1870–1939*, Clarendon Press, Oxford, 1985, 168–70.

162 Rose Gamble, *Chelsea Child*, Ariel Books, BBC Books, 1982, 38–9.

163 Goss, op. cit., 54–65.

164 Pember Reeves, op. cit., 195–200.

165 Rowntree and Lasker, op. cit., 224–8.

166 *Hard Up Husband. James Turner's Diary, Halifax, 1881/2*, (Ellisons' Editions, 1981).

167 Charity Organisation Society, 18th Annual Report (1884), 36.

168 Stamper, op. cit., 31.

169 Quoted Harris, op. cit., 36, ref. 5.

170 Belchem, op. cit., 183.

171 Frederick Charles Wynne, *Old Pompey and Other Places*, TS. Brunel University Archive, 8.

172 E. Robinson, *I Remember*, Brunel University Archive, 11–12.

173 Ben Turner, *About Myself, 1863–1930*, Cayme Press, 1930, 51.

174 William Wright, *A Few Memories of Tottenham in the 'Eighties*, Edmonton Historical Society, Occasional Paper No. 1, June, 1959, 3.

175 The Robert Tressell Papers, op. cit., 53–5.

176 Harry McShane, op. cit., 24–5.

177 For a full discussion of unemployment policies in the period, see the excellent account by Jose Harris, *Unemployment and Politics, A Study in English Social Policy, 1886–1914*, Oxford, 1972: only a brief review is necessary in the present volume.

178 Beveridge, op. cit. (1909), 157–62.

179 Sidney Pollard, *A History of Labour in Sheffield*, Liverpool University Press, 1959, 111–12, 182–4.

180 The Robert Tressell Papers, op. cit., 51–67.

181 General Booth, *In Darkest England*, op. cit., 91 et seq.

182 Harris, op. cit., Table 4, 376.

183 Treble, op. cit., 141–2.

184 Beveridge, op. cit. (1909), footnote, 152.

185 Harris, op. cit., Table 1, 373.

186 Alden and Hayward, op. cit., 8.

187 Harris, op. cit., 76.

188 Ronald C. Davison, *The Unemployed, Old Policies and New*, Longmans, Green and Co., 1929, 35; Beveridge, op. cit. (1909), 155.

189 Beveridge, op. cit. (1930), Table XXVI, 448–9.

190 Beveridge, op. cit. (1909), 162–91, provides a full and critical commentary on the 1905 Act.

191 Beveridge, op. cit. (1930) 302, and Table XXXV, 305.

192 Cited Bentley B. Gilbert, *The Evolution of National Insurance in Great Britain: The Origins of the Welfare State*, Michael Joseph, 1966, 264.

193 Pat Thane, *The Foundations of the Welfare State*, Longman, 1982, 95.

194 G. N. Barnes, *The Problem of the Unemployed*, ILP Pamphlet, c. 1907, 9–11.

195 John Burns, 'The Unemployed', *The Nineteenth Century*, CXC, Dec. 1892, reprinted as Fabian Tract No. 47, 1893, 1906, 10–15.
196 T. Good, 'Unemployment from the "Unemployed" Point of View', *The Nineteenth Century and After*, Vol. XIX–XX, Jan.–June, 1909, 155–6.
197 Cyril Jackson, *Unemployment and Trade Unions*, Longmans, Green and Co., 1910, 40–75.
198 Full accounts of the Right to Work movement are in Brown, op. cit., Chs 3, 4, 5, and Harris, op. cit., Ch. V. A popular, illustrated account is Sarah Cox and Robert Golden, *Down the Road, Unemployment and the Fight for the Right to Work*, Writers and Readers Publishing Co-operative, 1977.
199 Royal Commission on the Poor Laws, Cd. 4,499 (1909). Majority Report, Part IX, para. 142. Cited Harris, op. cit., 260.

6 'THE WORST OF TIMES?' UNEMPLOYMENT BETWEEN THE WARS

1 W. H. Beveridge, *Unemployment. A Problem of Industry*, Longmans, Green and Co., new edition, 1930, 345.
2 John Stevenson, *British Society, 1914–1945*, Allen Lane, 1984, 104.
3 As suggested by Martin Weiner in *English Culture and the Decline of the Industrial Spirit, 1850–1980*, 1985.
4 Ronald C. Davison, *The Unemployed. Old Policies and New*, Longmans, Green and Co., 1929, 80.
5 F. W. Pethick Lawrence, *Unemployment*, Humphrey Milford, Oxford University Press, n.d., *c.* 1922, 27.
6 Beveridge, op. cit., 353.
7 W. R. Garside, *British Unemployment, 1919–1939. A Study in Public Policy*, Cambridge University Press, 1990, Table 3, 8.
8 ibid., Table 2, 5, adapted from C. H. Feinstein, *Statistical Tables of National Income, Expenditure and Output of the U.K., 1855–1965*, Cambridge University Press, 1972, Table 58.
9 Of the many accounts of the inter-war economy and unemployment, the fairest summary is Stephen Constantine, *Unemployment in Britain between the Wars*, Longman, 1980.
10 Derek H. Aldcroft and Harry W. Richardson, *The British Economy, 1870–1939*, Macmillan, 1969, 238–9.
11 Constantine, op. cit., 14–15.
12 Beveridge, op. cit., 359.
13 Davison, op. cit., 179–80.
14 Daniel K. Benjamin and Levis A. Kochin, 'Searching for an Explanation for Unemployment in Interwar Britain', *Journal of Political Economy*, Vol. 87, 3, 1979, quoted Sean Glynn, *No Alternative? Unemployment in Britain*, Faber & Faber, 1991, 67.
15 *Report of Industrial Transference Board* (Ministry of Labour), Cmnd. 3156, 1928, 36–7.
16 Garside, op. cit., 26.
17 S. Glynn and J. Oxborrow, *Interwar Britain. A Social and Economic History*, 1976, 157–8.
18 Garside, op. cit., 4.
19 ibid., Table 2, 5. Adapted from Feinstein, *Statistical Tables of National Income, Expenditure and Output of the U.K., 1855–1965*, Cambridge University Press, 1972, Table 58.

20 Davison, op. cit., Table, 166.

21 B. Seebohm Rowntree, *Poverty and Progress. A Second Social Survey of York*, Longmans, Green and Co., 1941, 47.

22 A. L. Bowley and Margaret H. Hogg, *Has Poverty Diminished?*, 1st edn, P. S. King, 1925; reprint Garland Publishing Inc., New York, 1985, 152.

23 Noel Whiteside, *Bad Times. Unemployment in British Social and Political History*, Faber & Faber 1991, 83.

24 A. D. K. Owen, *A Survey of Juvenile Employment and Welfare in Sheffield*, Sheffield Social Survey Committee, Report No. 6, 1933, Table, 15.

25 ibid., 31–2.

26 Ministry of Labour, *Report of an Inquiry into the Personal Circumstances and Industrial History of Boys and Girls registered for Employment*, 1926, cited Davison, op. cit., 187.

27 Wal Hannington, *Ten Lean Years. An Examination of the Record of the National Government in the Field of Unemployment*, Victor Gollancz, 1940. Table, 284.

28 Constantine, op. cit., 24.

29 Beveridge, op. cit., Table XXXVII, 350.

30 Davison, op. cit., 177.

31 Beveridge, op. cit., 351–2.

32 Stevenson, op. cit., Table 19, 270.

33 Ministry of Labour Reports, *Investigations into the Industrial Conditions in certain Depressed Areas*, Cmnd. 4728, 1934.

34 Ellen Wilkinson, *The Town That Was Murdered. The Life-story of Jarrow*, Victor Gollancz, 1939, 259.

35 Katharine Nicholas, *The Social Effects of Unemployment on Teesside, 1919–39*, Manchester University Press, 1986, 25, 35–6.

36 *Investigations into . . . Depressed Areas* (Ministry of Labour), op. cit., 71–6.

37 ibid., 5, 9.

38 ibid., 130–48.

39 ibid., 201–18.

40 *Men Without Work. A Report made to the Pilgrim Trust*, Cambridge University Press, 1938, 4.

41 ibid., 7–10. The total numbers of long-term unemployed fell from 480,000 in July 1933 to 265,000 in August 1937, but the proportion rose from 25 to 27 per cent.

42 ibid., Table II, 13.

43 ibid., 26.

44 ibid., 24.

45 Rowntree, op. cit., 46. These periods of unemployment do not include occasional odd weeks of casual or relief work.

46 Wilkinson, op. cit., 262.

47 Rowntree, op. cit., 44.

48 E. Wight Bakke, *The Unemployed Man. A Social Study*, Nisbet and Co. Ltd., 1933, Introduction, vii.

49 ibid., 2–3.

50 ibid., 10.

51 Almost all working-class autobiographers of this period make mention of unemployment: some 200 of these have been consulted, many of which are cited in the following sections.

52 Lottie Barker, 'My Life as I Remember It, 1899–1920', TS. Brunel University Archive, 63.

53 Eva Shilton, 'School and Family Life in Coventry, 1913–1921', TS. Brunel University Archive.

54 Amy Frances Gomm, 'Water Under the Bridge', TS. Brunel University Archive.

55 Joseph Stacey, *Diary of a Tramp*, John D. Vose, ed., United Writers Pubs. Ltd., 1981, 13.

56 Mrs N. Jones, *Autobiographical letters*, Brunel University Archive, 9, writing of her husband.

57 Henrietta Burkin, 'Memoirs of Henrietta Burkin', TS. Brunel University Archive, 10.

58 Kenneth Maher, 'Caerphilly', in Nigel Gray, *The Worst of Times. An Oral History of the Great Depression in Britain*, Wildwood House Ltd., Aldershot, 1985, 30–1.

59 ibid., 32.

60 Dick Beavis, *What Price Happiness? My Life from Coal Hewer to Shop Steward*, Strong Words Publications 1980, 33.

61 J. H. Armitage, 'The Twenty-Three Years, or The Late Way of Life and of Living, by "The Exile" ', TS. Brunel University Archive, 134.

62 Wilkinson, op. cit., 191–2.

63 Arthur Barton, *Two Lamps in Our Street: A Time Remembered*, New Authors Ltd., Hutchinson, 1967, 169.

64 Jack Shaw, 'Ashton-under-Lyne', in Gray, op. cit., 84–5.

65 Armitage, op. cit., 200. He lost his job at the Airedale Foundry in Leeds, at seventeen.

66 Tom Blackman, in *Hastings Voices. Local people talking about their lives in Hastings and St. Leonards before the Second World War*, Hastings Modern History Workshop, 1982, 46–7.

67 Donald Kear, 'Forest of Dean', in Gray, op. cit., 163.

68 Charles Graham, 'South Shields', in Gray, op. cit., 103.

69 Harry Fletcher, *A Life on the Humber: Keeling to Shipbuilding*, Faber & Faber, 1975, 112.

70 Ernie Benson, *To Struggle is to Live. A Working Class Autobiography*, People's Publications, 1979, Vol. 1, 192.

71 John Evans, in *Time to Spare. What Unemployment Means, by Eleven Unemployed*, Felix Greene, ed., Allen & Unwin, 1935, 73.

72 Olive Doris Gold, 'My Life', TS. Brunel University Archive.

73 'A Skilled Wood-Carver', in *Memoirs of the Unemployed*, H. L. Beales and R. S. Lambert, eds, Victor Gollancz, 1934; reprint by Garland Publishing Inc., New York, 1985, 114–15.

74 Arthur Newton, *Years of Change. The Autobiography of a Hackney Shoemaker*, Hackney WEA and Centerprise Publications, 1974, 16, 55–6.

75 Mick Burke, *Ancoats Lad: The Recollections of Mick Burke*, Neil Richardson, 1985, 41.

76 Will Paynter, *My Generation*, Allen & Unwin, 1972, 48.

77 Arthur Horner, *Incorrigible Rebel*, Macgibbon and Kee, 1960, 9.

78 Edward Cain, 'Reminiscences from the Life Story of Edward Cain', TS. Brunel University Archive, 7.

79 George Bestford, in *Hello, Are You Working? Memories of the Thirties in the North-East of England*, Keith Armstrong and Huw Beynon, eds, Strong Words Publications, 1977, 78.

80 Harry McShane (and Joan Smith), *No Mean Fighter*, Pluto Press, 1978, 113.

81 George Hodgkinson, *Sent to Coventry*, Robert Maxwell and Co., 1970, 67.

82 Jack and Bessie Braddock, *The Braddocks*, Macdonald and Co., 1963, 68.

83 Mary Brooksbank, *No Sae Lang Syne. A Tale of this City*, Dundee Printers Ltd., 1971, 29–30.

84 Bakke, op. cit., 129.

85 ibid., 128.

86 ibid., 134–7.

87 Walter Greenwood, *How the Other Man Lives*, Labour Book Service, n.d., *c.* 1930, 38.

88 Sir Hubert Llewellyn-Smith, ed., *The New Survey of London Life and Labour*, Vol. III, *The Eastern Area*, P. S. King and Son, 1932, 161–4.

89 ibid., 174.

90 Greenwood, op. cit., 41–3.

91 John Jewkes and Allan Winterbottom, *Juvenile Unemployment*, Allen & Unwin, 1933, 45–6.

92 Peter Donnelly, *The Yellow Rock*, Eyre & Spottiswoode, 1950, 85.

93 Kay Garrett, Untitled TS. Brunel University Archive, 3–4. In 1945 Kay Garrett became 'Mary Brown', the well-known columnist of the *Daily Mirror*, a post she held for seventeen years.

94 Arthur Barton, *School for Love*, Hutchinson, 1976, 103–5.

95 Kathleen Betterton, 'White Pinnies, Black Aprons', TS. Brunel University Archive, 190.

96 Alice Pidgeon, 'Looking Over my Shoulder to Childhood Days and After', TS. Brunel University Archive, 15.

97 Jack Jones, *Unfinished Journey*, Oxford University Press, 1937, 185, 246. Jack Jones became a professional author, publishing two autobiographical novels and two radio plays by 1936, when the autobiography ends.

98 Joseph Halliday, *Just Ordinary, but . . . An Autobiography*, published by the author, Waltham Abbey, Essex, 1959, 158, 161.

99 Fletcher, op. cit., 114–15.

100 Joe Loftus, 'Lee Side', TS. Brunel University Archive, 149.

101 Max Cohen, *I Was One of the Unemployed* (Foreword by Sir William Beveridge), 1st edn 1945, repub. by E. P. Publishing Ltd., 1978, 28.

102 Wal Hannington, *Unemployed Struggles, 1919–1936. My Life and Struggles amongst the Unemployed*, E. P. Publishing Ltd., 1977, 181.

103 Lionel Rose, *'Rogues and Vagabonds'. Vagrant Underworld in Britain, 1815–1985*, Routledge, 1988, 146.

104 Armitage, op. cit., 211 et seq.

105 Charlie Potter, *On the Tramp in the 1930's*, Your Own Stuff Press, 1983, 46–7.

106 John Brown, *I Was A Tramp*, Selwyn and Blount Ltd., London, 1934, 183. In 1932 Brown won a TUC scholarship to Ruskin College, Oxford, where he gained a Diploma in Economics and Political Science: his later career was as a journalist and political organizer.

107 Garrett, op. cit., 4.

108 Halliday, op. cit., 90, 131.

109 Cohen, op. cit., 15.

110 Hodgkinson, op. cit., 75.

111 Brown, op. cit., 179.

112 Mr Campbell, in Jeremy Seabrook, *Unemployment*, Quartet Books, 1982, 184.

113 Stacey, op. cit., 100.

114 Mick Burke, *Ancoats Lad*, op. cit., 67.

115 Beales and Lambert, op. cit., 120.

116 McShane, op. cit., 115, 128.

117 Wal Hannington, *Never On Our Knees*, Lawrence and Wishart, 1967, 63 et seq.

118 William Gallacher, *Revolt on the Clyde. An Autobiography*, Lawrence and Wishart, 1936, and *The Rolling of the Thunder*, Lawrence and Wishart, 1947.
119 Horner, op. cit.
120 John A. Garraty, *Unemployment in History. Economic Thought and Public Policy*, Harper Colophon Books, New York, 1978, 170–80 describe these international studies.
121 Marie Jahoda, Paul F. Lazarsfeld and Hans Zeisel, *Marienthal. The Sociography of an Unemployed Community*, first published in German, 1933; English edn by Tavistock Publications, 1972.
122 ibid., 22.
123 ibid., 77.
124 ibid., 56.
125 Bakke, op. cit., 63.
126 ibid., 64–7.
127 Pilgrim Trust, *Men Without Work*, op. cit., 150–3.
128 ibid., 136.
129 Hilda Jennings, *Brynmawr. A Study of a Distressed Area*, Allenson and Co., 1934, 138–9.
130 E. A. G. Paris, in Greene, ed., op. cit., 114.
131 Terence Monaghan, in Armstrong and Beynon, eds, op. cit., 11.
132 G. A. W. Tomlinson, *Coal-Miner*, Hutchinson and Co., 1937, 183–4.
133 Cohen, op. cit., 59–60.
134 Donnelly, op. cit., 85.
135 Syd Metcalfe, 'One Speck of Humanity', ts. Brunel University Archive, 118.
136 Brown, op. cit., 197.
137 John Rankin, in Greene, ed., op. cit., 46.
138 Fletcher, op. cit., 115.
139 John Edmonds, 'The Lean Years', ms. Brunel University Archive, 6.
140 Loftus, op. cit., 149–51.
141 'A Skilled Engineer', in Beales and Lambert, eds, op. cit., 76.
142 Cohen, op. cit., 98.
143 Halliday, op. cit., 184.
144 Beales and Lambert, eds, op. cit., 137.
145 ibid., 218.
146 Burke, op. cit., 58.
147 Benson, op. cit., Vol. 2, 18–19.
148 Seabrook, op. cit., 2.
149 Nicholas, op. cit., 102.
150 'A Village Carpenter', in Beales and Lambert, eds, op. cit., 193.
151 'A Young Casual Labourer', ibid., 229.
152 'A Young Electrician', ibid., 253.
153 Sean Glynn and Alan Booth, eds, *The Road to Full Employment*, Allen & Unwin, 1987, 25.
154 Nicholas, op. cit., Table 38, 111.
155 ibid., Table 40, 113.
156 Ifan Edwards, *No Gold on My Shovel*, Porcupine Press, 1947, 208.
157 Seabrook, op. cit., 4–5.
158 Barton, *School for Love*, op. cit., 75.
159 Mrs Pallas, in Greene, ed., op. cit., 32, 39.
160 Garrett, op. cit., 1.
161 S. P. B. Mais, in Greene, ed., op. cit., 14–15.
162 Bakke, op. cit., 186–9.

163 Will Oxley, 'Are You Working?', in *Seven Shifts*, Jack Common, ed., 1st edn 1938; repub. E. P. Publishing, 1978, 117.
164 Jennings, op. cit., 130.
165 Pilgrim Trust, op. cit., 159.
166 Revd Cecil Northcott, 'Filling in the Workless Day', in Greene, ed., op. cit., 122.
167 George M. Ll. Davies, 'Unemployment in the Rhondda Valleys', ibid., 124.
168 Bakke, op. cit., 201.
169 Northcott, op. cit., 114.
170 Fletcher, op. cit., 112, 118.
171 Edmonds, op. cit., 32 et seq.
172 Pallas, in Greene, ed., op. cit., 27, 33.
173 Evans, ibid., 71.
174 Loftus, op. cit., 152–3.
175 Pilgrim Trust, op. cit., 171.
176 Bakke, op. cit., 194.
177 Kear, in Gray, op. cit., 166.
178 Paynter, op. cit., 33.
179 Oxley, op. cit., 110–11.
180 Beales and Lambert, op. cit., 70, 74, 133, 234.
181 Jones, op. cit., 265–6.
182 Bakke, op. cit., 193.
183 ibid., 199.
184 ibid., 178–80.
185 Clifford Steele, 'Barnsley', in Gray, op. cit., 124. (The 'kazoo' was a tin pipe with a hole at the top covered with thin paper. It made a sound like paper and comb, and could be bought at Woolworths for 3d. or 6d.)
186 Tomlinson, op. cit., 192.
187 ibid., 195–6.
188 Halliday, op. cit., 104.
189 Beales and Lambert, op. cit., 118.
190 Jennings, op. cit., 124, n. 1 and p. 132, Appendix 1.
191 Barton, op. cit., 108.
192 Pilgrim Trust, op. cit., 306.
193 Martin, in Greene, ed., op. cit., 81.
194 Keen, ibid., 86.
195 O'Neill, ibid., 99.
196 Brooksbank, op. cit., 21.
197 Harry Goldthorpe, *Room At The Bottom*, Sunbeam Press, 1959, 22–4.
198 Clarence Muff, *Unbelievable, But True!*, Bradford Libraries division, Occasional Local Papers No. 6, 1984, 27–8.
199 Goldthorpe, op. cit., 7.
200 A. L. Bowley and Margaret H. Hogg, *Has Poverty Diminished? A Sequel to 'Livelihood and Poverty'*, 1st edn P. S. King and Son, 1925; repub. Garland Publishers Inc., New York, 1985, Table D, 17.
201 Sir Hubert Llewellyn Smith, ed., op. cit., 89.
202 B. Seebohm Rowntree, op. cit., 460–61.
203 Herbert Tout, *The Standard of Living in Bristol. A Preliminary Report of the Work of the University of Bristol Social Survey*, Arrowsmith, Bristol, 1938, 28.
204 Rowntree, op. cit., 39.
205 Llewellyn Smith, op. cit., 90, 159.
206 Nicholas, op. cit., Table 11, 44.

207 Pilgrim Trust, Table XXXII, 119.
208 ibid., 120.
209 George Orwell, *The Road to Wigan Pier,* Victor Gollancz, London, 1937, 94.
210 *British Medical Association Report of Committee on Nutrition,* BMA, 1933, 42.
211 G. C. M. M'Gonigle and J. Kirby, *Poverty and Public Health,* Victor Gollancz, 1936, 118.
212 Rowntree, op. cit., 264.
213 Llewellyn Smith, op. cit., Table VIII, p. 53.
214 Jennings, op. cit., Appendix 2, 171.
215 Margery Spring Rice, *Working-Class Wives: Their Health and Conditions,* 1st edn Penguin, 1939: repub. Virago, 1981, 181.
216 On these, see John Macnicol, *The Movement for Family Allowances, 1918–1945,* Heinemann, 1980.
217 *Annual Report of the M.O.H. for the City and County of Newcastle-upon-Tyne on the Sanitary Condition of the City, 1936,* Appendix A, 23 et seq.
218 On diets generally, see my *Plenty and Want. A Social History of Food in England from 1815 to the Present Day,* 3rd edn Routledge, 1989, Ch. 12, 'Between the Wars'.
219 A. Fenner Brockway, *Hungry England,* Victor Gollancz, 1932, 223.
220 Orwell, op. cit., 7.
221 Spring Rice, op. cit., 166.
222 Tomlinson, op. cit., 200–3.
223 Mrs Pallas, in Greene, ed., op. cit., 33–4.
224 Evans, ibid., 69.
225 Mrs Keen, ibid., 83.
226 Cohen, op. cit., 44.
227 Brown, op. cit., 277.
228 'A Skilled Wood-Carver', in Beales and Lambert, eds, op. cit., 116.
229 Edmonds, op. cit., 37–8.
230 Cited in K. Laybourn, *Britain on the Breadline* (Alan Sutton, Gloucester, 1990), 52.
231 Clifford Steele, in Gray, op. cit., 125.
232 Paynter, op. cit., 36–7.
233 Tom Blackman, in *Hastings Voices,* Hastings Modern History Workshop and University of Sussex Centre for Continuing Education, 1982, 45.
234 Oxley, in Common, ed., op. cit., 137.
235 Cohen, op. cit., 44.
236 Major Blackburn, in Greene, ed., op. cit., 106.
237 Ministry of Health, *Report on Investigation in the Coalfields of South Wales and Monmouth,* Cmnd. 3272, 1929, cited Bakke, op. cit., 52.
238 Ministry of Health, *Annual Report for the Year 1932,* 21–2, cited Laybourn, op. cit., 42.
239 B. R. Mitchell and Phyllis Deane, *Abstract of British Historical Statistics,* Cambridge University Press, 1962. Population and Vital Statistics, 12, 37.
240 Laybourn, op. cit., Table 2.6, 57.
241 G. C. M. M'Gonigle and J. Kirby, op. cit., 267, 273.
242 Charles Webster, 'Healthy or Hungry Thirties?' *History Workshop Journal,* Vol. 13, Spring, 1982, 110.
243 ibid., 112.
244 Nicholas, op. cit., 94.
245 Pilgrim Trust, op. cit., Table XXVIII, 66.
246 ibid., 134.

247 Jennings, op. cit., 157.
248 Pilgrim Trust, op. cit., 127.
249 Jennings, op. cit., 157.
250 Spring Rice, op. cit., 170.
251 Bakke, op. cit., 60–2, 149–50, 236.
252 Constantine, op. cit., 42.
253 Richard Croucher, *We Refuse to Starve in Silence. A History of the National Unemployed Workers' Movement, 1920–46*, Lawrence and Wishart, 1987, 148–9. This is an authoritative, impartial account of the movement, contrasting with Hannington's personal accounts in *Unemployed Struggles, 1919–36* (1937) and *Never On Our Knees* (1967).
254 Arthur Horner, *Incorrigible Rebel*, MacGibbon and Kee, 1960; William Gallacher, *Revolt on the Clyde* and *The Rolling of the Thunder*, Lawrence and Wishart, 1936 and 1947; Harry McShane, *No Mean Fighter*, Pluto Press, 1978; Jack Jones, *Unfinished Journey*, Oxford University Press, 1937; Jack and Bessie Braddock, *The Braddocks*, Macdonald and Co., 1963; Wal Hannington, op. cit. John McGovern also took a leading part in the marches, but was an ILP member and opponent of Communism. His autobiography, *Neither Fear Nor Favour*, Blandford Press, London, 1960, presents some different perspectives.
255 'An Unemployed Businessman', in Beales and Lambert, op. cit., 61.
256 'A Skilled Engineer', in ibid., 72.
257 Evans, in Greene, ed., op. cit., 72–3.
258 Benson, op. cit., Vol. 2, *Starve or Rebel, 1927–1971*, 8.
259 Edmonds, op. cit., 60.
260 Beavis, in Armstrong and Beynon, eds, op. cit., 20.
261 Oxley, in Common, ed., op. cit., 136.
262 Paynter, op. cit., 104.
263 For full accounts of the marches, see Peter Kingsford, *The Hunger Marchers in Britain, 1920–1939*, Lawrence and Wishart, London, 1982; Ian MacDougall, *Voices from the Hunger Marchers. Personal Recollections by Scottish Hunger Marchers*, Polygon, 1990.
264 For example, W. R. Garside, *British Unemployment, 1919–1939. A Study in Public Policy*, Cambridge University Press, 1990; Bentley B. Gilbert, *British Social Policy, 1914–1939*, Batsford, 1970.
265 Alfred Smith, *A Cottage and an Acre. The Remedy for Unemployment, Poverty and the House Famine*, published by the author, London, 1923.
266 Ernest Bevin, *My Plan for 2,000,000 Workless*, Clarion Press, n.d., *c.* 1930.
267 D. Lloyd George and Seebohm Rowntree, *How to Tackle Unemployment*, Liberal Party, 1930.
268 Garside, op. cit., 266.
269 'A Skilled Wire-Drawer', in Beales and Lambert, op. cit., 179.
270 Tomlinson, op. cit., 198.
271 Loftus, op. cit., 149.
272 Cohen, op. cit., 3–8, 39.
273 Brown, op. cit., 192.
274 Edwards, op. cit., 214.
275 Horner, op. cit., 113.
276 Rankin, in Greene, ed., op. cit., 44.
277 Travis, in Seabrook, op. cit., 173.
278 Alf Hodd, in *Hastings Voices*, op. cit., 65.
279 Fletcher, op. cit., 114.
280 Divers, in Greene, ed., op. cit., 52.

281 Halliday, op. cit., 139 et seq.
282 Kear, in Gray, op. cit., 169.
283 Edmondson, in Armstrong and Beynon, eds, op. cit., 66.

7 BACK TO UNEMPLOYMENT, 1970–90

1 Brian Showler and Adrian Sinfield, *The Workless State. Studies in Unemployment*, Martin Robertson, Oxford, 1981, 61–3.
2 *Report of the Inter-Departmental Committee on Social Insurance and Allied Services*, Cmnd. 6404, 1942, 164, para. 441.
3 W. H. Beveridge, *Full Employment in a Free Society*, Allen & Unwin, 2nd edn, 1960, 20, 128.
4 M. J. Hill, R. M. Harrison, A. V. Sargeant and V. Talbot, *Men Out Of Work. A Study of Unemployment in Three English Towns*, Cambridge University Press, 1973, 6.
5 F. W. Paish, 'How the Economy Works', *Lloyds Bank Review* April 1968, 16, cited Hill et al., ibid., 7.
6 W. R. Garside, *The Measurement of Unemployment in Great Britain, 1850–1979*, Basil Blackwell, Oxford, 1980, Table 11, 88.
7 Showler and Sinfield, 76.
8 Adrian Sinfield, *What Unemployment Means*, Martin Robertson, Oxford, 1981, 11.
9 *Social Trends 21*, HMSO, 1991, 75.
10 *Social Trends 23*, HMSO, 1993, 62.
11 Showler and Sinfield, 8–9.
12 Kevin Hawkins, *Unemployment*, Penguin Books, 3rd edn, 1987, 17.
13 Carey Oppenheim, *Poverty. The Facts*, Child Poverty Action Group, London, 1990, 65.
14 Jon Shields, ed., *Conquering Unemployment. The Case for Economic Growth*, Macmillan in association with The Employment Institute, 1989, 4.
15 Hawkins, op. cit., 18.
16 Clive Jenkins and Barrie Sherman, *The Collapse of Work*, Eyre Methuen, 1979, 26.
17 Richard Layard, *How To Beat Unemployment*, Oxford University Press, 1986, 23.
18 W. W. Daniel, *A National Survey of the Unemployed*, PEP, The Social Science Institute, 1974, 53 et seq.
19 Santos Mukherjee, *Through No Fault of Their Own. Systems for Handling Redundancy in Britain, France and Germany*, PEP Report, Macdonald, 1973, Table 1, 29.
20 Will Paynter, *My Generation*, Allen & Unwin, 1972, 133 et seq.
21 Cited Peter Kelvin and Joanna E. Jarrett, *Unemployment. Its Social Psychological Effects*, Cambridge University Press, 1985, 91.
22 Andrea Garman and Gerry Redmond, 'The Changing Characteristics of Unemployed Men', *Employment Gazette*, Special Feature, Sept. 1990, 472–3.
23 Arnold Cragg and Tim Dawson, *Unemployed Women. A Study of Attitudes and Experiences*, Department of Employment, Research Paper 47, 1984, 8, 17, 70.
24 Jeremy Moon and J. J. Richardson, *Unemployment in the United Kingdom. Politics and Policies*, Gower Publishing, Aldershot, 1985, 12.
25 ibid., 25.
26 Nick Hedges and Huw Beynon, *Born to Work. Images of Factory Life*, Pluto Press, 1982, 78.

27 Derek H. Aldcroft, *Full Employment. The Elusive Goal,* (Harvester Wheatsheaf, 1984), Table 1. 4, 9.

28 *British Labour Statistics. Historical Abstracts, 1886–1968,* Department of Employment and Productivity and *Department of Employment Gazette,* cited Aldcroft, ibid., 5–6.

29 *Social Trends 21,* Table 4.11, 71, and Oppenheim, op. cit., 109–110.

30 *The Smiths. One Family's Experience of Trying to Stay in Work,* BBC Education, 1987. Only the names of the family have been disguised.

31 ibid., 9–22.

32 P. E. Hart, *Youth Unemployment in Great Britain,* National Institute of Economic and Social Research, Cambridge University Press, 1988, 1.

33 Daniel, op. cit., 7.

34 Hawkins, op. cit., 98–9.

35 Kelvin and Jarrett, op. cit., 34.

36 Daniel, op. cit., 7–8.

37 Hawkins, op. cit., 94.

38 Michael Young and Tom Schuller, *Life After Work. The Arrival of the Ageless Society,* HarperCollins, 1991, 66–8.

39 Jeremy Seabrook, *The Leisure Society,* Basil Blackwell, Oxford, 1988, 83.

40 Daniel, op. cit., 9.

41 Sheila Allen, Alan Watson, Kate Purcell and Stephen Wood, eds., *The Experience of Unemployment,* Macmillan, 1986, 41.

42 Cragg and Dawson, op. cit., 7, 47, 64, 71.

43 *Unemployment and Homelessness. A Report by the Reference Division,* Community Relations Commission, HMSO, 1974, 7, 17, 27.

44 Mike Campbell and Douglas Jones, *Racial Discrimination Against Asian School Leavers,* Unemployment Unit Bulletin No. 5, 1982, 4, cited Moon and Richardson, op. cit., 29.

45 *Employment Gazette,* Department of Employment, March 1990, cited Oppenheim, op. cit., 80.

46 Hill et al., op. cit., 57–8.

47 Layard, op. cit., 22.

48 *Social Trends 21,* Table 4.28, 77.

49 Oppenheim, op. cit., Table 22, 112.

50 Hawkins, op. cit., 98–9.

51 Daniel, op. cit., 144.

52 Maureen Colledge and Richard Bartholomew, *A Study of the Long-Term Unemployed,* Manpower Services Commission, 1980, 5.4.

53 Kelvin and Jarrett, op. cit., 32.

54 Garman and Redmond, op. cit., 474.

55 Colledge and Bartholomew, op. cit., 5, 12.

56 Roger Clarke, *Work in Crisis. The Dilemma of a Nation,* Saint Andrew Press, Edinburgh, 1982, 32, citing *Employment Gazette,* August 1981, Labour Market Supplement, 536.

57 *The Smiths,* op. cit., 11, 19.

58 Colledge and Bartholomew, op. cit., 5.12, 5.20.

59 Daniel, op. cit., 72.

60 Michael White, *Long-term Unemployment and Labour Markets,* Policy Studies Institute, 1983, 104.

61 Colledge and Bartholomew, op. cit., 5.15.

62 Dennis Marsden and Ewan Duff, *Workless. Some Unemployed Men and Their Families,* Penguin Books, 1975, 100.

63 ibid., 106.
64 Daniel, op. cit., 156.
65 ibid., 74.
66 Young and Schuller, op. cit., 64.
67 Tony Novak, *Poverty and Social Security*, Pluto Press, 1984, 3–4.
68 Layard, op. cit., Table 5, 48.
69 Oppenheim, op. cit., 19.
70 ibid., 29.
71 J. Bradshaw, K. Cooke and G. Godfrey, 'The Impact of Unemployment on the Living Standards of Families', *Journal of Social Policy*, Vol. 12, Pt. 4, 1983, 433 et seq.
72 Daniel, op. cit., 44.
73 Ruth Cohen, Jill Coxall, Gary Craig and Azra Sadiq-Sangster, *Hardship Britain. Being Poor in the 1990s*, CPAG, 1992, 116.
74 *Food and Drink Manufacturing Economic Development Council*, 1983, 2 and 3, cited Moon and Richardson, op. cit., 31–2.
75 Mr Hawkins, quoted Oppenheim, op. cit., 64–5.
76 J. Bradshaw and H. Holmes, *Living On The Edge. A Study of the Living Standards of Families on Benefit in Tyne and Wear*, Tyneside CPAG, 1989.
77 *On The Stones*, Newcastle-on-Tyne Trades Council Centre for the Unemployed, Sept. 1980, 3, 4, 24.
78 A Tyneside family, quoted in Sarah Cox and Robert Golden, *Down The Road. Unemployment and the Fight for the Right to Work*, The Writers and Readers Publishing Co-operative, 1977, 76, 79.
79 *The Smiths*, op. cit., 25–8.
80 Daniel, op. cit., 117–8.
81 Marsden and Duff, op. cit., 134.
82 Garman and Redmond, op. cit., 473–4.
83 Clarke, op. cit., 46.
84 Cited Aileen Ballantyre, *Guardian*, 18 November 1980.
85 Marsden and Duff, op. cit., 146.
86 Adrian Sinfield, op. cit., 56.
87 Marsden and Duff, op. cit., 140.
88 *The Smiths*, op. cit., 80.
89 Adapted from B. Zawadski and P. Lazarsfeld, 'The Psychological Consequences of Unemployment', *Journal of Social Psychology*, Vol. 6, 1935, 224–51.
90 John Hayes and Peter Nutman, *Understanding the Unemployed. The Psychological Effects of Unemployment*, Tavistock Publications, 1981, 13–14.
91 Clarke, op. cit., 80.
92 Hill (1978), cited in Kelvin and Jarrett, op. cit., 24–5.
93 Based on Marie Jahoda, 'The Impact of Unemployment in the 1930s and the 1970s', 13th Annual Myer's Lecture, *Bulletin of the British Psychological Society*, Vol. 32, 1979, 313.
94 T. Gould and J. Kenyon, *Stories From The Dole Queue*, Temple Smith, 1972, 33.
95 Young and Schuller, op. cit., 62.
96 Marsden and Duff, op. cit., 190.
97 Jeremy Seabrook, *Unemployment*, Quartet, 1982, 122.
98 *On The Stones*, op. cit., 24.
99 Daniel, op. cit., 44–5.
100 White, op. cit., 139–44.
101 Mr Downing, cited Cohen, op. cit., 18.
102 Brian, cited Seabrook, op. cit. (1988), 71.

103 Marsden and Duff, op. cit., 177 et seq.

104 Gould and Kenyon, op. cit., 36–41.

105 Hayes and Nutman, op. cit., 30, 31, 49.

106 Cited Jahoda, *Employment and Unemployment. A Social-Psychological Analysis*, Cambridge University Press, 1982, 51.

107 *Fred's People. Young Bristolians Speak Out*, A Bristol Broadsides Booklet, n.d., *c.* 1983, 8, 9, 26.

108 *Unemployment and Homelessness*, Report by the Reference Division, Community Relations Commission, HMSO, 1974, 41–4.

109 Cragg and Dawson, op. cit., 16.

110 ibid., 50.

111 A woman, quoted in Jane Root, 'No Jobs For Girls', *Honey*, February 1982, cited Hedges and Beynon, op. cit., 88.

112 Colledge and Bartholomew, op. cit., 5.28 (c).

113 Seabrook, op. cit. (1982), 14–15.

114 Cited Seabrook, op. cit. (1988), 79.

115 Allen et al., op. cit., 144.

116 Seabrook, op. cit. (1982), 4–5.

117 Paynter, op. cit., 144.

118 Tony Parker, *Red Hill. A Mining Community*, Heinemann, 1986, 20, 43, 77.

119 *The Smiths*, op. cit., 29.

120 Marsden and Duff, op. cit., 194.

121 D. J. Smith, *Unemployment and Racial Minorities*, Policy Studies Institute, London, 1981, cited Jahoda, op. cit., 47.

122 White, op. cit., 147.

123 Hayes and Nutman, op. cit., 72.

124 ibid., 74–6.

125 *Office of Population, Censuses and Surveys*, 1983, cited Moon and Richardson, op. cit., 30.

126 Seabrook, op. cit. (1982), 114.

127 Stephen Platt, *Recent Trends in Parasuicide (Attempted Suicide) and Unemployment Among Men in Edinburgh*, in Allen et al., op. cit., 156, 159, 165.

128 Elvis, cited *Fred's People*, 32.

129 Seabrook, op. cit. (1982), 115–6.

130 Summarized in Iain Crow, Paul Richardson, Carol Riddington and Frances Simon, *Unemployment, Crime and Offenders*, Routledge, 1989, 31–4.

131 ibid., 9.

132 Marsden and Duff, op. cit., 264.

133 Jock Keenan, 'On the Dole', in Ronald Fraser, ed., *Work. Twenty Personal Accounts*, Penguin Books, 1968, 273–6.

134 Gould and Kenyon, op. cit., 41.

135 ibid., 175.

136 Daniel, op. cit., 51.

137 *Social Trends 21*, Table 10.6, 172.

138 Kelvin and Jarrett, 69–70.

139 Seabrook, op. cit. (1982), 136–7.

140 Jane Root, *Honey*, February 1982, cited Hedges and Beynon, op. cit., 91.

141 Seabrook, op. cit. (1988), 96.

142 Marsden and Duff, op. cit., 176–9.

143 R. E. Pahl, *Divisions of Labour*, Basil Blackwell, Oxford, 1984, 275–6.

144 ibid., 336.

145 Marsden and Duff, op. cit., 183–4.

146 Seabrook, op. cit. (1982), 125.
147 Pahl, op. cit., 339–40.
148 Cited Claire Wallace and Ray Pahl, *Polarisation, Unemployment and All Forms of Work*, in Allen et al., op. cit., 117.
149 *The Rayner Committee*, Department of Employment and Department of Health and Social Security, 1981, cited Layard, op. cit., 53.
150 Showler and Sinfield, op. cit., 157.
151 Marsden and Duff, op. cit., 116.
152 *Social Trends 21*, Table 4.12, 71.
153 Marsden and Duff, op. cit., 116.
154 *The Smiths*, op. cit., 132.
155 Marsden and Duff, op. cit., 210.
156 Paynter, op. cit., 132.
157 Cox and Golden, op. cit., 115.
158 See Ch. 13 of Gould and Kenyon, op. cit., which describes his work as Claimants' organizer.
159 *TUC Centres for the Unemployed. A First National Survey*, K. Forrester, K. Ward and B. Stinson, Prepared by the University of Leeds, July 1988.

CONCLUSION

1 John Burns, *The Unemployed*, Fabian Society Tract No. 47, Nov. 1893; reprinted March, 1905, 4.
2 Quoted Clive Jenkins and Barrie Sherman, *The Collapse of Work*, Eyre Methuen, 1979, 6.
3 A Journeyman Engineer (Thomas Wright), *Some Habits and Customs of the Working Classes*, Ch. 6, 'On the Inner Life of Workshops', 1st edn 1867; reprinted Augustus M. Kelley, New York, 1967, 83–108.
4 Quoted Nick Hedges and Huw Beynon, *Born to Work. Images of Factory Life*, Pluto Press, 1982, 14.
5 John Burnett, *Useful Toil. Autobiographies of Working People from the 1820s to the 1920s*, Penguin Books, 1984, 15–18.
6 Quoted Ronald Fraser, ed., *Work. Twenty Personal Accounts*, Penguin Books, 1968, Introduction, 8.
7 ibid., 273, 59.
8 Mr Keach, in Jeremy Seabrook, *Unemployment*, Quartet Books, 1982, 136.
9 For an excellent, brief account of theories about work, see Sean Sayers, 'The Need to Work', in *Radical Philosophy*, Vol. 46, Summer, 1987, 18–26.
10 Dennis Marsden and Ewan Duff, *Workless. Some Unemployed Men and their Families*, Penguin Books, 1975, 264.
11 Michael Young and Tom Schuller, *Life After Work. The Arrival of the Ageless Society*, HarperCollins, 1991, 123–4.

BIBLIOGRAPHY
Autobiographies, diaries and memoirs
(including collections)

Many of the following are referenced in *The Autobiography of the Working Class. An Annotated, Critical Bibliography,* John Burnett, David Vincent and David Mayall, eds, 3 vols, Harvester Press, Brighton, and New York University Press, 1984–9: the entries include brief life histories of the authors and full bibliographical details of any alternative editions of their works.

The place of publication is London unless otherwise stated.

Abbreviation   BUA – Brunel University Archive of Working-Class Autobiography.

Acorn, George (pseud.), *One of the Multitude,* William Heinemann, 1911.

Adams, W. E., *Memoirs of a Social Atom,* 2 vols, Hutchinson and Co., 1903.

Anon., *The Autobiography of a Working Man,* Hon. Eleanor Eden, ed., Richard Bentley, 1867.

Anderson, Isaac, *The Life History of Isaac Anderson, a Member of the Peculiar People,* Essex Record Office, n.d.

Arch, Joseph, *The Autobiography of Joseph Arch,* John Gerard O'Leary, ed., Macgibbon and Kee, 1966.

Armitage, J. H., 'The Twenty-Three Years, or The Late Way of Life and of Living', TS. BUA, n.d.

Ashworth, Cornelius, *The Diary of Cornelius Ashworth,* in Frank Atkinson, ed., *Some Aspects of the Eighteenth Century Woollen and Worsted Trade in Halifax,* Halifax Museums, 1956.

Bain, Alexander, *Autobiography,* Longmans, Green and Co., 1904.

Bamford, Samuel, *Passages in the Life of a Radical,* Macgibbon and Kee, 1967.

Barker, Lottie, 'My Life as I Remember It, 1899–1920', TS. BUA.

Barnes, George N., *From Workshop to War Cabinet,* Herbert Jenkins, 1924.

Barrett, W. H., *A Fenman's Story,* Routledge and Kegan Paul, 1965.

Barton, Arthur, *Two Lamps In Our Street: A Time Remembered,* New Authors Ltd., Hutchinson, 1967.

Barton, Arthur, *School for Love,* Hutchinson, 1976.

Beales, H. L., and R. S. Lambert, eds, *Memoirs of the Unemployed,* Victor Gollancz, 1934; reprint by Garland Publishing Inc., New York and London, 1985. (Contains twenty-five autobiographies.)

Beavis, Dick, *What Price Happiness? My Life from Coal Hewer to Shop Steward,* Strong Words, Whitley Bay, 1980.

Benson, Ernie, *To Struggle is to Live. A Working Class Autobiography,* 2 vols, People's Pubs., Newcastle-upon-Tyne, 1979.

Bestford, George, in Keith Armstrong and Huw Beynon, eds, *Hello, Are You Working?*

Memories of the Thirties in the North-East of England, Strong Words, Whitley Bay, 1977. (Contains sixteen autobiographies.)

Betterton, Kathleen, 'White Pinnies, Black Aprons', TS. BUA.

Bezer, John James, *Autobiography of One of the Chartist Rebels of 1848*, in David Vincent, ed., *Testaments of Radicalism. Memoirs of Working Class Politicians, 1790–1885*, Europa, 1977.

Blackburn, Major, in Felix Greene, ed., *Time to Spare. What Unemployment Means, by Eleven Unemployed*, Allen & Unwin, 1935.

Blackman, Tom, in *Hastings Voices. Local People Talking about their Lives in Hastings before the Second World War*, Hastings Modern History Workshop, 1982.

Blow, John, *The Autobiography of John Blow*, J. Parrott, Leeds, 1870.

'Bourne' (Sturt), George, *The Bettesworth Book. Talks with a Surrey Peasant*, Duckworth, 1920.

Bowd, James, 'The Life of a Farm Worker', in *The Countryman*, Vol. 51, Pt 2, 1955.

Bower, Fred, *Rolling Stonemason. An Autobiography*, Jonathan Cape, 1936.

Braddock, Jack and Bessie, *The Braddocks*, Macdonald and Co., 1963.

Bray, John Francis, *A Voyage from Utopia*, M. F. Lloyd-Prichard, ed., Lawrence and Wishart, 1957.

Brierley, Ben, *Home Memories, and Recollections of a Life*, Abel Heywood and Son, Manchester, 1886.

Broadhurst, Henry, MP, *The Story of his Life from a Stonemason's Bench to the Treasury Bench. Told by Himself*, Hutchinson and Co., 1902.

Brooksbank, Mary, *No Sae Lang Syne. A Tale of this City*, Dundee Printers Ltd., 1971.

Brown, John, *I Was A Tramp*, Selwyn and Blount, 1934.

Buckmaster, John, *A Village Politician. The Life Story of John Buckley*, Introduction by John Burnett, Caliban Books, Horsham, 1982.

Burgess, J. T., *The Life and Experiences of a Warwickshire Labourer . . . as Told by Himself*, Routledge, 1872.

Burke, Mick, *Ancoats Lad. The Recollections of Mick Burke*, Neil Richardson, Swinton, 1985.

Burkin, Henrietta, 'Memoirs of Henrietta Burkin', TS. BUA.

Burn, James Dawson, *The Autobiography of a Beggar Boy*, David Vincent, ed., Europa, 1978, 1st edn William Tweedie, 1855.

Burrows, Mrs, 'A Childhood in the Fens about 1850–60', in Margaret Llewelyn Davies, ed., *Life As We Have Known It*, by Co-Operative Working Women, Virago, 1977, 1st edn, 1931.

Cain, Edward, 'Reminiscences from the Life Story of Mr E. Cain, MBE', TS. BUA.

Carnegie, Andrew, *The Autobiography of Andrew Carnegie*, Constable and Co., 1920.

Carter, Thomas, *Memoirs of a Working Man*, Charles Knight and Co., 1845.

Castle, John, 'The Diary of John Castle', MS., Essex County Record Office.

Clare, John, *John Clare's Autobiographical Writings*, Eric Robinson, ed., Oxford University Press, 1983.

Cobbett, William, *Rural Rides, 1821–32*, Introduction by Asa Briggs, Everyman's Library, 1967.

Cohen, Max, *I Was One of the Unemployed*, E. P. Publishing Ltd, Wakefield, 1978, 1st edn Victor Gollancz, 1945.

Colin (pseud.), *The Wanderer Brought Home. The Life and Adventures of Colin. An Autobiography*, Revd H. Richings, ed., 2nd edn William Tweedie, 1864.

Common, Jack, ed., *Seven Shifts*, E. P. Publishing Ltd, Wakefield, 1978, 1st edn Secker and Warburg, 1938. (Contains seven work histories.)

Darby, Aubrey S., *A View from the Alley*, Borough of Luton Museum and Art Gallery, 1974.

Davies, Margaret Llewelyn, ed., *Life As We Have Known It*, by Co-operative Working Women, Virago, 1977.

Donnelly, Peter, *The Yellow Rock*, Eyre & Spottiswoode, 1950.

Edmonds, John, 'The Lean Years', MS., BUA.

Edmondson, Len, in Keith Armstrong and Huw Beynon, eds, *Hello, Are You Working? Memories of the Thirties in the North-East of England*, Strong Words, Whitley Bay, 1977.

Edwards, George, *From Crow-Scaring to Westminster. An Autobiography*, Labour Publishing Co., 1922.

Edwards, Ifan, *No Gold on My Shovel*, Porcupine Press, 1947.

Elliott, Bill, *Piano and Herrings. Autobiography of a Wolverton Railway Worker*, People's Press, Milton Keynes, 1975.

Emsley, J. W., *Social Questions and National Problems . . . with Autobiographical Introduction*, 2nd edn, Matthews and Brooke, Bradford, 1902.

Evans, John, in Felix Greene, ed., *Time to Spare. What Unemployment Means, by Eleven Unemployed*, Allen & Unwin, 1935.

Evett, Paul, 'My Life In and Out of Print', TS. BUA.

Fairbairn, William, *The Life of Sir William Fairbairn, Bart., Partly Written by Himself*, William Pole, ed., Longmans, Green and Co., 1877.

Farish, William, *The Autobiography of William Farish. Struggles of a Hand-Loom Weaver, with Some of his Writings*, Printed for private circulation, 1889.

Fletcher, Harry, *A Life on the Humber: Keeling to Shipbuilding*, Faber & Faber, 1975.

Francis, W. J., *Reminiscences*, Francis and Sons, Southend-on-Sea, 1926.

Fraser, Ronald, ed., *Work. Twenty Personal Accounts*, Penguin Books, Harmondsworth, 1968.

Fred's People, 'Young Bristolians Speak Out', a Bristol Broadsides Booklet, n.d. (*c.* 1983).

Gallacher, William, *Revolt on the Clyde. An Autobiography*, Lawrence and Wishart, 1936.

Gallacher, William, *The Rolling of the Thunder*, Lawrence and Wishart, 1947.

Gamble, Rose, *Chelsea Child*, Ariel Books, BBC Books, 1982.

Garrett, Kay ('Mary Brown' of the *Daily Mirror*), untitled TS. BUA.

Gold, Olive Doris, 'My Life', TS. BUA.

Goldstein, Samuel, 'Résumé of the Life, Business and Social Activities, etc.' TS. BUA.

Goldthorpe, Harry, *Room at the Bottom*, Sunbeam Press, Bradford, 1959.

Gomm, Amy Frances, 'Water Under the Bridge', TS. BUA.

Goss, Frank, 'My Boyhood at the Turn of the Century. An Autobiography', BUA.

Gould, T., and J. Kenyon, *Stories From the Dole Queue*, Temple Smith, 1972.

Gray, Nigel, *The Worst of Times. An Oral History of the Great Depression in Britain*, Wildwood House Ltd., Aldershot, 1985.

Greenwood, Joseph, 'Reminiscences of Sixty Years Ago', in *Co-Partnership*, New Series, Vols XV–XVII, Nos 177–200, 1909–11.

Gutteridge, Joseph, *The Autobiography of Joseph Gutteridge*, in Valerie E. Chancellor, ed., *Master and Artisan in Victorian England*, Evelyn, Adams and Mackay, 1969.

Haggard, Lilias Rider, ed., *I Walked by Night, Being the Life and History of the King of the Norfolk Poachers, Written by Himself*, Boydell Press, 1974.

Halliday, Joseph, *Just Ordinary, but . . . An Autobiography*, published by the author, Waltham Abbey, Essex, 1959.

Hannington, Walter, *Never On Our Knees*, Lawrence and Wishart, 1967.

Hannington, Walter, *Unemployed Struggles, 1919–1936. My Life and Struggles amongst the Unemployed*, E. P. Publishing Ltd., Wakefield, 1977.

Hanson, William, *The Life of William Hanson, written by himself (in his 80th year)*, Whitaker and Son, Halifax, 1883.

Haw, George, *From Workhouse to Westminster: The Life Story of Will Crooks, M.P.*, Cassell and Co., 1907.

Heaton, William, *The Old Soldier, The Wandering Lover etc., Together with a Sketch of the Author's Life*, Simpkin, Marshall and Co., 1857.

Herbert, George, *Shoemaker's Window. Recollections of Banbury in Oxfordshire before the Railway Age*, Christiana S. Cheney, ed., Phillimore, for the Banbury Historical Society, 2nd edn 1971.

Hockley, John, *The Autobiography of John Hockley*, in Mark Sorrell, *The Peculiar People*, Paternoster Press, Exeter, 1979.

Hodd, Alf, in *Hastings Voices. Local People Talking about their Lives in Hastings before the Second World War*, Hastings Modern History Workshop, 1982.

Hodge, Herbert, *It's Draughty in Front. The Autobiography of a London Taxidriver*, Michael Joseph, 1938.

Hodgkinson, George, *Sent To Coventry*, Robert Maxwell and Co., Oxford, 1970.

Holroyd, Abraham, 'Autobiographical Note' in Charles F. Forshaw, ed., *The Poets of Keighley, Bingley, Haworth and District*, W. W. Morgan, 1893.

Horner, Arthur, *Incorrigible Rebel*, Macgibbon and Kee, 1960.

Ireson, Alfred, 'Reminiscences', TS. BUA.

Jones, Jack, *Unfinished Journey*, Oxford University Press, 1937.

Jones, Mrs N., 'Autobiographical Letters', BUA.

Kear, Donald, in Nigel Gray, ed., *The Worst of Times*, Wildwood House Ltd., Aldershot, 1985.

Keen, Mr, in Felix Greene, ed., *Time to Spare*, Allen & Unwin, 1935.

Keenan, Jock, 'On The Dole', in Ronald Fraser, ed., *Work*, Penguin Books, Harmondsworth, 1968.

Kemp, John, *Memoir of John Kemp, First Pastor of 'Ebenezer' Strict Baptist Chapel, Bounds Cross, Biddenden, Kent*, C. J. Farncombe and Sons, 1933.

Kitchen, Fred, *Brother to the Ox. The Autobiography of a Farm Labourer*, J. M. Dent and Sons, 1940.

Lanigan, Jack, 'The Kingdom Did Come', TS. BUA.

Leno, John Bedford, *The Aftermath: with Autobiography of the Author*, Reeves and Turner, 1892.

Livesey, Joseph, *The Life and Teaching of Joseph Livesey*, National Temperance League, 1885.

Loftus, Joe, 'Lee Side', TS. BUA.

Lovett, William, *The Life and Struggles of William Lovett in his Pursuit of Bread, Knowledge and Freedom*, Mary Thale, ed., Cambridge University Press, 1972.

Luck, Lucy, 'A Little of My Life', J. C. Squire, ed., *London Mercury*, Vol. XIII, No. 76, 1925–6.

MacDougall, Ian, *Voices From The Hunger Marches*, Polygon, Edinburgh, 1990. (Contains eighteen autobiographies.)

MacGill, Patrick, *Children of the Dead End. The Autobiography of a Navvy*, Introduction by John Burnett, Caliban Books, Ascot, 1980. 1st edn Herbert Jenkins, 1914.

Marcroft, William, *The Marcroft Family, and the Inner Circle of Human Life*, E. Wrigley and Sons, Rochdale; revised edn 1888.

Marsden, Dennis and Ewan Duff, *Workless. Some Unemployed Men and their Families*, Penguin Books, Harmondsworth, 1975. (Contains sixteen autobiographies.)

Mayett, Joseph, *Autobiography of Joseph Mayett of Quainton, 1783–1839*, Ann Kussmaul, ed., Buckinghamshire Record Society, 23, 1986.

McGovern, John, *Neither Fear nor Favour*, Blandford Press, 1960.

McShane, Harry, *No Mean Fighter*, Pluto Press, 1978.

Mead, Isaac, *The Story of an Essex Lad, Written by Himself*, A. Driver and Sons, Chelmsford, 1923.

Metcalfe, Syd, 'One Speck of Humanity', TS. BUA.

M'Gonagall, W., *The Authentic Autobiography of the Poet M'Gonagall, Written by Himself*, Luke Mackie and Co., Dundee, n.d.

Milne, William J., *Reminiscences of an Old Boy, and Autobiographic Sketches of Scottish Rural Life from 1832 to 1856*, John MacDonal, Forfar, 1901.

Monaghan, Terence, in Keith Armstrong and Huw Beynon, eds, in *Hello, Are You Working?*, Strong Words, Whitley Bay, 1977.

Muff, Clarence, 'Unbelievable, But True!' Bradford Libraries Division, Occasional Local Papers No. 6, 1984.

Newton, Arthur, *Years of Change. The Autobiography of a Hackney Shoemaker*, Hackney WEA and Centerprise Publications, 1974.

O'Neil, John, *The Journals of a Lancashire Weaver, 1856–60*, Mary Briggs, ed., Record Society of Lancashire and Cheshire, Vol. CXXII, 1982.

Oxley, Will, 'Are You Working?', in Jack Common, *Seven Shifts*, E. P. Publishing Ltd., Wakefield, 1978.

Pallas, Mrs, in Felix Greene, ed., *Time To Spare*, Allen & Unwin, 1935.

Paris, E. A. G., in Felix Greene, ed., *Time To Spare*, Allen & Unwin, 1935.

Parkin, Frederick, 'Autobiography of a Pottery Trade Unionist. Reminiscences of 45 Years', MS. Horace Barks Reference Library, Hanley, Stoke-on-Trent.

Paynter, Will, *My Generation*, Allen and Unwin, 1972.

Pidgeon, Alice, 'Looking Over my Shoulder to Childhood Days and After', TS. BUA.

Place, Francis, *The Autobiography of Francis Place, 1771–1854*, Mary Thale, ed., Cambridge University Press, 1972.

Plastow, William, 'William Plastow's Story', TS. Modern Records Centre, University of Warwick.

Potter, Charlie, *On the Tramp in the 1930s*, Your Own Stuff Press, Nottingham, 1983.

Powell, J. H., *Life Incidents and Poetic Pictures*, Trubner and Co., 1865.

Pugh, Albert, 'I Helped to Build Railways', Charles Madge, ed., *Pilot Papers: Social Essays and Documents*, Vol. 1, No. 4, Nov. 1946.

Randell, Arthur R., *Sixty Years a Fenman*, Routledge and Kegan Paul, 1966.

Rankin, John, in Felix Greene, ed., *Time To Spare*, Allen & Unwin, 1935.

Ricketts, Joseph, *Notes on the Life of Joseph Ricketts, Written by Himself*, Wiltshire Archaeological and Natural History Magazine, Vol. 60, 1965.

Robinson, E., 'I Remember', TS. BUA.

Rowles, George, 'Chaps Among the Caps', TS. BUA.

Rymer, Edward A., *The Martyrdom of the Mine, or A 60 Years' Struggle for Life*, Introduction by Robert Neville, *History Workshop Journal*, Spring 1976, first published 1893.

Santer, Louise, in *Hastings Voices*, Hastings Modern History Workshop, 1982.

Shilton, Eva, 'School and Family Life in Coventry, 1913–1921', TS. BUA.

Smith, Charles Manby, *The Working Man's Way in the World*, Printing Historical Society, 1967, 1st edn 1853.

Smiths, The, *One Family's Experience of Trying to Stay in Work*, BBC Education, 1987.

Snell, Lord, *Men, Movements and Myself*, J. M. Dent, 1936.

Somerville, Alexander, *The Autobiography of a Working Man, by One Who Has Whistled at the Plough*, Robert Hardwicke, 1855.

Southgate, Walter, *That's the Way it Was. A Working-Class Autobiography, 1890–1950*, New Clarion Press, Oxted, 1982.

Spurr, Robert, *The Autobiography of Robert Spurr. A Social Study of Nineteenth-Century Baptist Working Class Fortitude*, R. J. Owen, *Baptist Quarterly*, Vol. 26, April 1976.

Stacey, Joseph, *Diary of a Tramp*, John D. Vose, ed., United Writers, Cornwall, 1981.

Stamper, Joseph, *Less than the Dust. The Memoirs of a Tramp*, Hutchinson and Co., 1931.

Stewart, Robert, *Breaking the Fetters. The Memoirs of Bob Stewart*, Lawrence and Wishart, 1967.

Thom, William, *Rhymes and Recollections of a Handloom Weaver*, W. Skinner, ed., Alexander Gardner, Paisley, 1880.

Thorne, Will, *My Life's Battles*, George Newnes, 1925.

Thurston, Mark, *Happy Countryman. The Reminiscences of Mark Thurston*, C. Henry Warren, ed., Geoffrey Bles, 1939.

Tillett, Ben, *Memoirs and Reflections*, John Long Ltd., 1931.

Tomlinson, G. A. W., *Coal-Miner*, Hutchinson and Co., 1937.

Turner, Ben, *About Myself, 1863–1930*, Cayme Press, 1930.

Turner, James, *Hard Up Husband. James Turner's Diary, Halifax, 1881–2*, Ellisons' Editions, Orwell, 1981.

Varley, Julia, 'Life in the Casual Ward. Experiences of an ex-Bradford Guardian On the Road and In the Workhouse', Varley Papers, Brynmor Jones Library, Hull University.

Varley, William, *Diary of William Varley of Higham. Memorandum Book for the Year of Our Lord, 1820*, in W. Bennett, *The History of Burnley*, Burnley Corporation, Vol. 3, 1948.

Wallis, T. W., *Autobiography of Thomas Wilkinson Wallis*, J. W. Goulding and Son, Louth, 1899.

Watson, W. F., *Machines and Men. An Autobiography of an Itinerant Mechanic*, Allen & Unwin, 1935.

Williams, Thomas (Lord Williams of Barnburgh), *Digging for Britain*, Hutchinson, 1965.

Wood, John, *Autobiography of John Wood, Written in the 75th Year of his Life, Chronicle and Mail*, Bradford, 1877. (Local Studies Department, Bradford Central Library.)

Wood, Thomas, *Autobiography by Thomas Wood, 1822–1880*, offprint from serialized version in the *Keighley News*, 3 March–14 April 1956.

Wright, William, 'A Few Memories of Tottenham in the 'Eighties', Edmonton Historical Society, Occasional Paper No. 1, June 1959.

Wynne, Frederick Charles, 'Old Pompey and Other Places', TS. BUA.

Yearn, Mrs, 'A Public-Spirited Rebel', in Margaret Llewelyn Davies, *Life As We Have Known It*, Virago, 1977.

INDEX